WASHINGTON
STATE · PARKS

A COMPLETE
RECREATION
· GUIDE ·

SECOND EDITION

MARGE&TED
MUELLER

THE MOUNTAINEERS

 Published by
The Mountaineers
1001 SW Klickitat Way, Suite 201
Seattle, WA 98134

First edition, 1999

Published simultaneously in Great Britain by Cordee, 3a DeMontfort Street, Leicester, England, LE1 7HD

Manufactured in the United States of America

Edited by Christine Clifton-Thornton
Maps by the authors
All photographs by the authors
Cover design by Mountaineers Books
Book design and layout by Gray Mouse Graphics

Front cover photograph: *Native Pacific Rhododendron, the state flower of Washington* © H. Richard Johnston/ Definitive Stock
Back cover photos by the authors: *Clamming at Dosewallips State Park* (top); *Sunset at Shallow Bay, Sucia Island Marine State Park* (middle); *Camping at Chief Timothy State Park* (bottom)
Frontispiece: *Palouse Falls, in eastern Washington, pours over a 198-foot basalt cliff.*

Library of Congress Cataloging-in-Publication Data

Mueller, Marge.
    Washington State parks : a complete recreation guide / Marge & Ted Mueller. — 2nd ed.
        p.   cm.
    Includes bibliographical references (p.) and index.
    ISBN 0-89886-642-1 (pbk. : perm. paper)
    1. Outdoor recreation —Washington (State) Directories. 2. Parks —Washington (State) Directories. 3. Washington (State) Guidebooks. I. Mueller, Ted. II. Title.
    GV191.42.W2 M85 1999
    333.78'3'0257797— dc21

                                                99-6431
                                                  CIP

CONTENTS

Chapter 8: SOUTHEAST WASHINGTON   199

APPENDICES   227

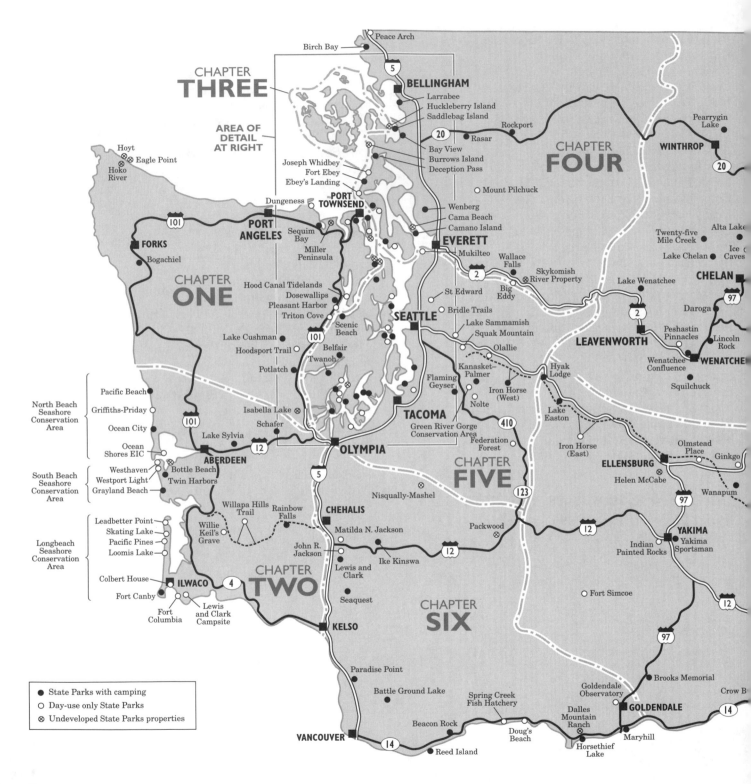

CHAPTER **THREE**

AREA OF DETAIL AT RIGHT

CHAPTER **FOUR**

CHAPTER **ONE**

CHAPTER **FIVE**

CHAPTER **TWO**

CHAPTER **SIX**

Birch Bay
Peace Arch
BELLINGHAM
Larrabee
Huckleberry Island
Saddlebag Island
Rockport
Rasar
Bay View
Burrows Island
Deception Pass
Joseph Whidbey
Fort Ebey
Ebey's Landing
Mount Pilchuck
WINTHROP
Pearrygin Lake

Hoyt
Eagle Point
Hoko River
Dungeness
PORT TOWNSEND
Wenberg
Cama Beach
Camano Island
EVERETT
Twenty-five Mile Creek
Alta Lake
Ice Caves
Lake Chelan

FORKS
PORT ANGELES
Sequim Bay
Miller Peninsula
Mukilteo
Wallace Falls
Skykomish River Property
Lake Wenatchee
CHELAN

Bogachiel
Hood Canal Tidelands
Dosewallips
Pleasant Harbor
Triton Cove
St Edward
Big Eddy
Bridle Trails
Daroga
LEAVENWORTH
Peshastin Pinnacles
Lincoln Rock
WENATCHEE

Lake Cushman
Hoodsport Trail
Scenic Beach
Belfair
SEATTLE
Lake Sammamish
Squak Mountain
Olallie
Wenatchee Confluence
Squilchuck

Twanoh
Potlatch
Kanasket-Palmer
Iron Horse (West)
Hyak Lodge

North Beach Seashore Conservation Area
Pacific Beach
Griffiths-Priday
Ocean City
Flaming Geyser
Nolte
Lake Easton
Olmstead Place
Ginkgo

Isabella Lake
Schafer
TACOMA
Green River Gorge Conservation Area
Federation Forest
Iron Horse (East)
ELLENSBURG
Helen McCabe
Wanapum

Ocean Shores EIC
Lake Sylvia
OLYMPIA

South Beach Seashore Conservation Area
Westhaven
Westport Light
Grayland Beach
ABERDEEN
Bottle Beach
Twin Harbors
Nisqually-Mashel
YAKIMA
Yakima Sportsman
Indian Painted Rocks

Longbeach Seashore Conservation Area
Leadbetter Point
Skating Lake
Pacific Pines
Loomis Lake
Willapa Hills Trail
Rainbow Falls
CHEHALIS
Matilda N. Jackson
Packwood

Willie Keil's Grave
John R. Jackson
Lewis and Clark
Ike Kinswa
Fort Simcoe

Colbert House
ILWACO
Fort Canby
Fort Columbia
Lewis and Clark Campsite
Seaquest
Paradise Point
Battle Ground Lake
Brooks Memorial
Goldendale Observatory
Crow B

VANCOUVER
Beacon Rock
Spring Creek Fish Hatchery
Dalles Mountain Ranch
GOLDENDALE

Reed Island
Doug's Beach
Horsethief Lake
Maryhill

KELSO

- State Parks with camping
- Day-use only State Parks
- Undeveloped State Parks properties

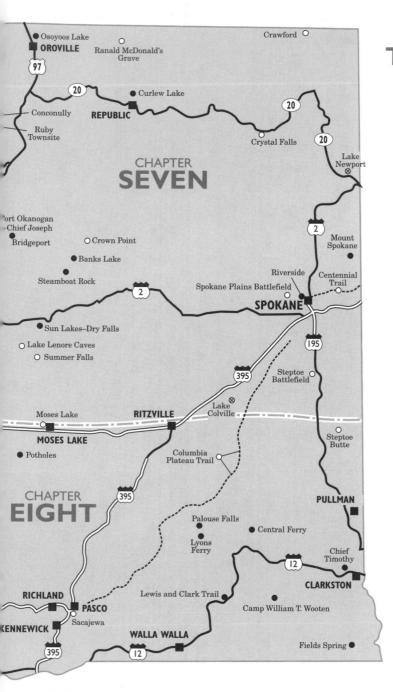

CHAPTER SEVEN

Osoyoos Lake
OROVILLE
97
Ranald McDonald's Grave
Crawford
20
Curlew Lake
REPUBLIC
20
Conconully
Crystal Falls
20
Ruby Townsite
Lake Newport

CHAPTER EIGHT

Fort Okanogan –Chief Joseph
Bridgeport
Crown Point
2
Mount Spokane
Banks Lake
Steamboat Rock
2
Riverside
Centennial Trail
Spokane Plains Battlefield
SPOKANE
Sun Lakes–Dry Falls
195
Lake Lenore Caves
Summer Falls
395
Steptoe Battlefield
Moses Lake
RITZVILLE
Lake Colville
MOSES LAKE
Steptoe Butte
Potholes
Columbia Plateau Trail
PULLMAN
395
Palouse Falls
Central Ferry
Lyons Ferry
Chief Timothy
12
CLARKSTON
RICHLAND
Lewis and Clark Trail
Camp William T. Wooten
PASCO
Sacajewa
KENNEWICK
WALLA WALLA
Fields Spring
395
12

WASHINGTON

CHAPTER THREE

Patos Island
Sucia Island
Matia Island
BELLINGHAM
Stuart Island
Jones Island
Moran
Clark Island
Larrabee
Posey Island
Doe I
Huckleberry Island
Saddlebag Island
Burrows Island
Bay View
Lime Kiln
James I
CHAPTER FOUR
Blind Island
Turn Island
SAN JUAN ISLANDS
Deception Pass
5
Spencer Spit
Undeveloped Islands
Joseph Whidbey
Fort Ebey
Ebey's Landing
Fort Casey
Cama Bay
Camano Island
PORT TOWNSEND
Keystone Spit
Fort Worden
Rothschild House
South Whidbey
EVERETT
Anderson Lake
Old Fort Townsend
Useless Bay
CHAPTER ONE
Fort Flagler
Mystery Bay
Kinney Point
PUGET SOUND
Wolfe Property
Shine Tidelands
Kitsap Memorial
Old Man House
Fay-Bainbridge
Illahee
DETAIL
Manchester
Fort Ward
Harper
Blake Island
Square Lake
SEATTLE
Belfair
Stretch Point
Haley Property
5
Cutts Island
Kopachuck
Saltwater
Twanoh
Dash Point
West Hylebos
Jarrell Cove
Penrose Point
Harstine Island
McMicken Island
Hope Island
TACOMA
Eagle Island
CHAPTER FIVE
Tolmie
Joemma Beach
OLYMPIA

MAP SYMBOLS

Picnic area	ORV riding	Boat launch
Standard campsites	Alpine skiing	Boat put-in (hand carry)
Primitive campsites, group camp	Ski lift	Marine pumpout station
No camping permitted	Cross-country skiing	Sailing
RV sites with hookups	Snowmobiling	Power boating
Trailer dump station	Sledding	Paddling or rafting
Ranger station or park manager's office	Kite flying	Rowing
Lighthouse	Birdwatching	Scuba diving
Navigation beacon	Bird blind	Windsurfing
Concession stand	Wildlife might be seen	Surfboarding
Scenic attraction	Swimming	Water skiing
Nature trail	Shellfish (clams, oysters)	Paragliding
Mushrooming	Crabs	Wagon rides
Disabled access	Tide pools, marine life	Golf
Hiking	Fishing	Tennis
Rock climbing	Mooring buoys	Airfield
Horseback riding	Anchorage	Buildings
Bicycling		Cemetery
		Mine

Trail (hiking, bicycling, or equestrian) ....

Gated road (walkable but not open to vehicles) ----|----------

Unpaved road ==========================

Paved road ——————————

Highway ══════════════

Railroad +++++++++++++++++

Bridge][

Park boundary – ·· – ·· – ·· – ·· –

Mountain peak ▲

River/stream

Waterfall

Intermittent stream

Body of water

Dock or pier

Artificial reef

Sand

Marsh

Bluff

INTRODUCTION

Washington residents can be justifiably proud of their superb state park system. The quantity of parks, and their diversity in features and recreation, are second to none in the nation. In what other state does the park system include such gems as:

- A 1,100-foot-long limestone cave
- An astronomical observatory open to public use
- Four abandoned railroad beds now converted to multi-use trails, ranging up to 130 miles long.
- More than 70 miles of ocean beach
- Two dozen large islands
- Numerous relics of historic forts
- A petrified forest
- Rock pinnacles and walls that challenge climbers
- An oceanfront whale-watching site

And much more. . . .

Recreation is also unlimited. In addition to the usual camping and picnicking, state parks provide a wondrous array of summer and winter activities, ranging from the sedate to the thrilling, that includes birdwatching, mushrooming, kite flying, fishing, bicycling, kayaking, horseback riding, windsurfing, hang gliding, cross-country skiing, rock climbing . . . and the list goes on.

Sucia Island Marine State Park, in the San Juan Islands, is one of the premier saltwater attractions in Washington's park system.

Mount Spokane State Park offers a wealth of activities, including camping, hiking, skiing, and superb sightseeing from the top of the mountain's 5,881-foot summit.

Although the parks are most heavily concentrated around Puget Sound population centers and the vacation centers of the coast and San Juan Islands, they are scattered to every corner of the state, providing a full inventory of the state's geographical and natural features, from the crashing waves of the coast to the blue-hazed hills of the Palouse.

STATE PARKS—NATURALLY!

Why state parks? In Washington, state parks offer a special outdoor experience. Their combination of recreational diversity, natural setting, and facilities are not found in places such as forest service campgrounds, national parks, or commercial campgrounds.

At forest service campgrounds, recreation is usually limited to what is available nearby, such as fishing, hiking, or hunting. Although they often are in pleas-

ant natural settings, facilities are rustic, and a ranger is rarely seen. At the other end of the spectrum, commercial campgrounds frequently provide play facilities ranging from children's swings to miniature golf courses and heated swimming pools, along with comfortable, well-tended accommodations, but rarely much in the way of nature or solitude. Washington's national parks and monuments undeniably are spectacular. They feature grand scenery and educational displays, and often have nice campgrounds. Recreation there is what the natural environment provides—hiking, mountain climbing, fishing; however, sometimes usage is restricted, with permits required for backcountry trips.

Although state parks vary (which is part of their appeal), they incorporate facets of all these other kinds of parks, but fill a different niche. Park settings are each a unique delight. Depending on the park, visitors enjoy a multitude of

activities, all set in nature's splendor. Families can devote an afternoon or a long vacation to safe, healthy fun in a relaxed environment, all for a reasonable fee, or no fee. Group camps and Environmental Learning Centers offer an enriched state park experience for school and church groups, family reunions, and other gatherings. Campgrounds are often nicely appointed, with level RV pads and restrooms with showers. Rangers or campground hosts usually are available when needed. Interpretive centers and displays at many of the parks give visitors fascinating insights into such things as the Lewis and Clark Expedition, or the state's geology and wildlife.

But how did these parks come to be?

When Washington embarked on its state parks program in 1913, it was among the first few states to set aside land for public recreation. Unfortunately, the Parks Board was not given guidance from the legislature as to its mission and received no funding for park acquisitions. Two years later the Parks Board accepted donation of its first two properties: the John R. Jackson House and Larrabee State Park. The parks system grew rapidly in the 1920s, as did park usage, and Washington's parks began to receive national recognition as well as visitors from across the country. With the growth of the state highway system, the Parks Committee added "auto campgrounds"; by 1928 these included Twanoh, Bay View, Sequim Bay, and Dry Falls.

In 1933, in order to combat the Depression, the new administration of Franklin D. Roosevelt created the Civilian Conservation Corps (CCC), which put unemployed young men to work on public construction projects. Washington State was quick to take advantage of the CCC, and it appropriated funds for a parallel program. The CCC refurbished existing park facilities and added campgrounds, picnic and kitchen shelters, bathhouses, restrooms, water and septic systems, and trail networks. Even today this work is evident in the older state parks, where the sturdy rock and log structures of the CCC are easily recognized.

By the late 1940s prosperity had returned to the state and nation, and the growing availability of money and free time put a mushrooming demand on recreational facilities. In addition, the state began to realize the economic value of tourism—and it certainly had the natural attractions to capitalize on it! By 1960 the park system saw over 7 million visits annually.

With the explosion of boating in the Puget Sound region, the need for marine parks became evident, and the commission began acquiring island property in the San Juan Islands and shorefront property elsewhere in Puget Sound. In a grand move to benefit the recreational public and to prevent ocean beaches from being pillaged, in 1967 the state declared as public all seashores bounding the Pacific Ocean, from the high-tide level to extreme low tide, with the exception of Indian reservations. Jurisdiction for these beaches was placed with the Parks Commission.

After a period of growing acquisition and development, by the 1980s the commission had to refocus on acquisition of critical property of unique historical or natural significance along with maintenance and renovation of existing parks. Preservation of the state's natural, historical, and cultural heritage is a crucial park role. Critical wetlands, bird nesting areas, old-growth forests and other vital habitat are protected through our state parks.

Today the parks system includes over 150 developed parks, and some 80 additional properties that are only nominally developed, are reserved for future development, or are held in their natural state. Total park areas exceed 240,000 acres, and over 50 million people visit the parks annually. All of this would not be possible were it not for the foresight and astute management of the State Parks and Recreation Commission and the dedication, courtesy, and pride in their parks of the hundreds of park managers, rangers, aides, interpreters, and volunteers.

Into the future—how you can help

As the state parks system enters the twenty-first century, all is not serene, as the parks, like any other state agency, are locked in a continual battle for funding, and their very popularity stretches maintenance dollars to the limit.

If even a small proportion of the millions of recreationists who visit the state parks each year make their pleasure of using the parks and their support of them known to the managers, the Parks Commission, and their lawmakers, Washington will continue to have the most outstanding parks in the nation—now, and when their grandchildren and great-grandchildren start to enjoy them. Without this active support and funding, parks will deteriorate and close, and present and future generations will have lost a priceless recreational, historical, and cultural heritage.

In addition, you can hold out your hand to help. Clubs can pitch in to assist with the maintenance of nearby parks. For individuals, a volunteer program has been established to aid rangers and provide service to the visiting public. Volunteers may become campground hosts at a particular park for a minimum period of time, ranging from a week to thirty days, and serve as greeters, provide information to visitors, and do some nominal work such as pick up litter. In return, the volunteers receive a free campsite (with hookups, in most cases), and all the fresh air and relaxation they can soak in—what a way to spend a vacation or retirement! A parallel program has been instituted for marine parks. For information about these programs, contact the volunteer coordinator at the state parks address listed in Appendix A on pages 227–230.

USING THE STATE PARKS

Parks that have overnight camping usually observe standard hours and gates are closed at night. Late-arriving campers or those who leave the premises in the

Bill and Ellen Schirmer spend their summers as hosts in various parks around the state, donating their time to help the rangers and visitors.

evening might find themselves locked out. If planning an early departure, check the gate hours before rolling out of the sack for naught.

Some parks close during winter months due to lack of use, while other parks cut back on their hours between Labor Day and Memorial Day or close facilities, such as interpretive centers and sections of campground, in order to reduce operating expenses. In the off-season, avoid disappointment by confirming that a park is open before planning a visit.

Reservations

A centralized computer system makes telephone reservations for selected Washington state parks. Campgrounds that accept reservations between April 1 and September 30, as of 1999, are listed in the sidebar on page 17. A non-refundable reservation fee and the first night's campsite fee are charged at the time of reservation. The reservation phone number is (800) 452-5687.

At reservation parks, any unreserved campsites are available on a first-come, first-served basis. Check-in time at reserved campsites is after 3:00 P.M. If a reserved campsite has not been checked into by 9:00 P.M., the site will be made available to others. If you know you will be arriving late, you can make arrangements by calling the park.

Generally, reservations for group day-use facilities such as kitchen shelters and playfields must be made with the individual park. Holiday dates for group facilities in popular parks are usually filled soon after reservations open in January, so plan ahead for that family reunion.

PARK FACILITIES AND REGULATIONS

DISABLED FACILITIES. The newer state parks have disabled access to restrooms, picnic sites, campsites, and interpretive features. Because several of the state parks date back to the 1930s, easy disabled access is not available in every park, although it is a high priority when facilities are remodeled. In most parks paths can be maneuvered by a wheelchair, although hiking trails might not be barrier-free.

CONCESSION-OPERATED SERVICES. At some larger parks where no towns are nearby, private concessionaires provide necessary goods and services ranging from groceries, snacks, restaurants, boat rentals, fishing supplies, and horse rentals to cabins, golf courses, and ski lifts. Concessions, with the exception of ski lifts, are typically open only during heavy-use summer months, even though the park might be open longer.

Platform tents (top) and yurts (bottom) are two types of accommodations that can be rented at the state parks.

DAY-USE FACILITIES. There is no charge for entering any state park or for day-use of the facilities, with the exception of areas that are reserved for groups. Interpretive centers may charge a small fee, or request a donation. Except for some marine state parks, picnic areas usually have drinking water at the site or nearby, trash containers, and restrooms or toilets. Individual picnic sites have picnic tables and braziers or fireplaces. Typically, there are also a few shelters for bad weather or for reservation by groups. On ocean beaches or in open areas of eastern Washington many picnic sites have windscreens.

HERITAGE SITES, INTERPRETIVE FACILITIES, AND PROGRAMS. The state parks include nearly 40 Heritage Sites that are of unique historical, geological, archeological, scientific, or cultural significance. Some of these are in conjunction with other state parks and others are stand-alone parks. All have plaques or exhibits telling of their particular significance. Some have volunteer-staffed interpretive centers with artifacts, exhibits, and audio-visual programs.

Although funding for staff to provide interpretive programs is extremely limited, a few of the parks offer guided tours or interpretive campfire programs, either on a scheduled or request basis. Where they are available, the programs are excellent; be sure to take advantage of them.

CAMPSITES. Over half the state parks offer some type of camping facilities. A fee is charged for overnight stays. Use of hook-up campsites is an additional fee. A fee is charged for use of trailer dump facilities, but use is free to those who pay a campsite fee. Camping is limited to 10 consecutive days at any one park. Except for reservation campgrounds, campsites are on a first-come, first-served basis. Staking out campsites with personal property, signs, or camping equipment to reserve them for friends is prohibited, as well as blatantly discourteous.

LODGING. Some parks offer rental lodging that appeals to those who like their park experience unique and a little less primitive, and their indoor accommodation inexpensive. All should be reserved ahead of time, although when you arrive you might be fortunate enough to find some open and available.

Buildings: Historic structures such as lighthouse keeper's residences and military housing are rented at some parks.

Furnishings vary, but usually are of comfortable period decor.

Camping: Cozy cabins, yurts, large tents, and Quonset-like weather ports usually include a couch that converts to a double bed, a bunk bed with double mattress below and single or three-quarters mattress above, a heater, and an outside picnic table and fire brazier. All have wooden floors and electricity for heat and lights; bathroom facilities are nearby restrooms. You provide bedding or sleeping bags and all cooking needs.

Hostels: Two parks—Fort Worden and Fort Flagler—have hostels operated by American Youth Hostels, Inc., which offers inexpensive dormitory-style lodging for bicyclists and travelers. It is not necessary to be a member of the organization to stay there.

USING THIS BOOK

At the beginning of each park description, the shaded area on the small state map indicates the region covered by the chapter, and the black dot shows the park location. A tent icon indicates that camping is available, and a trailer icon indicates that some sites have RV hookups.

Information blocks at the beginning of each park description contain the vital statistics of each park.

In the **Season/Hours** listing, "standard park hours," which are applicable in most parks, are 6:30 A.M. to 10:00 P.M. from April 1 through October 15, and 8:00 A.M. to 5:00 P.M. from October 16 through March 31, if the park remains open during the winter. A few parks have unique hours, which are indicated.

Barrier-free facilities are indicated by (☐). Note that facilities so designated might not meet the rigorous criteria of the Americans with Disabilities Act, but they are accessible with little difficulty.

In the **Camping Facilities** listing, the following campsite categories are described:

RV site: Campsites with power, water, and sewer connections for RVs and trailers. Where only one or two of the connections is provided, this is indicated by (E) for electricity or (W) for water. If nothing is indicated, all three are provided.

Standard campsite: A vehicle pull-off, picnic table, fireplace, and a space for pitching a tent or setting out gear. These sites are grouped on loops that have water, sink waste drains, solid waste-disposal containers, and a restroom.

Walk-in campsite: Similar to a standard site, but vehicle parking is nearby, not at the site itself.

Primitive site: Facilities vary, but usually includes a picnic table, fire grate, and tent space, but only nearby vault or pit toilets. They generally have no vehicle access, and might not have water. Marine state parks with onshore camping have only primitive campsites, and several do not have potable water. Primitive sites often appeal to bicyclists, as they usually have space available, and they offer accommodations at lower rates. Large groups of cyclists should contact the park in advance to be assured of space.

Cascadia Marine Trail site: Some saltwater parks have a few primitive campsites at beach level. These sites are restricted to kayaks, canoes, or small motorless boats that can be beached. For a more complete description of the Cascadia Marine Trail, contact the Washington Water Trails Association at the address listed in Appendix A.

"Restrooms" are those facilities with running water that have sinks for washing and flush toilets. "Toilets" are Sanicans, pit toilets, and vault toilets that do not have running water.

RESTROOMS, SHOWERS, AND DUMP STATIONS. All the larger state parks that have overnight camping have restrooms with coin-operated showers. Parks with swimming beaches often provide bathhouses with changing rooms and showers. Some parks might have restrooms in the main camping areas, but have only toilets in outlying camp areas or in group camps.

Larger state parks have dump stations for trailers, and several state parks that have boating facilities have marine pumpout stations or portable toilet dump stations.

FIRES. Fireplaces (low concrete enclosures topped with a metal grate) or braziers (metal enclosures on a waist-high metal stand) are provided in all areas where fires are permitted, and some parks have beach fire-rings. Bring wood or charcoal briquettes with you, or purchase them from the ranger or concessionaire if it is available. It might not be the pioneer way, but it is the most ecological. Cutting or damaging living trees is prohibited, as is removing dead or downed wood, as this disturbs the natural ecosystem, which relies on decaying wood for nutrients. Similarly, driftwood helps stabilize beaches, and its use for firewood is prohibited.

All fires must be confined to provided fireplaces. Picnic tables, docks, and other wooden structures must be adequately protected from portable barbecues to prevent any damage to them.

GARBAGE. Most public areas of state parks have solid waste-disposal containers. However, undeveloped or natural areas and several marine state parks do not have garbage pickup; there you are expected to pack your garbage out with you. Even in parks with garbage pickup, you are urged to take cans and bottles home with you and recycle them. Boaters should not toss their trash overboard, as it can pollute the water, create hazards for marine life, and eventually end up on the beach as litter.

A few of the parks have problems with raccoons, bears, or other scavenging wildlife. Garbage should be placed in the animal-resistant trash containers provided as soon as possible to prevent raids.

GROUP-USE AREAS AND PLAYFIELDS. Some state parks have reservable day-use facilities with picnic tables and kitchen shelters that accommodate groups of 20 or more for activities such as picnics, church services, or office get-togethers. Many state parks that offer camping also have one or more areas set aside for group camping. These areas often include open fields for play activities, space for pitching tents, picnic tables, fire grates, toilets, one or more picnic shelters, and in some cases adirondack shelters. Parks with these facilities are shown in Appendix B and are noted as such in the park information blocks.

Many parks have places for organized sports, such as softball diamonds, volleyball courts, tennis courts, horseshoe pits, and even golf courses. Visitors must bring their sports equipment with them. Use of these facilities is on a first-come, first-served basis, unless prior arrangements for group use have been made.

ENVIRONMENTAL LEARNING CENTERS (ELCs). The most comprehensive group overnight facilities are at ELCs. These most closely resemble the summer camps fondly (or not) remembered from our youth, and they were originally established to provide youth a place to enjoy, experience, and learn from camping.

Today ELCs may be reserved by any organized group, young or not-so-young, such as scout troops, church groups, school classes, seminars, or family reunions. Although ELCs vary in their facilities, most include a kitchen/mess hall, rustic sleeping cabins, playfields, campfire circles, and classroom space. Others have tennis courts, swimming pools, adirondack shelters, canoes, cook cabins, and infirmaries. Your group must provide supervisory personnel, food, bedding, and other supplies, and you must plan your own activities, although sometimes park personnel will, on request, provide interpretive talks or hikes.

Fees for ELCs vary with the facilities available. Only one group at a time may use a group camp or ELC. For information and reservations contact state park headquarters in Olympia.

CONFERENCE CENTER. The most elaborate group facilities are found at Fort Worden, where, in addition to all of the amenities found in group camps or ELCs, the park has facilities that can accommodate from 12 to 400 people, including conference rooms, three dormitories, a dining hall, a restaurant, and 24 refurbished officers' quarters with kitchens. A similar ELC/Conference Center, Hyak Lodge, has recently been established in an old Department of Transportation bunkhouse at Snoqualmie Pass.

MARINE AND FRESHWATER FACILITIES. Many state parks with water frontage have docks, floats, or mooring buoys available for overnight use by visiting boaters. Fees, based on boat length, are charged for overnight use of park docks, floats, and buoys. Continuous moorage at any one facility is limited to three consecutive nights. There is no fee or time limit for anchoring. Rafting on docks and floats is not required, but is encouraged (with permission of inboard boaters).

On buoys, rafting is subject to the following limits: for boats up to 24 feet, four boats maximum on a buoy; for boats between 25 and 36 feet, three boats; for boats between 37 and 45 feet, two boats; for boats over 45 feet, one boat. Exceeding these limits can dislodge a buoy.

Nearly all parks with water frontage have launch ramps for trailered boats, most with adjacent boarding floats. A fee is charged for use of launch ramps; the amount varies with the quality of the ramp. For those camping in the state park, launch ramp use is covered by the campsite fee. Moorage at these floats is restricted to 30 minutes or less. Boaters should launch or recover boats as rapidly as possible and move cars and boat trailers to separate parking areas to make room for others.

A few parks also have launch areas dedicated to hand-carried boats. Lakes within parks are often restricted to hand-powered or battery-run boats; check park rules before using motors. Many parks have water access suitable for dropping in hand-carried boats, even though a specific spot is not designated.

Use of mooring and launch facilities is on a first-come, first-served basis, and neither buoys nor dock space may be reserved by tying dinghies or personal property on them (actions that might result in that property being cut loose). Boaters who anchor off state parks should make sure that hooks are solidly set and ample swing room is left to avoid bumping into others, especially at low tide.

PARK ACTIVITIES—SAFETY AND REGULATIONS

WATER SPORTS. Swimming, windsurfing, surfboarding, waterskiing, and use of motorized water bikes (personal water craft, or PWCs) are popular at various parks (although PWCs are prohibited in San Juan County). Many parks with freshwater frontage have roped-off swimming beaches during summer months. Beaches usually have shallow wading areas, deeper swimming areas, and sometimes swim floats. Budget cuts in 1992 eliminated all lifeguards. Swimming is at your own risk.

A few parks also have floats for use by water skiers. Buoys offshore from swimming beaches mark the limits where boats must operate at no-wake speeds. When engaged in any of these water sports, it is your responsibility to use care in regard to your safety and the safety and enjoyment of others using the park. Wear proper safety equipment, and be aware of natural conditions and your own limitations. Rules with respect to safety and courtesy are posted at all parks.

OCEAN BEACH ACCESSES. Along the Pacific coast, in addition to ocean beach parks, the state parks maintain numerous Ocean Beach Access Points. Most of these access points have hard-packed roads

through the dunes and across the soft sand to the drivable beach.

Within Washington, drivable public beaches on the Pacific Ocean are legally considered part of the highway system. In this case, "drivable" means only that portion of hard-packed wet sand above the courtesy poles designating razor clam beds; driving is not permitted in the soft sand higher on the beach or on the dunes. Because this area is legally a highway, vehicles must be street-legal and licensed, drivers must be licensed, and traffic laws are strictly enforced. The speed limit is 25 mph, and pedestrians always have the right-of-way. All regulations apply to any motorized vehicle, including mopeds.

In some areas, because of heavy pedestrian use, beach driving is prohibited from April 15 to the day after Labor Day, except during razor clam season; other areas do not have the razor-clam-season exception. The text describing the individual Seashore Conservation Areas defines these limits and where they are

applicable. Driving is prohibited year-round at a few areas of high pedestrian concentration or unique wildlife habitats.

FISHING, SCUBA DIVING, AND BEACH FORAGING. Within state parks the only living beach life that may be taken are those forms that are edible and under regulation by the Department of Fish and Wildlife. It is unlawful to remove any inedible living animals, such as starfish, sand dollars, or sea anemones. Valid state licenses are required to take shrimp, razor clams, or fresh- or saltwater fish within state parks. State Department of Fish and Wildlife regulations govern the taking of fish and shellfish.

A number of artificial underwater reefs have been built near state parks to encourage growth of marine life. Most of these are open to scuba diving, but many are classified as underwater sanctuaries, and taking of living creatures is prohibited. Check with park regulations before using underwater spearfishing gear.

Bivalve shellfish, such as clams, oysters, mussels, and scallops, which feed by filtering sea water, concentrate toxic substances in the water in their bodies. In certain areas toxic chemical wastes, effluents, bird and mammal feces, or poisonous algae blooms ("red tide," which causes paralytic shellfish poisoning [PSP]) might be concentrated at levels that make shellfish unsafe for human consumption. The Department of Health regularly monitors all shellfish harvesting areas in the state, and when contaminants near unsafe levels, beaches are closed to taking of shellfish. Closure notices are publicized in newspapers, on a Department of Health "hot line," and on bulletin boards at individual parks.

Razor clams, once the greatest trophy of ocean beaches, unfortunately have suffered serious setbacks. In 1984 and 1985 the season was closed due to a parasite that, although harmless to humans, attacked the clams and caused devastation to their population. In 1991 and 1992 the high levels of domoic acid, which causes nausea in people who consume the clams,

Digging for razor clams and harvesting other types of seafood are popular at many state parks that have saltwater beaches. Be sure to follow state regulations regarding season, limits, and licenses.

A great blue heron shops for lunch among old pilings at Fort Canby State Park.

caused a closure of the digging season. Razor-clamming seasons are generally short—one or two weeks a year—and vary with the condition of the clam beds. Such careful management will help this important resource return to its glory in future years.

WALKING AND HIKING. Although hiking is listed as an attraction at many state parks, hiking trails vary dramatically from park to park. Hikes range from short (0.25 mile or less) paved walks in smaller parks to many miles of hiking trails at some parks. Unfortunately, in parks with extensive trail systems, back-country trail maintenance may suffer because of budget limits. Before hiking on a remote park trail, check with local rangers about its condition. Long hikes require the same attention to clothing, footgear, backpacks, food, and emergency supplies as on other remote forest trails. Walkers should re-

member that on equestrian trails they share, horses have the right-of-way; move to the side of the trail and stand quietly while they pass.

Many parks have short interpretive nature walks. Sometimes these walks have brochures that are keyed to numbered stations describing the flora, fauna, geology, history, or ecology; a few parks leave it to the visitor to identify features found there. Groups can often arrange for guided nature walks by advance request to the park manager.

EQUESTRIAN USE. Eleven state parks have designated trails open to equestrian use, and many of these have trailer unloading facilities. No fees are charged for riding horses in state parks. Lake Wenatchee and Riverside State Parks have concessionaire-operated horse rentals; at Ocean Shores and a few other state parks, privately operated horse rentals

are nearby. Horses are not permitted in swimming, camping, or picnicking areas, and must never be left unattended or insecurely tied. Riders are responsible for keeping their mounts under control.

Horseback riding is allowed year-round on all Pacific Ocean beaches in the Seashore Conservation Areas (essentially from Moclips to Ilwaco). Horses are permitted only on the hard-sand area above the clam beds; riders must yield to pedestrians and must walk their mounts through areas of heavy pedestrian concentration.

BICYCLING. Bicycling is becoming increasingly popular in Washington state parks as both transportation and recreation. All roads within parks are open for bicycle use, but bicyclists must obey all traffic laws, ride single file on the shoulder in the direction of traffic flow, use adequate lighting after dark, and exercise courtesy.

Restrictions on trail use by bicycles vary by park. Check with local park rangers to find out which trails are open to bicycles. Bicycles may only be used on roads and designated trails, and may not be ridden cross-country, or on lawns or natural vegetation.

WINTER RECREATION. A number of the state parks at higher elevations that receive substantial snowfall are as heavily used in winter as in summer. Cross-country skiing and snowshoeing are the most common winter fun at these parks, but at Mount Spokane concessionaires operate ski lifts and tows for alpine skiing, and a sledding hill is maintained at Fields Spring. A few other parks have roads that are open to snowmobiling.

Cleared parking areas are provided at these parks, but a Sno-Park permit must be displayed on the vehicle. Fees generated by the Sno-Park program go to maintaining trails. The park headquarters in Olympia sells a pocket guide to Sno-Park ski trails; many retail sporting goods stores sell Sno-Park permits.

METAL DETECTORS. Use of metal detectors

is regulated in nearly 100 of the state parks. From the Friday before Memorial Day through Labor Day, use of metal detectors is permitted in the day-use areas of those parks only in the morning, from park opening time to 10:00 A.M. During the rest of the year, metal detecting is allowed all hours that those parks are open to the public. Persons planning to metal detect must register with the park office.

PETS. Pets must be on a leash less than 8 feet long and must be under control at all times. With the exception of dogs assisting disabled persons, pets are not allowed on any swimming beach or in any public building. Pets are not permitted to molest, annoy, or disturb the peace of other visitors. Owners are responsible for cleaning up pet excrement by putting it in a paper or plastic bag and depositing it in a solid-waste container. Use special care

that dogs are on a leash and under control in equestrian areas.

ALCOHOL. Alcoholic beverages may be consumed only in designated areas (typically individual campsites). Kegs of beer are prohibited.

NOISE. Tastes in music might differ, but at a certain decibel level it's all offensive noise. Please don't inflict your choice on

CURRENT FEES

The following information is as of 1999. It is provided as general reference regarding fees, and is subject to change. For more details and information about reservations contact Washington State Parks, 7150 Cleanwater Lane, Box 42650, Olympia, WA 98504-2650; (360) 902-8500. Website: http://www.parks.wa.gov

Parks That Accept Campsite Reservations

Battle Ground Lake	Lake Easton	Scenic Beach
Belfair	Lincoln Rock	Seaquest
Birch Bay	Manchester	Sequim Bay
Central Ferry	Maryhill	Spencer Spit
Chief Timothy	Millersylvania	Steamboat Rock
Dash Point	Moran	Sun Lakes
Dosewallips	Ocean City	Twenty-five
Fort Canby	Pacific Beach	Mile Creek
Fort Flagler	Pearrygin Lake	Twin Harbors
Grayland Beach	Penrose Point	Wenatchee Con-
Ike Kinswa	Potholes	fluence
Lake Chelan	Rasar	Wenberg
Lake Cushman		

Fees

Standard campsite: $11
Campsite with utilities: $16
Primitive site, motorized access: $8
Primitive site, no motorized access: $6; motorized access: $8
Extra vehicle or unattended overnight vehicle permit: $6
Campsite reservation fee: $6, non-refundable
A $1 popular-destination camping surcharge is also collected at the most heavily used parks from April 1 through September 30.

Group camping: $2 per person per night, or the appropriate campsite fee; $25 non-refundable reservation/registration fee; minimum fee, $15
Cascadia Marine Trail Campsite: $7 per person
Limited income and disability: No charge
Group day-use: $50 to $500+, based on group size (20 to 500+)
Trailer dump fee, per use: $3 (no charge for those paying overnight camping or moorage fees)
Mooring buoys: $5 per night
Docks and floats: Boats under 26 feet, $8 per night; 26 feet and over, $11 per night
Boat launch fee: $4 per day at sites with restrooms, parking, and boarding docks; $3 per day for hard surface sites without one or more of these three features. (No charge for those paying overnight camping or moorage fees.)
Environmental Learning Centers: Overnight use, $6.25 per person per day (Camp Wooten, $7.55). Day-use only, $2 per person. Minimum charges vary by location and season. Deposit is a one-day minimum occupancy.
Daily Sno-Park fee per vehicle: $8; three-day pass, $10; seasonal pass, $20.
Interpretive Center entrance fee: $2.

Annual passes and permits

Off-season senior citizen camping pass: $30 (October 1 to March 31, and Sunday through Thursday in April)
Annual moorage permit: Boats under 26 feet, $50; 26 feet and over, $80
Annual boat launch permit: $40
Annual Cascadia Marine Trail Campsite permit: $20

neighboring campers. Park campers are requested to observe quiet hours from 11:00 P.M. to 6:30 A.M. Generators may only be operated between 8:00 A.M. and 9:00 P.M.

THE NATURAL ENVIRONMENT AND VANDALISM. It is unlawful to hunt or harass wildlife in a state park, and discharge of firearms or fireworks is prohibited. Trees, bushes, and other vegetation within the park, including flowers, may not be picked or damaged. Gathering edible berries and mushrooms for personal consumption is permitted.

Destruction or defacing of park property is senseless, as well as illegal, since it prevents others from enjoying the very things that you and they have come to the park to experience, and costs state residents scarce tax dollars to repair. Sometimes damage results from ignorance or thoughtlessness; these people need to be educated. Deliberate vandalism—restroom fixtures broken, docks damaged, graffiti spray-painted on old fort bunkers—is inexcusable. Anyone seen destroying either the natural environment or park property should be promptly reported to authorities.

SAFETY CONSIDERATIONS AND EMERGENCIES

Visitor safety is a primary concern in the design and maintenance of park facilities, but mishaps can occur. Children should not roam unsupervised. Not all the areas described in this book are suitable at all times, or for all people: Dangerous undertows can occur on ocean beaches, trails can be treacherously slippery in bad weather, old army bunkers can be dangerous to the unwary, and storms can make beach approach by boat hazardous. At all times independent judgment and common sense must be used to ensure that your visit is a safe and enjoyable one.

It is hoped that no emergency will mar your stay at a state park. But if one should, the park manager or ranger will render assistance. If there is no resident manager at the park you are visiting, the county sheriff has legal authority in all unincorporated areas. There usually are telephones within the park or nearby.

For boaters, the U.S. Coast Guard has primary responsibility for safety and law enforcement. The Coast Guard continuously monitors marine VHF channel 16, and that should be the most reliable means of contact for emergencies on the water. The Coast Guard also monitors Citizen's Band channel 9 at some locations and times. Several volunteer groups monitor the CB emergency frequency and will assist with relaying an emergency request to the proper authorities. Cellular telephone companies in the Puget Sound area provide a quick-dial number, *CG, that will immediately connect a cell phone to the Coast Guard Vessel Traffic Center in Seattle. This center coordinates all marine safety and rescue activities for the region.

CHAPTER ONE

THE OLYMPIC PENINSULA

BOGACHIEL STATE PARK

Camping, picnicking, fishing, rafting, paddling

SEASON/HOURS: Year-round, some campsites closed in winter.

AREA: 123.1 acres; 2,800 feet of freshwater shoreline on the Bogachiel River.

OVERNIGHT AND DAY-USE FACILITIES: 6 RV sites (E), 34 standard campsites, 2 primitive campsites, group camp (20 persons), 3 picnic sites, picnic shelter, 2 restrooms with showers, trailer dump station.

RECREATIONAL FACILITIES: 0.5-mile nature trail.

CAR ACCESS: On US 101, 4.4 miles south of Forks.

The scenic grandeur and recreational attractions of the Olympic Peninsula are so fine that much of its mountainous heart and wave-swept ocean shores has been set aside as national park. The only developed state park in the northwest peninsula area is Bogachiel, a park modest in size but impressive in its beauty. The park's entrance road drops down through a striking stand of hemlock, a reminder of the ancient forest that once

At Fort Worden State Park, several trails lead through bright yellow lupine to the beach.

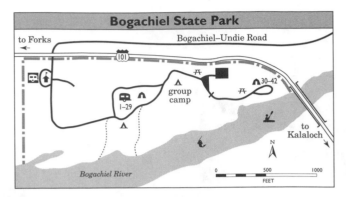

Bogachiel State Park

to Forks
Bogachiel–Undie Road
101
group camp
1–29
30–42
to Kalaloch
N
Bogachiel River
0   500   1000
FEET

Large, old spruce frame picnicking and camping sites at Bogachiel State Park.

blanketed the region. A campground and picnic shelter sit in tall spruce; a pair of primitive walk-in/bicycle campsites and a small group camp lie in the trees nearer the wide Bogachiel River. Beyond the upper campground, the road swings downhill past a rustic kitchen shelter to more campsites. Paths lead through the forest to the riverbank.

In all but high-water season the river bed is an expanse of water-worn rocks, with intermittent pools where trout lurk. A state steelhead-rearing area 8 miles downstream contributes to excellent runs of winter steelhead. Put in here for paddling trips down the quiet river to its confluence with the Sol Duc, some 15.5 river miles away. At this point the merged waterways become the Quillayute River and flow on for 5 more miles to reach the Pacific Ocean.

HOYT PROPERTY

Beach walking, shellfish

AREA: 36.8 acres; 1,520 feet of saltwater shoreline on the Strait of Juan de Fuca.
CAR ACCESS: On both sides of SR 112, 5 miles west of Sekiu.

East of the mouth of the Sekiu River, SR 112 parallels the shore. The land north of the highway as well as a small inland segment is a portion of undeveloped Hoko River State Park. This Strait of Juan de Fuca sand-and-gravel beach is flat and exposed, except for a narrow forested strip at either end. Several gravel pulloffs on the beach side of the highway provide easy access over the low bank to the beach.

EAGLE POINT PROPERTY

Beach walking, tide pools

AREA: 52.9 acres; 5,730 feet of saltwater shoreline on the Strait of Juan de Fuca.
BOAT ACCESS: 3.5 miles west of Sekiu, northeast of Eagle Point Road.

A second isolated strip of park beach property is about 2 miles east of the Hoyt Property, on the east side of Eagle Point. The mile-long beach, which can be reached only by boat, is sand above and hardpan below mid-tide levels, displaying primarily piddock clams and mussels, but no harvestable shellfish.

DUNGENESS STATE PARK

Boating, paddling, fishing

SEASON/HOURS: Year-round.
AREA: 0.5 acres; 1,943 feet of saltwater shoreline on the Strait of Juan de Fuca.
DAY-USE FACILITIES: 2 toilets.
RECREATIONAL FACILITIES: 1-lane paved boat ramp.
CAR ACCESS: From US 101 in Sequim, turn north at Sequim Avenue. Follow this road for 4.7 miles, to where it bends west and becomes East Anderson Road. In 0.9 mile turn north on Marine Drive, and continue 0.9 mile to the junction with Cline Spit Road. Take this road downhill for 0.3 mile to the park.

This small piece of beach is owned by State Parks, but has been developed for a launch ramp by Clallam County. The ramp leads down to a shallow lagoon on the inside of Cline Spit. A narrow channel, tenuous at minus tides, threads through the bay behind Dungeness Spit to offer boating access to the Strait of Juan de Fuca. Not bothered by the shallow lagoon waters, kayakers find this an excellent launch spot.

SEQUIM BAY STATE PARK

Camping, picnicking, hiking, scuba diving, beach walking, shellfish, fishing, boating, paddling

SEASON/HOURS: Year-round, some campsites closed in winter; reservations accepted in summer.

AREA: 92.4 acres; 4,909 feet of saltwater shoreline on Sequim Bay.

OVERNIGHT AND DAY-USE FACILITIES: 26 RV sites (&), 60 standard campsites (&), 3 primitive campsites, group camp with kitchen shelter

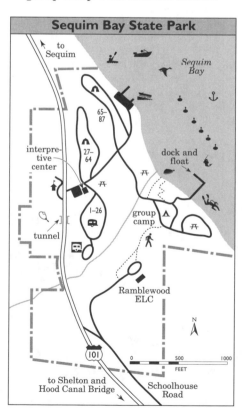

Boaters row ashore from their quiet anchorage at Sequim Bay State Park.

(75 persons), 20 picnic sites, 2 kitchen shelters (1 reservable), 2 group day-use areas (50 persons and 100 persons), 5 restrooms (3 with showers) (&), trailer dump station.

RECREATIONAL FACILITIES: 1 mile of hiking trail, baseball field, 2 tennis courts, quarter basketball court, 2-lane paved boat ramp with boarding float, dock and float (removed in winter), 6 mooring buoys.

EDUCATIONAL FACILITIES: Interpretive displays.

RAMBLEWOOD ELC: Kitchen, dining hall, lodge with fireplace, 8 adirondack shelters, restroom with showers, volleyball area, accommodates 100 persons day-use, 75 persons overnight.

CAR ACCESS: On US 101, 4 miles southwest of Sequim.

BOAT ACCESS: Follow the marked channel between the two parallel sandspits at the entrance to Sequim Bay. The park is on the southwest side of the bay.

The two parallel sandbars that guard the entrance to Sequim Bay hid it from the first three expeditions to visit the area; neither Quimper in 1790, Eliza in 1791, nor Vancouver in 1792 recorded the inlet. It was not until 1841 that it was finally discovered by the Wilkes Expedition, which named it Washington Harbor. It was later renamed to the Clallam Indian word meaning "quiet water." The same sandbars that slowed the discovery of the bay challenge boaters today. The channel between them is marked by navigation aids, but it is narrow and shallow. Once in the bay, however, the placid waters live up to their Native American name.

The park is on the southwest end of the harbor on a terraced bluff. A fishing and moorage float, reached by a dock extending far out over shallow water, is removed in the winter. The water outboard of the float is rather shallow, so use caution when approaching at minus tides. Six buoys with more water under them than the float are set offshore; a seventh buoy to the south is private. At the north end of the park, a paved road drops down the bluff to a two-lane launch ramp.

A small interpretive center near the entrance, open from 9:00 A.M. to 9:00 P.M. daily, offers displays and a short video program that teach you about harvesting shellfish and crabs, boating safely, filleting fish, and other interesting park-related topics.

A campground at the north end of the park is laid out in two loops. The lower loop holds a few sites with water views, but most are tucked into the wooded hillside. Sites in the upper loop are in open timber with no views of the bay, and might pick up traffic noise. A hookup campground loop, with a trailer dump station and a group picnic site with swing sets, lies in conifer-shaded grass south of the campground entrance road.

A dead-end road leads south from a bluff-top picnic shelter, past primitive walk-in campsites and a deep stream-carved ravine, to the group camp. A canopy of western red cedar with a few Douglas-fir and grand fir shades this more rustic campsite. Short trails throughout the park connect picnicking, camping, and shore areas—walk and see what you discover. A path from the picnic area leads through a concrete underpass beneath the highway to sports fields near the ranger's residence.

A separate road at the south end of the park leads to Ramblewood, which is connected to the main portion of the park by trails. The popular ELC, which is open year-round, offers extensive facilities for group camping and recreation.

MILLER PENINSULA

Beach walking

AREA: 2,843.34 acres; 11,400 feet of saltwater shoreline on the Strait of Juan de Fuca.
BOAT ACCESS: The beach runs west for just over 2 miles from Thompson Spit, 1.5 miles west of Diamond Point.

State Parks acquired this property on the Miller Peninsula due to a failed resort project and a complex sequence of land swapping. However, State Parks, perpetually strapped for dollars, has not come up with funding for park development.

There is no feasible land access to the property's fine 2-mile-long sand and gravel beach that lies below a 200-foot-high sandy bluff; however, it can be reached by a beachable boat. For those who don't mind a long beach hike, the park beach is a part of DNR Beach 411, which continues westward to the tip of Travis Spit at the entrance to Sequim Bay. A tiny Clallam County park provides beach access 0.5 mile west of Rocky Point. To reach this park, turn off US 101 onto East Sequim Bay Road at either Old Blyn Road or Blyn Crossing. Follow East Sequim Bay Road north along the east side of the bay for 4.5 miles to Panorama Boulevard. Here turn east, and in 0.75 mile turn east again onto Buck Loop. Find the park in another 0.25 mile at the intersection of Buck Loop and Deer Court. At all but extreme high tide levels the beach can be walked east to the park property.

ANDERSON LAKE STATE PARK

Hiking, fishing

SEASON/HOURS: Closed November 1 through April 15.
AREA: 423 acres; 8,250 feet of freshwater shoreline on Anderson Lake.
DAY-USE FACILITIES: Picnic site, 2 toilets.
RECREATIONAL FACILITIES: 4.4 miles of

Two young anglers are fascinated by polliwogs along the shore of Anderson Lake.

hiking trail, 1-lane paved boat ramp (*only electric motors permitted*).

CAR ACCESS: Drive SR 20 south from Port Townsend for 6.7 miles, or north 3.7 miles from US 101, and turn east on Anderson Lake Road to reach the park in another 1.1 miles.

The mirrored surface of Anderson Lake reflects the surrounding forested hillsides and shoreside marshes, hiding cutthroat and rainbow trout that lure anglers to its waters. Park facilities are minimal: a pair of toilets, a single-lane launch ramp, a water faucet, and a solitary picnic table beneath a towering Douglas-fir at water's edge.

The 59-acre lake, which is only 25 feet deep at its deepest spot, was once choked by algae, threatening the fish; however, an aeration system has restored the oxygen balance, and thus the viability of the lake's aquatic population. A sometimes muddy trail that circles the lake helps fishermen reach shoreside accesses.

OLD FORT TOWNSEND STATE PARK

Camping, picnicking, nature interpretation, hiking, scuba diving, shellfish, fishing, crabbing, boating, paddling, historical interpretation

SEASON/HOURS: Closed mid-September to mid-April.

AREA: 367.73 acres; 3,960 feet of saltwater shoreline on Port Townsend Bay.

OVERNIGHT AND DAY-USE FACILITIES: 40 standard campsites, 3 primitive campsites, group camp (80 persons), 43 picnic tables, 3 kitchen shelters (1 reservable), 3 fire rings, group day-use area (100 persons), 2 restrooms (1 with shower), 6 toilets, trailer dump station.

RECREATIONAL FACILITIES: 6.5 miles of hiking trail (biking on some), 4 mooring buoys.

EDUCATIONAL FACILITIES: 0.25-mile nature trail, 0.25-mile historical interpretive trail.

CAR ACCESS: From SR 20, 2.2 miles south of Port Townsend, turn east on Old Fort Townsend Road and reach the park in 0.5 mile.

BOAT ACCESS: Buoys lie 1 mile south of Glenn Cove on the west side of Port Townsend Bay. Nearest launch ramps are at Port Townsend, Fort Flagler, and Hadlock.

Although most of the well-known forts on Puget Sound are of World War I vintage, this one harkens back to the short-lived Indian War of 1855–56. That uprising struck sufficient fear into the hearts of the local settlers that Company I of the Fourth Infantry was sent to Puget Sound. Construction of their garrison, Fort Townsend, began in 1856. Two years later, Company I was relocated to Fort Steilacoom, and the fort was placed in caretaker status until 1874. In July of that year political pressure applied by the scions of Port Townsend caused the fort to be reactivated, over the objections of many regional military commanders who felt it was a poor defensive position and tried (unsuccessfully) to shut it down. In January 1895 an accident accomplished what 20 years of protest through military channels could not, when a lamp exploded and burned down the barracks, and the post was permanently abandoned a few months later. The fort retained its "never say die" character, however, when it was used during World War II as an enemy munitions defusing station. It was finally transferred to state parks in 1953.

Today a row of campsites line up with military precision above the wide grass terrace that once held the officers'

Mount Baker is framed by old offshore pilings at Old Fort Townsend State Park.

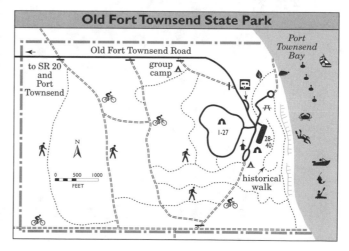

Old Fort Townsend State Park

houses. The remainder of the campground is along a loop road heavily wooded with cedar and Douglas-fir, with a thick ground cover of salal, ferns, thimbleberry, and rhododendron. Primitive walk-in campsites sit on a flat lawn above the ranger's residence. Picnic sites, ball fields, and a children's play area are all found on the grassy field that once was the post parade ground.

A gated service road drops down the steep bluff to a gently tapering rock and cobble beach and a line of pilings that supported the fort's wharf. Mooring buoys are offshore. Steep underwater walls and the old pilings provide fine opportunities for scuba diving.

A self-guided nature trail that parallels the service road passes stations identifying local flora. A second historical interpretive trail starts at the display kiosk in the heart of the park and circles the perimeter of the parade grounds, where 13 stations have informational displays about features of the 1877 post. The park ranger conducts interpretive walks on Saturdays and by request, and supports an active Junior Ranger interpretive program in the park.

The munitions defusing station has now been transformed into a group camp, and more than 6 miles of trails and fire roads thread through the woods southwest of the campground loop. Since portions of the unimproved forest within the park have been classified as a Natural Forest Area, bicycles are permitted on only a few of these trails; park informational displays tell which ones are open to bicycles.

ROTHSCHILD HOUSE HERITAGE AREA

Historical interpretation

SEASON/HOURS: Daily April through October; weekends only the remainder of the year.
AREA: 0.54 acre.
DAY-USE FACILITIES: Picnic table.
EDUCATIONAL FACILITIES: Restored historic house (fee for tour).
CAR ACCESS: From SR 20, entering Port Townsend from the south, bear uphill to the left on Washington Street. In 10 blocks turn left on Taylor Street. The home is 1 block north at the intersection of Taylor and Franklin.

This historic home is not as elaborate as some of the showcase Victorian-era homes in Port Townsend, but it is an excellent example of typical architecture and furnishings of the period. The wood frame house, which is listed on the national Register of Historic Places, as well as the state register, was built in 1868 by D. C. H. Rothschild, a German immigrant who became a prominent Port Townsend merchant.

The original carpets, wallpaper, woodwork, and landscaping of the home have been carefully restored and maintained. Many of the furnishings are those of the original owners, and over 2,500 antiques are incorporated into the decor. The gardens, which are representative of those in the late 1800s, include herbs and old-fashioned roses, peonies, and lilacs. A fee is charged to tour the house; volunteers answer your questions about the home's history and its antique furnishings.

The kitchen at Rothschild House stands ready to serve up a hearty meal.

FORT WORDEN STATE PARK AND CONFERENCE CENTER

Camping, picnicking, kite flying, hiking, bicycling, scuba diving, beach walking, fishing, boating, historic sites, military museum, marine science center, conferences, cultural arts

SEASON/HOURS: Year-round; housing and campsite reservations accepted in summer.

COMMANDING OFFICER'S HOUSE: 10:00 A.M. to 5:00 P.M. daily June through August; weekends 1:00 P.M. to 4:00 P.M. from March through May, September through October, and selected holidays (visitor fee charged).

PUGET SOUND COAST ARTILLERY MUSEUM: 11:00 A.M. to 4:00 P.M. daily June through August; weekends only 11:00 A.M. to 4:00 P.M. from March through May and September through October (visitor fee charged).

MARINE SCIENCE CENTER: Noon to 6:00 P.M. Tuesday through Sunday mid-June through Labor Day; noon to 4:00 P.M. weekends April through mid-June and Labor Day through October; noon to 4:00 P.M. the Friday and Saturday following Thanksgiving (visitor fee charged).

AREA: 433.56 acres; 11,020 feet of saltwater shoreline on Admiralty Inlet and the Strait of Juan de Fuca.

OVERNIGHT AND DAY-USE FACILITIES: 80 RV sites (30 EW) (7 &), 5 primitive campsites, fire ring, Cascadia Marine Trail campsites, 60 picnic sites, reservable kitchen shelter, 5 restrooms with showers (3 &), 5 toilets, trailer dump station, laundromat.

LODGING: Extensive rental options ranging from dormitory-style housing in enlisted men's barracks to family housing in refurbished Victorian homes and a youth hostel (27 persons). Contact the park for full descriptions and reservations.

RECREATIONAL FACILITIES: 8 miles of hiking trail (&), bicycle trails, ball field, gymnasium, 2 tennis courts, outdoor basketball court, volleyball court, bathhouse, underwater marine park, 2-lane paved boat ramp with boarding float, 3 mooring floats (128 feet of space, *floats removed in winter*), 8 mooring buoys.

EDUCATIONAL FACILITIES: Abandoned Coast Artillery fortifications, Puget Sound Coast Artillery Museum, Commanding Officer's House, Centrum, Marine Science Center, Centennial Rhododendron Garden.

CONCESSIONS: Snack bar/grocery, cafeteria, restaurant (May through October).

OTHER: Conference center (10–400 persons) with extensive meeting room and recreation options. Contact the park for full descriptions and reservations.

CAR ACCESS: From Port Townsend follow the well-signed route north to the

Fort Worden beach activity is overseen by the Point Wilson lighthouse.

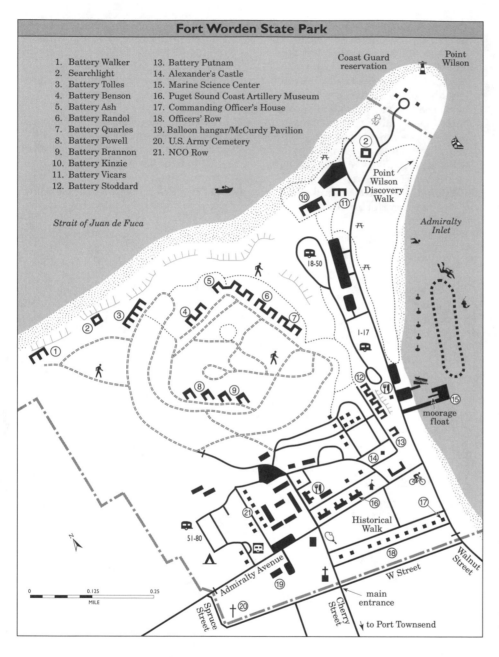

Fort Worden State Park

1. Battery Walker
2. Searchlight
3. Battery Tolles
4. Battery Benson
5. Battery Ash
6. Battery Randol
7. Battery Quarles
8. Battery Powell
9. Battery Brannon
10. Battery Kinzie
11. Battery Vicars
12. Battery Stoddard
13. Battery Putnam
14. Alexander's Castle
15. Marine Science Center
16. Puget Sound Coast Artillery Museum
17. Commanding Officer's House
18. Officers' Row
19. Balloon hangar/McCurdy Pavilion
20. U.S. Army Cemetery
21. NCO Row

Strait of Juan de Fuca

park entrance at the intersection of Cherry and W Streets.

BOAT ACCESS: Moorage docks and buoys are on Admiralty Inlet, 1 mile north of Point Hudson, or 1 mile south of Point Wilson.

Fort Worden, which was once an imposing fortification, has, improbably, become a popular center for recreation and performing arts. This was one of three major Coast Artillery forts built in the early 1900s to protect Puget Sound. Its design incorporated the defensive technology of the period—massive concrete emplacements with huge guns mounted on barbette carriages, groups of mortars in concrete-rimmed pits protected from direct naval fire, and smaller batteries intended to prevent naval landing attacks. The fort was activated in 1902, and over the next 10 years, the fortifications were supplemented by newer batteries with guns on disappearing carriages (which could be raised out of their protective emplacements so that the guns were exposed only long enough to fire), and more advanced rapid-fire gun batteries were added. However, this was a period of transition in naval technology; battleships were designed with increasingly bigger and more accurate guns, and the fort's batteries became obsolete almost as soon as they were placed.

Changes in U. S. naval operating strategies, improved shipboard fire control systems, and the advent of military aircraft finally tolled a death knell for these large Coast Artillery dinosaurs. Most of the guns and mortars were removed from the fort and sent to Europe during World War I, where they were mounted on rail cars to serve as mobile heavy artillery. In 1920 antiaircraft guns were mounted in some of the old emplacements in tacit recognition of the latest change in military technology. During World War II the fort was headquarters of the Harbor Defense of Puget Sound, which monitored new underwater sonar and sensing devices and radar sites, and coordinated Canadian and U.S. defensive activities in the Strait of Juan de Fuca and Puget Sound. The last of the fort's big guns were scrapped in the early 1940s, and in 1953 the Harbor Defense Command was deactivated, ending forever the fort's coastal defense role. No shots were ever fired in actual defense of Puget Sound from any of the region's forts.

Enjoying the Fort's History

Although the guns themselves are gone, the massive concrete emplacements remain as silent witnesses to a half century of change in defensive strategies and technology. The fort is now on the National Register of Historic Places and is designated as a National Historic Landmark. Because the road to upper hill emplacements is closed to cars, many visitors view only those few batteries found near the road to the beach. To gain a better appreciation of the history of the fort, pick up one of the park brochures describing the gun batteries and walk the road to the top of the hill or follow the trail uphill from the campground. It is here that a major portion of the original emplacements remain.

A less strenuous historical walk loops through the "people" portion of the old fort, passing the post headquarters, barracks, hospital, officers' row, and numerous other buildings. The Puget Sound Coast Artillery Museum occupies a portion of one of the barracks north of the parade ground. Photos, displays, a short video, and a working, 1/10-scale model of a disappearing gun bring the military era to life. A volunteer interpreter answers questions on the history of coastal fortifications.

Pick up another descriptive brochure and tour the Commanding Officer's House,

The old Fort Worden bunkers are fascinating to explore.

one of the fort's finest buildings. This fully refurbished example of Victorian architecture and decor, which was completed in 1904, has each of its twelve rooms decorated in a style typical of the time that the fort was active.

Using the Park Today

Thirty-three housing units that were originally residences for officers and non-commissioned officers now serve as unique vacation housing. Larger groups can be accommodated in barracks converted to dormitories, complete with a cafeteria. For the economy-minded, a youth hostel is also available.

The park has conference facilities available in some of the old fort buildings. Additionally, Centrum, a non-profit foundation for creative education and the arts, leases buildings for its residential programs, and hosts a wealth of cultural and educational events, including

workshops, seminars, and writers' conferences. The old balloon hangar, now converted into a performing arts pavilion, hosts symphony concerts, music festivals, folk dance festivals, and plays. Most performances are open to the public. Contact the park for schedules, or see what is going on when you arrive.

Its unique offerings notwithstanding, Fort Worden also has the usual state park trappings. Campsites are split between an open, windy flat between the beach and the bluff at the east side of the park and a wooded loop near the western edge of the upper park. Picnic sites are strung along the beach, while at the south end of the beach is a wharf that was used to bring in supplies, locomotives, construction materials, and guns at the time the Coast Artillery batteries were being built. Today the sturdy wharf protects boat ramps, a dock, and three small floats for visiting boaters.

A building at the end of the wharf houses a marine science center, which is operated by the Port Townsend Marine Science Society as a resource for teachers and school marine programs. The center also conducts classes in marine ecology and offers beach walks, slide shows, workshops, and fish printing sessions. For a small fee the public can view the

Displays at the Puget Sound Coast Artillery Museum include a scale model of a disappearing gun.

facilities' glass tanks and open "wet tables" with live marine life and intertidal creatures.

The Natural Setting

The waters south of Point Wilson are designated a marine underwater park; spearfishing is not permitted. Scuba divers explore rocky pinnacles that rise from the bottom on the north side of the point. The sandy bottom of the east shore and pilings of the old wharfs provide more varied opportunities to view marine life. The swift current is a hazard.

The park's beaches are a study in contrasts. The narrow, rocky north beach, facing the Strait of Juan de Fuca, lies below 200-foot-high bluffs and is exposed to the wild wave action from winds that sweep in from the Pacific. At low tide this portion of the beach can be walked west to North Beach County Park. The beach on the east side of the park, south of Point Wilson, is more sedate, with beach grass and low dunes tapering to a broad sandy beach. It can be walked from the Point Wilson lighthouse all the way south to Chetzemoka City Park.

The U. S. Coast Guard's Point Wilson lighthouse, at the northeast end of the beach, is not open to the public. A beachfront trail, the Point Wilson Discovery Walk, avoids the beach by the lighthouse and heads east across a meadow near the park boundary, passes a searchlight tower, and circles Battery Kinzie.

FORT FLAGLER STATE PARK

Camping, picnicking, hiking, bicycling, windsurfing, scuba diving, beach walking, shellfish, fishing, crabbing, boating, historical interpretation

SEASON/HOURS: Campground closed November 1 through February 28; day-use open year-round; campsite reservations accepted in summer.

AREA: 783.28 acres; 19,100 feet of saltwater shoreline on Admiralty Inlet, Port Townsend Bay, and Kilisut Harbor.

OVERNIGHT AND DAY-USE FACILITIES: 14 RV sites (&), 102 standard campsites (&), 4 primitive campsites, 2 group camps (40 and 80 persons), Cascadia Marine Trail campsite, 59 picnic sites, reservable kitchen shelter, group day-use area (100 persons), 4 restrooms (3 with showers) (&), toilet, trailer dump station.

LODGING: 4 units rental housing (4 to 8 persons), youth hostel (14 persons).

RECREATIONAL FACILITIES: 4 miles of hiking trail, bicycle trails, underwater park, 2 single-lane paved boat ramps, moorage dock and 256 feet of float space (removed in winter), 7 mooring buoys.

EDUCATIONAL FACILITIES: Nature trail, interpretive displays, abandoned Coast Artillery fortifications, music and theater performances.

CONCESSIONS: Snacks, groceries.

ELC: Kitchen, dining hall, auditorium,

Deer graze the lawns at Fort Flagler.

recreation room, fire circles, sports fields, volleyball court, half basketball court, classrooms, 3 barracks-type living units with restrooms and showers (40–180, 25–52, and 15–112 persons).

CAR ACCESS: 1 mile south of Hadlock on Oak Bay Road (SR 116) turn east on

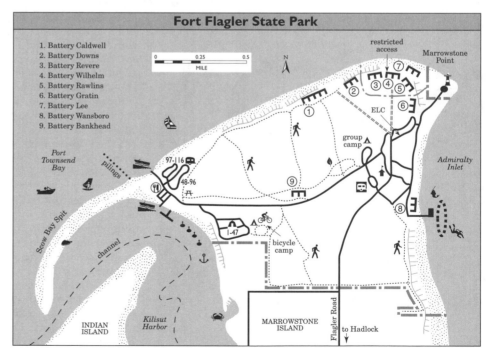

Fort Flagler State Park

1. Battery Caldwell
2. Battery Downs
3. Battery Revere
4. Battery Wilhelm
5. Battery Rawlins
6. Battery Gratin
7. Battery Lee
8. Battery Wansboro
9. Battery Bankhead

restricted access

Marrowstone Point

0   0.25   0.5
MILE

N

Port Townsend Bay

pilings

Scow Bay Spit

97-116

48-96

ELC

group camp

Admiralty Inlet

bicycle camp

I-47

channel

INDIAN ISLAND

Kilisut Harbor

MARROWSTONE ISLAND

Flagler Road

to Hadlock

Flagler Road, cross onto Marrowstone Island, and follow the road 6.9 miles north to the park entrance.

BOAT ACCESS: Enter the west end of the marked channel behind the sandspit at the head of Kilisut Harbor. Moorage is at the east end of the first leg of the channel.

Fort Flagler, the first of the three major Coast Artillery forts at Admiralty Inlet to be activated, beginning in 1899 served as the headquarters for the Harbor Defense of Puget Sound. However, the remote tip of Marrowstone Island was a long haul from civilization, and in 1904 the headquarters was relocated to Fort Worden, although the fort itself remained active. The commanding officer and his staff were then closer to the swinging social life at Port Townsend, and the town gained the musical talents of the Artillery Band.

Because the main gun batteries at Fort Flagler were installed during a period of transition in the technology of artillery, they were of the older style, on fixed barbette mounts, and thus were always exposed to potential enemy fire, even though they were set in massive emplacements. Mortar batteries in concrete pits were protected from direct fire by a small hill at the center of the fort. Smaller guns designed to hold off landing parties were later added to the fortifications; two more batteries, which incorporated newer-design guns on disappearing carriages, were added in 1907.

In World War I the fort served as a training center for army troops, and most of its guns and mortars were removed and sent to Europe. After the war the fort was used only for National Guard and Reserve Officer training camps. During World War II inductees were again trained here; it was home to a few engineering support units until it was permanently deactivated in 1953.

Emplacements for 3- and 6-inch batteries can be seen along the road on the east side of the park; a similar pair are found above the north shore at the end of a gated service road. These batteries, along with mortar emplacements on the north side of the road that leads to the campgrounds, are open to the public. Because they are unsafe, the fort's main gun batteries are not open to visitors.

Using the Park Today

What remains of the fort's barracks, houses, and other buildings now comprise the park's rental facilities and its ELCs, available for use by organized groups. This area surrounds the old parade ground on the open bluff above the east side of the point. A group camp with picnic shelter and campfire circle lies to the west.

The park's camping is divided between two areas. Sites at the upper campground line a loop on a heavily wooded bluff at the southwest corner of the park. Walk-in bicycle campsites are available at the east end. The northwest tip of the park holds picnic sites, a small store, and the lower campground loops, which sit in open grass above the beach. One of two boat ramps drops north into Port Townsend Bay; the second runs west into Kilisut Harbor. A dock with a mooring float and a string of mooring buoys are also at this bend of the channel as it flows into Kilisut Harbor.

The Natural Setting

The north end of the harbor is blocked by the 0.75-mile-long finger of Scow Bay Spit; the channel into the harbor runs along its south side. The spit is partially submerged at high tide, but not enough so for safe boat passage over it. At low tide, park visitors can search the soft sandy spit for clams and probe seaweed for elusive crab. A moldering set of pilings running north from the spit toward Port Townsend once anchored an anti-submarine net that stretched across this span of water during World War II.

The Marrowstone Point lighthouse, on

Family picnicking is one of the many attractions at Fort Flagler State Park.

the northeast tip of the beach, is not open to the public. The adjacent Bureau of Sports Fisheries and Wildlife Research Lab, also closed to the public, provides tours of its facility on advance request. The old engineering wharf, used to bring in construction materials and supplies when the fort was built, juts far out into Admiralty Inlet just south of the ELC area. An underwater park on either side of the wharf attracts scuba divers. Unfortunately, because of a rotting section of deck, the pier is closed to public use until funds are available for its repair. At low tide beachcombers can walk the shoreline between the pier and the lighthouse.

A network of trails connects the camp areas, batteries, and a service road. Just west of the group camp is the self-guided Roots of the Forest interpretive trail, with 14 stations keyed to a park brochure describing the ecology.

Mystery Bay State Park is a favorite boating getaway.

MYSTERY BAY MARINE STATE PARK

Picnicking, shellfish, crabbing, boating

SEASON/HOURS: Year-round.
AREA: 10.09 acres; 685 feet of saltwater shoreline on Kilisut Harbor.
DAY-USE FACILITIES: 9 picnic sites, picnic shelter, 2 toilets, marine pumpout station, portable toilet dump station, single-lane paved boat ramp, dock with floats (683 feet of float space), 7 mooring buoys.
CAR ACCESS: 1 mile south of Hadlock on SR 116 (Oak Bay Road), continue east on SR 116 (Flagler Road), cross the bridge to Marrowstone Island, and follow the road 5 miles to Nordland and 1 more mile to the park entrance.
BOAT ACCESS: Follow the marked channel behind the sandspit at the head of Kilisut Harbor. *Caution: The narrow, shallow channel makes an S-curve at the entrance; any deviation from the center of the channel can lead to grounding.* Mystery Bay is on the east side of the harbor, 2 miles south of the entrance.

Back in Prohibition days, smuggling booze from Canada was a profitable and somewhat honored occupation in the remote waters of northwest Washington. Sequestered between Marrowstone and Indian Islands, Kilisut Harbor was one refuge used by smugglers to evade Coast Guard vessels. The smugglers' shallow-draft boats were readily hidden in overhanging trees at a small bay near the end of the harbor, and their regular disappearance here was categorized by the Coast Guard as "mysterious"; hence the name for the bay.

The park is categorized as a marine recreation area, as its facilities are primarily of interest to boaters. A pier leads out to a long float that is available for overnight moorage for boats, or for fishing by land-bound visitors. Several buoys provide additional moorage. A single-lane launch ramp drops down the gently sloping beach west of the float. Clams and oysters can be found on the beach at low tide, and crabbing is good offshore.

KINNEY POINT PROPERTY

Beach walking, shellfish

AREA: 76 acres; 683 feet of saltwater shoreline on Admiralty Inlet and Oak Bay.
BOAT ACCESS: Kinney Point is at the south end of Marrowstone Island, accessible only by beachable boats. The nearest launch ramp is at Oak Bay County Park.

Kayakers have proposed this property for one of the Cascadia Marine Trail campsites. Unfortunately, the gradual beach stretching below high bluffs disappears at higher tide levels, thus a suitable camping location needs to be found and sanitation problems must be resolved before the campsite becomes a reality. Until then, the property is accessible only for day-use at mid- or lower tide levels by beachable boats.

OLD MAN HOUSE STATE PARK

Picnicking, shellfish, historical display

SEASON/HOURS: Year-round.
AREA: 1.05 acres.
DAY-USE FACILITIES: 2 picnic sites, water, fire ring, toilet.
RECREATIONAL FACILITIES: Interpretive display.
CAR ACCESS: *From the Kingston ferry terminal,* follow SR 104 northwest for

The interpretive kiosk at Old Man House State Park reflects the architecture of a Northwest Indian longhouse.

2.5 miles, then turn south on Hansville Road NE, which becomes Miller Bay Road NE, and in 5.7 miles reach Suquamish. Continue south on Suquamish Way NE for 0.2 mile, then turn south on Division Avenue NE. In 0.2 mile the road bends east and becomes NE McKinstry Street, which in 1 block Ts into Angeline Avenue S NE at the park. *From the Bainbridge Island ferry terminal,* follow SR 305 north to the Agate Passage Bridge. Just north of the bridge, turn north on Suquamish Way NE and reach Division Avenue NE in 1.3 miles.
BOAT ACCESS: The park lies at the north end of Agate Passage. Nearest launch ramp is to the north in Suquamish.

This sandy stretch of shoreline at the entrance to Agate Passage was once the site of one of the largest Northwest Indian longhouses ever built. Archeological digs indicate that the structure, which was occupied by multiple families from the Suquamish tribe, stretched from 500 to 900 feet long. This was believed to have been the birthplace of Chief Sealth, for whom the city of Seattle was named. His grave is just a few blocks away, in Memorial Cemetery in the town of Suquamish. Federal Indian agents burned the longhouse in the late 1800s, hoping that eradicating the native's custom of communal living would force them to adopt the white man's lifestyle.

An informational kiosk at the park tells the story of the longhouse. The display itself incorporates posts, beams, and a short section of cedar roofing typical of Native American construction techniques.

The small park's tree-studded grass terraces stretch down to a broad sandy beach, with views of Port Madison and Agate Passage. Hand-carried boats can be launched here. The park is sometimes used as an entry point for scuba divers; only experienced divers should attempt to explore the channel, due to the swift tidal currents.

SHINE TIDELANDS STATE PARK AND WOLFE PROPERTY

Camping, windsurfing, scuba diving, beach walking, shellfish, crabbing, fishing, boating, paddling

SEASON/HOURS: Closed November 1 through March 31.
AREA: 134.6 acres; 16,092 feet of saltwater shoreline on Hood Canal.
FACILITIES: Shine Tidelands: 16 primitive campsites; toilets; Wolfe Property: none.
CAR ACCESS: At the west end of the Hood Canal Bridge, turn northeast onto Paradise Bay Road, then immediately southeast onto Termination Point Road. At the bottom of the hill a dirt road heads northeast to the Shine Tidelands camping area. The beach can also be reached by continuing northeast on Paradise Road for 0.5 mile, then turning north on Seven Sisters Road, a narrow paved road.

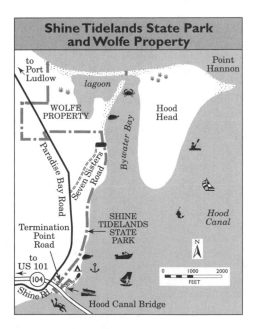

31

Oyster pickers clean Hood Canal booty.

In another 0.5 mile reach a parking area and the Wolfe Property access.

BOAT ACCESS: The park is on the west shore of Hood Canal, immediately north of the Hood Canal bridge.

A narrow sandspit, built by wave action, attaches Hood Head to the mainland and encloses Bywater Bay. The shores of the shallow bay, the end of which becomes a mudflat at minus tide, are prime areas for seeking clams, oysters, and crab that hide in seaweed in shallow water. Public tidelands run from the west end of the Hood Canal Bridge to the head of the bay. On the northwest side of the bay, a densely wooded section of property enclosing a saltwater lagoon is undeveloped park property.

Such park improvement as there is lies at the south end of the tidelands, where a single-lane dirt road leads to primitive campsites along the beach. Toilets and a self-administered pay station are the sole amenities. Garbage is pack-it-in, pack-it-out. Camping is rough, but the sites are nearly always full during minus tides when clamming and crabbing are best. Boaters also use the campsites and the launch ramp just north of the bridge; however, the beach tapers so gently that unless boats can be beached they must be anchored well offshore and the shore reached by dinghy or wading.

To the north, tideflats on the Wolfe Property access have been planted with shellfish for public harvest, and both clams and oysters are plentiful (in season) for shellfish lovers.

HOOD CANAL STATE PARK TIDELANDS

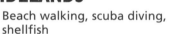

Beach walking, scuba diving, shellfish

FACILITIES: None.
ACCESS: Boat access only, except for Lilliwaup Tidelands.

Four stretches of saltwater tidelands on Hood Canal are under the State Park Commission's administration. The beaches are open to public usage below mean high-tide level; only one has land access. Harvesting clams and oysters is subject to the usual Department of Fish and Wildlife regulations. Be aware that additional closures will occur during red tide warnings.

TOANDOS TIDELANDS. 10,455 feet of tidelands on the south end of the Toandos Peninsula between Tskutsko Point and Oak Head, and east of Fisherman Harbor.

H. J. CARROLL PROPERTY. 2.8 acres; 560 feet of tidelands and 2.8 acres of undeveloped uplands 0.2 mile north of Pulali Point on the west side of Dabob Bay.

RIGHT SMART COVE TIDELANDS. 1 acre; 200 feet of tidelands 5 miles north of Brinnon and 0.3 mile west of Wawa Point on the west side of a creek draining a saltwater estuary.

LILLIWAUP TIDELANDS. 4,122 feet of tidelands lying below a gravel parking lot on the east side of US 101, 0.5 mile north of Lilliwaup. Crude access trails lead down the bluff at either end of the beach. The property line is marked with state park boundary signs.

DOSEWALLIPS STATE PARK

Camping, picnicking, wildlife watching, mushrooming, hiking, shellfish, shrimping, fishing

SEASON/HOURS: Year-round; campsite reservations accepted in summer.
AREA: 424.5 acres; 5,500 feet of saltwater shoreline on Hood Canal.
OVERNIGHT AND DAY-USE FACILITIES: 40 RV sites, 88 standard campsites, 3 platform tents, 3 primitive campsites, group camp (25–50 persons), group camp with picnic shelter (50–135 persons), 40 picnic sites, picnic shelter, 3 restrooms (2 with showers) (&), 6 toilets, trailer dump station.

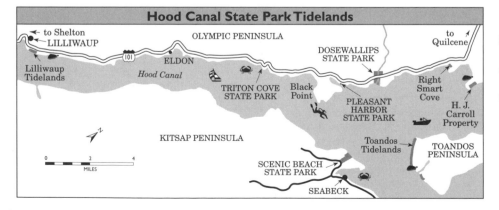

RECREATIONAL FACILITIES: 4 miles of hiking/biking trails.
EDUCATIONAL FACILITIES: Wildlife viewing platform.
CAR ACCESS: The park is 1 mile south of Brinnon or 40 miles north of Shelton on US 101.

From its headwaters in the heart of the Olympics, the Dosewallips River tumbles down the glacier-scooped valley, past the precipitous south ridge of Mount Constance, to deliver its icy waters to Hood Canal. Sediments clawed from the upper course of the river settle at its mouth, forming a broad sand and mud fan that extends into Hood Canal. Dosewallips State Park occupies the south bank of the river, straddling the river mouth and the alluvial plain of Brinnon Flats.

The major portion of the campground lies in an evergreen-shaded flat west of the highway, where hookup sites radiate in wagon wheel fashion around a series of loops. An older campground is situated in open woods along the riverbank both east and west of the highway. Low clearance (10 feet) under the end of the bridge precludes use of the area east of the highway by RVs or trailers; none of these older sites have hookups. A recent addition to the overnight facilities are three platform tents, replicas of old-style camping accommodations, although with more modern furnishings. The tents are on the northwest road loop, by group camp B.

The picnic area east of the highway, at the south end of the park, theoretically fronts on the beach; however, a morass of marshes, saltwater channels, and dense brush prevents reaching the beach at this point. A trail leads from here through the older section of the campground to the bridge and connects to the beach trail.

To reach the beach area, cross the highway bridge to the north side of the river. Here a trail starts along the bank and travels through the alder and cedar woodland that give way to beach grass. A wildlife viewing platform is found where the trail breaks out onto the beach. Near high-tide level the trail picks its way around

Dosewallips State Park is a favorite for family clam digging.

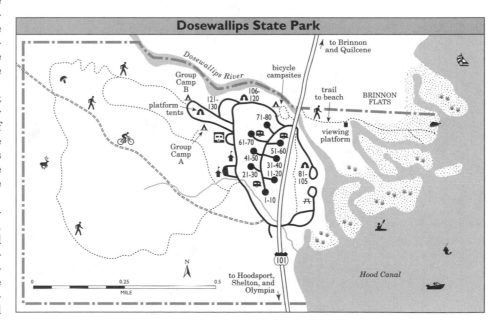

33

slick, grass-covered mud hummocks, then vanishes onto the broad, flat cobble beach. At minus tides the beach is bared out for another 0.25 mile.

This transition zone from fresh to salt water, which nurtures a wide variety of plants, birds, waterfowl, fish, and intertidal creatures, is a fascinating place to explore. The beach is a prime area for harvesting clams and oysters. In recent years the beach was contaminated with the feces of seals that had dramatically increased in number in the vicinity, leading to a ban on gathering shellfish here. An offshore haul-out float for seals and fences around the creek areas have led to the reopening of the beach to shellfish harvesting.

A loop trail that circles the inland part of the park starts at the park administration area and meanders through forest along the west boundary of the park before returning to its starting point. A service road diagonaling through this section of the park breaks the trail into a pair of loop possibilities. In winter a quiet hiker might see some of the elk herd that retreats to the park from snow at higher elevations. In August look for delicious chanterelles. If you don't enjoy eating mushrooms, please don't destroy them— leave them for those who love them.

PLEASANT HARBOR STATE PARK

Scuba diving, boating

SEASON/HOURS: Year-round.
AREA: 0.84 acre; 100 feet of saltwater shoreline on Hood Canal.
DAY-USE FACILITIES: Picnic table, toilet.
RECREATIONAL FACILITIES: Dock with float (218 feet of float space).
CAR ACCESS: Follow US 101 along the west side of Hood Canal to 1.25 miles south of Brinnon. The dock is at the end of a narrow paved road that leaves the highway 0.2 mile north of the marked entrance to the Pleasant Bay Marina.
BOAT ACCESS: Pleasant Harbor lies behind Black Point on the west side of Hood Canal. The second dock inside the harbor entrance belongs to the park. Nearest launch ramps are at Triton Cove on the west shore of the canal and at Misery Point on the east shore.

The Hood Canal shoreline has few coves or indentations, and the beaches drop off steeply in rock walls, except at the alluvial fans of the large rivers that drain the Olympics. As a result, safe, bombproof refuges for boaters are scarce and coveted when storm winds whistle up and down the canal. A good place to wait out bad weather or enjoy beautiful calm evenings is tucked behind the small peninsula of Black Point on the west shore of the canal, due west of Seabeck.

The entrance to Pleasant Harbor is through a narrow channel on the northwest side of the point, which leads into a cove surrounded by steep forested hillsides—a moorage as enticing as its name implies. Two private marinas are in the bay. The good-sized marina at the head of the harbor has fuel, water, and transient moorage. The state park, however, is rather small and spartan, but more private. It consists of just a dock and float and a few feet of shorefront. The park is on the west side of the harbor, just inside the entrance. Look for the park sign on the dock, as all other docks nearby are private.

The moorage at Pleasant Harbor State Park is well protected from weather.

TRITON COVE STATE PARK

Picnicking, fishing, boating

SEASON/HOURS: Year-round.
AREA: 28.1 acres; 555 feet of saltwater shoreline on Hood Canal.
DAY-USE FACILITIES: 3 picnic sites, toilet (&), fishing pier, boat ramp with boarding float.

CAR ACCESS: Triton Cove is on US 101, 6 miles south of Brinnon and 7 miles north of Eldon.

BOAT ACCESS: Triton Cove is on the west side of Hood Canal, 4 miles north of the mouth of the Hamma Hamma River and 2.5 miles south of the mouth of the Dosewallips River.

A defunct, privately owned RV park and boat launch on Triton Cove has become a nice little access to Hood Canal. State Parks acquired the property in 1990 and replaced the old weathered launch ramp, float, and on-shore facilities with a new ramp and dock, a new and easier access road to the ramp, a spacious parking lot for cars and boat trailers, and picnic sites. There is no camping now. The handicapped-accessible dock offers a fine spot for near-shore fishing.

HOODSPORT TRAIL STATE PARK

Picnicking, mushrooming, hiking

SEASON/HOURS: Closed October 1 through April 30.

AREA: 80 acres.

DAY-USE FACILITIES: 3 picnic sites, toilet.

RECREATIONAL FACILITIES: 2 miles of hiking trail.

EDUCATIONAL FACILITIES: 0.5 mile interpretive trail.

CAR ACCESS: At Hoodsport on US 101, turn west on SR 119 (Lake Cushman Road) to reach the park in 3.1 miles.

Here is a chance for an easy sampling of the wealth of flora to be found in second-growth Olympic forests. A parking area just off Lake Cushman Road holds a few picnic tables, a toilet, and the start of the park's trails. Although it is small, an amazing amount of trail mileage has been squeezed into the park's compact area. Signs at the trailhead

A rustic bridge in Hoodsport Trail State Park spans a small creek.

indicate two loops: the lower, 0.5 mile long, and the upper, 1.5 miles long (although, in fact, a third trail segment cutting diagonally across the upper loop offers yet another option).

The trail first passes through second-growth fir and cedar at the top of a bank along the south side of Dow Creek, where a wide variety of mushrooms bursts through the pine-needle ground cover in fall. Near the north park boundary a rustic wooden bridge crosses the creek and the trail swings back, parallel to the north side of the creek, continuing on to a Y-intersection. Here the north leg heads uphill to the upper loop and the south leg continues along the creek drainage. An expansive grove of mature alder straddles the creek.

Shortly, another Y-intersection is reached; the south leg leads through brush to a second bridge, then up the bank to the return route of the lower loop. From the other leg of the Y, the upper loop soon pulls away from the creek, heading past huge stumps of the logged old-growth cedar, some as much as 8 feet in diameter.

At the eastern park boundary, the trail

starts gently uphill in a series of lazy switchbacks. After skirting the park's northern boundary, near the top of a gentle hill, the trail switchbacks down to the initial Y-intersection. The diagonal trail across the upper loop, and the spur heading southeast out of the park at the return leg of the lower loop, make route finding more complicated.

LAKE CUSHMAN STATE PARK

Camping, picnicking, mushrooming, hiking, swimming, waterskiing, fishing, boating

SEASON/HOURS: Closed October 31 through March 31, upper campground and group camp closed September 15 through April 15; campsite reservations accepted in summer.

AREA: 602.9 acres; 41,500 feet of freshwater shoreline on Lake Cushman.

OVERNIGHT AND DAY-USE FACILITIES: 30 RV sites (2 ♿), 50 standard campsites, 2 primitive campsites, group camp with picnic shelter (60 persons), 40 picnic sites, picnic shelter, 3 restrooms (2 with showers) (♿), 4 toilets, trailer dump station.

RECREATIONAL FACILITIES: 4 miles of hiking trails, 3-lane paved boat ramp, unguarded swimming beach, amphitheater, horseshoe pit.

CAR ACCESS: At Hoodsport, turn west from US 101 onto SR 119 (Lake Cushman Road) to reach the park in 7.2 miles.

Even in the early 1900s little Lake Cushman was popular with hunters and anglers, and two rustic resorts flourished on its shores. A hydroelectric dam constructed in 1926 flooded the resorts and increased the surface of the lake a hundredfold. New resorts and lakeshore developments sprang up along the shoreline,

and in time a section of land halfway up the east shore of the lake, surrounding a long, narrow inlet below Big Creek, was acquired as a state park.

Big Creek Inlet, a deep, 0.75-mile-long inlet that divides the park in two, gives it even more shoreline than would be expected for its size. The main park facilities (a day-use area, boat launch, and campground) lie on the southeast side of the inlet. A second park entrance 0.7 mile farther north up the road leads to a second campground, group camp, and much of the inland area of the park. At the south section of the park a three-lane concrete launch ramp and paved parking lot, capable of holding more than fifty vehicles with trailers, is a testimony to the boating popularity of the park.

A forest of mixed conifers with a heavy undergrowth of salal surrounds the day-use area. A swimming beach fronts the picnic area, and a gravel island just offshore sits at the apex of a roped-off beach. A campground loop north of the picnic area has sites framed by stands of small conifers. Two primitive walk-in sites are found at the northeast corner of the loop. Park rangers give nature slide shows on

Lake Cushman State Park offers fine boating and swimming.

weekends in summer at a small amphitheater near the entrance to the campground loop. A second smaller campground loop and a group camp lie a scant 2,000 feet away on the north side of Big Creek Inlet. To reach them, however, unless a boat is at hand, it is necessary to drive or hike more than 1.5 miles around the narrow finger of the inlet.

In the north section of the park, over 4 miles of trails lead through the forest and along the Big Creek shoreline. Rhododendrons add their pink blush in spring. Chanterelles and other mushrooms begin to emerge in late July and linger until September, depending on the rainfall and the timing of the first hard frost.

DEER MEADOWS

Picnicking, boating, fishing (day-use only)

AREA: 1.5 acres, 500 feet of shoreline on Lake Cushman.
FACILITIES: 4 picnic sites, toilet.
BOAT ACCESS: At the south end of Lake Cushman west of the dam spillway.

For boaters, a hidden treasure exists at the south end of Lake Cushman, where a tiny segment of park property, Deer Meadows, surrounds a small spit west of the Lake Cushman Dam spillway. This day-use area, accessible only by boat, is a quiet, relaxing nook for a picnic.

DRY CREEK

Fishing, boating, hiking, nature study (day-use only)

AREA: 1 acre.
FACILITIES: None.
CAR ACCESS: From the main entrance to Lake Cushman State Park continue

north on SR 119 and in 2.2 miles head west on Forest Road 24. In another 5.8 miles turn west on Forest Road 2451, cross the inlet to Lake Cushman, and take the first primitive road to the south to the Dry Creek trailhead. The park property is 1.3 miles to the south by trail.
BOAT ACCESS: From Lake Cushman State Park head northwest for 4.5 miles. Look for a tiny island at the mouth of Dry Creek to identify the property.

A small section of lakeshore at the mouth of Dry Creek on the northwest side of Lake Cushman is undeveloped park property. The trail leaves a short road spur south of FR 2451 and continues along the edge of the lake below a steep forested hillside. In about a mile the main trail turns inland and starts to climb steeply. Shortly a spur trail to the southeast drops down to the mouth of Dry Creek and the park property.

POTLATCH STATE PARK

Camping, picnicking, birdwatching, hiking, scuba diving, shellfish, fishing, boating, paddling

SEASON/HOURS: Campground closed end of October through end of March, day-use area open year-round.
AREA: 56.95 acres; 9,470 feet of saltwater shoreline on Hood Canal.
OVERNIGHT AND DAY-USE FACILITIES: 18 RV sites, 17 standard campsites, 2 primitive campsites, 81 picnic sites, reservable kitchen shelter, 2 restrooms (1 with showers), trailer dump station.
RECREATIONAL FACILITIES: 0.5 mile of hiking trail, horseshoe pit, 4 mooring buoys.
CAR ACCESS: The park is on US 101, 12 miles north of Shelton, or 3 miles south of Hoodsport.

The entire family goes clamming at Potlatch State Park.

BOAT ACCESS: The park is on the west side of Hood Canal on Annas Bay, 3 miles south of Hoodsport. Nearest boat ramps are at Union and Tacoma City Light's Potlatch Boat Launch.

The potlatch was an important tribal ceremony common to Northwest Native Americans. At a potlatch a chief might designate an heir, family rights might be bestowed on children, a dead chief might be mourned and a new one recognized, or a social misadventure (such as the chief's "loss of face" by stumbling or falling in public) might be acknowledged and repaired. Protocol required that the guests—the witnesses who validated the claims—be given gifts by the host. The more esteemed the host and the more auspicious the occasion, the grander the gifts. Potlatch State Park holds forth at a site once used by local tribes for these festivities.

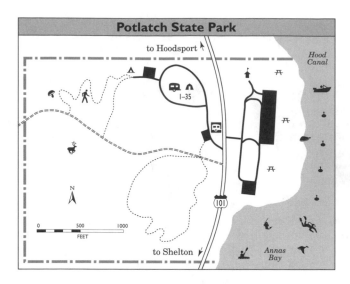

Potlatch State Park

to Hoodsport

Hood Canal

I-35

N

0   500   1000
FEET

101

to Shelton

Annas Bay

US 101 splits the park, with the campground on the west side of the highway and day-use and picnic areas to the east along the Hood Canal shoreline. The wooded campground is relatively small, so campsites are snugly packed together. A few primitive walk-in sites are at the west end of the loop.

The large parking lot and spacious, table-filled lawn of the picnic area attest to the park's day-use popularity. The cobble-strewn mud beach tapers gently into Annas Bay, exposing a broad foreshore at a minus tide for digging clams and picking oysters. Mooring buoys are situated well offshore in deeper water. Canoes or kayaks can be carried to the beach for paddle exploration of the Great Bend of Hood Canal or the nearby estuary of the Skokomish River. Seals often forage in these waters. Flocks of water birds seek shelter in the protected channels; watch for yellow-billed loons as well as more common birds. The bay is also a popular scuba diving site, with only nominal tidal currents to concern novice divers.

The park's upland has two short trail loops that weave through a cedar forest, offering a chance to see squirrels, rabbits, deer, and a wide variety of birds that make the forest home.

ISABELLA LAKE STATE PARK

Picnicking, hiking, birdwatching

AREA: 182 acres; 1,835 feet of shoreline on Isabella Lake.
FACILITIES: None.
CAR ACCESS: At Shelton, take the SR 3 exit from US 101. Head west, then south on W Golden Pheasant Road. In 1 mile turn west on Delight Park Road and arrive at the park property in 0.5 mile.

This state park property is identified by small signs at gates on either side of Delight Park Road. A single line of tall firs edges the road. Behind these sentinels is a strip of young pine trees and, below, a broad mown field sweeps gradually down to thick brush cover along the edge of the lake. A few former farm buildings are on the property. The area is open for day-use hiking and picnicking; however, dense shore brush prevents lake access. To the south, the partially wooded property extends about 0.75 mile to abut Fredson Road. It takes little imagination to visualize what a wonderful recreation site this impressive piece of property could be, if developed.

Morning arrives at the Potlatch State Park anchorage.

CHAPTER TWO
SOUTHWEST WASHINGTON

SCHAFER STATE PARK

Camping, picnicking, hiking, wading, fishing, rafting

SEASON/HOURS: Campground closed October 1 through April 30, open to day-use year-round.

AREA: 119.11 acres; 4,200 feet of freshwater shoreline on the Satsop River.

OVERNIGHT AND DAY-USE FACILITIES: 6 RV sites, 34 standard campsites, 2 primitive campsites, 75 picnic sites, 2 kitchen shelters, 2 group day-use areas (50 and 200 persons), 2 restrooms, trailer dump station.

RECREATIONAL FACILITIES: 2 miles of trails and fire roads for hiking/biking, children's play equipment.

CAR ACCESS: At Exit 104 (US 101 N, Aberdeen, Port Angeles) from I-5 at Olympia, take US 101 west for 6.2 miles, then SR 8 west for 27.9 miles to the exit signed to Brady and Schafer State Park. Drive north on Monte–Brady Road for 0.3 mile; at the intersection with Monte Elma Road, continue straight ahead (north) on Brady–Matlock Road. At a Y-intersection with West Satsop Road in 5 miles, continue northeast on Brady–Matlock Road for another 3.6 miles. Here turn east on West Schafer Park Road and reach the park in 1.3 miles.

A clam digger shows off her catch of prime razor clams.

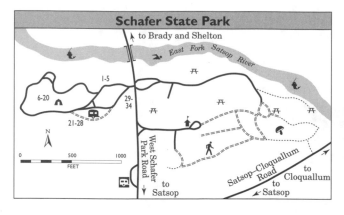

Schafer State Park

to Brady and Shelton

East Fork Satsop River

I-5

6-20

29-34

21-28

N

0   500   1000
FEET

West Schafer Park Road

Satsop-Cloquallum Road

to Satsop

to Cloquallum

to Satsop

In the early 1900s the three Schafer brothers began an ox-team operation and developed it into one of the largest and most successful logging companies in this part of the Olympic Peninsula. The Schafers reserved one of the prettiest corners of their land as a site for company picnics. The loggers and their families gathered here, by the meandering East Fork of the Satsop River, to picnic, hold log-rolling contests, dance, and enjoy serenades by a brass band. Today groups of all sizes meet on the banks of the river to picnic, camp, fish, and enjoy

The shallow river at Schafer State Park is always an attraction.

the murmuring river. Anglers use the park heavily; the river offers steelhead in winter, while mid-July to October brings sea-run cutthroat, followed by spawning salmon.

West Schafer Park Road divides the park; all campsites lie on the west side of the road, some on the river and some inland, while the day-use areas are on the east. A few picnic tables beside the river just inside the campground entrance are reserved for bicyclists and walk-in campers. Beyond here a loop road meanders through moss-covered maples and past campsites. A few hookup sites are lined up near the entrance. Rustic restrooms have sturdy walls of river stones.

Picnic spots spread along the riverbank east of the road are rimmed with ancient oak, alder, and Douglas-fir. East of here the forest is laced with a series of abandoned roads that once led to other picnic sites, evidenced by a few moss-encrusted tables. A quiet walk along these old roads offers the opportunity to observe the squirrels, rabbits, deer, and birds that inhabit this less-frequented portion of the park; in fall, chanterelles and other forest-loving mushrooms appear.

LAKE SYLVIA STATE PARK

Camping, picnicking, team sports, hiking, swimming, fishing, boating, paddling, birdwatching

SEASON/HOURS: Year-round; campground closed October 1 through April 1, but camping is permitted in the day-use area in the off season.
AREA: 233 acres; 15,000 feet of freshwater shoreline on Lake Sylvia.
OVERNIGHT AND DAY-USE FACILITIES: 35 standard campsites, 2 primitive campsites, group camp (120 persons), 118 picnic sites, 2 kitchen shelters, group day-use area (200 persons), 2 restrooms (&), trailer dump station.
RECREATIONAL FACILITIES: 2-mile lakeshore trail, children's play equipment, swimming beach, swim float, bathhouse, fishing platform (&), boat ramp *(no gasoline motors)*.
EDUCATIONAL FACILITIES: Trailheads for 2-mile interpretive Sylvia Creek Forestry Trail on adjacent land, historical display.
CONCESSIONS: Food, groceries, boat rental.
CAR ACCESS: From US 12 at its junction with SR 107, turn north into Montesano. Take Main Street north to E Spruce Street, turn west on it, and in 3 blocks turn north on N 3rd Street. Follow 3rd as it winds uphill, then downhill, and reach the park in 0.7 mile.

The slender thread of Lake Sylvia is actually a backwater pond behind a dam that was built in 1878 to create a log pond for a sawmill; the dam was reconstructed in 1909 to create a water reservoir and electric power plant for the city of Montesano. Because of the 31-acre lake's long shape, nearly every park campsite has a nice waterfront view. The camping area lies on a narrow peninsula; a narrow channel separates the southern tip of the peninsula from a tiny island that holds a single old fir surrounded by deciduous growth. The campground is closed in winter, but RV camping is permitted in the parking lot of the day-use area on the northwest side of the lake.

Shaded picnic sites line the east side of the lake between the entrance and the campground peninsula. More picnic sites, a children's play area, a swimming beach, and a boat ramp are northwest of a bridge that spans the lower end of the lake. A footbridge across a tiny cove west of the day-use area serves as a fishing platform. Fishing lines and lures resplendent on the power lines above testify to a

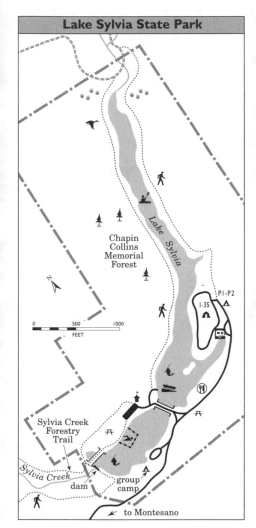

Lake Sylvia State Park

Chapin Collins Memorial Forest

Lake Sylvia

P1-P2

1-35

Sylvia Creek Forestry Trail

Sylvia Creek

dam

group camp

to Montesano

A wooden footbridge at Lake Sylvia State Park is a fine spot for fishing.

few rainbow trout that escaped an angler's hook. The trail continuing beyond the bridge leads to the dam. Here the 2-mile-long Sylvia Creek Forestry Trail leaves the park and loops down one side of the stream and up the other. A brochure describes features along the way such as logging sites, beaver dams, and salmon spawning pools.

The park serves as a virtual museum to logging. A wooden ball, nearly 4 feet in diameter, hangs beneath a kiosk at the day-use area. A local logger, Purl Stone, carved this ball from the trunk of a Sitka spruce in 1925. The surefooted Stone regularly outdid other loggers, who had trouble even staying on the ball, by standing atop it and rolling it in the water from the bridge to the dam and back.

North of the day-use area is the start of an old railroad-bed trail that passes two fishing docks, then continues along the north lakeshore to the Chapin Collins Memorial Forest, which reaches far beyond the park boundary. Hundreds of acres that have been logged over the years have been replanted with Douglas-fir and western hemlock. Ever present are huge stumps from the original forest; many of these ancient stumps now nurse full-grown trees.

A maze of marshy islands separated by narrow channels choke the north end of the lake—a canoer's paradise. Silent paddlers or shore hikers will discover great blue heron, grebes, mergansers, Canada geese, and other waterfowl. At the lake's end, a narrower trail heads back along the east shore, crossing side drainages on log bridges, seldom far from the lake.

BOTTLE BEACH STATE PARK

Birdwatching, wildlife watching, nature study, beach walking

SEASON/HOURS: Year-round.
AREA: 70.21 acres; 6,500 feet of saltwater shoreline on Grays Harbor.
FACILITIES: None.
CAR ACCESS: Drive SR 105 west from Aberdeen for 14.4 miles, or east from Twin Harbors State Park for 4.5 miles, to Ocosta Third Street at Ocosta Flats. A stub road on the opposite (north) side of the highway ends at the gated park access and limited parking.

This wildlife-filled mudflat on Grays Harbor remains undeveloped to preserve it as Ruby Egbert Natural Area, named for the woman responsible for its preservation. From the park gate, follow remnants of the road a short distance to reach a bridge over a freshwater marsh, probably rousing a quacking flurry of waterfowl. West of the bridge a foot-beaten path continues through head-high Scotch broom to reach the beach on South Bay. The southwest park boundary is adjacent to the spot where the path breaks onto the beach. The other boundary is about a mile to the northeast.

At minus tides the bay becomes a mudflat up to 0.5 mile wide. The park is named for a bottle factory that once existed here. Rotted pilings well offshore bear testimony to the length of the pier that was required for boats to reach safe depths. The shoreline is covered with thick growths of Scotch broom, willow, and shore pine that provide cover for local wildlife. Explore the mudflats and try to identify the animal tracks you spot—deer, marten, gulls, Canada geese, and more.

NORTH BEACH SEASHORE CONSERVATION AREA

Both horses and riders enjoy the beach near Chance a la Mer.

Picnicking, kite flying, birdwatching, horseback riding, surfboarding, beach walking, shellfish, surf-fishing, paddling

SEASON/HOURS: Day-use year-round.
AREA: 22 miles of saltwater shoreline on the Pacific Ocean.
BEACH DRIVING RESTRICTIONS:
Open all year: Moclips Gap to Analyde Gap, immediate vicinity of Roosevelt Gap, Copalis Head to the Copalis River, Benner Gap to Ocean City Beach access, Ocean City Beach access to Chance a la Mer access, Pacific Way access to Marine View Drive.
Prohibited April 15 through the day after Labor Day, except during razor clam season: Quinault Indian Reservation to Moclips Gap, Analyde Gap to Roosevelt Gap, Roosevelt Gap to Copalis Head, Ocean City Beach access to 1.8 miles north, Chance a la Mer access to Pacific Way access, Marine View Drive to North Jetty.
Prohibited all year, except during razor clam season: Copalis River to Benner Gap.
Prohibited year-round: Damon Point, Protection Island.
FACILITIES: Moclips: Restroom (&). **Roosevelt:** Toilet. **Ocean City Beach:** 10 picnic sites, restroom (&). **Oyhut:** 9 picnic sites, restroom. **Chance a la Mer:** Restroom (&). **North Jetty:** Restroom (&), water fountain, interpretive display. **Damon Point:** 5 picnic sites, 4 toilets, parking. No vehicle access to the beach.
CAR ACCESS: See following.

The true recreational shores of Washington State run south along the Pacific Ocean from the Quinault Indian Reservation to the mouth of the Columbia River. Grays Harbor and Willapa Bay divide the shore into three sections: North Beach, South Beach, and Long Beach. This sectioning prevents a continuous north–south flow, although the beaches are quite similar in character.

North Beach begins at Moclips and runs south for 22 miles to Ocean Shores at the tip of Point Brown. Some steep cliffs extending from Pacific Beach to Copalis Rock are a last, faint echo of the rugged cliffs and offshore rocks of the northern coast. From here south the landscape flattens, and sandy beach reaches out to greet crashing surf. Beach grass-anchored dunes back the shores, while farther inland low spots hold bogs and shallow lakes. Salt marshes and protected estuaries provide nesting areas for several species of plovers. These are also favored stopovers for migratory birds along the Pacific Flyway; in winter many uncommon birds might be spotted here and in the dunes, as well as huge flocks of birds that normally range along the coast.

All the ocean beaches are open to the public; however, the uplands are private except for the accesses listed here and the developed state park lands. Vehicles may be driven onto the beach at all

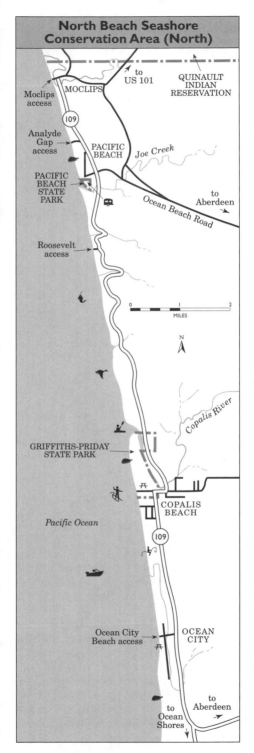

North Beach Seashore Conservation Area (North)

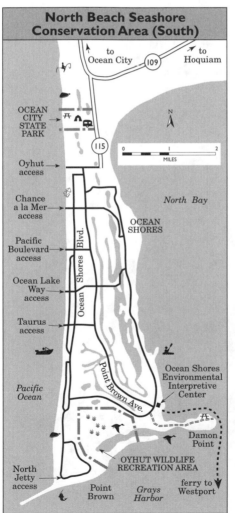

North Beach Seashore Conservation Area (South)

accesses, except as noted. The introduction to this book lists beach regulations.

MOCLIPS. On the north side of Moclips, 1 block west of SR 109 at the junction of Railroad Avenue and 2nd Street.

ANALYDE GAP. At the north end of Pacific Beach, turn west from SR 109 onto First Street, and in 0.1 mile, at the intersection of Homer Street and Analyde Gap Road, turn north on a gravel road leading downhill to the beach access.

ROOSEVELT. At the end of Roosevelt Beach Road, 0.2 mile west of SR 109, 5 miles north of Copalis Beach (3.4 miles south of Pacific Beach).

OCEAN CITY BEACH. At the end of 2nd Avenue in Ocean City, 1.9 miles north of the junction of SR 109 and SR 115.

OYHUT. At the west end of Damon Road (SR 115), 0.3 mile west of the entrance to Ocean Shores.

CHANCE A LA MER. Turn west from Point Brown Road onto W Chance a la Mer Road NW 0.7 mile south of the entrance to Ocean Shores.

PACIFIC BOULEVARD. Turn west from Point Brown Avenue onto Pacific Boulevard, 1.8 miles south of the entrance to Ocean Shores.

OCEAN LAKE WAY. Turn west from Ocean Shores Boulevard onto Ocean Lake Way, 2.5 miles south of the entrance to Ocean Shores.

TAURUS. Turn west on Taurus Boulevard from Ocean Shores Boulevard, 3.4 miles south of the entrance to Ocean Shores.

NORTH JETTY. No hard-pack access to the beach. Drive to the end of Ocean Shores Boulevard, 6.5 miles south of the entrance to Ocean Shores.

DAMON POINT. No vehicle access to the beach. At the end of Point Brown Avenue, 6 miles south of the entrance to Ocean Shores, turn south on Marine View Drive and in 0.2 mile turn southeast on the gravel access road that runs to the end of the point. Damon Point hosts over 200 species of bird and marine life. It marks the northernmost range of the snowy plover and the southernmost range of the semipalmated plover, and is the only place in the world where both species are known to breed. Except for the beach, the area south of the access road is closed from March 15 to August 31 to protect nesting birds.

PACIFIC BEACH STATE PARK

Camping, picnicking, kite flying, birdwatching, beach walking, shellfish, surf-fishing, paddling

SEASON/HOURS: Year-round; campsite reservations accepted year-round.
AREA: 10.21 acres; 2,300 feet of saltwater shoreline on the Pacific Ocean.
OVERNIGHT AND DAY-USE FACILITIES: 31 RV sites (E) (&), 31 standard campsites (&), 2 primitive campsites, 10 picnic sites, 2 restrooms with showers (&), trailer dump station.
CAR ACCESS: From Hoquiam drive SR 109 west, then north along the coast for 29.1 miles to the park, on Joe Creek, on the southwest edge of the town of Pacific Beach. Alternatively, at the Y-intersection 8 miles west of Hoquiam, head north on Ocean Beach Road to reach Pacific Beach in 16 miles. The park entrance is at the end of Second Street. *No vehicle access to the beach.*

Pacific Beach State Park is a small flat rimmed on the outside by a riprap wall between the park and the beach. Low bushes edge a short row of RV pads. Seven additional RV sites and the primitive walk-in campsites are gravel surfaced. Sites are jammed together, but that suits most RVers, whose main interest is easy beach access to succulent razor clams. There's no shade here in sunny weather, and nothing to temper winds.

Beachcombing is great, and a good steady northerly makes for prime kite flying. At the south edge of the park, in the shallow flow near the mouth of Joe Creek, watch gulls and pelicans splash their wings against the water as they herd small schools of fingerlings into belly-filling concentrations. The beach is closed to vehicles, thus the park is popular with families; children can romp on the expanses of sand without fear of being run over by hot-rodding drivers.

GRIFFITHS-PRIDAY STATE PARK

Picnicking, kite flying, birdwatching, hiking, horseback riding, beach walking, shellfish, paddling

SEASON/HOURS: Day-use year-round.
AREA: 364.18 acres; 8,316 feet of saltwater shoreline on the Pacific Ocean; 9,950 feet of freshwater shoreline on the Copalis River.
DAY-USE FACILITIES: 7 picnic sites (2 with wind screens), reservable picnic shelter, group day-use area (75 persons), restroom (&).
RECREATIONAL FACILITIES: Boardwalk through dunes to the beach (closed from March 15 to August 31).
CAR ACCESS: From Hoquiam take SR 109 west, then north along the coast for 19.6 miles to the town of Copalis Beach. In the center of the town turn west on Benner Road, signed to the park.

Over the centuries, the mouth of the Copalis River has been driven north by a narrow, accreted peninsula that is bordered on the west by the Pacific Ocean and on the east by the Copalis River. Today, at the heart of this spit are grass-covered dunes surrounded by sandy beaches on both the ocean and river sides. The entire spit comprises Griffiths-Priday State Park.

A boardwalk leads through the environmentally sensitive, grassy dune area to the beach. A car access point is immediately adjacent to the park, at the end of Benner Road.

At one time this was a nesting area for the snowy plover; unfortunately, the bird has not been seen here for many years. Other shore birds do nest here, between the high-tide level and the dune grass, so use care when walking during breeding season. Any disturbance might cause birds to leave their nests or young unprotected, and the fragile eggs are easily

Masses of gulls and a single pelican congregate at the mouth of Joe Creek at Pacific Beach State Park.

broken by people walking where eggs are buried.

The beach below the high-tide line is open to horseback riding, beachcombing, or seasonal razor clamming; the mouth of the river is a good spot to try surf-fishing for redtail surfperch. On the river side of the peninsula, paddling the protected waters of the Copalis River offers water-side views of birds and other wildlife.

OCEAN CITY STATE PARK

Camping, picnicking, kite flying, birdwatching, mushrooming, horseback riding, surfboarding, beach walking, shellfish, surf-fishing, paddling

SEASON/HOURS: Year-round; campsite reservations accepted in summer.
AREA: 169.8 acres; 2,980 feet of saltwater shoreline on the Pacific Ocean.
OVERNIGHT AND DAY-USE FACILITIES: 29 RV sites (&), 149 standard campsites (&), 3 primitive campsites, group camp with picnic shelter (40 persons), 10 picnic sites, 2 picnic shelters, 4 restrooms (3 with showers) (&), trailer dump station.
CAR ACCESS: From Hoquiam take SR

109 west for 15.5 miles to its intersection with SR 115. Turn south and reach the park in 1.2 miles.

Although it is rather compact, Ocean City State Park holds a remarkable variety of ocean beach habitat. The park's foredunes are separated from the beach by the trickle of a small creek, stained a rainbow of colors by the algae and shore plants that flourish in the merging of fresh and salt waters. Sandpipers and plover wade the creek and skitter about in search of snacks, while farther out on the beach clusters of gulls screech out the local gossip. Sharp beach grass cloaks the dunes, sprinkled with flashes of color from buttercups, wild beach strawberry, lupine, vetch, red clover, and northern dune tansy.

Dense thickets of shore pine and kinnickinnick hide the campground loops, protecting them from wind and offering seclusion. A few hundred yards farther inland, deciduous trees mix with the pine, and freshwater marshes coalesce into a series of small ponds. A variety of ducks, both resident and transient, feed along the pond's reedy banks, and unseen birds chirp and twitter in nearby brush.

Four forested campground loops and a group camp in a wide green field lie inland from the dunes. The day-use area consists mainly of a parking lot near the edge of the dunes with a path leading west for foot access to the beach. Picnic shelters and a few tables sit beneath the trees on either side of the lot.

If returning from the beach, watch for a tall white pole with orange stripes atop the foredunes that marks the trailhead back to the park. Two of the small inland ponds have short trails leading from nearby parking to breaks in their marshy shoreline.

Beach strawberries grow in the sand at Ocean City State Park

The paths wander through a marshy profusion of rhododendron, salal, skunk cabbage, and seasonal mushrooms.

OCEAN SHORES ENVIRONMENTAL INTERPRETIVE CENTER

Environmental and historical interpretation

SEASON/HOURS: Open Thursday through Monday from Memorial Day to Labor Day.
AREA: 0.2 acre.
DAY-USE FACILITIES: 4 picnic tables.
RECREATIONAL FACILITIES: Nature displays, historical displays.
CAR ACCESS: At the intersection of Point Brown Avenue and Discovery Avenue SE, 6 miles south of the entrance to Ocean Shores, turn north

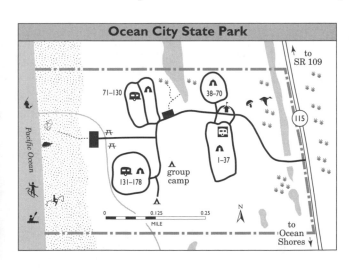

Ocean City State Park

71–130
38–70
131–178
1–37
group camp
115
Pacific Ocean
to SR 109
to Ocean Shores
0   0.125   0.25
MILE
N

Starfish cling to jetty rocks at Ocean Shores.

and in 1.1 miles arrive at the center at the intersection of Discovery Avenue SE and Catala Avenue SE.

Point Brown, the 6-mile-long and 2-mile-wide peninsula that shelters the upper half of Grays Harbor, was used as a clamming and trading site by local Native American tribes long before the arrival of outsiders. It was first noted by white men when Captain Robert Gray sailed his ship, the *Columbia Rediviva,* into present-day Grays Harbor in 1792.

The Ocean Shores Environmental Interpretive Center traces the natural and human history of the point. Pictorial displays describe the process of accretion by which the peninsula was built and is still being built—today's Damon Point, at the tip of present-day Point Brown, was an island until the early 1900s. The center also shows collections of rocks, beach flowers, Native American baskets and projectile points, the skeleton of a whale, and stuffed birds and animals that live in the dunes of the point. Several "touch and feel" displays are especially popular with

children. The staff of local volunteers can tell you all about the history and ecology of the area.

SOUTH BEACH SEASHORE CONSERVATION AREA

Picnicking, kite flying, birdwatching, horseback riding, surfboarding, beach walking, shellfish, surf-fishing, paddling

SEASON/HOURS: Day-use year-round.
AREA: 19 miles of saltwater shoreline on the Pacific Ocean.
BEACH DRIVING RESTRICTIONS:
  Open all year: Schafer Road Access to Warrenton Cannery Road Access.
  Prohibited April 15 through the day after Labor Day, except during razor clam season: Westhaven State Park to Westport Light State Park, Westport Light State Park to Schafer Road Access, Warrenton Cannery Road Access to Willapa Wildlife Refuge.
  Prohibited April 15 through the day after Labor Day, including razor clam season: Westport Light State Park.
  Prohibited year-round: Westhaven State Park beach.
FACILITIES: Schafer Road: 21 picnic tables, 2 windscreens, restroom (&), parking. **Bonge Avenue:** 3 picnic tables, restroom (&), parking. **Cranberry Road:** Restroom (&), parking. **Cranberry Beach Road:** Restroom (&), parking. **Warrenton Cannery Road:** Restroom (&), parking.
CAR ACCESS: See following.

South Beach runs for 19 unbroken miles between Grays Harbor and Willapa Bay. At its north end the town of Westport, which is oriented to sport fishing, boasts a fleet of charter boats. Boats aren't essential, however, as first-class fishing

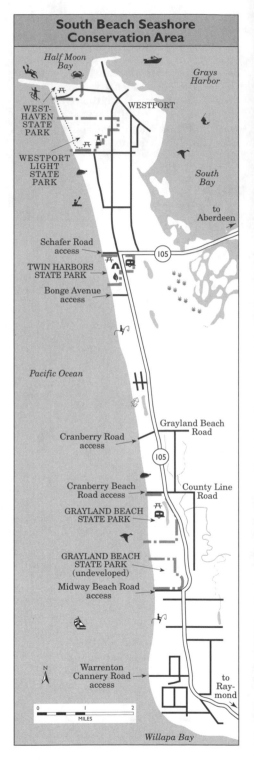

South Beach Seashore Conservation Area

can be had from the jetties or shore. Surf-fishers can have success with even a light or medium spinning rod if the surf is not too rough.

To many people Washington beaches mean razor clams, and South Beach is a prime spot for pursuing them. When digging seasons are officially opened in fall and spring, throngs descend in search of the Cadillac of clams. Buckets of succulent bivalves are soon carted away to a loving home where they are breaded, fried, and enshrined on a dinner plate. Vehicles can be driven onto the beach at all accesses, except as noted. The introduction to this book lists beach regulations.

SCHAFER ROAD (also known as Twin Harbor approach). No vehicle access to the beach. At the intersection of SR 105 E/W and 105 N/S, head west along the north side of Twin Harbors State Park to reach the beach in 0.2 mile.

BONGE AVENUE. From the intersection of SR 105 E/W and 105 N/S, head south for 0.7 mile to Bonge Avenue, then turn west and reach the beach in 0.4 mile.

CRANBERRY ROAD (also known as Grayland Beach approach). From the intersection of SR 105 E/W and 105 N/S, head south for 3.6 miles to an intersection where Cranberry Road goes west and Grayland Beach Road heads east. Follow Cranberry Road to the beach.

CRANBERRY BEACH ROAD (also known as County Line approach). From the intersection of SR 105 E/W and 105 N/S, head south for 4.9 miles to County Line Road, at the north side of Grayland Beach State Park. Turn west and reach the beach in 0.5 mile.

MIDWAY BEACH ROAD. From the intersection of SR 105 E/W and 105 N/S, head south for 6.8 miles to Midway Beach Road, then turn west and reach the beach in 0.4 mile.

WARRENTON CANNERY ROAD (also known as North Cove approach). From the intersection of SR 105 E/W and 105 N/S, head south for 8.5 miles to Warrenton Cannery Road, then turn west and reach the beach in 0.9 mile.

WESTHAVEN STATE PARK

Picnicking, kite flying, hiking, horseback riding, surfboarding, paddling, scuba diving, beach walking, crabbing (in Half Moon Bay), surf-fishing

SEASON/HOURS: Year-round.
AREA: 79.06 acres; 1,215 feet of saltwater shoreline on the Pacific Ocean.
DAY-USE FACILITIES: 2 picnic sites, drinking fountain, restroom (&), outside shower.
RECREATIONAL FACILITIES: City of Westport dune trail with viewing platforms and interpretive display.
CAR ACCESS: From US 101 on the south side of Aberdeen, take SR 105 west for 19 miles, then 105 Spur north for 2 miles to its end at the intersection of W Ocean Avenue and S Forrest Street. Continue north on Forrest, which becomes E Wilson Avenue as it bends eastward and in 1.1 miles intersects N Montesano Street. Turn northwest on Montesano, and in 0.2 mile the signed road to the park heads to the west. The park boundary is reached in 0.5 mile, and the beach parking lot in 1 mile. *No vehicle access to the beach.*

A long rock jetty built in the 1940s to reduce silting in the mouth of Grays Harbor led to the accretion of grass-covered dunes and the broad sandy shore that is now Westhaven State Park. Rolling breakers from the Pacific Ocean make this the state's most popular surfing beach. Sea kayakers are also drawn here to test their skills maneuvering through the crashing waves.

The beach will hold a moderate swell from almost any direction, but those from the north and northwest tend to be the cleanest (best for holding their shape and form). Since the bottom is all sand, it is difficult for storm surf or swells over 7 feet to hold their shape. Low and incoming

Razor clam season attracts throngs to South Beach.

Westhaven State Park offers great surfboarding.

tides usually produce the most rideable surf, no matter what the direction of the swell is, while high tide will ruin just about any swell, large or small.

Summer surf usually is slow and lazy, but very playful; fall and spring surf requires strong paddling muscles. When swells are large, there is usually a rip current along the jetty to help surfers paddle out. Wet suits are needed to survive the frigid ocean water, which doesn't warm above 60 degrees, even in summer. Warm summer days might require only a half wet suit, but in midwinter boots, gloves, and hood along with a full wet suit are the dress code.

In summer the wide beach attracts other kinds of recreationists. Kids create sand castles while Mom and Dad comb the beach for sand-buffed agates or treasures brought in by the surf. Winter storms in 1993 ripped through the peninsula

between the jetty and Half Moon Bay, slicing a 50-foot-wide channel through the park property into the bay, and cutting off access to fishing from the jetty. The breach was successfully refilled with dredged slurry, but the fill has built a steep, 8-foot-high bank above the beach that might be difficult for some people to negotiate. Beach fishing and crabbing are popular activities in the placid waters along the shoreline of Half Moon Bay. The trail between Westhaven and Westport Light is described in Westport Light State Park.

WESTPORT LIGHT STATE PARK

Picnicking, kite flying, hiking, horseback riding, surfboarding, beach walking, shellfish, surf-fishing

SEASON/HOURS: Day-use, year-round.
AREA: 212.18 acres; 3,397 feet of saltwater shoreline on the Pacific Ocean.
DAY-USE FACILITIES: 15 picnic sites (5 with wind screens), restroom (&).
RECREATIONAL FACILITIES: City of Westport dune trail between Westhaven and Westport Light State Parks with viewing platforms and interpretive displays.
EDUCATIONAL FACILITIES: Westport lighthouse.
CAR ACCESS: From US 101 on the south side of Aberdeen, take SR 105 west for 19 miles, then 105 Spur north for 2 miles to its end at the intersection of W Ocean Avenue and S Forrest Street. Turn west on Ocean Avenue, and reach a platform with views of the lighthouse in 0.3 mile, and the parking lot, beach, and trail access at 0.8 mile.

Westport lighthouse is unique in several ways: At 107 feet, it is the tallest lighthouse on the West Coast of the U.S., and it is one of the few lighthouses where

most of the original lighting system is still intact. The French-built Fresnel lens, originally assembled for it in 1895, and the vents in the tower walls, used to adjust the draft for the original oil lamps, are still in place, even though the present light source is a 1,000-watt lamp producing a beam of 1,520,000 candlepower, visible up to 25 nautical miles away. A sign on a small viewing platform tells the story of the light.

Rolling dunes covered with beach grass and shore pine form the inland portion of the park. All the facilities—a parking lot, restrooms, and windscreened picnic sites—are found just above the beach at the southeast corner of the park. The road along the south edge of the park (W Ocean Avenue) continues through the foredunes to the beach. Beachcombing is especially popular during the winter, when storms bring treasures from the Pacific.

Westport Light Trail, a 1.4-mile-long blacktopped path, wanders along the top of the foredunes between Westport Light and Westhaven State Parks. Three viewing platforms en route have interpretive panels describing the ecosystem of the dunes and history of the area.

TWIN HARBORS STATE PARK

Camping, picnicking, kite flying, horseback riding, beach walking, shellfish, surf-fishing

SEASON/HOURS: Day-use, year-round. Closed to camping between November 1 and February 28; campsite reservations accepted in summer.
AREA: 239.09 acres; 6,414 feet of saltwater shoreline on the Pacific Ocean.
OVERNIGHT AND DAY-USE FACILITIES: 49 RV sites, 249 standard campsites (3 &), 5 primitive campsites, group camp with picnic shelter, fire ring, and barbeque (80 persons), 12 picnic sites, kitchen shelter, group day-use

area (100 persons), 6 restrooms with showers (&), trailer dump station.

RECREATIONAL FACILITIES: 0.75-mile nature trail, children's play area, shellfish cleaning area.

CAR ACCESS: From US 101 on the south side of Aberdeen, take SR 105 west for 18.8 miles. The main park entrance is on the south side of the highway, 0.2 mile east of the intersection with 105 Spur to Westport. Traffic through the main park area is one-way, entering from SR 105 on the north side of the park, and exiting to SR 105 on the west side. Additional camping areas are on the west of the highway 0.2 mile south of the main camp exit. Vehicles may reach the beach via Bonge Avenue, on the south side of the park; there is no vehicle access at Twin Harbors Gap Road, on the north side of the park.

The largest of the two state park campgrounds in the South Beach area, Twin Harbors, attracts capacity crowds in summer as well as during spring and fall razor clamming seasons, with over 500,000 people visiting the park annually. The extensive camping areas sit on both sides of SR 105. Hookup sites lie just inside the entrance of the eastern section of the park. The remaining sites on this side of the highway line a series of loops, shaded by brush and shore pine. Flooding might cause some of these campsites to be closed during rainy months. A children's play area includes the hull of a boat for fanciful ocean voyages by young skippers.

Camping on the west side of SR 105 is along a road adjacent to the highway or on a large loop closer to the beach. These sites are more open than those to the east, but they are bordered with enough shore pine to provide a bit of privacy and a little shade, as well as protection from the wind. Trails linking the camp areas and the individual sites eventually lead to the beach. This camp area might be closed in winter.

While the beach habitat might, on the surface, seem to be a simple one of sand, grass, and scrub, it is in reality complex, and includes a wealth of interdependent plant communities. A park brochure describes ecological features at 20 numbered stations along the Shifting Sands Nature Trail. The path begins on the west side of the highway about 50 feet beyond campsites 285–307 and loops counterclockwise through the dune area south of the campground. The start of the trail might be poorly marked, and some station posts might be obscure or missing.

Shore pine, wild strawberry, evergreen huckleberry, black twinberry, and kinnickinnick soon crowd the trail. In 0.25 mile the route breaks out in beach grass, then climbs to the top of the foredune overlooking the beach. Although unmarked and obscured by beach grass, the trail now heads south along the top of the dunes to the return leg; don't drop down to the

Knowledgeable clam diggers bring their boots for wading and their barbecue for cooking their trove.

beach, as you will have trouble finding the start of the return leg. On the final trail section shore pine arches cathedral-like over the trail. Walk quietly and you might see brush rabbits, field mice, and possibly even deer.

GRAYLAND BEACH STATE PARK

Camping, picnicking, kite flying, hiking, horseback riding, beach walking, shellfish, fishing

SEASON/HOURS: Year-round; campsite reservations accepted in summer.
AREA: 433.5 acres; 7,749 feet of saltwater shoreline on the Pacific Ocean.
OVERNIGHT AND DAY-USE FACILITIES: 60 RV sites (2 ♿), 3 primitive campsites, picnic table, restroom (♿), toilet.
CAR ACCESS: From US 101 on the south side of Aberdeen, take SR 105 west for 19 miles to its intersection with 105 Spur to Westport. Here continue south on SR 105 for 4.8 miles to Cranberry Beach Road. Head west on this road and reach the park entrance in 0.2 mile.

Grayland Beach State Park is the second of the two parks on South Beach that have camping. Sites arranged around the perimeter of six paved circles are

A tiny sanderling forages in mud at Grayland Beach State Park.

hugged by dense 12-foot-high growths of shore pine and kinnickinnick. A few primitive campsites are hidden in the woods just inside the park entrance. There is no designated day-use area for picnickers; most will choose to pack their lunch to the shore.

The beach, of course, is the main reason for visiting here. A short trail leaves the center of the campground and leads through dense shrubs to the foredune and the beach. On sunny summer days steady northwest winds lure kite flyers to the beach, and on blustery winter days flotsam at the high-tide line holds beachcombers' treasures. During razor clamming season the beach is a favorite spot for those pursuing this tasty bivalve. An 8-mile-long strip of beach north and south of the park is open to motorized vehicles.

A second, undeveloped portion of land that is part of the park lies 2 miles south, on the north side of the Midway Beach Road access. A primitive, rutted jeep road running north and south through the property can be walked.

LONG BEACH SEASHORE CONSERVATION AREA

Picnicking, kite flying, birdwatching, horseback riding, surfboarding, beach walking, shellfish, surf-fishing, paddling

SEASON/HOURS: Day-use, year-round.
AREA: 29 miles of saltwater shoreline on the Pacific Ocean.
FACILITIES: Oysterville, Ocean Park, Klipsan Beach, and Cranberry Road: Toilet. **Bolstad:** Restrooms (♿), paved bicycle path, picnic tables, 2 wind screens, paved dune trail, boardwalk (to the south). **10th Avenue:** Restrooms (♿), wind screen, paved dune trail, boardwalk (to the north). **Seaview:** 2 restrooms (♿).
CAR ACCESS: See following.
BEACH DRIVING RESTRICTIONS:
Open all year: Oysterville Access to Bolstad Access, Seaview Access to

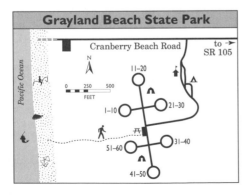

Grayland Beach State Park

Cranberry Beach Road

to → SR 105

Pacific Ocean

N

0   250   500
FEET

11–20
21–30
1–10
51–60
31–40
41–50

Fort Canby State Park.
Prohibited April 15 through the day after Labor Day, except during razor clam season: Leadbetter Point State Park to Oysterville Access, Seaview Access to Bolstad Access, Warrenton Cannery Road Access to Willapa Wildlife Refuge.
Prohibited all year except during razor clam season: Leadbetter Point State Park
Prohibited year-round: Fort Canby State Park.

Long Beach is the grandest of the state's three recreational ocean beaches. Claimed to be the longest unbroken stretch of beach in the world, it sweeps southward for 29 miles from Willapa Bay to the mouth of the Columbia River.

Surf, sand, and dunes offer all the fun found on the two northern beaches; Fort Canby State Park, at the southern tip of the Long Beach peninsula, is the jewel in this recreational crown. The fare at other Long Beach state parks ranges from birdwatching to camping to golf. Ilwaco, which faces on Baker Bay on the Columbia River, is a commercial and sport fishing center, with numerous charter offices booking trips for salmon, tuna, sturgeon, and bottom fish. If time does not allow for one of these excursions, the jetty at Fort Canby offers good fishing as well as views of the fishing fleet. Birdwatching groups can also charter boats for offshore observation of spectacular flocks of hundreds of thousands of migratory birds.

Unlike North Beach and South Beach, Long Beach is edged by water for most of its east side as well as its west; Leadbetter Point State Park has shoreline on both Willapa Bay and the Pacific Ocean. Tidelands on Willapa Bay are private, except for those in the state park or Willapa National Wildlife Refuge. Vehicles can be driven onto the beach at all accesses, except as noted. The introduction to this book lists beach regulations. The following driving directions all begin at the intersection of US 101 and SR 103 (Pacific Highway) at Seaview.

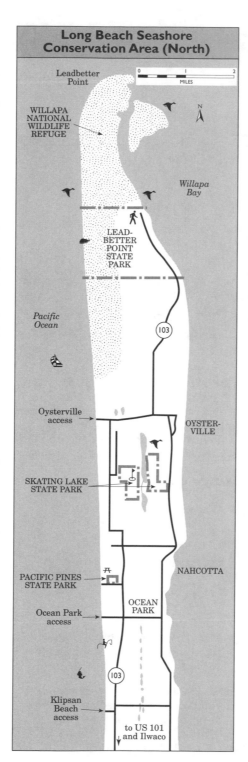

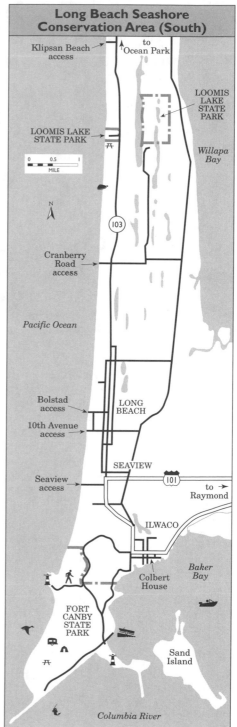

A galaxy of kites fills the air at the Long Beach Kite Festival.

OYSTERVILLE. Head north on SR 103 for 11.5 miles to Ocean Park. Follow it west through Ocean Park on Bay Avenue. In 0.8 mile SR 103 turns north as Sandridge Road. At a T-intersection in 4.2 miles, head west on Oysterville Gap and reach the beach in 1.5 miles.

OCEAN PARK. Drive north on SR 103 for 11.5 miles to Ocean Park. Turn west on Bay Avenue and reach the beach in 0.4 mile.

KLIPSAN BEACH. Head north on SR 103 for 9.6 miles to 225th Street, then west for 0.2 mile to the beach access.

CRANBERRY ROAD. Head north on SR 103 for 4.6 miles to Cranberry Road, then west for 0.4 mile to the beach access.

BOLSTAD. Go north on SR 103 for 1.5 miles to Bolstad Street, then west for 0.1 mile to the beach access, the north end of the Long Beach Boardwalk along the foredunes, and an intersection with the dune trail.

10TH AVENUE. Drive north on SR 103 for 1.1 miles to 10th Street in Long Beach, then west for 0.3 mile to the beach access at the south end of the Long Beach Boardwalk along the foredunes, and an intersection with the dune trail.

SEAVIEW. Turn south on SR 103, then in 0.1 mile head west on 38th Place to reach the beach in 0.5 mile.

LEADBETTER POINT STATE PARK

Picnicking, hiking, bicycling, wildlife watching, beach walking, shellfish, fishing

SEASON/HOURS: Day-use year-round, except dune area closed mid-March through August for snowy plover nesting.
AREA: 1,184.45 acres; 15,840 feet of saltwater shoreline on the Pacific Ocean and Willapa Bay.
DAY-USE FACILITIES: 2 toilets (&).
RECREATIONAL FACILITIES: 6.3 miles of hiking trail (1.1 miles open to mountain bikes).
CAR ACCESS: From the intersection of US 101 and SR 103 at Seaview, take SR 103 (Pacific Highway) north for 11.5 miles to Ocean Park. Turn east on Bay Avenue, and in 0.8 mile, north on Sandridge Road. In 4.2 miles, at a T-intersection, head west on Oysterville Road, then in 0.3 mile go north on Stackpole Road. Reach the park entrance in another 3 miles, and the road end in 4.5 miles. *No vehicle access to the beach.*

Leadbetter Point State Park encompasses a band of land that stretches across the Long Beach peninsula, giving it beach frontage on both the ocean and Willapa Bay. The road runs in timber near the east shore; parking areas are midway at Stackpole Slough and at the road end at the far north end of the park.

A remarkable transition in ecology occurs in little over a mile, east to west. On Willapa Bay a grassy marshland reaches east to the shoreline along the protected waters. To the west, cedar, spruce, hemlock, and alder make up the forest, which merges with a dense growth of kinnickinnick, shore pine, blackberries, and huckleberries, and becomes more sparse as the ocean beach is neared. Saltwater marshes amid the dunes nourish arrowgrass and pickleweed. Rolling dunes stabilized by hardy beach grass, wild beach strawberry, gorse, sand verbena, lupine, and beach pea finally give way to the wide, windswept sandy beach facing on the ocean. The dunes running north from the park to the tip of the peninsula are one of three parts of the Willapa National Wildlife Refuge; Long Island near the south end of Willapa Bay and shorelands at the end of the bay are its two other sections.

Four trails, each with color-coded trail markers, start at the road-end parking

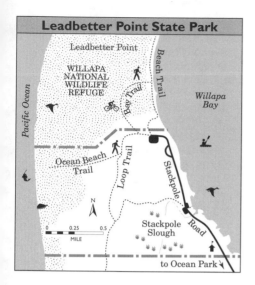

pipits that in spring nest in alpine meadows and on arctic tundra. From mid-July through October, you might see brown pelicans that have wandered north from their California breeding grounds. The north end of the wildlife refuge is closed to the public from April through August, when snowy plovers nest there. Aside from the bird population, the state park is home to raccoons, deer, berry-seeking black bears . . . and clouds of mosquitoes in early summer.

SKATING LAKE STATE PARK

Golfing, birdwatching, nature study

SEASON/HOURS: Day-use year-round.
AREA: 340.64 acres.
CONCESSION: Golf course.
CAR ACCESS: Follow Vernon Avenue

north from Ocean Park to Joe Johns Road, turn west on it, then north on H Street, west on 295th Street, and north on I Street. At 315th Street turn east for one block, then north on J Place to reach the Surfside Golf Club parking lot.

Diversity is the norm in Washington's state parks, and Skating Lake State Park proves it. This property, acquired from the Department of Natural Resources, includes a nine-hole golf course, operated by a concessionaire. The state's prime interest, however, is preservation of the wetlands that border the east side of the golf course. The property includes the middle portion of Skating Lake, a slender, 1.5-mile-long combination marsh and pond that is a wintering site for trumpeter swans and other waterfowl. Trailheads from the north and south boundaries of the park and paths through the wetlands are planned for the future.

lot. The longest, the 2.1-mile-long Loop Trail, heads west then bends south and eventually links to the Stackpole Slough parking area. The trail, mostly in open shore pine, within sound but not sight of the ocean, has a loose sand base that makes it slow and tiring to walk. The 1.3-mile Ocean Beach Trail shares the first 0.75 mile with the Loop Trail, then branches west to reach the Pacific Ocean beach. Both trails are subject to deep flooding from October through May. The 1.8-mile Beach Trail, which begins to the east of the road-end, shortly breaks onto the beach at Willapa Bay. The sandy shoreline is followed north out of the park into the wildlife refuge at the tip of the peninsula. The Bay Trail branches west from this eastern Beach Trail in about 0.5 mile and returns inland, joining the trails to the west. This is the only trail on which bicycles are permitted.

Leadbetter Point is a "Holiday Inn" on the Pacific Flyway; among the migratory birds that stop here from fall through spring are sooty shearwaters, Canada geese, white-fronted geese, brant, pintails, shovelers, canvasbacks, and buffleheads. Clouds of dunlins and sanderlings frequent the beaches, while dunes provide winter refuge for birds such as Lapland longspurs, horned larks, and water

Geese and swans winter over at Skating Lake.

53

PACIFIC PINES STATE PARK

Picnicking, kite flying, hiking, beach walking, shellfish, surf-fishing

SEASON/HOURS: Closed November 1 through mid-March.
AREA: 10.8 acres; 590 feet of saltwater shoreline on the Pacific Ocean.
DAY-USE FACILITIES: 8 picnic sites, restroom (&), paved parking lot.
RECREATIONAL FACILITIES: Hiking trail to the beach, horseshoe pits.
CAR ACCESS: From the intersection of US 101 and SR 103 at Seaview, take SR 103 north for 11.5 miles to Ocean Park. Continue north on Vernon Avenue for 0.6 mile, then head west on 274th Place for 0.2 mile to reach the park. *No developed vehicle access to the beach.*

A section of land north of Ocean Park that once was platted for a real estate development has, instead, become a small state park. Only the name given it by the realtor remains as an echo of its intended destiny. The park is little more than a glorified beach access, but its few amenities of restrooms, picnic tables, and horseshoe pits are very nice. Shore pine provides some sheltered spots for lunching when winds are too brisk on the beach. The unimproved road here through the dunes to the beach is not a legal access point.

LOOMIS LAKE STATE PARK

Picnicking, kite flying, birdwatching, beach walking, shellfish, fishing

SEASON/HOURS: Year-round.
AREA: 295.1 acres; 425 feet of saltwater shoreline on the Pacific Ocean.
DAY-USE FACILITIES: 7 picnic sites with wind screens (3 &), fire braziers, restroom (&).
RECREATIONAL FACILITIES: Paved path to a viewing platform (&), with a continuing trail to the beach.
NEARBY: Department of Fish and Wildlife boat launch and fishing pier on Loomis Lake.
CAR ACCESS: From the intersection of US 101 and SR 103 at Seaview, take SR 103 north for 10.9 miles. The eastern, undeveloped portion of the park is on the east side of Loomis Lake, and includes Mallard Lake, Lost Lake, and the north end of Island Lake. The west portion of the park is at the end of an unnamed road west of the highway between 179th Street and 188th Place. *No vehicle access to the beach.*

The developed portion of Loomis Lake State Park is a 13.5-acre strip of land that faces the ocean, but doesn't touch the lake itself. A king-sized parking lot provides a spot for beachgoers to leave their cars when heading for clam digging or other enticing beach activities. Picnic tables with windscreens are handy for a picnic stop before hiking the short distance to the shore. A barrier-free path leads to a dune-top viewing deck overlooking the beach; from here a sand trail continues to the shore.

The 280-acre section of park that lies on the west shore of the lake is undeveloped. The property and the small ponds that it encompasses are a wintering habitat for trumpeter swans. These magnificent birds were nearly hunted to extinction; in 1931, a mere 35 birds were counted. By virtue of conservation measures, they have made a remarkable comeback, and large flocks now range in the western U.S. and Canada. The park lands will remain undeveloped in order to preserve the wildlife habitat.

Loomis Lake, at 2.5 miles long, is the largest lake on the Long Beach peninsula, and the only one that is planted with rainbow trout. A Department of Fish and Wildlife boat launch and public fishing dock is on its west shore at the end of a gravel road opposite 188th Place. The state park property is on the opposite side of the lake.

Tracks in beach sand tell a tale of previous visitors.

FORT CANBY STATE PARK

Camping, picnicking, birdwatching, hiking, beach walking, shellfish, boating, fishing, historical interpretation, lighthouse tours

SEASON/HOURS: Year-round; campsite reservations accepted in summer.

AREA: 1,884.06 acres; 42,600 feet of salt-water shoreline on the Pacific Ocean and the mouth of the Columbia River.

OVERNIGHT AND DAY-USE FACILITIES: 87 RV sites (27 EW), 155 standard campsites, 5 primitive campsites.

LODGING: 3 cabins, 3 yurts (5 persons each) (&), North Head lighthouse keeper's house rental, 50 picnic sites, 8 restrooms (&) (7 with showers), 2 toilets, trailer dump station.

RECREATIONAL FACILITIES: 5.5 miles of hiking trail; 2-lane paved boat ramp with boarding float, viewing platform.

EDUCATIONAL FACILITIES: 1.5-mile nature trail, 2 lighthouses (1 open for tours), Lewis and Clark Interpretive Center with gift shop, historic Coast Artillery gun emplacements.

CONCESSIONS: snacks, groceries, fishing and camping supplies.

CAR ACCESS: From Ilwaco, at the stoplight on US 101 at 1st Street and Spruce Street SE, head west on Spruce Street, which becomes Robert Gray Drive. Reach the park boundary and the road to Beards Hollow in 1.8 miles, the road to North Head lighthouse in 2.1 miles (RVs prohibited), and the park entrance in 3.5 miles.

BOAT ACCESS: Fort Canby lies at the mouth of the Columbia River, south of Ilwaco.

This stretch of bluffs and beach at the southern tip of the Long Beach peninsula is among the most historically significant in the state; in fact, the Cape Disappointment area has been declared

The North Head lighthouse, which was the second navigational beacon to be installed at Fort Canby, was visible by ships traveling from the north.

a National Historic District. It was here, in November 1805, that the Lewis and Clark Expedition first touched the waters of the Pacific Ocean. William Clark carved his name on a nearby tree.

As Oregon Territory was settled, the site became vital to commerce, maritime safety, and the military defense of the mouth of the mighty Columbia River. Treacherous currents at the bar that lies at the mouth of the river caused the area to become known as the "Graveyard of the Pacific." The Cape Disappointment lighthouse, which marks the river and

warns sailors of the bar, began operation in 1856, and was the first lighthouse in Washington. A second lighthouse was added at North Head in 1898, to assist mariners traveling from the north who were unable to spot the Cape Disappointment light.

The 584-acre military reservation, created in 1852, was the first site north of San Francisco considered worthy of military defenses. Smooth-bore cannons placed here in 1862 to guard the river's entrance were the first generation of Coast Artillery. During the early 1900s the

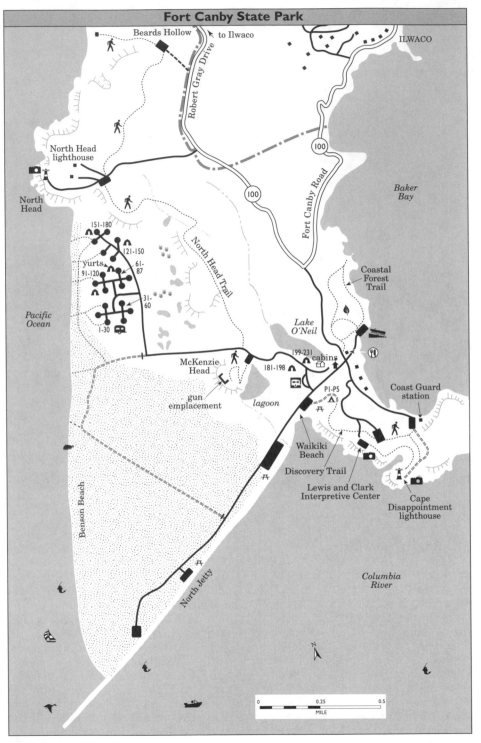

Fort Canby State Park

Beards Hollow — to Ilwaco

ILWACO

Robert Gray Drive

100

North Head lighthouse

North Head

Fort Canby Road

Baker Bay

151-180

121-150

yurts

61-87

91-120

North Head Trail

31-60

1-30

Pacific Ocean

Coastal Forest Trail

Lake O'Neil

199-231 cabins

McKenzie Head

181-198

gun emplacement

lagoon

P1-P5

Coast Guard station

Waikiki Beach

Discovery Trail

Lewis and Clark Interpretive Center

Cape Disappointment lighthouse

Benson Beach

Columbia River

North Jetty

N

0   0.25   0.5
MILE

fortifications were upgraded with new gun and mortar batteries and control centers for underwater mines that were laid beneath the entrance to the Columbia. World War II saw the addition of a modern, armored, long-range rapid-fire battery atop McKenzie Head. The fort was deactivated after World War II and became a state park.

The Park Today

The rich history of Fort Canby State Park is rivaled only by its varied recreation, which draws nearly 1 million visitors each year. Weekends during salmon fishing season see long lines of trailered boats waiting to be launched at the boat ramp facing on the Columbia River, just east of the park entrance gate.

Heading for North Jetty, the park road passes Waikiki Beach, a tiny, secluded cove holding the day-use and primitive camping areas. The road continues out to the 800-yard-long rock jetty, constructed to help control the wave action and erosion at the mouth of the Columbia. The jetty provides superb fishing for rockfish, perch, and even some salmon. Benson Beach, north of the jetty, is excellent for surf-fishing. Birdwatchers on the jetty can sometimes spot stray birds, such as albatross, that normally would be seen farther offshore, as well as plenty of more commonly seen ones.

One camping area lies in tree-shaded flats near the park entrance, on the edge of marshy Lake O'Neil. Here also are three one-room rental cabins with small porches overlooking the lake. Across the road from Lake O'Neil is a small parking area and the unmarked path to McKenzie Head, a 150-foot-high wooded knob. This trail climbs steeply around the south side of the head before arriving at the remnants of the World War II gun battery. The two armored 6-inch guns are gone, but the bunker is open to exploration; a flashlight is needed to poke into the dark rooms inside the tunnel between the two gun emplacements.

The park's main campground area, near the beach below North Head, contains numerous wagon-wheel circles nestled in shore pine. Three of these sites hold yurts—cozy wood-floored, canvas-walled accommodations. Some of the campsites are interspersed with 50-foot-high rock outcroppings that offer challenges for young rock scramblers—far more fun than a jungle gym. Trails lead through the dunes to the sandy 2-mile-long expanse of Benson Beach.

Behind the protective mass of Cape Disappointment is the only Coast Guard motor lifeboat station in the world that trains coxswains for heavy weather and heavy surf operations; however, it is not open to the public. From the parking lot at the station, a steep gated road can be walked uphill to the Cape Disappointment lighthouse.

The Lewis and Clark Interpretive Center perches on a 200-foot-high cliff. A short path switchbacks uphill from the parking lot to the center; disabled parking is adjacent to the center. By means of a "time line" with descriptive panels that follow a ramp spiraling down two flights and then back up, the interpretive center tells the story of the Lewis and Clark Corps of Discovery as it traveled from St. Louis to the Pacific Ocean. The lower level of the ramp holds more displays and a multimedia theater offering short programs. The ramp returns to the main floor, where an expanse of windows reveal breathtaking views of the Cape Disappointment lighthouse, the Columbia River, the western reaches of the park, and the Pacific Ocean. Other presentations tell more about the maritime and military history of the area. This bluff was originally the site of the turn-of-the-century Coast Artillery Battery Harvey Allen. The massive concrete emplacement that housed the battery is immediately behind the interpretive center.

Near the northern park boundary, a road leads to the North Head lighthouse. At road's end a short path leads through woods of Sitka spruce to a kinnickinnick-lined path to the lighthouse, perched above precipitous cliffs overlooking the crashing waves of the Pacific.

Over 5 miles of trails lace the park, wending through forest and marshland to arrive at lighthouses, viewpoints, or campgrounds; walk to see what you can discover. The Coastal Forest Trail, a 1.5-mile-long loop nature trail north of the boat launch, circles through a forest of 300- to 500-year-old Sitka spruce and hemlock, which has been undisturbed by man from the time of the original explorers.

Beards Hollow

Tucked away in a far north section of the park is Beards Hollow. The road to this one-time quarry has disappeared into a lush growth of alder, fir, and oak nurtured by moist clouds off the Pacific. The lagoons you see here were freshwater marshes that survived behind the barriers of ocean-built dunes, but were occasionally inundated by salt water driven by midwinter storms. The resulting brackish water killed some of the old cedars, which persist as old silver ghosts above green, algae-covered ponds.

A huge Fresnel lens in the Lewis and Clark Interpretive Center is typical of those used in lighthouses.

The Lewis and Clark Interpretive Center sits atop the high cliffs of Cape Disappointment, at the mouth of the Columbia River.

A trail with muddy sections leads to views overlooking the breakers of the Pacific. The cliff walls of North Head and a 100-foot-high basalt outcrop to its northeast stand in marked contrast to the dune grass flat that comprises most of the hollow.

COLBERT HOUSE HERITAGE AREA

Historical interpretation

SEASON/HOURS: Open weekends during summer months, 1:00 P.M. to 4:00 P.M.

AREA: 0.36 acre.

EDUCATIONAL FACILITIES: Historic home (fee for tour).

CAR ACCESS: In Ilwaco at the corner of Quaker and Lake Streets.

This beautifully maintained and furnished house represents a typical Ilwaco home of the late 1800s. The center part of the house was originally built in nearby Chinookville in 1871 by Fred and

A bedroom at Colbert House displays period furnishings.

Catherine Colbert. It was barged to this site in 1883. A sitting room, bedrooms, kitchen, and loft were added later. One room holds a plumbed bathtub; however, Catherine Colbert felt it was unsanitary for people to relieve themselves in the house, so an outhouse was used for many years.

Colbert, a Swedish immigrant, fished, manufactured fishing nets, and ran a livery stable and carriage house. The family of twelve lived here, and at times up to four other Swedish immigrants lived in the loft of the house where fishing nets were manufactured. Volunteers conduct tours on weekend afternoons during the summer.

FORT COLUMBIA STATE PARK

Picnicking, hiking, historic fortifications, historic military barracks restoration, local and Native American historical displays

SEASON/HOURS: Closed October 1 through mid-April, open June 1 to September 30.

AREA: 592.6 acres; 6,400 feet of freshwater shoreline on the Columbia River.

DAY-USE FACILITIES: 26 picnic sites, 2 restrooms (&).

LODGING: Steward's House vacation rental.

EDUCATIONAL FACILITIES: Historic gun batteries, 2 historic interpretive centers, 1-mile historic walk.

OTHER: Battery 246 conference rental.

CAR ACCESS: On US 101, drive 2.6 miles west of the junction of 101 and SR 401 at the north end of the Columbia River Bridge from Astoria, or 0.9 mile east from Chinook.

Fort Columbia was one of several Coast Artillery forts built between 1885 and 1905 on the West Coast during the period of frenzied construction of defensive fortifications. To destroy enemy ships that

might attempt to enter the mouth of the Columbia River, huge batteries, some on disappearing carriages, were mounted in massive concrete emplacements. Strings of underwater mines laid along the river bottom were to be detonated from a shore-based control center when enemy ships passed. A smaller rapid-fire battery protected the minefields from attempts to disarm them via small boats, and also prevented landing parties from attacking the fort. In World War II a new battery with long-range rapid-fire guns in armored turrets supplemented the older, outmoded batteries.

The Park Today

As with most of these early forts, the property is now a state park, with restored buildings and historical displays providing a glimpse into this military era. Recreational facilities are limited to short trails and some picnic tables below the upper gun battery emplacement. Although the park fronts on the Columbia River, steep bluffs prevent access to the water. It was these cliffs,

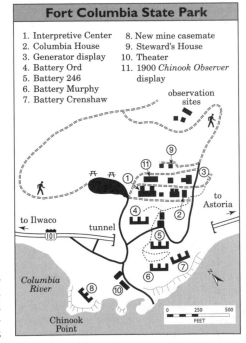

Fort Columbia State Park

1. Interpretive Center
2. Columbia House
3. Generator display
4. Battery Ord
5. Battery 246
6. Battery Murphy
7. Battery Crenshaw
8. New mine casemate
9. Steward's House
10. Theater
11. 1900 *Chinook Observer* display

observation sites

to Ilwaco
tunnel
to Astoria

Columbia River

Chinook Point

0   250   500
FEET

Restored barracks, officers' housing, and other buildings at Fort Columbia State Park provide a glimpse of World War I Army life.

which made enemy attacks impossible, that made the site ideal for a fort.

The enlisted men's barracks at Fort Columbia serve as a historical interpretive center. The restored kitchen, mess hall, and squad room evoke memories of lines of uniformed artillery men, eagerly waiting to be served from huge steaming pots. A taped voice of an army cook explains what you see and describes his daily duties. A mess table set with dishes is attended by a mannequin in a period Coast Artillery uniform. An upstairs squad room contains cots and lockers; posters remind soldiers of their duties and responsibilities. Other rooms in the building hold displays detailing the post's fortifications and regional history; an excellent video presentation tells of the creation of the fort and its transition to a state park.

A historic walk starts at the interpretive center in the old enlisted men's barracks, then pauses at the Columbia House, the former commandant's home, which has been restored and decorated with period furnishings. From here the path passes the old powerhouse then heads downhill through the various gun battery emplacements and exceptionally beautiful grounds shaded by tall, old spruce and enormous big-leaf maple. The most modern of these emplacements, Battery 246, which was constructed in the early 1940s, has two of the original 6-inch shielded guns, only six of which are known to exist today. A second leg of the walk follows old roads up Scarboro Hill to the site of the fire control observation posts.

Above the interpretive center, the quartermaster's storehouse has one room that shows the newspaper office of the *Chinook Observer* as it looked at the turn of the century. The paper is still published today.

LEWIS AND CLARK CAMPSITE HERITAGE AREA

Picnicking, historical interpretation

SEASON/HOURS: Day-use year-round.
AREA: 0.8 acre.
DAY-USE FACILITIES: 2 picnic tables.
EDUCATIONAL FACILITIES: Historical display.
CAR ACCESS: On US 101, drive 1.9 miles west of the junction of 101 and SR 401 at the north end of the Columbia River Bridge from Astoria. The site is on the north side of the road.

In mid-November of 1805 Lewis and Clark paused in their westward journey and camped here. It was from this spot that they first saw the breakers of the Pacific Ocean and realized they had accomplished the mission set for them by President Thomas Jefferson.

This road wayside contains a carved wooden statue depicting the explorers. A small grassy meadow next to the memorial has a couple of picnic tables.

WILLIE KEIL'S GRAVE HERITAGE AREA

Historical interpretation

SEASON/HOURS: Day-use year-round.
AREA: 0.34 acre.
EDUCATIONAL FACILITIES: Historical display.
CAR ACCESS: On the south side of SR 6, 3.3 miles east of Raymond, or 2.1 miles west of Menlo.

A poignant, macabre, or hilarious tale, depending on your viewpoint: Willie Keil was a 19-year-old man who had been designated to drive the lead wagon for a group of settlers headed west from Bethel, Missouri, along the Oregon Trail. In May of 1855, four days before the group's departure, he died. His overwhelming desire to go west with the colony led them to preserve his body in a metal-lined casket filled with alcohol (some accounts claim it was whiskey), converting the lead wagon to a makeshift hearse. Willie led the group west both in body and spirit(s). On November 26, 1855, he was finally laid to rest on a hillside above the tranquil Willapa River—his wish to reach the promised land fulfilled.

A wayside stop along SR 6 marks his gravesite. The ornately carved sign depicts the long journey west. Nearby is a granite marker commemorating the first fort, school, and post office in the Willapa Valley near this spot.

WILLAPA HILLS TRAIL

Hiking, bicycling, fishing, horseback riding

AREA: 762.24 acres, 56.2 linear miles; 13,000 feet of freshwater shoreline on the Chehalis and Willapa Rivers.

DAY-USE FACILITIES: Picnic tables, toilets between Raymond and South Bend, restrooms (&) at Pe Ell, toilet (&) at Ceres.

RECREATIONAL FACILITIES: Paved bicycle trail along the old road bed between Raymond and South Bend, with a detour across the South Fork of the Willapa River. Undeveloped access points at several other locations between Raymond and Chehalis, with improved grade between Pe Ell and Ceres Hill. Thirty-three trestles and bridges and an historic railway swing bridge.

CAR ACCESS: The east end of the trail is on the west side of I-5 at Chehalis. Immediately west of the freeway, head south from SR 6 onto Riverside Road, which shortly changes to Newaukum Avenue SW. In 0.5 mile turn east on SW Sylvenus Street, signed to the nearby steam train ride. At the steam train parking lot turn south on SW Hillburger Road, which crosses the trail in 0.4 mile. Newaukum Avenue intersects the trail 0.6 mile south of Sylvenus Street, and the steam train tracks also intersect the trail a little over a mile to the west. The west end of the trail is at the east side of South Bend, adjacent to US 101. Developed access points are at various street crossings between South Bend and Raymond. The map shows other main access points along the route.

This spur line of the Northern Pacific Railway was built between 1891 and 1893 to link Chehalis to South Bend, and to speed the area's economic development. With disastrous timing, the railroad came into existence during a major depression, and it wasn't until the early 1900s that the line, then known as the Yakima and Pacific Coast Railroad, began to haul freight and passengers.

The abandoned railroad station at Pe Ell can be seen along the Willapa Hills Trail.

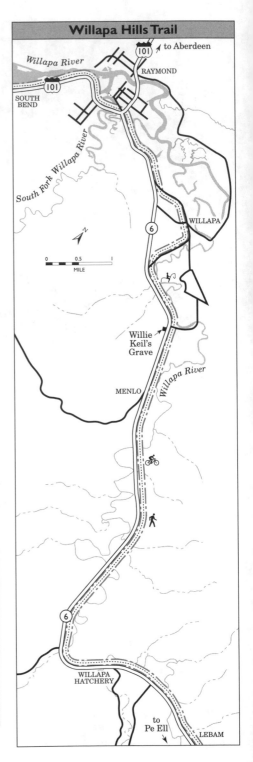

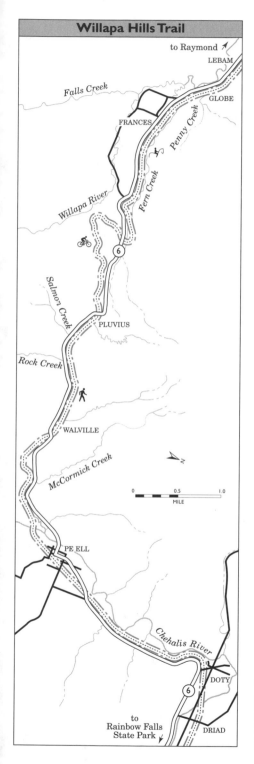

Willapa Hills Trail

to Raymond ↗
LEBAM

Falls Creek

GLOBE

FRANCES

Penny Creek

Fern Creek

Willapa River

6

Salmon Creek

PLUVIUS

Rock Creek

WALVILLE

McCormick Creek

N

0   0.5   1.0
MILE

PE ELL

Chehalis River

6

DOTY

to
Rainbow Falls
State Park ↓

DRIAD

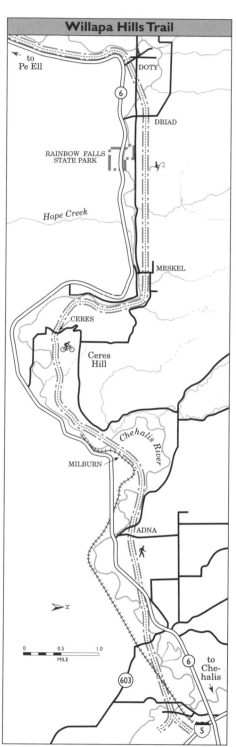

Willapa Hills Trail

to
Pe Ell

DOTY

6

DRIAD

RAINBOW FALLS
STATE PARK

Hope Creek

MESKEL

CERES

Ceres
Hill

Chehalis River

MILBURN

N

0   0.5   1.0
MILE

ADNA

6   to
Che-
halis

603

5

The railroad saw several other name changes over the ensuing years, including "the Ghost Line" during the depression years of the 1930s. Eventually the Burlington Northern ended up with the track, which was last active in 1993. State Parks acquired the railbed under a federal "rail banking" law that permits interim public recreational use of old rail corridors until such time, if ever, that rail service is reactivated.

Ties and rails have been removed, and vehicle-blocking gates have been installed at most of the obvious access points. The only complete trail development has been within the city of Raymond, where a paved trail and parking have been constructed along Alder Street, southeast of the historic railroad swing bridge across the South Fork of the Willapa River. Since the bridge is no longer functional, the trail has been rerouted along US 101 and city streets until it once more joins the old railroad bed about 0.25 mile to the west. It continues to the South Bend city limits as a bicycle trail, with occasional picnic tables and toilets en route.

A phased development of the remainder of the trail is planned, with primitive trailside camping sites at a few trailheads. The map shows existing facilities (as of 1999), and those planned.

RAINBOW FALLS STATE PARK

Camping, picnicking, nature study, hiking, fishing, paddling, rafting

SEASON/HOURS: Closed October 1 through March 31, except for weekends and holidays.

AREA: 129.37 acres; 3,400 feet of freshwater shoreline on the Chehalis River.

OVERNIGHT AND DAY-USE FACILITIES: 47 standard campsites, 3 primitive campsites, group camp with kitchen shelter (56 persons), 65 picnic sites, reservable kitchen shelter, picnic shelter, group day-use area (150 persons), restroom with showers (&), trailer dump station, 4 toilets.

RECREATIONAL FACILITIES: Suspension footbridge, 6 miles of hiking trails, children's play equipment, baseball field, horseshoe pits.

EDUCATIONAL FACILITIES: 0.5-mile nature trail (&), fuschia garden.

CAR ACCESS: From I-5 take Exit 77 (SR 6W, Pe Ell, Raymond), and take SR 6 west for 17.3 miles to the park entrance.

This venerable state park remains as charming today as when it was established as a community park in the early 1900s. Because of its long history, some

Rainbow Falls on the Chehalis River is just one of the state park's many nice attractions.

centuries-old trees remain, providing shade for the park and nurturing a unique forest habitat. Most of the facilities, including the sturdy log residence of the ranger and the suspension bridge across the Chehalis River, are CCC-constructed. The Rainbow Falls for which the park is named are low and relatively small, except during spring runoffs. However, most of the year the foaming river water that surges through the narrow neck between two large rock outcroppings lifts a fine mist that, when hit by sunlight, creates a distinct rainbow. The falls and their rainbow namesake are best seen from the vintage, springy suspension footbridge that crosses the river just downstream from them. Anglers try for cutthroat and rainbow trout that frequent pools above and below the falls, and in summer kayakers and rafters paddle miles of the slow-moving river, with a portage around the falls.

The park's picnic area is a shaded meadow. Tables line the perimeter, and a ball diamond sits in one corner. Campsites along the loop road are in immense old fir, alder, and cedar, with an understory of salal and ferns. East of the entrance to the campground, a small group camp in a clearing has a picnic shelter and toilet. The flagpole in front of the park office is surrounded by a split-rail fence that encloses a garden with over 40 identified varieties of fuschias.

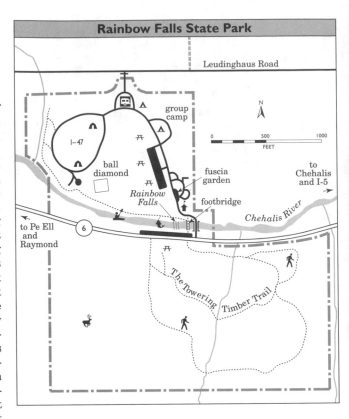

Rainbow Falls State Park

Leudinghaus Road

group camp

I-47

ball diamond

Rainbow Falls

fuscia garden

footbridge

Chehalis River

to Pe Ell and Raymond

to Chehalis and I-5

6

The Towering Timber Trail

N

0   500   1000
FEET

Although its main facilities are to the north, a major portion of the park's acreage lies south of SR 6. The wide shoulder along the north side of the highway provides parking for visitors using this part of the park. Aside from a picnic table in a small clearing, this part of the park is devoted to hiking trails. The shortest of these, "The Towering Timber Trail," is a 0.5-mile-long interpretive trail. A park brochure identifies mosses, various species of ferns, and other plants along the trail. Douglas-fir and western hemlock 175 to 200 feet tall give the trail its appropriate name. Other, longer trails that meander about this section of the park for several miles lead to additional grand views of spectacular trees.

CHAPTER THREE

THE SAN JUAN ISLANDS

PATOS ISLAND MARINE STATE PARK

Camping, hiking, picnicking, scuba diving, beach walking, tide pools, fishing, boating, paddling

SEASON/HOURS: Year-round.

AREA: 207.4 acres; 20,000 feet of saltwater shoreline on the Strait of Georgia.

OVERNIGHT AND DAY-USE FACILITIES: 7 primitive campsites (*no water, no garbage collection*), 3 toilets.

RECREATIONAL FACILITIES: 1.5 miles of hiking trail, 2 mooring buoys.

BOAT ACCESS: Patos Island lies 5.5 miles north of Orcas Island in the San Juan archipelago. Nearest launch facilities are at North Beach and West Beach on Orcas Island, or on the mainland at Bellingham, Larrabee State Park, Anacortes, or Hale Passage.

Patos Island, which sits near the Canadian border at the junction of Haro Strait and the Strait of Georgia, is the northernmost of all of the San Juan Islands. Its beacon on Alden Point marks the turning point for vessels headed to and from the Vancouver and Fraser River areas. Back in the days when lighthouses were manned, the entire island

Lime Kiln Lighthouse State Park in the San Juan Islands is dedicated to viewing whales such as these orcas.

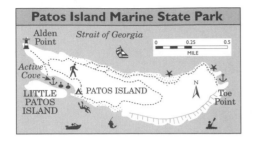

Patos Island Marine State Park

Alden Point · Strait of Georgia · Active Cove · LITTLE PATOS ISLAND · PATOS ISLAND · Toe Point · N · 0 0.25 0.5 MILE

was a lighthouse reserve; now the lighthouse is automated and the island owned by the Bureau of Land Management, but managed as a marine state park.

The only improved anchorage is Active Cove, a narrow protected cove with a wave-carved sandstone shore, at the west tip of the island. The cove has two mooring buoys and space for anchorage, although eelgrass along the bottom makes setting a hook challenging. Boats of any draft must enter the cove from the west, as the narrow channel at the east end of Little Patos Island is shallow and swept by tidal currents. Patos Island's few primitive campsites lie on a low, grassy flat above the gravel beach at the east end of Active Cove.

A 1.5-mile-long loop trail that circles the wooded center of the island begins at the campground and proceeds along the south-shore bluff before turning inland through brushy woods. After starting its return leg on the north flank of the island, the trail touches the shore, offering beach access. From the north beach access, the island loop trail cuts back inland, crossing the low backbone of the island near the lighthouse. From here an old road leads back to the trail's starting point.

The beach hike on the north shore of Patos Island to Toe Point, 0.75 mile away, is a delight. Each of the series of slight coves holds unique treasures. One cove might have seaweed creating abstract patterns on water-worn boulders; the next, rippled sandstone coated with thousands of indigo mussels; another displays fanciful, wave-carved sandstone.

Toe Point is finally reached at the east end of the island, where sandstone headlands frame a tiny cove and icy Mount Baker provides a backdrop. Although the hike is most enjoyable at a minus tide, tide level should pose no hazard for the trip as low headlands between the beaches are easily crossed by inland scrambles. Upland areas east of the loop trail are designated as a natural area, and hiking should be confined to the beach. The southern shoreline, east to Toe Point, is a rocky, inaccessible bluff.

The cove at Toe Point is also an excellent anchorage, especially when winds sweeping the Strait of Georgia make Active Cove uncomfortable.

SUCIA ISLAND MARINE STATE PARK

Camping, picnicking, birdwatching, fossil hunting, hiking, swimming, scuba diving, beach walking, tide pools, shellfish, crabbing, fishing, boating, paddling

SEASON/HOURS: Year-round. Little Sucia Island and the east half of Justice Island are closed to the public from January 1 through August 15, but are open for day-use at other times.

AREA: 564.08 acres; 77,700 feet of saltwater shoreline on the Strait of Georgia.

OVERNIGHT AND DAY-USE FACILITIES: 55 primitive campsites, 2 group camps (16 and 25 persons), 16 picnic sites,

Active Cove offers a snug anchorage at Patos Island Marine State Park.

3 picnic shelters, 12 toilets, 2 portable toilet dump stations (*no water October through March*).

RECREATIONAL FACILITIES: 6.2 miles of trail and 3.5 miles of service road for hiking, underwater artificial reef, 2 docks with floats (778 feet of float space), 48 mooring buoys.

BOAT ACCESS: Sucia Island is 2.5 miles north of Orcas Island. Nearest launch ramps are at North Beach and West Beach on Orcas Island, or on the mainland at Bellingham, Larrabee State Park, Anacortes, or Hale Passage.

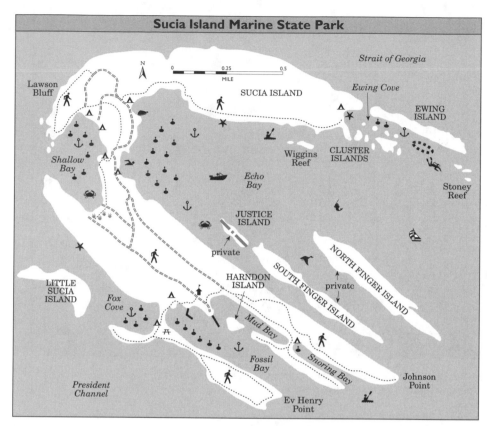

Dramatic geological formations and sandstone monoliths standing at water's edge, where waves have chiseled them from beach walls, make Sucia Island the crown jewel of Washington's marine state parks. Five layers of alternately hard and softer sandstone and shale form the island; these layers were deposited 65 million years ago in a great sea, and over time were severely folded and tilted. The island's horseshoe shape is due to this folding, while the erosion patterns are a result of glaciers that covered the area and the ocean waters that followed them.

The inland portions of the island are densely covered with brush and trees broken only by former logging roads that link the bays to the center of the island. Nine clearings at the heads of the bays have designated campgrounds, with the most developed facilities at Fossil Bay; the park's office is also there. Snoring Bay and Ewing Cove have a few primitive campsites. Camping is permitted only in designated areas—those who randomly pitch their tents might find themselves cited by a ranger.

The largest of the island's inlets is Echo Bay, which opens southeastward. More than a dozen mooring buoys line its head; anchorages here can be bouncy when southeasterly winds from Rosario Strait push swells into the shallow head of the bay. Two long, wooded islands in Echo Bay, North Finger and South Finger, are the only privately owned islands of the Sucia Group. The east half of the small island off the inner tip of South Finger holds nesting eagles and a seal rookery.

The arm of Sucia that forms the northern shore of Echo Bay ends at narrow Ewing Cove, framed on the south by a chain of rock islets—the Cluster Islands and Stoney Reef—and on the north by the long sandstone finger of Ewing Island. The hull of an old vessel has been sunk just beyond the outer mooring buoy to form a fish habitat for an underwater park. Boaters should enter the cove cautiously from the east, keeping an eye out for the rocks of Stoney Reef. The small channel at the west end of Ewing Island is too shallow and raked by tidal currents to provide a safe passage.

The end of Sucia's south arm is indented by two more bays, Snoring Bay and Fossil Bay. Fossil Bay sees the most

Saltwater erosion creates fascinating patterns in Sucia Island sandstone.

MATIA ISLAND MARINE STATE PARK

Camping, picnicking, birdwatching, hiking, fishing, scuba diving, beach walking, tide pools, shellfish, crabbing, boating, paddling

SEASON/HOURS: Year-round.

AREA: 5 acres; 680 feet of saltwater shoreline (the remainder of the island is a wildlife refuge).

OVERNIGHT AND DAY-USE FACILITIES: 6 primitive campsites (*no water, no garbage collection*), picnic site, toilet.

RECREATIONAL FACILITIES: 1-mile loop trail in the adjoining wildlife refuge, dock with float (144 feet of float space, *float removed in winter*), 2 mooring buoys.

BOAT ACCESS: Matia Island is 2.5 miles north of Orcas Island and 1.5 miles east of Sucia Island. Nearest launch facilities are at North Beach and West Beach on Orcas Island, and on the mainland at Bellingham, Larrabee State Park, Anacortes, and Hale Passage.

Fantastic sandstone formations, worn by water and weather, are a hallmark of Sucia Island Marine State Park.

activity; in addition to a crowd of mooring buoys, it has two docks and the greatest number of developed camping facilities. Small Snoring Bay is favored by kayakers who wish to avoid the crowds of the larger anchorages.

To escape the bustle of Fossil Bay, yet not forego its shoreside amenities, stay in Fox Cove. This beautiful sandy-beached cove is protected on the south by a thin rock finger from the main island and on the west by Little Sucia Island. It is best to approach Fox Cove from the northwest, as the narrow channel on the south side of Little Sucia is bordered by unmarked submerging rocks. Fires and overnight camping are prohibited on Little Sucia.

Shallow Bay, which offers the best protection in heavy weather, lies on the west side of Sucia Island. Although rocks encroach on the entrance on both sides, day marks show a safe channel. When mooring or anchoring here, be sure to check the depth and tide level, for its name was not chosen whimsically, and portions of the bay dry at minus tides. Chinaman Rock, an especially interesting sandstone formation, is found at the edge of the trees at the northeast side of Shallow Bay: legend has it that during the late 1800s worn hollows and body-sized caves that pock the sandstone face were used by smuggled Chinese aliens as hiding places to avoid immigration patrols.

A day or more can be spent exploring trails that probe the extended arms of the island. Paths run through dense forest or touch down at beaches. Look down into secret coves that might hold otters or herons; follow trails that climb to vistas that provide stomach-wrenching views down cliffs and north to Patos Island; discover sandstone walls carved by waves in an endless variety of shapes and textures; or find fossil seashells embedded in stratified walls.

Although it is a companion to popular Sucia Island State Park, scarcely more than 1.5 miles to the northwest, Matia sees far fewer visitors due to its limited anchorage and camping space. Only 5 acres at the west end of Matia are developed for public use; the remainder of the island is a wildlife refuge, with access permitted only as long as wildlife and seabirds remain undisturbed.

Tiny Rolfe Cove, where the state park lies, is enclosed by sandstone cliffs on the south side and by a small, steep-walled rock island on the north. A dock with float at the head of the cove and two mooring buoys provide the only other moorage. Anchorage here is chancy, as the gravel bottom is poor holding ground, and tidal currents swirling around the small island tend to swing boats about their anchor point, pulling on the hook

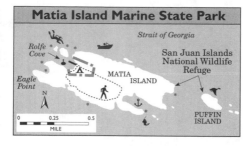

Matia Island Marine State Park

Strait of Georgia

Rolfe Cove

San Juan Islands National Wildlife Refuge

Eagle Point

MATIA ISLAND

N

PUFFIN ISLAND

0   0.25   0.5
MILE

from undesired directions. Six campsites lie in the trees above the beach, and an ingenious, high-tech marvel—a self-composting toilet—rises at the base of a nearby hill.

A loop trail leads beyond the campground into the wildlife reserve, with one leg heading down the center of the island to emerge at the head of another long cove at the southeast side. The return loop of the trail runs along the south side of the island past faint traces of what once were the cabin and gardens of a recluse, Elvin Smith. Smith lived here for nearly 30 years, during which time he gained a reputation as a mystic and mail-order faith healer. He and a friend disappeared in 1921 in heavy weather while rowing from Orcas Island.

The cove on the island's southeast side that is protected from the south by a long finger ridge would make a choice anchorage but for rocks near its entrance and a very shallow bottom. However, with caution it can still be used by keeping north of the entrance rocks and anchoring well out from the end of the cove.

To protect wildlife and nesting birds, public access to the northwest end of the island is prohibited.

CLARK ISLAND MARINE STATE PARK

Camping, picnicking, birdwatching, hiking, scuba diving, beach walking, tide pools, shellfish, fishing, boating, paddling

SEASON/HOURS: Year-round.
AREA: 55.05 acres; 11,292 feet of saltwater shoreline on the Strait of Georgia.
OVERNIGHT AND DAY-USE FACILITIES: 8 primitive campsites (*no water, no garbage collection*), 2 picnic sites with fire rings, 2 toilets, 9 mooring buoys.
BOAT ACCESS: Clark Island is 1.75 miles north of Lawrence Point, the northeast tip of Orcas Island. Nearest launch facilities are at North Beach and Obstruction Pass on Orcas Island, or on the mainland at Bellingham, Larrabee State Park, Anacortes, and Hale Passage.

Clark Island, Barnes Island, and The Sisters are a group of small islands off the northeast tip of Orcas Island. Barnes is privately owned, The Sisters are part of the San Juan Islands National Wildlife Refuge, and Clark Island is a marine state park. The north half is covered with impenetrable brush and trees, which makes the narrow, steep, rocky shoreline on this part of the slender island accessible only by small boat or kayak. However, the undersea walls interest scuba divers, who see starfish, sea urchins, anemones, and sea squirts there. All the seashores and the seabed of the San Juan archipelago are a marine sanctuary. The taking or destruction of any marine specimen, except for food, is prohibited.

The south end of the island has two broad beaches—pea gravel on the east and sand on the west—separated by a strip of brush and trees that protects eight primitive campsites. Trails that run through the campsites join the two

Rolfe Cove at Matia Island Marine State Park holds mooring buoys and a short float.

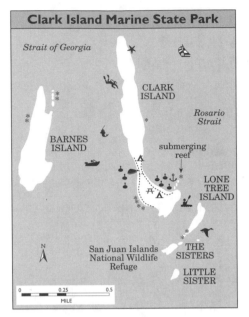

Clark Island Marine State Park

Strait of Georgia

CLARK
ISLAND

*Rosario
Strait*

BARNES
ISLAND

submerging
reef

LONE
TREE
ISLAND

N

San Juan Islands
National Wildlife
Refuge

THE
SISTERS

LITTLE
SISTER

0   0.25   0.5
MILE

beaches. Other paths lead south below the edge of the bluff above the beach, dipping into small pocket coves with tide pools that harbor a wondrous array of marine creatures.

Mooring buoys are set on both sides of the island, just off the south beaches. Those on the east side lie in a basin behind a baring rock reef; avoid the reef by approaching cautiously from the north near the shore.

STUART ISLAND MARINE STATE PARK

Camping, picnicking, sightseeing, hiking, shellfish, crabbing, fishing, boating, paddling

SEASON/HOURS: Year-round.
AREA: 88 acres; 7,600 feet of saltwater shoreline on Reid and Prevost Harbors.
OVERNIGHT AND DAY-USE FACILITIES: 19 primitive campsites (*no water October through March*), Cascadia Marine Trail campsite, 2 picnic sites, 4 toilets, marine pumpout station.
RECREATIONAL FACILITIES: Hiking trails, both in and outside the park, docks and floats (621 feet of float space in Reid Harbor, 256 feet in Prevost Harbor), 23 mooring buoys.
BOAT ACCESS: Stuart Island lies on the northeast side of Haro Strait, 5 miles northwest of San Juan Island. Nearest launch ramps are at West Beach on Orcas Island, and Roche Harbor, Mitchell Bay, or Jackson Beach on San Juan Island.

For diversity as well as beauty, few parks in the San Juan Islands can challenge Stuart Island. Reid Harbor, one of the two large bays that bracket the park land, is a miniature fjord with steep hillsides, while the second harbor, Prevost, is more shallow and open, with one side defined by a low, wooded islet. At the far end of Stuart Island, Turn Point offers stunning vistas of the rugged outlines of Canada's Gulf Islands. The beach at the end of Reid Harbor is one of the better areas in the San Juans for littleneck and butter clams. Eelgrass in Prevost Harbor hides Dungeness crabs, and a crab pot dropped over the side might result in a gourmet evening meal.

The state park laps over a high spine of timber-covered rock that separates its two anchorages. Campsites are found on this ridge and in the woods at the head of Reid Harbor. Cascadia Marine Trail campsites are on the east edge of this campground. Both campgrounds have drinking water—a rarity in San Juan marine parks.

Satellite Island encloses the northeast side of Prevost Harbor. The channel on the south is laced with rocks and reefs; boats of any draft should enter the harbor from the north, between the north end of Satellite Island and Charles Point. Mooring buoys and a dock and

A wooden staircase descends to the mooring float at Reid Harbor in Stuart Island Marine State Park.

float mark the park. There is ample room for anchorage in the harbor's uniform 6-fathom depth, but eelgrass makes it a challenge to set a hook.

The entrance channel to Reid Harbor passes to the west of tiny Cemetery and Gossip Islands, which are closed to public access to protect their rare and fragile plant communities. Once inside the harbor, steep hillsides rise abruptly on either side of the long, narrow waterway, while

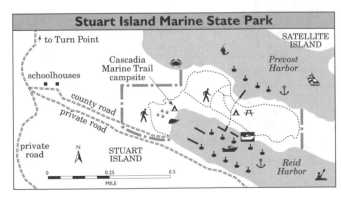

Stuart Island Marine State Park

to Turn Point

SATELLITE
ISLAND

Cascadia
Marine Trail
campsite

*Prevost
Harbor*

schoolhouses

county road

private road

private
road

N

STUART
ISLAND

*Reid
Harbor*

0   0.25   0.5
MILE

the head of the harbor has a gently sloping beach. More than a dozen park mooring buoys ring the head of the harbor; two sets of floats and a marine head pumpout station have been built around offshore pilings. On the north side of the harbor, a dock and float lead to a stairway that climbs up the ridge separating Reid and Prevost Harbors.

Trails join the camping areas; one follows the ridgeline to the northwest, where a series of staircase switchbacks descend to the Reid Harbor beach. At the west side of the beach a county road climbs past the park boundary to a schoolyard with a classic one-room, white clapboard schoolhouse. Across the yard is another school of more modern design—still one room, however.

A short way beyond the schoolyard, a dirt road leads northwest for 2.5 miles to the old Turn Point Light Station. When the lighthouse was automated, the site was turned over to the Bureau of Land Management. Be awed by expansive views of the Gulf Islands marine traffic on Haro Strait, and boiling tide rips at the base of the cliffs where the waters of the strait twist around the point.

The Turn Point Light Station on Stuart Island is now automated.

POSEY ISLAND MARINE STATE PARK

Camping, picnicking, scuba diving, beach walking, tide pools, fishing, paddling

SEASON/HOURS: Year-round.
AREA: 1 acre; 1,000 feet of saltwater shoreline on Spieden Channel.
OVERNIGHT AND DAY-USE FACILITIES: Cascadia Marine Trail campsite, overnight usage limited to 16 persons (*no water, no garbage collection*), 2 picnic sites with fire rings, toilet.
BOAT ACCESS: Posey Island is 0.25 mile north of Roche Harbor on San Juan Island. Nearest launch ramp is at Roche Harbor.

Minuscule Posey Island perches off the northwestern corner of Pearl Island, near the entrance of Spieden Channel as it flows into Roche Harbor. Surrounding waters are quite shallow, so visits must be made by dinghy, kayak, or canoe. The island is a short mile by water from the Roche Harbor Resort via the channel on the east side of Pearl Island. The spartan onshore facilities include a few picnic tables. Most of the flat island is covered with beach grass and brush and a few small picturesquely scrubby trees. Its location makes it the object of hordes of kayakers, which has led to a limit of 16 people for overnight camping.

Why come here at all? For at least two reasons: to enjoy the wildflowers that bloom here in late spring and early summer (look, but don't pick or stomp on, please), and to have a ringside view of a spectacular local phenomenon—afterglow.

When the sun sets behind the western, rainy side of Vancouver Island, the blue-black island silhouettes are painted against a blazing golden sky, which slowly fades to orange, then crimson, then a lingering pastel glow of pink.

JONES ISLAND MARINE STATE PARK

Camping, picnicking, hiking, scuba diving, beach walking, shellfish, fishing, boating, paddling

SEASON/HOURS: Year-round.
AREA: 188.09 acres; 25,000 feet of saltwater shoreline on Spieden Channel and Spring Passage.
OVERNIGHT AND DAY-USE FACILITIES: 21

Mirror-calm water and early morning light work their magic on a Jones Island anchorage.

available; however, the rocky, steeply sloping bottom makes it difficult to set an anchor securely. Two small coves on the island's south side also have mooring buoys, but waves generated by traffic in Spieden Channel often make stays here rather rough.

Onshore, campsites are among the trees near the mooring areas, and a group camp with a picnic shelter is in an old orchard above the south cove. Campsites on the south side of the island are set on headlands that have more open and scenic views than those on the north. In the winter of 1990, a devastating storm with 100-mph winds toppled many of its old-growth trees. Downed timber still presents a potential fire hazard during dry months; please be careful with fires.

A trail leading across the island connects the anchorages. A loop trail departs from the main cross-island trail near the

north cove, skirts the bluffs above the beach, then crosses a headland to reach the Cascadia Marine Trail campsite on the northwest side of the island before returning to the dock area. At the south cove, a trail skirts the southwestern shoreline and meets the trail from the north cove at the Cascadia Marine Trail site.

Raccoons, weasels, mink, eagles, a variety of seabirds, and a small herd of black-tailed deer inhabit the island. The deer have become so tame that they regularly mooch from campers—for their sake, resist their appeals. People food is unhealthy for them and leads to dependence on humans.

DOE ISLAND MARINE STATE PARK

Camping, picnicking, hiking, scuba diving, beach walking, fishing, boating, paddling

SEASON/HOURS: Year-round.
AREA: 6.1 acres; 2,049 feet of saltwater shoreline on Rosario Strait.
OVERNIGHT AND DAY-USE FACILITIES: 5 primitive campsites (*no water, no garbage collection*), toilet.
RECREATIONAL FACILITIES: 0.5-mile loop trail, dock with float (60 feet of float space, *float removed in winter*).
BOAT ACCESS: Doe Island lies just east of the southeast side of Orcas Island near Doe Bay. Nearest launch ramps are at North Beach and Obstruction Pass on Orcas Island, or on the mainland at Bellingham, Larrabee State Park, or Anacortes.

Tiny Doe Island, hidden away on the southeast side of Orcas Island immediately south of Doe Bay, is a bit out of the way for most San Juan boaters, and is not as heavily used as the other marine state parks. A small anchorage behind its north side, protected from the winds and waves of Rosario Strait, holds a short

primitive campsites, group camp (30 persons), Cascadia Marine Trail campsite, water (April to September, but often dry by mid-August), 6 toilets.
RECREATIONAL FACILITIES: 1 mile of hiking trail, dock with float (264 feet of float space, *float removed in winter*), 7 mooring buoys.
BOAT ACCESS: Jones Island is 1 mile west of the southwest tip of Orcas Island. Nearest launch ramps are at West Beach on Orcas Island, and Roche Harbor and Jackson Beach on San Juan Island.

Lying just off the southwest tip of Orcas Island at the confluence of San Juan, Spieden, and President Channels, Jones Island is a popular midway stop for boaters in the San Juan Islands. Mooring buoys and a dock with float are found in a well-protected cove on the north side of the island, but the island generally attracts more boats than these can accommodate. Anchoring space is

Jones Island Marine State Park

Cascadia Marine Trail campsite

JONES ISLAND

Spring Passage

group camp

San Juan Channel

0   500   1000
FEET

N

dock. Mooring buoys in the area are all private, so visitors should be prepared to anchor unless their boats can be beached. At minus tides Doe Island is almost connected to Orcas by a tideflat off its northwest tip. Kayakers come ashore at coves on the eastern tip and along the south side of the island.

A few primitive campsites are set in the trees above the dock. Others with views of Cypress Island and Rosario Strait are found in clearings above the south shoreline. A trail circles the edge of the island, passing the campsites and wave-carved coves along the southern shore. Noisy flocks of gulls and seabirds rest on the rocky headland at the southern tip of the island. Spring and early summer bring a profusion of wildflowers, adding splashes of color along the trail.

area (no livestock ramps), nature trail, 2 swimming beaches, swim float, 2 bathhouses with outside showers (&), dock, 2 boat ramps (*no gasoline motors*).

EDUCATIONAL FACILITIES: 3 interpretive displays, mountaintop viewing area and viewing tower.

CONCESSIONS: Food service, boat rentals, firewood.

ELC: 9 cabins and 3 duplex buildings (70–156 persons summer, 50–100 persons winter) (main camp 40–88 persons, minicamp 10–12 persons), dock, kitchen, dining hall, kitchen shelter, staff quarters, infirmary, basketball and volleyball courts, amphitheater.

CAR ACCESS: From the Orcas Island ferry landing, follow the Horseshoe Highway north to Eastsound, then continue east and south to the park in 13 miles.

Strangely, in the San Juan Islands, where the focus is saltwater, boating, and all the accouterments, one of the biggest visitor attractions is a state park that cannot be approached by boat and has no saltwater activities. True, part of the park touches the Strait of Georgia, but the frontage is a steep rocky cliff of interest only to seabirds. Obviously, the park offers plenty to compensate for its lack of saltwater, including two large trout-stocked lakes and three smaller ones; a mountain (the highest point in the San Juan Islands), from which can be seen all the archipelago, as well as a goodly part of the Gulf Islands; and several days' worth

Moran State Park

Camping, picnicking, scenic views, birdwatching, nature trails, hiking, bicycling, horseback riding, swimming, paddling, fishing, interpretive displays

SEASON/HOURS: Year-round, some facilities closed in winter; campsite reservations accepted in summer.

AREA: 5,252 acres; 1,800 feet of saltwater shoreline on the Strait of Georgia; 45,300 feet of freshwater shoreline on Cascade, Mountain, Twin, and Summit Lakes.

OVERNIGHT AND DAY-USE FACILITIES: 136 standard campsites, 15 hiker/biker sites (7 with vehicle parking) with adirondack shelter, 54 picnic sites, 5 picnic shelters, group day-use area (100 persons), children's play equipment, 4 restrooms with showers (2 &), 5 toilets, trailer dump station.

RECREATIONAL FACILITIES: 45 miles of trails (some closed to mountain bikes and horses), 2.4 miles of unimproved road, equestrian load/unload

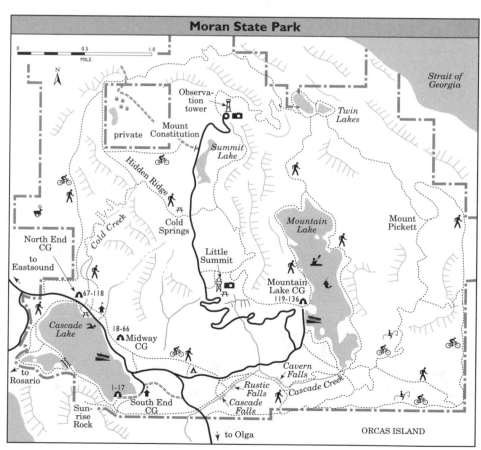

Moran State Park

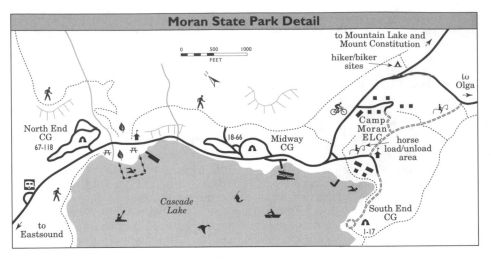

Moran State Park Detail

North End CG 67-118

Cascade Lake

to Eastsound

18-66

Midway CG

to Mountain Lake and Mount Constitution

hiker/biker sites

Olga

Camp Moran ELC

horse load/unload area

South End CG 1-17

of trails along ridge, lake edge, and forest. Forest and shore provide habitat for nearly every animal found in the San Juans. Black-tailed deer are often seen in the campgrounds or along the trails and roads. Twilight lures out nocturnal animals such as raccoons, minks, otters, and muskrats.

The park is so popular that the campsites are usually full all summer long. Three of the park's four campgrounds, North End, Midway, and South End, are at Cascade Lake. Additional sites are at Mountain Lake Landing, where there is a small campground west of the parking lot, and on a pretty little peninsula nearby. The large day-use area at Cascade Lake includes picnic areas, a swimming beach, bathhouses, a dock, and boat rentals. A short nature trail that explains the natural environment of Orcas Island wanders in the trees west of the picnic area. Nearby, a display describes the forces of nature that are at work in the forest environment. Another day-use picnic area is found at Cold Springs, and picnic tables are at Little Summit and the top of Mount Constitution. The ELC is just off the south end of Cascade Lake. The well-equipped facility, which is available for rental by large groups, has its own swimming beach and dock.

Moran's clear, cold lakes make boating and fishing a favorite pastime. Paddle boats and rowboats can be rented at Cascade Lake, and a launch ramp for trailered boats is at Midway Campground. Mountain Lake also has rowboat rentals and a launch ramp. Both of these large lakes provide excellent fishing for rainbow, eastern brook, and cutthroat trout, and kokanee salmon. Summit Lake is a marsh-rimmed, 0.5-mile-long pond, with only scramble access to launch a canoe and commune with the frogs. Twin Lakes, which are reached via trail, are not stocked, although they hold some trout.

Thousands of visitors come to the park for just a day to enjoy its scenic attractions. They usually begin at spectacular Cascade Falls, where crystalline water fans over a 70-foot-high cliff and plunges into a pool. The falls is at its best from winter through early summer, when the water flow is greatest, but it is well worth the 0.25-mile walk to see it any time of year. Rustic Falls and Cavern Falls, two smaller cataracts that lie upstream, are less impressive than Cascade Falls, but are beautiful nonetheless.

The climax of Moran State Park is Mount Constitution and the views from its summit. The road that switchbacks to the top provides several pulloffs for enjoying the ever-expanding views of the islands. The road straightens out as it breaks out onto the south end of the summit plateau. Here at Little Summit, a path from a small parking area leads to picnic tables and dramatic views south

The view tower at Moran State Park is patterned after a twelfth-century Caucasian Mountain fortress.

over Entrance Mountain to the islands of Lopez Sound. On a clear day the ragged peaks of the Olympic Range and the distant ice cone of Mount Rainier pierce the blue sky.

The fascinating stone observation tower at the summit of Mount Constitution was patterned after a twelfth-century Caucasian Mountain fortress. Plaques along the inside winding staircase tell the story of its construction. Other plaques at the top of the tower identify the jumble of islands lying below and the army of peaks stretched along the horizon.

From October through April the road is usually gated at 5:00 P.M. at its starting point, just past Cascade Lake, but during fishing season it is left open as far as Mountain Lake. In the summer it remains open to the top until 10:00 P.M. to permit watching the stunning sunsets and to accommodate straggling hikers. The drive to the top of the mountain is not recommended for trailers, buses, or large mobile homes due to the many steep grades and sharp hairpin curves. For bicyclists, the uphill pedal to the summit of Mount Constitution is a strenuous haul, with over 2,000 feet of elevation gained in 6 miles (have brakes in good shape for the descent).

Hiking, Bicycling, and Equestrian Trails

The more than 33 miles of hiking trails that interweave in the park provide countless options for long or short, level or steep hikes. Hikers with friends often start at the top of the mountain and arrange to be picked up at the bottom, avoiding the long haul back to the top. Distances can vary considerably, depending on which side trails or alternate routes are taken.

Bicycle usage of park trails varies by trail and season; some trails in the southeast portion of the park are open to equestrian use. Maps at interpretive kiosks show the restrictions for each trail. Severe winter storms periodically wreak havoc on the trails. Because funds for trail maintenance are limited, some of the less frequently used trails might not

The view from the top of Mount Constitution spreads south to Mountain Lake and distant islands.

be in the best of condition. Check with a ranger before striking out on the more remote trails.

The Cascade Lake Loop is a 2.7-mile-long, mostly level circuit of the lake along road and trail. A 0.75-mile-long side trail circles Rosario Lagoon, an arm of Cascade Lake.

A very steep, 0.5-mile-long trail begins at the South End Campground and climbs to views at the top of Sunrise Rock, overlooking Cascade Lake.

The most popular walk in the park is the one to Cascade Falls, which lies an easy 0.25 mile from the road. Continue upstream another 0.25 mile to reach two smaller falls.

A trail from Mountain Lake follows Cascade Creek past Cascade Falls all the way down to the South End Campground

at Cascade Lake. The total distance is 2.75 miles.

Another level hike is at Mountain Lake, where a 3.9-mile-long trail circles the lake.

A service road follows the long ridge of Mount Pickett above Mountain Lake. Begin the hike at Cascade Falls and end it at Twin Lakes. The distance is 4.4 miles.

For a challenge, an occasionally maintained, strenuous trail branches from the Mount Pickett trail, follows the southeast boundary, and ends up at the road that runs along the park's south boundary. Spur trails provide other possibilities; the longest trail option is about 5 miles.

From the top of the mountain, a steep 1.5-mile trail drops to Twin Lakes. From here another trail continues to the north end of Mountain Lake and joins the loop trail around the lake. The total distance from the summit to the parking lot at Mountain Lake is 3.7 miles.

A trail with loads of views starts at the top of the mountain and traverses the plateau down to Little Summit, 2.25 miles away. A branch trail continues to Mountain Lake, reaching it in a little over 1 mile.

From the Cold Springs picnic area a trail follows Hidden Ridge and then switchbacks down Cold Creek to arrive at Cascade Lake in 2 miles. A 1-mile-long side path continues along Hidden Ridge to join the West Boundary Trail.

A 4.7-mile-long trail follows the west boundary of the park. It branches from the North Side Trail and drops down to the road near the northwest park entrance.

The North Side Trail branches from the Twin Lakes trail, swings along the north edge of the park, and in 2.2 miles reaches a junction with the Hidden Ridge Trail and the West Boundary Trail.

once the home of a local hermit fisherman who built a cabin and shed here and scratched out a garden. The only remaining sign of his habitation is some concrete around a small spring (the water here is not potable).

Four mooring buoys are set off the south side of the island in Blind Bay. Because partially submerged rocks and reefs extend across the channel west of the island, the bay must be entered on its east side. Even here caution is required, as a baring rock rib protrudes into the channel from the east. The end of it has been marked with a pole by residents, but for safety's sake favor the west (Blind Island) side of the channel.

Because the island faces Harney Channel, immediately adjacent to the ferry landing at Shaw Island and directly across from the one at Orcas, ferry watching is a major attraction. After dusk the reflection in the channel of brightly lit decks makes them appear as huge leviathans.

Lime Kiln lighthouse guides boats in Haro Strait.

BLIND ISLAND MARINE STATE PARK

Camping, picnicking, birdwatching, fishing, boating, paddling

SEASON/HOURS: Year-round.
AREA: 3 acres; 1,280 feet of saltwater shoreline on Harney Channel.
OVERNIGHT AND DAY-USE FACILITIES: 4 Cascadia Marine Trail campsites (*no water, no garbage collection*), toilet, 4 mooring buoys.
BOAT ACCESS: Blind Island is immediately west of the Shaw Island ferry landing. Nearest launch ramps are at Obstruction Pass on Orcas Island, or Odlin County Park on Lopez Island.

At the entrance to Blind Bay, on the north side of Shaw Island, is a 3-acre rock with some struggling vegetation: Blind Island Marine State Park. The island was

LIME KILN POINT STATE PARK

Picnicking, hiking, whale watching

SEASON/HOURS: Year-round.
AREA: 32.56 acres; 2,550 feet of saltwater shoreline on Haro Strait.
DAY-USE FACILITIES: 10 picnic sites (*no water*), 2 toilets (♿).
RECREATIONAL FACILITIES: Trail to beach (♿), 0.25-mile trail.
EDUCATIONAL FACILITIES: Interpretive displays, interpretive programs in summer, whalewatch site, lighthouse.
CAR ACCESS: From the ferry landing at Friday Harbor, drive west on Spring Street for 1.5 blocks, north on 2nd Street for 3 blocks, west on Guard for 1 block, then north on Tucker. At a Y-intersection in the road, bear left on Roche Harbor Road. In 9 miles head south on West Valley Road,

and in 3.25 miles head west on Mitchell Bay Road. In 0.75 mile turn south on West Side Road, reaching the park in another 6.5 miles.

Since 1914 the sequence of three flashes of white light from Lime Kiln lighthouse has guided ships in Haro Strait on the west side of San Juan Island. Vessels are not the only things that utilize Haro Strait. Whales were here long before there was marine traffic, and they remain—although not in such great numbers as formerly. Whales cruise the nearby shoreline, feeding on offshore marine life and salmon headed for spawning grounds in the Fraser River.

The lighthouse still serves as a navigational beacon, although now it has been automated. Except for the lighthouse, this is now a state park dedicated to whale watching. Trails reach overlooks where benches and picnic tables furnish spots to wait while watching for telltale riffles, a dorsal fin breaking the water's surface, or the exciting sight of the giant mammals leaping into the air as they breach.

Displays here tell of the various whales that patrol the area: pods of *Orcinis orca*, the toothed "killer whale" whose fierce reputation fades with more knowledge of the species; minke whales, a baleen whale that strains sea water through comblike structures to collect the small arthropods that comprise its diet; Dall's porpoises, smaller mammals with traits and markings similar to the orca; pilot whales; and harbor porpoises. Volunteers from the Whale Museum are available during the late summer through fall season, when whales are most likely to be present, to answer questions.

A short trail leads north from the parking lot to two historic old lime kilns. Plans call for restoring at least one of these to working order and installing interpretive signs. Property east and north of the kilns belongs to the San Juan Land Bank; trails there are primitive and potentially dangerous.

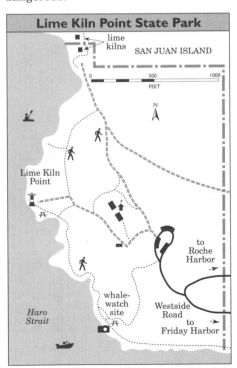

TURN ISLAND MARINE STATE PARK

Camping, picnicking, birdwatching, hiking, scuba diving, beach walking, tide pools, shellfish, crabbing, fishing, boating, paddling

SEASON/HOURS: Year-round.
AREA: 35.15 acres; 16,000 feet of saltwater shoreline on San Juan Channel.
OVERNIGHT AND DAY-USE FACILITIES: 13 primitive campsites (*no water, no garbage collection*), picnic site, 2 toilets.
RECREATIONAL FACILITIES: 3 miles of hiking trail, 3 mooring buoys.
BOAT ACCESS: Turn Island is off the northeast tip of San Juan Island, 1.75 miles from Friday Harbor. Nearest launch ramps are at Jackson Beach on San Juan Island and Odlin County Park on Lopez Island.

Only a narrow waterway separates Turn Island from its large brother, San Juan Island. Although the channel looks as if it could almost be waded at low tide, with sufficient care, boats can pass safely even at low water. Turn Island is within range of Friday Harbor for easy day trips by kayak or canoe.

At the west end of the island, picnic and camping sites sit in timber above a gravel beach. Wakes from boat traffic in San Juan Channel slosh the three offshore mooring buoys, so boaters riding the buoys overnight are guaranteed to be rocked to sleep. At minus tide, a small spit that reaches toward San Juan Island becomes a tideflat with rocky tide pools harboring multihued marine life. All the seashores and the seabed of the San Juan archipelago are a marine sanctuary, and the taking or destruction of any marine specimen, except for food, is prohibited.

All but the south end of Turn Island, where the park facilities are found, is a wildlife refuge. Public access is permitted to the refuge, provided wildlife and

birds remain undisturbed. A trail follows the high bluff around the perimeter of the island, with a shortcut crossing the center. Spur paths lead to some secluded sandy coves below the steep headland

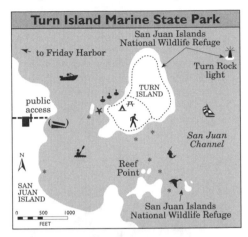

A picturesque red-barked madrona overhangs the beach at Turn Island Marine State Park.

on the southeast side, but most of the east and north sides of the island are high rocky cliffs with no accessible beach below.

A bald eagle nest once filled the top of one of Turn Island's stately trees, but a storm downed the tree. The nest has been reestablished, and eagles are frequently seen here. Turn Rock, off the northeast tip of the island, which is capped by a navigation light, is usually crowded with pelagic cormorants and hundreds of noisy gulls.

SPENCER SPIT STATE PARK

Camping, picnicking, birdwatching, hiking, beach walking, shellfish, crabbing, fishing, boating, paddling

SEASON/HOURS: Closed November 1 through February 28.

AREA: 129.6 acres; 7,840 feet of saltwater shoreline on Lopez Sound.

OVERNIGHT AND DAY-USE FACILITIES: 30 standard campsites (♿), 7 primitive campsites, group camp with 2 adirondack shelters (9 persons), group camp (30 persons), Cascadia Marine Trail campsite, 26 picnic sites (6 ♿), 2 picnic shelters, group day-use area with picnic shelter (50 persons), 2 restrooms (♿), toilet, outdoor shower, trailer dump station.

RECREATIONAL FACILITIES: 4 miles of hiking trails, 16 mooring buoys.

CAR ACCESS: From the Lopez ferry landing, drive 1.2 miles to the first road junction and turn east on Port Stanley Road. In 3.8 miles turn east on Baker View Road and reach the park in 1 mile.

BOAT ACCESS: Spencer Spit lies on the east side of Lopez Island at the north end of Lopez Sound. Nearest mainland launch ramps are at Bellingham, Larrabee State Park, Anacortes, and Deception Pass State Park.

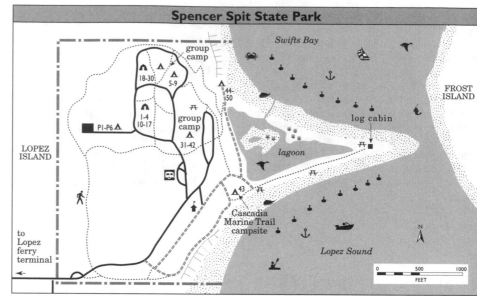

As one of the few state parks in the San Juan Islands accessible by land (with the help of a ferry), and as the only state park on Lopez Island, Spencer Spit is immensely popular with visitors. Campsites are often filled every night in July and August. A sign at the Anacortes ferry terminal usually warns when parks are filled and visitors should make alternate plans. Spencer Spit is equally popular with visitors who arrive by water and claim one of the array of mooring buoys

The ubiquitous San Juan bunnies seen at Spencer Spit State Park are a crossbreed of wild rabbits and domestic ones that were turned loose many years ago.

strung along both sides of the spit, or one of the good anchorages in muddy bottom found nearby.

Most campsites are along a pair of loops in the wooded upland of the park. Bicycle campsites, walk-in sites, a Cascadia Marine Trail site, two group camps, and a group picnic area are spread around the park, some in forest, others with shoreside ambiance. Water is always scarce in the park, and in summer when the fire danger is high, open fires might be banned.

Paths lead through the woods between the campground and the park entrance and along the rim of the bluff at the south side of the park. Other wooded trails join the upland areas to the spit. Here a pair of long sandspits have joined over time to enclose a brackish saltchuck lagoon. The shallow lagoon is brightly painted with multihued algae and saltwater plants that flourish in this unique environment. Tiny sandpipers wade in the mud along its edge in search of tidbits, and in fall migratory waterfowl stop to rest. This unique ecosystem is very fragile; please stay out of the marsh and enjoy it from a distance.

A rock-framed log picnic shelter at the inland end of the spit is a remnant of a home built here by the Spencer family in the late 1800s. The original cabin collapsed but was rebuilt. Another Spencer legacy is a one-room log cabin at the tip of the spit, which they built as a guest house.

When a minus tide exposes the wide, gently sloping beaches on either side of the spit, dimples in the sand that spurt water mark sites to dig for clams. Rabbits that burrow in the hillside frequent the picnic areas; campsites might be visited by black-tailed deer or nosy raccoons.

To the north of Spencer Spit are the barren knob of little Flower Island and a chain of rocks that ends in Leo Reef, which is marked by a navigation light. These are part of the San Juan Islands National Wildlife Refuge; clusters of seabirds rest here, and seals and sea lions are frequently seen hauled out on the rocks. In the channel just beyond, glowing lights reflect in the water after dusk as ferries pass by en route to island stops.

Classic hull lines and baggy wrinkles (the padding wrapped around the stays) make this boat anchored at James Island Marine State Park a scenic delight.

JAMES ISLAND MARINE STATE PARK

Camping, picnicking, hiking, scuba diving, fishing, boating

SEASON/HOURS: Year-round.
AREA: 113.65 acres; 12,335 feet of saltwater shoreline on Rosario Strait.
OVERNIGHT AND DAY-USE FACILITIES: 13 primitive campsites, Cascadia Marine Trail campsite (*no water, no garbage collection*), picnic shelter, 4 toilets.
RECREATIONAL FACILITIES: 1.5 miles of hiking trails, dock with float (134 feet of float space), 5 mooring buoys.

BOAT ACCESS: James Island is 0.25 mile east of Decatur Island, just south of Thatcher Pass. Nearest mainland launch ramps are at Anacortes, Bellingham, Larrabee State Park, and Deception Pass.

The cliffy headlands of this dogbone-shaped island are squeezed at the center by small coves on its east and west sides. The two tiny coves on the east have a pair of mooring buoys each, but the small island gives the moorages little protection from wind and waves from Rosario Strait, so mooring here can become exciting in foul weather.

The cove on the west side of the island, which is just across the channel from Decatur Head, has a dock with a float at

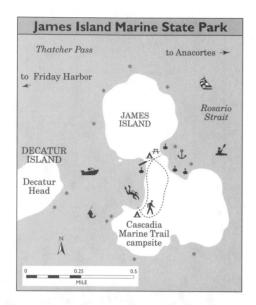

James Island Marine State Park

Thatcher Pass

to Anacortes →

to Friday Harbor ←

JAMES ISLAND

Rosario Strait

DECATUR ISLAND

Decatur Head

Cascadia Marine Trail campsite

N

0   0.25   0.5
MILE

the head of a rock-rimmed gravel beach and a single mooring buoy. Swirling tidal currents and a steeply sloping bottom often frustrate boaters' attempts to drop a secure anchor here.

Most campsites are scattered among fir trees on the saddle of land between the two coves; a few are found just above the east cove beach, and three Cascadia Marine Trail campsites sit above a staircase on the south side of the west cove. At night stow your food with you in your tent or on board your boat: resident raccoons will remind you (in the dead of night!) if you don't.

A short marked trail leads through the thick woods of the south lobe of the island to a tiny beach. Rock faces along the island's outer edges drop abruptly to the water.

STATE PARK PROPERTIES IN THE SAN JUAN ISLANDS

Scuba diving, fishing, boating, paddling, birdwatching

SEASON/HOURS: Year-round.
AREA: 9.65 acres total; 20,922 total feet of saltwater shoreline in the San Juan Islands.
FACILITIES: Olga: Dock and float maintained by the Olga Community Club, water available at the head of the dock; on the east side of East Sound at the community of Olga.
BOAT ACCESS: See following.

Several tiny islands, some scarcely larger than rocks, as well as a few sections of tidelands in the San Juans, are state park property. Although they are undeveloped (and will remain so), they are open to the public. All are accessible from the water, with varying degrees of difficulty. If you visit, do not disturb nesting birds or the natural habitat. Fires and overnight camping are prohibited; take all garbage with you when you leave.

Eighty-four rocks and small islands are set aside as the San Juan Islands National Wildlife Refuge, providing sanctuary for pelagic birds and animals. Going ashore on any of these refuge islands is prohibited. If unsure whether you are approaching a refuge island or one of the state parks lands, err on the side of caution and stay away.

FREEMAN ISLAND. 0.95 acre; 720 feet of saltwater shoreline; in President Channel, 0.3 mile off the northwest shore of Orcas Island between Point Doughty and West Beach.

LOPEZ ISLAND TIDELANDS. 4,332 feet of saltwater tidelands; includes all of the tidelands in front of Odlin County Park on the north end of Lopez Island.

Kayaks are an ideal means of reaching the many small, remote state park rocks and islands in the San Juans.

MUD BAY TIDELANDS. 11,360 feet of saltwater tidelands; includes all of the southwest end of Mud Bay, at the south end of Lopez Sound, and the southeast shore of the bay up to Shoal Bight, with the exception of about 1,000 feet of private tidelands near the end of a road spur on the southeast side of the bay.

NORTHWEST McCONNELL ROCK. 2.5 acres; 2,000 feet of saltwater shoreline; just off the northwest tip of McConnell Island in Wasp Channel, and connected to the island by a sandspit at low tide.

OLGA. 0.2 acre; 60 feet of saltwater shoreline on Orcas Island.

SKULL ISLAND. 1 acre; 750 feet of saltwater shoreline; on the south side of Orcas Island in West Sound, at the north end of Massacre Bay.

VICTIM ISLAND. 5 acres; 1,700 feet of saltwater shoreline; on the south side of Orcas Island along the west side of West Sound, 0.3 mile north of Double Island.

Two of the three tiny Cone Islands are state park property; the islands are favorite scuba diving sites.

CONE ISLANDS

Scuba diving, paddling

AREA: 9.85 acres; 2,500 feet of saltwater shoreline on Bellingham Channel.
FACILITIES: None.
BOAT ACCESS: The Cone Islands are between the east shore of Cypress Island and the north tip of Guemes Island. Nearest launch ramps are at Anacortes and Larrabee State Park.

The Cone Islands are a grouping of three tiny, picturesque islands near Cypress Island. The two southernmost islands are state park property. Steep, rocky slabs drop from their tree-tufted tops into the water without pausing to form a beach, making landing on the islands difficult.

The underwater walls and nearby kelp beds are popular scuba diving spots. Eagles frequent the taller trees.

HUCKLEBERRY ISLAND

Scuba diving, paddling

AREA: 10 acres; 2,900 feet of saltwater shoreline on Padilla Bay.
FACILITIES: None.
BOAT ACCESS: Huckleberry Island lies at the north end of Padilla Bay, 0.3 mile east of Long Bay on the southeast end of Guemes Island. Nearest launch ramps are at Anacortes, Larrabee State Park, Bay View, and the north end of the Swinomish Channel.

The north, east, and south sides of Huckleberry Island are sheer rock faces that dive sharply into the water, then continue underwater to depths of 60 feet or more. On the southwest side of the island, a white clay bluff drops to a reasonably wide gravel beach. This beach, which is a nice spot for a visit by kayak or a beachable boat, remains exposed except at extreme high tides. Although the water offshore from the beach is shallow enough for anchoring, it is unprotected from wind and waves, and several offshore rocks are potential hazards.

SADDLEBAG ISLAND MARINE STATE PARK

Camping, picnicking, hiking, scuba diving, shellfish, crabbing, fishing, boating, paddling

SEASON/HOURS: Year-round.
AREA: 23.20 acres; 6,250 feet of saltwater shoreline on Padilla Bay.

OVERNIGHT AND DAY-USE FACILITIES: 5 primitive campsites, Cascadia Marine Trail campsite (*no water*), toilet.

RECREATIONAL FACILITIES: 1 mile of hiking trail.

BOAT ACCESS: Saddlebag Island is in the north end of Padilla Bay, 2 miles northeast of Anacortes. Nearest launch ramps are at Anacortes, Larrabee State Park, Bay View, and the north end of the Swinomish Channel.

Saddlebag Island earns its name from its shape—a pair of rocky brush- and timber-covered headlands, linked by a narrow flat between coves that pinch the center of the island. Since the city of Anacortes is only a little over 2 miles to the southwest, many visitors stop by for a day of fishing or to drop a crab pot in the hope of landing some of the island's renowned supply of Dungeness.

Dungeness crab can be caught right from your anchorage in either of the coves at Saddlebag Island State Park.

Huckleberry and Saddlebag Island Marine State Parks

0   0.25   0.5
MILE

Padilla Bay

HUCKLEBERRY ISLAND

N

SADDLEBAG ISLAND

Cascadia Marine Trail campsite

DOT ISLAND

GUEMES ISLAND

San Juan Islands National Wildlife Refuge

Guemes Channel

The island sits at the north end of the shallow estuary of Padilla Bay, and at a minus tide a large portion of the bay for a mile to the east dries to a seaweed-covered mudflat. The shallow underwater shelf on which Saddlebag Island sits drops away steeply to the west. Approach by boat should be made from the west to avoid possible grounding.

Park facilities are a few primitive campsites secluded in trees above the two coves. There are no mooring buoys, so boaters must either anchor in the island's two small coves or have a beachable boat. Holding ground for anchoring is solid in either cove; however, the larger one on the north has a softer bottom, and is generally favored. Neither cove offers much protection in heavy weather, but with a safe haven nearby in Anacortes, few boaters would elect to ride out foul weather here.

A quick circuit of the island on trails that have been cut or beaten along the top of the bluff of the two headlands offers views of its neighbors, Dot and Hat Islands immediately to the south, and across the channel to the west to Huckleberry and Guemes Islands. Nearby Dot Island, which is a bird-nesting area of the San Juan Islands Wilderness, usually teems with seabirds; boaters might also spot otters or harbor seals.

CHAPTER FOUR

NORTH PUGET SOUND

PEACE ARCH STATE PARK

Picnicking, horticultural displays, interpretive signs, historic arch

SEASON/HOURS: Year-round.
AREA: 19.95 acres.
DAY-USE FACILITIES: 100 picnic sites, reservable kitchen shelter, group day-use area (300 persons), 2 restrooms (&).
RECREATIONAL FACILITIES: 0.8-mile interpretive trail (&).
EDUCATIONAL FACILITIES: Historic arch.
CAR ACCESS: Take Exit 276 (SR 548S, Blaine City Center, Peace Arch Park) from I-5 just before reaching the U.S.-Canada border. The off-ramp comes to the junction of 2nd Street and D Street. Follow signs on 2nd Street, which ends at the park entrance immediately north of B Street.

The two mottoes, "Children of a Common Mother" and "Brethren Dwelling Together in Unity," emblazoned on either side of the magnificent white concrete arch that straddles the U.S.-Canada border at Blaine, set the theme for Peace Arch State Park. The park and Canada's Provincial Park, its companion on the north side of the border, were completed in 1931 to commemorate 100 years of

A trail switchbacks down to the beach at Fort Ebey State Park on Whidbey Island.

open, undefended boundary between the two countries, and to acknowledge their shared origins. The parks flow together in wide lawns on the median and on both sides of the highway lanes between the two customs stations. A series of displays tells the history of the park and the significance of its construction. The columns of the 67-foot-high arch contain metal caskets that hold pieces of the Canadian steam vessel *Beaver,* brought to the Northwest by the British in 1837, and the Pilgrim ship *Mayflower.*

The park has become a meeting place for groups devoted to international peace and brotherhood; thousands of people gather here every year on the second Sunday in June for a celebration sponsored by the International Peace Arch Association. The gardens themselves are enough reason for many visitors to pause at the park. Rhododendrons, azaleas, and heather blaze forth in shades of red, pink, and purple in spring; by summer, masses of annuals march in bright array along the borders of green lawns.

BIRCH BAY STATE PARK

Camping, picnicking, birdwatching, volleyball, kite flying, hiking, crabbing, shellfish, waterskiing, windsurfing, beachcombing, scuba diving, fishing, boating, paddling, guided interpretive walks

SEASON/HOURS: Year-round, some campsites closed in winter; campsite reservations accepted in summer.
AREA: 193.30 acres; 8,285 feet of saltwater shoreline on Birch Bay; 14,933 feet of freshwater shoreline on Terrell Creek.
OVERNIGHT AND DAY-USE FACILITIES: 20 RV sites (&), 147 standard campsites (&), 1 primitive campsite, primitive group camp with picnic shelter (40 persons), 235 picnic sites (&), 3 picnic shelters, 50 barbecues, 14 fire rings, 7 restrooms (5 with showers) (&), toilet, 2 trailer dump stations.

RECREATIONAL FACILITIES: 2.2 miles of hiking trail, 0.5-mile nature trail with interpretive stations, half basketball court, bathhouse, 1-lane unpaved boat launch.
CAR ACCESS: From I-5, take Exit 270 (Lynden, Birch Bay) 5 miles south of Blaine and head west on Birch Bay–Lynden Road.

For the campground entrance, in 3 miles turn south on Blaine Road (Highway 548); in another 2 miles turn west on Bay Road, at a T-intersection in 1 mile head south on Jackson Road, and in 0.3 mile head west on Helweg Road to reach the park.

For the day-use entrance, at the intersection of Bay Road and Jackson Road head north to reach the town of Birch Bay in 0.4 mile, then turn southwest on Birch Bay Drive to reach the park in 1 mile. The park can also be reached from Exit 266, 8 miles south of Blaine.

Because of its nearness to the international border, the resort community of Birch Bay draws many visitors from British Columbia, and the state park on the south side of the town is as popular with Canadians as it is with state residents.

The campground loops are on a forested flat above the beach. Short trails leading from the campground to the beach cross Terrell Creek on footbridges. A primitive boat ramp is found at the south park boundary; however, it is not paved, so use by trailered boats requires a towing vehicle that can handle the soft cobble-and-gravel beach. Because the bay is quite shallow, trailered boats can only be launched at high tides.

With more than 2 miles of superlative sandy beach, most activities are focused on the saltwater. Beachside picnicking, wading, waterskiing, windsurfing, volleyball, and kite flying are popular at any level of tide, but when minus tides expose large sections of the gently sloping beach, intertidal creatures are on display for a brief time before the water returns. Telltale dimples in the sand mark spots to dig

At Birch Bay State Park, driftwood logs, fantastic tree roots, and sandy beach are inviting places for kids to play.

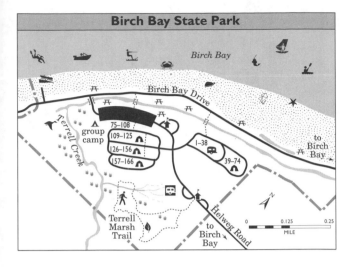

Birch Bay State Park

Birch Bay

Birch Bay Drive

Terrell Creek

group camp

75–108
109–125
126–156
157–166

1–38

39–74

to Birch Bay

Terrell Marsh Trail

Helweg Road

to Birch Bay

0   0.125   0.25
MILE

for clams, and seaweed can be probed for red rock crab. Please treat all organisms kindly, even those destined for the dinner pot.

The beach is not the sole attraction, however. Along the park's south edge, Terrell Creek trickles through a saltwater marsh before turning to flow northeast

Bright yellow skunk cabbage is a harbinger of spring at Birch Bay State Park.

above the beachfront for the length of the park. A 0.5-mile self-guided interpretive trail loops through the woodland northeast of the creek, reaching the edge of the marsh midroute. A brochure identifies trailside flora. Near the marsh edge, skunk cabbage blooms bright yellow in early spring. The marshland and beach grass are habitat for beavers, muskrats, opossums, and great blue heron. More than a hundred other species of birds live in or migrate through the area. Harlequin ducks, oldsquaws, and loons might be seen on the bay in winter.

LARRABEE STATE PARK

Camping, picnicking, hiking, bicycling, clamming, crabbing, beachcombing, waterskiing, scuba diving, fishing, boating, paddling

SEASON/HOURS: Year-round, some facilities closed in winter; campsite reservations accepted in summer.
AREA: 2,787.75 acres; 8,100 feet of saltwater shoreline on Samish Bay; 6,700 feet of freshwater shoreline on Fragrance and Lost Lakes and other small unnamed lakes.
OVERNIGHT AND DAY-USE FACILITIES: 26 RV sites (♿), 51 standard campsites (♿), 8 standard walk-in sites, 3 primitive campsites, group camp (40 persons), 67 picnic sites, 2 picnic shelters, group day-use areas with kitchen shelters (50 and 100 persons), amphitheater, 4 restrooms (3 with showers) (3 ♿), 3 toilets, trailer dump station.
RECREATIONAL FACILITIES: 6.5 miles of

road, 17.2 miles of hiking/biking trail, interurban bicycle trail to Bellingham, 2-lane paved boat ramp.
CAR ACCESS: From I-5 in Bellingham, take Exit 205 to SR 11 (Chuckanut Drive) and continue south for 7 miles to the park. Alternatively, from I-5 Exit 231, 4 miles north of Mount Vernon, take SR 11 northwest and reach the park in 17 miles. The launch ramp is off Cove Road, 0.7 mile north of the park entrance.

Larrabee State Park holds many distinctions, its unique one being that it was Washington's first official state park. The initial 20 acres of land was given to the state in 1915 by the Larrabee and Gates families; in 1923 it was dedicated as a park. The popular beach and camping areas that lie on the west side of Chuckanut Drive comprise only a very small portion of the park, which reaches 3 miles inland to include several small lakes and the 1,941-foot lower summit of Chuckanut Mountain's long massif.

Most of the park's campsites are packed along a pair of loops at the park's north end, between Chuckanut Drive and the shore. Railroad tracks that run along the bluff above the beach add to the constriction of the area. At the center of both camping loops, hookup sites are stacked side by side in cozy familiarity, and standard campsites rim the outside of the loops. A group camp and a string of walk-in sites lie west of the main campground loops. The picnic areas, south of the campgrounds between the highway and the railroad track, hold kitchen shelters and an amphitheater/stage.

Short trails from the picnic area lead through a concrete underpass beneath the railroad tracks to a T-intersection on the bluff above the beach. Here, the path to the north descends to a broad cobble beach. A rock finger separates this bay from Wildcat Cove to the north. Low tide uncovers wave-worn hollows in the rock inhabited by limpets, mussels, barnacles, tubeworms, and other intertidal creatures.

At the middle of Wildcat Cove, a steep

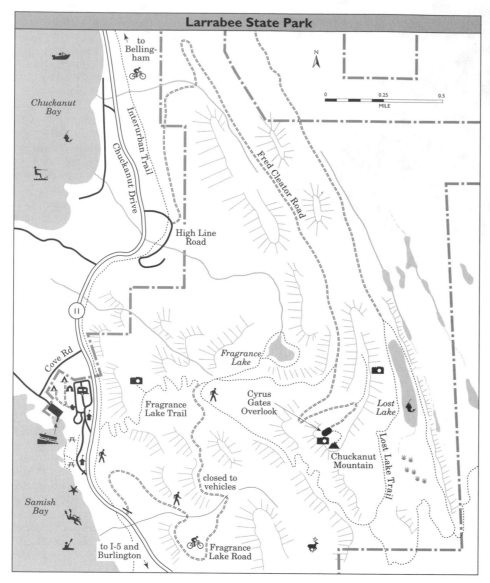

Larrabee State Park

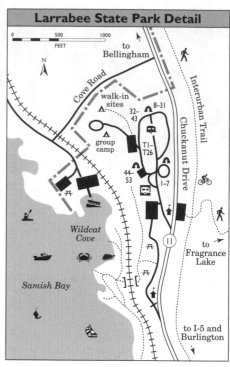

Larrabee State Park Detail

Fragrance and Lost Lake, two nice-sized lakes, offer good trout fishing and provide scenic destinations. These lakes, as well as several smaller potholes that snuggle in pockets below the bands of cliffs that form Chuckanut Mountain, can be reached by hiking from the campground.

A fine viewpoint, reached by gravel road, is gained by driving a mile north of the park boundary and turning east on High Line Road, which shortly becomes Fred Cleator Road, and winds up Chuckanut Mountain. At 2.5 miles a trail to the right heads to Fragrance Lake. The road reaches Cyrus Gates Overlook at 3.5 miles, 100 feet below the nearby summit ridge. Here are expansive views north to Bellingham and west over Lummi Island to the northern San Juan Islands. A short spur trail from the last switchback to a lower viewpoint below Cyrus Gates Overlook provides glimpses down the steep timbered east face of the mountain into Lost Lake, beyond to Lookout Mountain,

concrete boat ramp leads down to water's edge. This ramp area cannot be reached by road from the main portion of the park; access is from Cove Road, north of the park entrance.

The trail south of the T-intersection leads to rock fingers dropping to tiny coves that offer secluded outlooks for sunsets over the San Juan Islands. A second beach area, Clayton Beach, can be reached via

a trail from a gated service road 0.5 mile south of the main park entrance. Just above the highway a wide, flat trail runs through the park and north to the Fairhaven District of Bellingham. This is the old roadbed of the Mount Vernon to Bellingham Interurban Railway, now converted into a hiking/bicycling/equestrian trail. Total trail distance to Bellingham is 5.5 miles.

Rocky coves and gnarled, weather-torn trees at Larrabee State Park create a scene of rugged beauty.

boundary; some are abandoned, others are gated logging roads. They are scheduled for future integration into an 80-mile trail system.

The trail to 12-acre Lost Lake is a strenuous 2.5-mile-long route that begins near the end of the Fragrance Lake service road. It climbs in a series of switchbacks through old-growth forest to a 1,600-foot-high saddle before crossing to steep, timbered cliffs on the east side of the ridge. From here a long traverse across the face above the lake leads to the north end of the lake.

From this point a more faint trail follows the top of the rib along the east side of the lake, and south of the lake joins a logging road spur that heads uphill toward the southwest. A trail continues from the upper end of this road over the top of a wooded knob and then drops back down to meet the main trail at the saddle southwest of Lost Lake.

Another spur trail 0.25 mile north of the saddle leads downhill through bogs at the south end of the lake.

BAY VIEW STATE PARK

Camping, picnicking, birdwatching, swimming, fishing, paddling

SEASON/HOURS: Year-round, some campsites closed in winter; campsite reservations accepted in summer.

AREA: 25.17 acres; 1,320 feet of saltwater shoreline on Padilla Bay.

OVERNIGHT AND DAY-USE FACILITIES: 30 RV sites (WP) (&), 46 standard campsites (&), 3 primitive campsites, tent-only group camp (64 persons), 59 picnic sites, group day-use area with kitchen shelter (175 persons), restroom with shower, 5 toilets.

CAR ACCESS: From I-5 take Exit 231 (SR 11N, Chuckanut Drive, Bow–Edison), 5 miles north of Mount Vernon, and head west on Josh Wilson Road. In 6.5 miles, at the town of

and to Mount Baker in the distance. The unmarked trail continues north along the crest of Chuckanut Mountain to rejoin the road in another 1.5 miles.

Hiking the Park

But why drive a gravel road when you can walk and enjoy the beauty of the wildwood? The Fragrance Lake Trail (hikers only) begins across the road from the park entrance and switchbacks steeply uphill, gaining some 800 feet of elevation in 1.5 miles. Don't miss the viewpoint at 0.9 mile, with dizzying views down a cliff to Samish and Chuckanut Bays and out to a tapestry of islands and mountains.

As the path nears the lake, it is joined by a short side spur from the end of the Fragrance Lake service road/trail, then descends gently for 0.25 mile through cedar and hemlock forest to the edge of the 6.5-acre lake.

The gated, gravel, Fragrance Lake service road/trail, which starts 0.5 mile south of the park entrance, provides an alternate route up Chuckanut Mountain for hikers and mountain bikers. After intersecting the Lost Lake trailhead in 2.1 miles, the trail ends at a cul de sac at 2.2 miles, the junction with the trail from the Cyrus Gates Overlook. Primitive trails lace the backcountry beyond the park

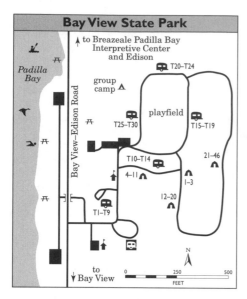

Bay View State Park

Padilla Bay

to Breazeale Padilla Bay Interpretive Center and Edison

group camp

playfield

T20–T24
T25–T30
T15–T19
T10–T14
21–46
4–11
1–3
12–20
T1–T9

Bay View–Edison Road

to Bay View

N

0   250   500
FEET

Bay View, turn north on Bay View–Edison Road. Follow this north 0.3 mile to the park entrance.

Bay View State Park is split into two sections by Bay View–Edison Road. The lower western section, reached by a tunnel under the highway, is a grassy day-use and picnic area fronting on Padilla Bay. The upper eastern area contains the park's campground, a meadowy playfield, and a wooded group camp.

The beach is the heart of activity in the park, with ample opportunity for picnicking, sunbathing, kite flying, and wading, or just exploring the mud of Padilla Bay at low tide. A reservable picnic shelter with three sides shielded from the wind, several picnic tables, and a volleyball area make up the beach amenities. Kayaks or small boats that can be carried the few feet from the parking lot to the water can be put in here for leisurely paddling on the bay. Most of the estuary is a mere 6 feet deep at high tide, so use care to avoid being stranded by an outgoing tide.

Over 11,000 acres of the marsh and tidelands of Padilla Bay are designated as a National Estuarine Sanctuary to protect its important ecological system. Breazeale Padilla Bay Interpretive Center, 0.5 mile north of the state park, has displays that describe the vegetation and wealth of creatures that live in the bay and along its shores. The protected estuary is an important migratory stop for waterfowl such as black brant and snow geese. Visitors often see hawks, eagles, owls, and herons along the shore.

Black brant geese, which winter in Padilla Bay because of the eelgrass found there, are often seen at Bay View State Park.

RASAR STATE PARK

Camping, picnicking, birdwatching, nature study, hiking, fishing, historical displays

SEASON/HOURS: Year-round.
AREA: 168.9 acres; 4,000 feet of freshwater shoreline on the Skagit River.
OVERNIGHT AND DAY-USE FACILITIES: 23 RV sites (2 &), 14 standard campsites, 3 hiker/biker sites, 13 primitive campsites (&) with 2 adirondack shelters, group camp, 28 picnic sites with barbecues, reservable kitchen shelter, 2 restrooms (&), trailer dump station.
RECREATIONAL FACILITIES: 4 miles of hiking trail (&), children's play equipment.
EDUCATIONAL FACILITIES: Interpretive displays.
CAR ACCESS: From SR 20 eastbound, 14.9 miles east of Sedro Wooley, turn south on Lusk Road. In 0.7 mile, turn east on Cape Horn Road and reach the park in another 0.8 mile. From SR 20 westbound, 5.6 miles west of Concrete, turn south on Russell Road. In 0.8 mile turn west on Cape Horn Road to reach the park in 1.4 miles.

This fine new addition to the state's array of parks occupies an old farm site along the meandering Skagit River. Two wooded campsite loops sit on a terrace near the road. New park buildings in the day-use area have fieldstone walls reminiscent of the 1930s' CCC construction style. From the day-use area, a paved, barrier-free trail wends down the bank to a hayfield, where a display describes how the Skagit Valley was settled by loggers first, and then farmers. Portions of the park are still maintained as a working farm, in order to preserve the legacy of farming in the Skagit Valley. As you walk, the sweet scent of hay mixes with the tangy aroma of conifers.

A barrier-free trail at Rasar State Park leads to interpretive displays.

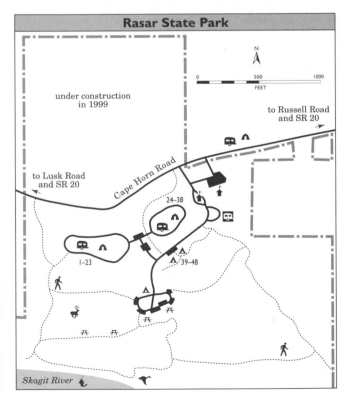

Rasar State Park

under construction in 1999

to Lusk Road and SR 20

to Russell Road and SR 20

Cape Horn Road

24–38

1–23

39–48

Skagit River

N

0   500   1000
FEET

gles feed on winter salmon runs in the Skagit River, making the park a prime spot for eagle watching.

ROCKPORT STATE PARK

Camping, picnicking, birdwatching, hiking

SEASON/HOURS: Closed November 1 through April 1.
AREA: 669.16 acres.
OVERNIGHT AND DAY-USE FACILITIES: 50 RV sites, 8 standard campsites, group camp (65 persons), 3 primitive campsites, 4 adirondack shelters, 33 picnic sites, kitchen shelter, 2 restrooms with showers, trailer dump station.
RECREATIONAL FACILITIES: 5 miles of hiking trail.
CAR ACCESS: From Exit 230 from I-5, 3 miles north of Mount Vernon, head east on SR 20 to reach the park in 35.5 miles.

The path weaves through a fern- and moss-encrusted forest of large cottonwood, Douglas-fir, cedar, and alder. Look for a magnificent old maple with nearly a dozen separate trunks. Its hollowed base holds a cave large enough for children to climb inside and imagine themselves as Peter Pan and his friends. At the riverbank the paved path ends and dirt trails head in both directions along the riverbank, eventually looping back through fields and forest to the parking lot.

You might see elk in the park, or at least their droppings and tree bark they have munched. Thousands of bald ea-

Here's one of the grandest chunks of forest primeval to be found in any of Washington's state parks. The preserve, which miraculously was spared the logger's blade, serves as a fitting monument to Scotsman David Douglas, who visited the Pacific Northwest in 1825 on a mission to collect botanical samples for the British Royal Horticultural Society. The gigantic Douglas-fir was one of his many discoveries. A plaque near the park entrance describes his achievements.

Impressive, 250-foot-tall specimens of the trees that bear Douglas's name fill the state park, and sunlight barely penetrates the thick forest canopy. Moss-draped cedar and slender stems of maple and alder that arch over trails add to the cathedral-like solemnity. Elderberry and salmonberry ripen on trailside bushes, and even the friendless devil's club bears fiery batons of red berries. Virtually every kind of Northwest fern carpets the

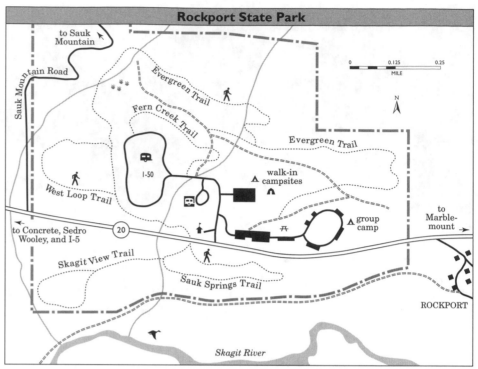

Rockport State Park

A downed Douglas-fir log is a super-highway for a small park visitor at Rockport State Park.

forest floor—count how many different ones you see. In July unique Indian pipe blossoms can be found in the moist, rich humus near the base of old firs. The bizarre, waxy white saprophyte (which has no chlorophyll) is rare, so treat it with care. The park surely is woodpecker nirvana; watch for pileated woodpeckers attacking enormous tree trunks.

The day-use picnic area is on the right, just inside the park entrance; a group camp lies on a grassy loop east of here. Walk-in sites with adirondack shelters are just a stroll away in the woods north of the picnic area. Campsites with utility hookups are on a loop road on the west side of the park, surrounded by dense undergrowth.

Trails range around the outer edges of the park and link together, forming a pleasant forest maze. On the south side of SR 20 between the road and the bank above the Skagit River drainage are two trail loops, Sauk Springs Trail and Skagit View Trail, both gentle and easily followed. River views are obscured by the thick forest.

The park lies at the edge of the Skagit River Bald Eagle Sanctuary, and in winter more than 100 eagles at a time might be seen. The huge raptors congregate along the river to feed on carcasses of spawned-out salmon.

BURROWS ISLAND

Beach walking, boating, paddling

AREA: 343.62 acres; 9,440 feet of saltwater shoreline on Rosario Strait.
FACILITIES: None.
BOAT ACCESS: Burrows Island is on the northwest side of Burrows Bay. Nearest launch ramp is at a marina on Flounder Bay or Bowman Bay in Deception Pass State Park.

State park property on Burrows Island adjoins the Coast Guard lighthouse property at the west tip of Burrows Island, and most of the park shoreline lies below steep cliffs along the northwest entrance to Allen Pass. In calm weather kayaks and other small boats can be beached in a cove on the north side of the lighthouse. A stairway leads up the bluff. Overnight camping is permitted; however, there is no water.

DECEPTION PASS STATE PARK

Camping, picnicking, sightseeing, birdwatching, interpretive trails, hiking, bicycling, swimming, fishing, scuba diving, beach walking, boating, paddling, interpretive center

SEASON/HOURS: Year-round, some facilities closed in winter; campsite reservations accepted in summer.

CCC INTERPRETIVE CENTER: May through September, 10:00 A.M. to 6:00 P.M., Wednesday through Sunday and holidays.

AREA: 3,158.29 acres; 77,000 feet of saltwater shoreline on Rosario Strait, Deception Pass, and Skagit Bay; 22,500 feet of freshwater shoreline on Cranberry, Pass, and Campbell Lakes.

OVERNIGHT AND DAY-USE FACILITIES:

Cranberry Lake and West Beach: 70 RV sites (E) (6 &), 152 standard campsites, 5 primitive campsites, 74 picnic sites, reservable kitchen shelter, 9 restrooms (6 with showers) (3 &), trailer dump station.

North Beach: 3 group camps with 4 adirondack shelters and 4 toilets (32, 32, and 64 persons); kitchen shelter, 2 picnic shelters, 12 picnic sites, reservable kitchen shelter, restroom, 6 restrooms at the Scenic Vista (2 &).

Bowman Bay: 16 standard campsites, Cascadia Marine Trail campsite, 35 picnic sites, 3 reservable kitchen shelters, picnic shelter, 2 restrooms with showers (&).

Pass Lake: 2 toilets.

Rosario Beach: 35 picnic sites, reservable kitchen shelter, 2 restrooms with showers (&), outside shower.

Cornet Bay: 6 picnic sites, restroom with showers, marine pumpout station.

Hope Island: 5 primitive campsites (no water, no garbage collection).

Heart Lake: 2 toilets.

RECREATIONAL FACILITIES: 25 miles of hiking trail. Gasoline motors prohibited on all lakes.

Cranberry Lake and West Beach: Amphitheater, freshwater and saltwater swimming beaches, fishing dock with floats, hand-carried boat launch.

Bowman Bay: Fishing dock, 1-lane paved boat ramp, offshore mooring float, 4 mooring buoys, dinghy float.

Pass Lake: Hand-carried boat launch.

Rosario Beach: Underwater marine park, dock with float.

Cornet Bay: 4-lane paved boat ramp with 2 boarding floats, 2 offshore mooring floats (1,140 feet of float space).

Skagit Island: 4 mooring buoys.

Heart Lake: Unpaved boat launch.

EDUCATIONAL FACILITIES: Nature trail, CCC Interpretive Center.

CORNET BAY ELC: 16 cabins (76–156 persons summer, main camp 40–76 persons winter, minicamp 30–38 persons winter), kitchen/dining hall, cook's cabin, infirmary, recreation hall, heated swimming pool, campfire circle, horseshoe pits, sports field, volleyball court, quarter basketball court.

CAR ACCESS: *From the north,* on Fidalgo Island, at a T-intersection 12 miles west of Mount Vernon, follow SR 20 as it turns south. In 6.5 miles reach the north entrance to the park at Pass Lake. The Bowman Bay and Rosario Beach areas are off Rosario Road, west of the lake. The entrance to the main and Cornet Bay portions of the park is 2 miles farther south.

From the south, on Whidbey Island head north on SR 525, which becomes SR 20. In 44.5 miles reach the south park entrance.

To reach Heart Lake, from SR 20 at the east end of Campbell Lake, head west on Campbell Lake Road and in 1.6 miles turn north on Heart Lake Road, which reaches the lake's parking area in 2 miles.

BOAT ACCESS: The park lies at the confluence of Rosario Strait and the Strait of Juan de Fuca. From the east side of Whidbey Island, it can be reached by following Saratoga Passage and Skagit Bay north.

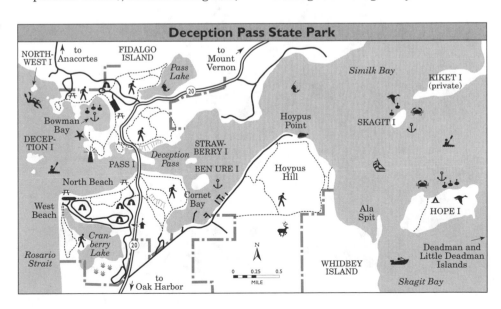

Deception Pass State Park

The Deception Pass bridge offers high views of sparkling water and steep cliffs.

When listing Washington state's super-latives, Deception Pass State Park must certainly be included, so stunning is its scenery, so monumental is its bridge, and so diverse are the activities that it offers. The more than 3.5 million people who visit here annually make it the most used of all the state parks. The park is large enough that it can accommodate the visiting hordes, aside from those campers who have not had the foresight to make reservations. On summer weekends parking might be difficult to find.

The park is split into several parts, each unique. Trails connect some; some sections are separated by waters of the pass. The main entrance and the major facilities are on the southwest side, off SR 20. Boating focuses on Cornet Bay, on the southeast; the park's ELC also is found there. The ELC site once was the CCC camp that housed the men who built the original park.

The focal point of the state park is the Deception Pass Bridge. Construction of the bridge in 1934-35 was so difficult, because of the distance and height, that it required the bridge to be built in two giant leaps from Fidalgo Island to Whid-bey Island, stopping midway on Pass Island between the watery channels of Canoe and Deception Passes. The bridge elicits breathless admiration from visitors star-ing from the decking down the steep chan-nel walls. Pulloffs at the north end of the bridge, at Scenic Vista at the south end of the bridge, and on Pass Island provide spots to leave cars and walk out onto the span. Impromptu paths on Pass Island work down slabs that are sprinkled with sedges, wildflowers, and gnarled pine trees. Three sides of the island end in cliffs; only at the eastern end is there any chance of getting near the shoreline, and even there the steep bank should be approached cautiously. *Use care!*

CRANBERRY LAKE AND WEST BEACH. The southwest corner of the park has a gener-ous helping of both freshwater and salt-water. West Beach offers a stark contrast between the wave-tossed driftwood shore on the saltwater side and the marsh-rimmed freshwater lake a few hundred feet inland. The two are not as different as they might seem, for Cranberry Lake once was a saltwater lagoon before wave-driven sand blocked its opening to saltwater, and upland streams filled the brackish lagoon to form a freshwater lake. A dock on Cranberry Lake lures anglers to test their mettle against the trout that are stocked in the lake.

The majority of the park's campsites are found in this part of the park, on a flat, densely wooded bluff above the beach. Late-arriving bicyclists usually will find tent space at walk-in sites, even if the park is filled with vehicle campers. A nature trail between the park headquarters and Cranberry Lake has stations that describe plants and trees seen on the short loop. A road branching north to picnic sites above North Beach passes three group camps. The two smaller camps, on the east side of the road, can be reserved as one large facility.

BOWMAN AND ROSARIO BAYS. Two inlets at the northwest corner of the park are reached by separate roads branching off Rosario Road. Bowman Bay is the west side refuge for boaters, who hang out on the mooring buoys or float, waiting for a favorable tide to run the pass. Sharpe Cove, on the north side of the bay, has the most protected moorage. Buoys and an offshore mooring float are in the middle of the bay. The long pier near the heart of the bay that rests on tall pilings is too high above the water to be used by boaters, but is ideal for fishing or crabbing. A small dinghy dock at its end permits boaters on buoys or the float to tie up a small boat and climb a ladder to reach shore. Both Coffin Rocks and Gull Rocks clutter the entrance to Bowman Bay; boaters should be cautious, and approach the bay along its southeast side.

Onshore are kitchen and picnic shelters and a host of picnic sites. Near the middle of the area, three sturdy rock and timber buildings house restrooms and the park's excellent CCC interpretive

center. Here, displays relate how this innovative 1930s Depression program put jobless men to work constructing public facilities, such as many of the park's buildings.

Rosario Bay, north of Bowman Bay, is headquarters for scuba divers headed to the underwater marine park at Northwest Island and nearby Urchin Rocks. At minus tides the near-shore rocks at Rosario Bay hold tide pools for exploration.

This is a protected marine sanctuary; taking of marine animals other than for food is prohibited. During slack currents experienced scuba divers can explore the underwater cliffs of Pass Island.

On the south side of Rosario Bay, a narrow peninsula reaching out to Rosario Head separates the bay from Sharpe Cove. On the peninsula is the Maiden of Deception Pass story pole. It illustrates a Samish tribe legend of a native woman

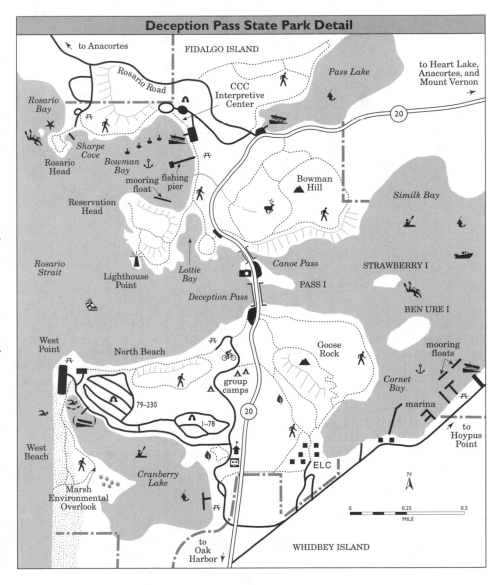

Sharpe Cove has the most protected moorage in Deception Pass State Park.

who agreed to marry a sea spirit and live with him below the waters of Deception Pass if he would restore scarce seafood to her people.

PASS LAKE. North of SR 20, on Fidalgo Island, a parking lot at the southern corner of Pass Lake provides a launch spot for fishing. The lake, which is governed under the Department of Fish and Wildlife, and has "catch and release" regulations, provides catches of good-sized rainbow trout and Atlantic salmon. Unimproved trails that start at the launch ramp allow shore access for anglers.

HEART LAKE. This 66-acre lily-pad lake, south of Anacortes on Heart Lake Road, is a separate parcel of property managed by Deception Pass State Park. A favorite with anglers, it is stocked with rainbow trout. A launch ramp and a pair of toilets are the day-use park's only amenities. A trail circling the lake offers spots to cast a line.

Boating Deception Pass Waters

Tidal currents in the narrow, cliff-bound channels of Deception Pass sometimes exceed 9 knots. Unless boaters are driving high-powered vessels, they must wait for slack tide to enter the channel rather than challenge the maelstrom during maximum tidal currents. Bowman Bay on the west side and Cornet Bay on the east side provide protected moorage.

On both the east and west sides of the park, kayakers will find waters ranging from protected to excitingly exposed. Easiest paddling is in Bowman and Cornet Bays, which have only weak currents and are well protected in most weather. Both of the channels of Deception Pass require intermediate paddling skills; because capsizing is a distinct possibility, kayakers are advised to wear wet suits or dry suits and to travel in a group in case rescue is necessary.

CORNET BAY. The center of saltwater boating is Cornet Bay, on the southeast side of Deception Pass. In addition to the park moorage facilities, a private marina farther into the bay offers fuel, food, overnight moorage, and fishing and marine supplies. The bay is quite shallow, but safe passage into it from the east is marked by pilings and day marks.

OFFSHORE ISLANDS. The park includes a number of small islands. Some have anchorages or mooring buoys, allowing approach by dinghy, while others are best reached by kayak. The nearer the pass, the more carefully the strength of the tide and the skill of the paddler should be considered.

In Rosario Strait, Deception Island, the offshore guardian of the west entrance to Deception Pass, is a rocky outcropping with a few trees and a craggy shoreline. A shallow underwater shelf between the island and the pass is a favorite salmon fishing spot. Beachable boats can land, with caution, on its rocky shoreline. The shelf on which the island lies drops away steeply to the west. Also on the west side, barren Northwest Island is a favorite of scuba divers.

Strawberry and Ben Ure Islands lie at the east end of Deception Pass. Kayaks or small boats capable of being beached can find spots to go ashore on Strawberry Island, especially at the more gently sloping east end of the tiny island. As of 1999, an effort to acquire Ben Ure Island as park property was underway.

Skagit Island, which along with Hope Island lies at the head of Skagit Bay, is a 21-acre island covered with trees and brush. A primitive trail follows the top of the bluff around the island. Mooring buoys are placed offshore along its north side. Camping is prohibited on the island due to the fire hazard.

Hope Island, whose 166 acres make it the largest of the park's islands, is an oversized twin of Skagit. It also has mooring buoys along its north side. A few primitive campsites are at Lang Bay on the north side. A trail crosses from the campsites to cliff-top views to the south. Eagles and great blue herons frequently sit in tall snags on both islands. Deadman and Little Deadman Islands are two small islands that lie southeast of Hope Island. Because the water around them is extremely shoal, they should only be approached at high tide, and even then with a shallow-draft boat and a whole lot of caution.

Hiking the Park

An extensive system of trails that threads through the park connects lakes, forests, cliff-rimmed beaches, and wide bays. Moderate to low tides offer added opportunities for long beach walks.

A trail from the Rosario Bay picnic area climbs to the top of Rosario Head and circles the top of the bluff; another branches east and follows the shores of Sharpe Cove and Bowman Bay. Trails that begin at Bowman Bay branch out to Reservation Head, Lighthouse Point, and Lottie Bay.

Unimproved trails on the east side of SR 20 circle Bowman Hill; trailheads are at the pullout just north of the bridge.

Cranberry Lake provides an interesting contrast to the bordering forest. A path along the west side of the lake leads to a viewing platform over a marsh, then returns across the grass-covered dunes.

At North Beach, north of Cranberry Lake, a trail loop connects the campgrounds. Side routes lead down to a pair of rock-rimmed sandy beaches and an impressive, CCC-vintage kitchen shelter. Marvel at startling views upward at the Deception Pass Bridge and watch boating traffic in the throat of Deception Pass. The trail up to the south end of the bridge passes concrete bases where, during World War II, rapid-fire guns defended the pass against enemy intrusion. A trail spur continues under the bridge to Goose Rock.

Routes around the slopes and over the top of Goose Rock offer high views, first in one direction, then in another. Rocky slabs at the top are ideal for sunning while catching your breath from the climb up.

The Discovery Trail, which begins at the ELC on Cornet Bay and runs northeast to the highway, has a number of stations along the way that identify flora and geological and ecological points of interest. This route links with other paths that crisscross Goose Rock.

East of Cornet Bay, quite a different kind of trail circles through the dense lowland old-growth forest of Hoypus Hill. Trailheads are at a gated side road and a gravel pit.

JOSEPH WHIDBEY STATE PARK

Camping, picnicking, beach walking, surf-fishing, paddling

SEASON/HOURS: Closed October 1 through March 31.

AREA: 112 acres; 3,100 feet of saltwater shoreline on the Strait of Juan de Fuca.

OVERNIGHT AND DAY-USE FACILITIES: Cascadia Marine Trail campsite, 20 picnic sites, picnic shelter, 2 toilets (*no water*).

RECREATIONAL FACILITIES: 1-mile beach hike.

CAR ACCESS: *From the south,* south of Oak Harbor, turn northwest from SR 20 onto Swantown Road. The park is reached in 3 miles, at the intersection of West Beach and Crosby Roads.

From the north, north of Oak Harbor, turn west from SR 20 onto Ault Field Road. In 2.2 miles turn south on Crosby Road, and reach the park in 2.3 miles.

Joseph Whidbey, a member of George Vancouver's 1792 expedition, explored the east side of Whidbey Island up to Deception Pass. When his group reached the north end of the passage, Whidbey

A great blue heron surveys the scene from a high perch.

took a small boat through Deception Pass, reaching the spot where he had been a few days before, thus becoming the first European to circumnavigate this 45-mile-long island (the longest in the U.S., by the way). Vancouver named the island for him.

Joseph Whidbey State Park boasts one of the grandest beaches on Whidbey Island. Paths lead from the picnic area to the broad sand and gravel beach facing on the Strait of Juan de Fuca. Logs and driftwood mark the high-tide line. Winds and waves rolling down the strait toss beachcombing treasures along the high-tide margins, especially during winter storms. In the distance the low silhouettes of Smith and Minor Islands can be spotted by the repeated solitary flash from the Smith Island lighthouse.

A second access to the beach can be found next to the first residence on the south side of the park, where a path leads directly to the beach. A Cascadia Marine Trail site, the only camping in the park, is in brush at the northeast end of a grass field above the beach.

FORT EBEY STATE PARK

Camping, picnicking, hiking, bicycling, surfboarding, beach walking, fishing, paddling, paragliding, interpretive programs, historic display

SEASON/HOURS: Day-use, year-round; campground closed from November 1 through February 28; campsite reservations accepted in summer.

AREA: 644.23 acres; 8,000 feet of saltwater shoreline on the Strait of Juan de Fuca; 1,000 feet of freshwater shoreline on Lake Pondilla.

OVERNIGHT AND DAY-USE FACILITIES: 4 RV sites (E), 42 standard campsites, 3 primitive campsites, group camp (50 persons), Cascadia Marine Trail campsite, 24 picnic sites, 2 restrooms with showers (&), toilets.

RECREATIONAL FACILITIES: 3 miles of hiking/biking trail.

EDUCATIONAL FACILITIES: Abandoned Coast Artillery fortification.

CAR ACCESS: From SR 20 on Whidbey Island, turn west on Libbey Road, 5.8 miles south of Oak Harbor. In 1 mile turn south on Hill Valley Drive, and reach the park in 0.4 mile.

Although many Washington park-goers are familiar with the 1900s-vintage Coast Artillery defenses of Forts Casey, Flagler, and Worden (all now state parks), far fewer people are aware of Fort Ebey, which was a Johnny-come-lately in the coastal defense business. The big, obsolete guns at the other forts had been removed long before Fort Ebey was built. The fortification at Point Partridge on Whidbey Island was one of three intended to protect Puget Sound from Japanese attacks during World War II; others were at Striped Peak, west of Port Angeles, and at Cape Flattery. Only the first two were completed by the time that U.S. air superiority in the Pacific and Gulf of Alaska made land-based coastal defense batteries obsolete, causing construction to be halted. Today only concrete platforms mark the gun locations, and the bunker now echoes with the voices and footsteps of youngsters playing hide-and-seek among its spooky, deserted rooms.

The state park includes several miles of hiker/biker trails, said to be the best on the island, that connect with a system of hiker/biker/equestrian trails through the "Ebey's Kettles," east of the park. The kettles are a unique geologic formation consisting of large depressions in the land left by receding continental glaciers some 15,000 years ago.

At the north end of the park, a short trail leads to tiny, bass-filled Lake Pondilla. Bald eagles often roost in nearby snags. A number of walk-in hiker/biker campsites are found along the shore. Forested campground loops lie south of the battery site. Paddlers approaching the park will find a Cas-cadia Marine Trail campsite on the beach below the Point Partridge lighthouse.

The southeast section of the park holds a group camp on the edge of a 200-foot-high bluff overlooking Admiralty Inlet and the Strait of Juan de Fuca. A trail from here descends down a gully to the beach; several delightful picnic sites sit on viewpoints along the trail. From the trail, breathtaking vistas spread west across the inlet and south to Perego's Lagoon.

Two trails from the day-use area drop down gentle bluffs to provide beachcombing access to the short stretch of wide sandy beach that lies north of the Point Partridge lighthouse. A hiking trail traverses the bluff above the Strait of

Fort Ebey State Park

Cascadia Marine Trail campsite
to SR 20
Libbey Road
Lake Pondilla
Point Partridge
Hill Valley Drive
WHIDBEY ISLAND
Bluff Trail
Watertower Trail
Raider Creek Trail
gun battery
Campground Trail
group camp
Admiralty Inlet

0   500   1000
FEET

Summertime picnicking at Fort Flagler State Park is great for family fun.

Juan de Fuca and has short connecting links to the campground and gun battery area. Still more hiker/biker trails weave through the thick forest east to the park boundary, some connecting with the county's Kettles Park trail system between there and SR 20.

EBEY'S LANDING STATE PARK

Hiking, birdwatching, beach walking, surf-fishing, paddling

SEASON/HOURS: Year-round.

AREA: 45.75 acres; 6,120 feet of saltwater shoreline on the Strait of Juan de Fuca.

DAY-USE FACILITIES: Toilet (*no water*).

RECREATIONAL FACILITIES: 1.5 miles of hiking trail.

EDUCATIONAL FACILITIES: Interpretive display, Ebey's Landing National Historic Reserve nearby.

CAR ACCESS: From SR 20 on Whidbey Island, turn south on Ebey Road, 0.2 mile west of Coupeville. The park is reached in 2.7 miles.

Ebey's Landing State Park offers some of the most scenic beach walking to be found.

Of the several ways to get a state park named for you, the way Colonel Isaac Ebey did it is not among those recommended. Ebey, the first white settler on Whidbey Island, homesteaded the rich farmland on the bluff above the park and held several bureaucratic offices in this virgin territory. Thus, when a group of Tlingit Indians sought revenge for the death of a chief at the hands of white men, they looked for a white "chief"—and found him in the person of Ebey. In August of 1857 they surprised him in his home, shot him, and carried his head home as a trophy.

Today the beach section of Isaac Ebey's property now comprises the state park named for him. The park adjoins Ebey's Landing National Historic Reserve, a joint federal and state effort to preserve the nineteenth-century agricultural character of this historic part of Whidbey Island.

Near the parking lot at the beach at Ebey's Landing, interpretive signs tell the story of Isaac Ebey and George Perego, a hermit who lived on the nearby windblown bluff. A 1-mile trail leads from the parking lot inland to Sunnyside Cemetery, which contains Ebey's grave and the James Davis blockhouse, one of the few remaining log forts built during the Puget Sound Indian Wars. The cemetery can also be reached by road.

Another trail (outside the state park boundary, but on National Park Service land) follows the lip of Perego's Bluff. In about 1.5 miles the path switchbacks down the face of the bluff to the beach. A shoreline trip, on the beach side of Perego Lagoon, returns to the Ebey's Landing starting point. Beachcombing opportunities abound on the wave-tossed beach.

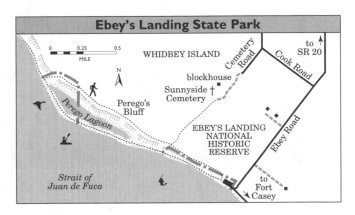

95

FORT CASEY STATE PARK

Camping, picnicking, hiking, scuba diving, beach walking, shellfish, fishing, boating, lighthouse/interpretive center, historic display, interpretive signs

SEASON/HOURS: Year-round.
LIGHTHOUSE INTERPRETIVE CENTER: Open 11:00 A.M. to 5:00 P.M., April through May, Thursday through Sunday and holidays; June through mid-September, Wednesday through Sunday and holidays; mid-September through October, Thursday through Sunday.

AREA: 142.07 acres; 8,305 feet of saltwater shoreline on Admiralty Inlet.
OVERNIGHT AND DAY-USE FACILITIES: 35 standard campsites (&), hiker/biker camp in the picnic area, 63 picnic sites, 5 restrooms (2 with showers).
RECREATIONAL FACILITIES: 1.25 miles of interpretive trail, 1 mile of beach walk, underwater park, 2-lane boat launch with boarding floats.
EDUCATIONAL FACILITIES: Historic Coast Artillery fortifications, lighthouse interpretive center.
CAR ACCESS: From SR 20 on Whidbey Island, turn south on Engle Road at Coupeville and reach the park in 3.2 miles.
Alternatively, 6 miles south of Coupeville, where the main north–south road changes from SR 20 to SR 525, follow SR 20 west and reach the park in 3.4 miles.

One wouldn't think an instrument of war could become a major recreational facility; however, such is the case with several old forts in the state. Admiralty Head was one of three sites selected in 1896 for the defense of Puget Sound. The batteries at Forts Casey, Worden, and Flagler were intended to form a "triangle of fire" that would rain death on enemy ships attempting to enter Admiralty Inlet. All are now state parks.

The initial gun and mortar emplacements, fire control systems, and searchlight batteries at Fort Casey were installed between 1899 and 1911. Although the fort was fully active when the U.S. entered World War I in 1917, improvements in naval guns, ship's armor, and fire control systems made these fixed coastal defense forts obsolete almost as quickly as they were finished. Most of the guns were removed in 1920 and sent to Europe to be mounted on railroad cars as artillery pieces. The fort was briefly armed again when some antiaircraft guns were placed here prior to World War II. Because its use as a coastal defense fortification proved impractical, the site was used primarily for the induction and training of troops during both world wars.

The four guns mounted today in batteries Worth and Trevor are not part of the original armament; they were originally at Fort Wint in the Philippines and were brought here for display. All of the old shot rooms and powder magazines and their interconnecting corridors beneath the gun emplacements are open for exploration. Battery Worth has interior lighting. If you plan to go into any of the other batteries, be sure to bring a flashlight—once past the steel outer doors, everything inside is black. Catwalks lead from the gun emplacements to concrete towers that served as fire control stations. Buried in the hillside above the south end of the batteries

The former Admiralty Head light, which was moved from its original site west of the present-day gun emplacements, now serves as an interpretive center.

are concrete-lined rooms from which targets were tracked and their positions plotted to provide data to the gun batteries. Lower on the bluff, below the gun emplacements, another bunker held a searchlight. At the east side of the fort, U-shaped emplacements held mortars.

Prior to its use as an army fort, Admiralty Head was a lighthouse reservation. The original light, which stood west of the present gun emplacements, first shone here in 1861. When the fort was constructed, the building was moved farther back on the bluff; it now serves as the park's interpretive center, with displays on the history of the fort and the natural history of Whidbey Island.

At Fort Casey, modern facilities include hilltop picnic sites in trees above the gun emplacements, and a campground loop on the flat, open beach area below the east side of the bluff. A trail leads from the campground up the bluff to the emplacements, or you can walk along the road. Other footpaths lace the bluff.

The campground sits on earth dredged from adjoining Keystone Harbor, where the ferry to Port Townsend lands. A two-lane boat ramp drops into the harbor from the spit on its east side. An underwater park just offshore in Admiralty Inlet attracts scuba divers.

Seattle Pacific University uses the old barracks, warehouses, and officers' quarters along the parade ground at the park's entrance as an extension campus.

Scuba divers leave the water after visiting the offshore reef at Keystone Spit State Park.

KEYSTONE SPIT STATE PARK

Picnicking, kite flying, birdwatching, windsurfing, scuba diving, beach walking, surf-fishing, interpretation

SEASON/HOURS: Year-round.
AREA: 279.8 acres; 7,330 feet of saltwater shoreline on Admiralty Bay; 7,000 feet of freshwater shoreline on Crockett Lake.
EDUCATIONAL FACILITIES: Interpretive displays.
CAR ACCESS: See directions to Fort Casey State Park.

Keystone Spit, a mile-long narrow gravel bar, separates Crockett Lake and Admiralty Bay, immediately adjoining the east side of Fort Casey State Park. In 1896 the land was acquired by the Army Corps of Engineers, who used the western portion of the spit for an engineering camp during the construction of Fort Casey. In order to improve on the primitive fire control methods used at the time the fort was constructed, new observation stations were built in 1908 at the east end of Keystone Spit and at other extreme ends

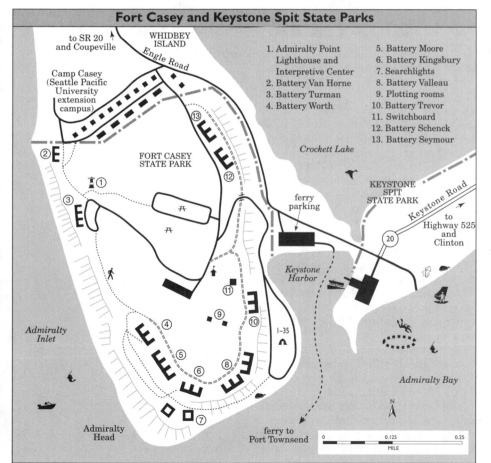

Fort Casey and Keystone Spit State Parks

to SR 20 and Coupeville

WHIDBEY ISLAND

Engle Road

Camp Casey (Seattle Pacific University extension campus)

FORT CASEY STATE PARK

Crockett Lake

KEYSTONE SPIT STATE PARK

Keystone Road

ferry parking

20

to Highway 525 and Clinton

Admiralty Inlet

Keystone Harbor

I-35

Admiralty Head

Admiralty Bay

ferry to Port Townsend

N

1. Admiralty Point Lighthouse and Interpretive Center
2. Battery Van Horne
3. Battery Turman
4. Battery Worth
5. Battery Moore
6. Battery Kingsbury
7. Searchlights
8. Battery Valleau
9. Plotting rooms
10. Battery Trevor
11. Switchboard
12. Battery Schenck
13. Battery Seymour

0   0.125   0.25
MILE

of the fort property to provide a long base-line for triangulating on targets and improving on the accuracy of position plots.

Today, a major portion of the spit, with freshwater shoreline on one side and saltwater on the other, is open for public enjoyment as a place to beach walk, birdwatch, fish, or fly kites. Crockett Lake, a 250-acre shallow marsh created by the gravel bar, is used by waterfowl as a place to pause or overwinter on their migratory flights. Other marsh-loving birds nest along its edges. Bring binoculars and see how many different species you can spot.

SOUTH WHIDBEY STATE PARK

Camping, picnicking, birdwatching, hiking, beach walking, shellfish, crabbing, fishing, interpretive programs

SEASON/HOURS: Closed November 1 through February 28.
AREA: 348.73 acres; 4,500 feet of saltwater shoreline on Admiralty Inlet.
OVERNIGHT AND DAY-USE FACILITIES: 2 RV sites, 53 standard campsites, 6 primitive campsites, group camp (144 persons), 26 picnic sites, picnic shelter, amphitheater, 2 restrooms (&), trailer dump station.
RECREATIONAL FACILITIES: 3.5 miles of hiking trail, 1-mile nature trail, 0.5-mile beach walk.
CAR ACCESS: From the ferry landing at Clinton on Whidbey Island, take SR 525 northwest for 9 miles, then turn west on Bush Point Road, which in about 3 miles joins Smugglers Cove Road. Continue north for 1.5 miles to the park entrance.

In most parks bordering on Puget Sound, the beach is the prime attraction, and any inland trails are nice added tidbits, but draw only limited interest. The case is just the opposite at South Whidbey,

Sun, a comfortable spot, and a best friend are all you need to enjoy the beach at South Whidbey State Park.

where the beach, although not to be denigrated, is not as interesting as its trails.

All of the park facilities lie on the west side of Smugglers Cove Road. Picnic sites are on a forested flat near the park entrance, and beyond are camping loops. Trees and dense brush provide campsite seclusion. At the end of the campground road, a small loop encircles a group camp. Groups may schedule guided interpretive walks with the rangers.

The Beach Trail, a 0.5-mile-long path to the beach, leaves the parking lot and campground and wanders through a forest of huge old Douglas-fir with a thick undergrowth of salmonberries, blackberries, and a healthy share of nettles. The final stretch descends to the shore on a wooden staircase. The narrow cobble beach lies below a high clay bank with exposed strata of sedimentary rocks.

At the south end of the park, the mile-long Forest Discovery Trail traces a pair of loops along the top of the bluff past alder, cedar, and fir, and Lilliputian forests of ferns. Bridges cross creeks and

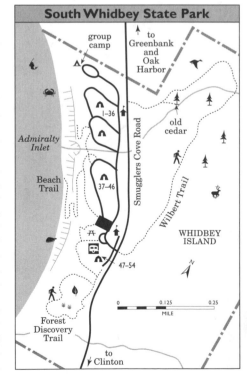

South Whidbey State Park

soggy spots; brilliant yellow skunk cabbage brighten the trail in spring.

The Wilbert Trail, which starts on the east side of the road opposite the park entrance, loops through a spectacular forest of 250-year-old western red cedar and Douglas-fir. Walk quietly and perhaps see black-tailed deer, or small animals who make the forest home. Look up to tree snags for bald eagles, ospreys, and pileated woodpeckers.

USELESS BAY TIDELANDS

Birdwatching, beach walking, shellfish

SEASON/HOURS: Year-round.
AREA: 21,120 feet of saltwater tidelands on Useless Bay.
DAY-USE FACILITIES: 2 toilets (&), picnic table (all in county park).
EDUCATIONAL FACILITIES: Interpretive display (in county park).
CAR ACCESS: From the ferry landing at Clinton on Whidbey Island, take SR 525 northwest for 8.2 miles, then turn south on Double Bluff Road, and follow it to a county park at the road end in 2.2 miles. The state park tidelands extend west from here to Double Bluff.

A really nice public beach is often hard to come by. Here, on the southwest end of Whidbey Island, road-end facilities are provided by Island County and two miles of prime shoreland is courtesy of the State Department of Natural Resources and state parks (and Mom Nature). The beach lies below 300-foot-high Double Bluff. The information kiosk at the parking lot points out fascinating geological formations in the soft glacial till of the bluff.

Walk the sandy beach, enjoying the wind and cry of gulls, or snooze on a piece of sun-warmed driftwood. Tiny backwater lagoons invite wading. Beware of being

High bluffs, deposited by an ancient glacier, help create the fine sandy beach on Useless Bay.

stranded by high tide. Several additional chunks of state park shorelands are scattered around Useless Bay, but are not accessible.

CAMANO ISLAND STATE PARK

Camping, picnicking, birdwatching, hiking, swimming, beach walking, shellfish, fishing, boating, paddling, nature study

SEASON/HOURS: Year-round, some campsites closed in winter.

AREA: 134.35 acres; 6,700 feet of saltwater shoreline on Saratoga Passage.
OVERNIGHT AND DAY-USE FACILITIES: 87 standard campsites (2 &), group camp (160–180 persons), Cascadia Marine Trail campsite, 113 picnic sites, picnic shelter, kitchen shelter, amphitheater, 4 restrooms (2 with showers) (&), 3 toilets, trailer dump station.
RECREATIONAL FACILITIES: 2.5 miles of hiking trail, 0.5-mile self-guided nature trail, 3-lane paved boat ramp.
CAR ACCESS: At Exit 212 (SR 532, Stanwood, Camano Island) from I-5, 18 miles north of Everett, head west 5.7 miles on SR 532 to Stanwood. Continue west for 4.5 miles to the

Camano Island State Park boasts a fine boat launch ramp and a gentle shore for beaching shallow draft boats.

few clams might even be found, and surf-fishing might yield a bottomfish or two. The wide beach-grass flat between high-tide debris and the bluff has ample room for flying kites, playing ball, tossing Frisbees, or picnicking. A freshwater marsh edged by a thicket of wild roses stretches along the base of the bluff behind the parking lot. A few primitive Cascadia Marine Trail campsites lie on the shoreline at the south end of this beach strip.

Campground loops lie in the woods at the top of the bluff. Most are in dense fir with brush providing campsite isolation; a few sites have expansive views across Saratoga Passage. The 0.5-mile-long Al Emerson Nature Trail, found here, has numbered stations identifying trailside flora and features such as signs of early logging.

South Cliff Trail leaves the campground and skirts the edge of the bluff. Views are south along Camano Island to its tip at Camano Head, to Gedney Island at the heart of Saratoga Passage, and across the passage to Whidbey Island. A second trail along the edge of the bluff links the North Beach picnic area with the campground and offers bird's-eye views across the backbone of Whidbey Island to the horizon-filling Olympic Mountains. A spur from this trail weaves through the woods to the group camp.

junction of East Camano and North Camano Drives, signed both ways to the park. Either road reaches the park in about 12 miles.

You've heard of instant coffee. Camano Island State Park probably could be called "instant park." In 1949, after the South Camano Grange successfully lobbied the DNR to make property available for a park, a group of 900 volunteers turned out and in one day developed the initial park improvements.

The 100-foot-high headland of Lowell Point divides the park. At a Y-intersection inside the park, one fork swings southwest then drops steeply to the north to a day-use area on a bench about 30 feet above the beach. From this picnic area a short trail leads down to the gradually tapering cobble beach. The beach along the northern two-thirds of the park is much narrower than the portion west of Lowell Point, and in places it nearly disappears at high tide.

The other road fork runs through the bluff-top campground area to Lowell Point. Here it cuts down the bluff to the wide, flat beach at the southwest side of the point, and a three-lane concrete boat launch ramp at the north end of Lowell Point, on Saratoga Passage. The ramp tapers gently into the water; however, there are no boarding floats, so wading becomes part of the launching ritual.

The broad rocky beach below the driftwood line is one of the best on Saratoga Passage for a lazy day of sunbathing while watching boats cruise the waterway. At a minus tide a

CAMA BEACH PROPERTY

Nature study, historical interpretation, beach walking

SEASON/HOURS: Day-use, open year-round.

AREA: 438 acres; 450 feet of saltwater shoreline on Saratoga Passage.

FACILITIES: None open to the public at present.

RECREATIONAL FACILITIES: Trail from Camano Island State Park.

CAR ACCESS: See directions to Camano Island State Park. The Cama Beach property is west of West Camano

Camano Island State Park

to I-5 Exit 212
Lowell Point Road
CAMANO ISLAND
Al Emerson Nature Trail
South Cliff Trail
North Beach
to Cama Beach State Park
group camp
43–88
I-42
Saratoga Passage
0   0.125   0.25
MILE
Cascadia Marine Trail campsite
Lowell Point

Drive, 0.2 mile north of Lowell Point Road.

There was a time when people spent their summer vacations in rustic beach resorts such as Cama Beach. When Camano Island became only a skip away from metropolises, Cama Beach ceased to be the popular getaway it once was, and closed. The property, along with a row of small beach cottages and some larger buildings, is now owned by state parks. Restoration of the buildings is scheduled when money is available. A 0.5-mile trail from Camano Island State Park permits day-use exploration of the beach. The buildings are off-limits at present, but are tentatively scheduled for opening in 2000.

MUKILTEO STATE PARK

Picnicking, kite flying, birdwatching, scuba diving, windsurfing, beach walking, fishing, boating

SEASON/HOURS: Year-round.
AREA: 17.82 acres; 1,495 feet of saltwater shoreline on Admiralty Inlet.
DAY-USE FACILITIES: 47 picnic sites, restroom with dressing rooms, 4-lane boat ramp with boarding floats.
EDUCATIONAL FACILITIES: Interpretive display, historic lighthouse nearby.
CAR ACCESS: At Exit 189 (SR 526, Mukilteo, Whidbey Island Ferry) from I-5, 6 miles south of Everett, head west on SR 526 for 4.2 miles to its intersection with SR 525 (Mukilteo Speedway). Turn north and arrive at the town of Mukilteo and the park in another 2 miles.

Although Mukilteo State Park is primarily a huge, blacktopped parking lot, over a million people visit it annually. What's the attraction? The strip of sandy beach is a nice place for local people to grab a quick picnic; it also is great for sunbathers, although strong currents and rapid dropoffs make the water unsafe for swimmers; windsurfers (in wet suits to protect themselves from the year-round icy water) take advantage of the winds sweeping along the shores of Possession Sound; and the less venturesome can use the same winds to fly kites.

The four-lane ramp, one of the park's main draws, drops gradually at high-tide levels, then very steeply near the low-tide line. The slope of the ramp, combined with winds and waves that frequently whip the point from the southwest, make it one of the more difficult to use on Puget Sound, but because it is the only one for some distance, it is heavily used. Boarding floats lie on the bottom at minus tides.

Two plaques at the park commemorate the location's historical significance as the site of the signing, in 1855, of the Point Elliott Treaty between Territorial Governor Isaac Stevens and the chiefs of the 22 Native American tribes living in the area. The chiefs, not understanding the language of the treaty, ceded their lands in exchange for meager reservations and trivial money. Unrest over this and other unfair treaties precipitated the Indian Wars of 1855–56.

WENBERG STATE PARK

Camping, picnicking, swimming, waterskiing, fishing, boating

SEASON/HOURS: Year-round, some campsites closed in winter; campsite reservations accepted in summer.
AREA: 45.86 acres; 1,140 feet of freshwater shoreline on Lake Goodwin.
OVERNIGHT AND DAY-USE FACILITIES: 33 RV sites (EW) (3 ♿), 45 standard campsites, 80 picnic sites, picnic shelter, group day-use area with picnic shelter (150 persons), 2 restrooms with showers (♿), trailer dump station.
RECREATIONAL FACILITIES: 0.5 mile of

The Mukilteo lighthouse adjoins Mukilteo State Park.

trail, children's play equipment, swimming beach, 2 swim/waterski floats, bathhouse (♿), 2-lane boat ramp with boarding float.
CONCESSIONS: Groceries, fast food, snacks.
CAR ACCESS: At Exit 206 from I-5, 7 miles north of Marysville, head west on 172nd Street NE, which at Meridian becomes 172nd Street NW. In 2.4 miles head northwest on Lakewood Road. In 2.7 miles turn south on E Lake Goodwin Road to reach the park in another 1.5 miles.

Wenberg State Park packs a lot of fun into a narrow strip of land fronting on Lake Goodwin. Since the park is close

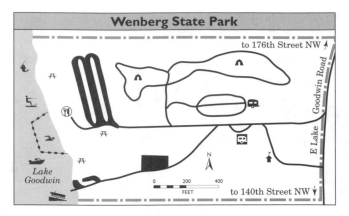

Wenberg State Park

to 176th Street NW

E Lake Goodwin Road

Lake Goodwin

N

to 140th Street NW

0   200   400
FEET

to Puget Sound's metropolitan areas, it is extremely popular, and the campground is nearly always full on weekends during summer months. The 545-acre lake is stocked with rainbow and cutthroat trout, and also holds bass and perch. Early season trout fishing is usually excellent.

A road leads down along the south side of the park to a two-lane paved boat ramp with a loading dock between the ramps. The park's uplands hold three campground loops—one a grassy strip with hookup sites, and the other two with standard campsites set among brush and maple.

The day-use area has a reservable group picnic shelter on the bluff between the campground and the beach. Short, paved trails lead from here down the wooded hillside to the lake. At the beach, a rolling lawn punctuated with stately grand fir, some more than 100 feet high, holds picnic sites and a small picnic shelter. Another strip of lawn, packed with sunbathers during the summer, tapers to the sandy shoreline of the beach, facing on a roped-off swimming area. A pair of floats serve as a take-off point for waterskiers.

MOUNT PILCHUCK STATE PARK

Scenic views, hiking, mountain climbing, ski mountaineering, snowshoeing

SEASON/HOURS: Year-round.
AREA: 1,893.02 acres; 6,000 feet of freshwater shoreline on various lakes and streams.
DAY-USE FACILITIES: Toilet.
RECREATIONAL FACILITIES: 2.5 miles of hiking trail, historical display.
EDUCATIONAL FACILITIES: Fire lookout with interpretive signs.
CAR ACCESS: From the northeast side of Granite Falls, take the Mountain Loop Highway north for 10.1 miles to the Verlot Ranger Station. In

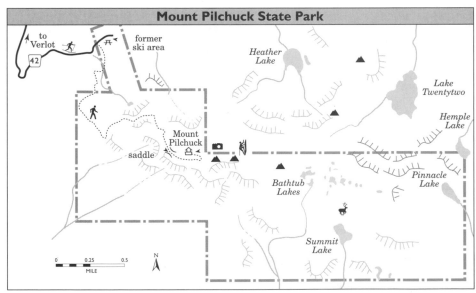

Wenberg State Park is popular for all kinds of water play.

Mount Pilchuck State Park

to Verlot

42

former ski area

Heather Lake

Lake Twentytwo

Hemple Lake

Mount Pilchuck

saddle

Bathtub Lakes

Pinnacle Lake

Summit Lake

0   0.25   0.5
MILE

N

another 0.9 mile, just beyond the bridge over the Stillaguamish River, turn south on Forest Road 42 (Heather Lake, Mount Pilchuck) and follow it uphill for 6.9 miles to the park.

Although its offerings of a hiking trail and a toilet seems meager compared to those of an upscale, multiactivity park, what the 5,340-foot-high summit of Mount Pilchuck offers is spectacular. No other spot in the western Cascades offers such views to any but skilled mountain climbers able to scale high peaks. The summit trail starts at the 3,160-foot level of the mountain, where a commercial ski area operated until it closed in the 1970s. Now only a parking lot and a battered toilet sit below the once-groomed slopes, now covered with 20-foot-high evergreens. In winter the road is gated at the Heather Lake trailhead, 5.5 miles downhill. The strenuous cross-country ski or snowshoe trip up the road to the old ski area is rewarded on a clear day with views of sharp, blazing-white peaks to the northeast.

The lower section of the hiking trail winds up the drainage of Rotary Creek before swinging west to the edge of clearcuts. The once muddy and tree-root-studded lower section of the trail has been rebuilt with bridges, staircases, and improved footing. At 4,100 feet the trees give way to rocky slopes and alpine meadows, and views up the high-angle granite slabs to the summit lookout. The path wends through heather-rimmed slabs and boulders up stairsteps and switchbacks to a 4,700-foot saddle west of the summit, then crosses the narrow ridge into alpine timber on the south side of the mountain. Although the ridgeline can be followed to the summit from the saddle and the way is marked with paint splotches, strenuous boulder scrambling is involved. The regular route is easier and faster, but a little longer. The final 100 yards leading to the lookout access ladder require some rock scrambling.

Although this is not a difficult hike, the elevation gain is over 2,200 feet in

The lookout on the top of Mount Pilchuck offers spectacular views.

about 2.5 miles, and a leisurely round trip will take about 5 hours. You will need routefinding experience on the upper portion of the trail in fog or when snow covers the upper rocky portions of the path; novice hikers have become lost or been injured here. The vertical northeast side of the mountain offers challenging routes for experienced mountain climbers.

Those old fire-watchers knew what they were doing when they chose this 5,340-foot summit for a lookout site. Peaks of the north Cascades spread in all directions, ranging from nearby Whitehorse and Three Fingers to the distant snowy masses of Shuksan, Baker, Glacier, and Rainier. Photographic displays inside the lookout tell its history and identify the major peaks.

WALLACE FALLS STATE PARK

Camping, picnicking, berry picking, nature study, hiking, mountain biking, fishing, scenic views

SEASON/HOURS: Closed September 30 through March 31.

AREA: 1,528.51 acres; 6,300 feet of freshwater shoreline on Wallace River and Wallace Lake.

OVERNIGHT AND DAY-USE FACILITIES: 6 standard campsites (walk-in), picnic tables, 2 picnic shelters, restroom (♿).

RECREATIONAL FACILITIES: 14 miles of hiking trails (some on adjoining DNR property).

EDUCATIONAL FACILITIES: Interpretive trail.

CAR ACCESS: At Gold Bar turn north from US 2 onto First Street, then in 0.4 mile head east on May Creek Road (Camp Huston, Wallace Falls State Park). In 0.7 mile turn north on Ley Road and arrive at the park in another 0.4 mile.

From the highway between Sultan and Gold Bar, Wallace Falls appears as a white ribbon pinned to the forested hillside. The 265-foot-high cataract visible from the highway on the north side of the Skykomish River valley is only one of a series of plunges on the South Fork of the Wallace River that drops a total of nearly 500 feet.

Camping is clearly secondary to the scenery at this state park. Six walk-in campsites are spread around a wooded loop on the west side of the parking lot. The hiking trail starts at the parking area and splits a short way uphill. The left branch, which follows the bed of an old logging railroad grade, is a longer but gentler alternative. The right branch, the Woody Trail, traces a steeper path through second-growth Douglas-fir, alder, and cedar above the riverbank. The Woody Trail is open only to foot travel, but bikers may use the railroad grade and the trails above it to Wallace Lake.

A short distance beyond the start of the Woody Trail is a logging interpretive trail. The 0.8-mile loop trail climbs steeply up a finger ridge, passing vestiges of past logging in the area. Displays with illustrations and photos explain interesting logging activities.

At the 1-mile point on the Woody Trail a spur path climbs up to join the railroad grade at its 2-mile point. The divergent paths meet again near the bridge over the North Fork of the Wallace River. The path now switchbacks steeply uphill, then levels at a picnic shelter where the first view of the falls is reached. This is a good destination for the faint of lung and leg; beyond here the route switchbacks relentlessly upward to two more views of the thundering falls, one of the tallest in the Cascades. One of a pair of log-fenced vistas at the top of the lower falls overlooks the Skykomish Valley, framed by uprising peaks. The second provides the most photogenic view of the spectacular upper falls. Total distance from the trailhead to this point is 2.5 miles via the Woody Trail and 3.5 via the railroad grade. The trail continues uphill through switchbacks, then diagonals across a steep hillside. In 0.5 mile it arrives at the lip of the upper falls, with views down the deep, plunging drainage of the Wallace River.

To reach Wallace Lake, continue on a marked but poorly maintained trail. In 0.25 mile reach an abandoned logging road and follow it north as it gradually ascends another 2.5 miles to Wallace Lake, framed by wooded cliffs more than 500 feet high. An alternative, signed route to

Wallace Falls State Park

Jay Lake

Pebble Beach

Wallace Lake

0   0.25   0.5
MILE

North Fork Wallace River

DNR Road

Upper Grade

Old Railroad Grade

to Gold Bar

Woody Trail

Small Falls Interpretive Trail

lower falls

upper falls

Wallace River

Wallace Falls plunges nearly 500 feet in a series of foaming cascades.

BIG EDDY SCENIC RIVER ACCESS

Fishing, paddling, picnicking

AREA: 10 acres; 1,000 feet of freshwater shoreline on the Skykomish River.
DAY-USE FACILITIES: 2 toilets.
CAR ACCESS: US 2 crosses a high bridge over the Skykomish River 1.6 miles southeast of Gold Bar. At the east end of the bridge, on the south side of the road look for a gravel road marked "Public Fishing." Follow this road 0.2 mile to the parking lots at the river access.

The take-out point for paddlers navigating a popular 7-mile-long rafting and kayaking whitewater river run is at Big Eddy, a small piece of state parks property. Scenic Skykomish River threads through the heavily forested valley floor overshadowed by the precipitous cliffs of Mount Index and Mount Persis. The section between the base of Sunset Falls, a mile east of Index, and Gold Bar is a continuous succession of rapids including the infamous "Boulder Drop."

The river offshore from the property is a broad, calm respite between two series of rapids. A sandy shelf extending into the water offers an easy haul-out spot. The boulder-and-sand shoreline makes a nice blanket picnicking spot, and also attracts anglers hoping to hook steelhead or Dolly Varden.

SKYKOMISH SCENIC RIVER RECREATION CORRIDOR

Fishing, rock climbing

AREA: 1,3771 acres; 2,600 feet of freshwater shoreline on the Skykomish River.
FACILITIES: None.

the lake leaves the end of the third switchback on the railroad grade at the 1.5-mile-point, and follows an abandoned road for 4.5 miles, joining the other route at the lake. The round trip, using either trail, is 12 miles.

CAR ACCESS: From US 2 take the Index–Galena road 1 mile to the northeast, then cross the bridge to the town of Index. In one block turn southwest on Index Avenue, which in 3 blocks bends south and becomes 2nd Street. At a T-intersection in a block turn southwest on Reiter Road (unmarked). In 0.6 mile look for a short, unmarked gravel road to a parking area on the north side of the road.

The impressive 1,200-foot granite cliffs of the Index Town Wall on the north side of the Skykomish River recently have been acquired by State Parks. The near-vertical Town Wall offers some of the state's most challenging rock climbing. The Lower Town Wall can be reached by crossing the railroad track above the parking area and following boot-beaten paths through forest to the base of the wall. More than 50 routes have been put up

this rock face, many rated between 5.11 and 5.13 (5.14 being the most difficult imaginable).

A gravel road parallel to the railroad track leads to an old quarry at the east side of the Lower Town Wall. Here, a steel door seals a 200-foot-long tunnel that was gnawed into the wall to test the machine that tunneled under the English Channel. The Upper Town Wall, the impressive granite face just above the town of Index, is reached by walking east along the railroad tracks to paths leading to its base, or picking up paths from Index. Some of the land between the railroad tracks and the wall is not public property.

Portions of state park property on the Skykomish River and its North Fork adjacent to the parking area provide fishing access to the river and an opportunity for primitive camping. Use care not to trespass on private property.

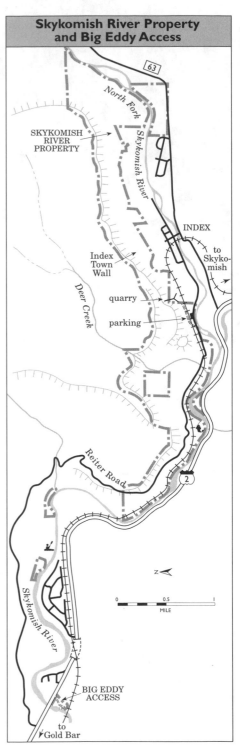

The Index Town Wall, part of recently acquired state park property, has long been a favorite rock climbing area.

CHAPTER FIVE

SOUTH PUGET SOUND

KITSAP MEMORIAL STATE PARK

Camping, picnicking, volleyball, hiking, shellfish, fishing, boating, paddling

SEASON/HOURS: Year-round.

AREA: 57.63 acres; 1,797 feet of saltwater shoreline on Hood Canal.

OVERNIGHT AND DAY-USE FACILITIES: 18 RV sites, 24 standard campsites (EW), group camp with 2 adirondack shelters (32 persons), 20 picnic sites, group day-use area with picnic shelter (75 persons), reservable community hall (200 persons), 2 restrooms (1 with showers) (&), 2 toilets, trailer dump station.

RECREATIONAL FACILITIES: 1 mile of hiking trail, playfields, children's play area, horseshoe pits, volleyball court, 1 mooring buoy.

CAR ACCESS: *From Kingston,* take SR 104 west to Port Gamble, then SR 3 south to the park; the distance is 11.5 miles.

From Bainbridge Island, take SR 305 north to its intersection with SR 3 west of Poulsbo, then SR 3 north to the park; the distance from Winslow is 16.2 miles.

At a quiet anchorage from Penrose Point State Park, Mount Rainier rises above Carr Inlet.

A wooden staircase descends to the narrow beach at Kitsap Memorial State Park.

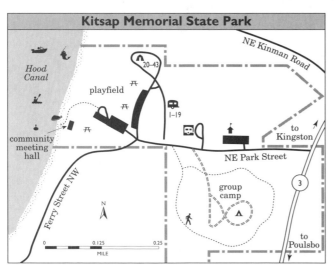

BOAT ACCESS: The park is on the east shore of Hood Canal, 3 miles south of the floating bridge. The nearest launch ramp is at Salisbury Point County Park.

Meadowlike playfields and a saltwater beach combine to make Kitsap Memorial one of the most popular day-use parks in the Bremerton/Poulsbo area. A large grass sports field and space for volleyball nets form the heart of the park. Half the park campsites, with hookups, are tightly packed along a strip of road east of this field; the remainder lie on a wooded loop to the north. An evergreen-shaded picnic shelter and several tables are scattered on the bluff above the beach, with views out to Hood Canal.

A short hiking trail that circles the group camp on the south side of the park leads through second-growth timber. Holes bored high in tree trunks bear evidence of bug-hungry flickers and pileated woodpeckers; listen for their noisy drilling.

A short path drops from the picnic area down the low bluff to the water. The beach, merely a thin strip of sand at high tide, is mostly barnacle-encrusted rock and cobble when exposed at lower water. While the rocky beach makes for difficult clam digging, the tidelands might reward explorers with close encounters with marine life such as starfish, mussels, tiny crabs, chitons, limpets, and an occasional oyster. Look, but don't disturb inedible forms; oysters are fair game for gourmets if current regulations permit.

The park's single mooring buoy is exposed to wind and tidal currents, which can cause a bumpy overnight stay for boaters.

SCENIC BEACH STATE PARK

Camping, picnicking, hiking, scuba diving, beach walking, shellfish, fishing, boating, paddling

SEASON/HOURS: Day-use year-round, campground closed September 30 through April 1; campsite reservations accepted in summer.

AREA: 88.24 acres; 1,487 feet of saltwater shoreline on Hood Canal.

OVERNIGHT AND DAY-USE FACILITIES: 52 standard campsites, group camp (48 persons), 56 picnic sites (2 &), kitchen shelter, fire braziers, group day-use area (100 persons), Emel House community center and Heritage Place (50 persons), gazebo, 3 restrooms (2 with showers) (&), bathhouse (&), toilet, trailer dump station.

RECREATIONAL FACILITIES: Walking paths (&), horseshoe pits, 2 volleyball courts, 2 children's play areas.

EDUCATIONAL FACILITIES: Recreation of historic log cabin, interpretive displays.

CAR ACCESS: From Bremerton, take SR 3 north for 4.6 miles to the Newberry Hill Road/Silverdale exit. Head west on Newberry Hill Road, which joins Seabeck Highway NW in 3 miles. Follow this highway south 4.4 miles to Seabeck, and in 0.7 mile turn west on Miami Beach Road NW. At a Y-intersection in 0.8 mile, turn southwest on Scenic Beach Road NW to reach the park in another 0.4 mile.

A Maytime profusion of pink native rhododendron blossoms makes Scenic Beach a favorite spring destination. At other times of the year, the picturesque setting on Hood Canal, with views across the water to the glacier-carved valleys of the Dosewallips and Duckabush Rivers and up to white Olympic peaks, provides ample reason to visit the park.

The western portion of this scenic site earned early favor as a private resort. Following the death of the resort owner, Joe Emel, Sr., the land became a state park. The Emel home is currently used as a community center and heritage place. The charming grounds, with orchards, a rustic bridge over a creek, and an attractive little gazebo, have adapted nicely to state park life. The eastern portion of the park was used by the Campfire Girls for a number of years.

Douglas-fir, western red cedar, and western hemlock soar skyward in stands of a dense, 100-year-old forest that rims the roads and campsites. These conifers, along with maple and alder, host an array of birds. Pileated woodpeckers, Steller's jays, juncos, towhees, and wrens are but a few that might be spotted. A short trail connecting the campground loops to the beach leads through the lush growth of salal, rhododendron, Oregon grape, and huckleberry that screens the campsites.

The park's eastern day-use area, set in open timber, has picnic sites, play equipment, a volleyball court, horseshoe pits, and a bathhouse. Below a short, steep

At Scenic Beach State Park wild native rhododendrons decorate a picnic site.

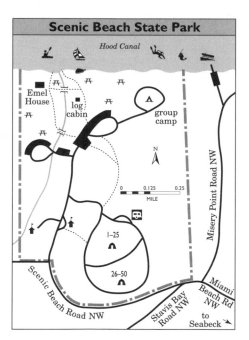

bank, the cobble beach drops gently into Hood Canal. On the west edge of this picnic area is a recreation of a one-room cabin built on the property in 1936 by Emel's sixteen-year-old son.

TWANOH STATE PARK

Camping, picnicking, hiking, swimming, waterskiing, fishing, boating

SEASON/HOURS: Closed November 1 through April 30.
AREA: 182.02 acres; 3,167 feet of saltwater shoreline on Hood Canal.

OVERNIGHT AND DAY-USE FACILITIES: 22 RV sites (&), 17 standard campsites (&), group camp (40 persons), 8 primitive campsites, 111 picnic sites, fireplaces, 5 kitchen shelters (1 reservable), group day-use area (150 persons), 4 restrooms (1 with showers) (&), bathhouse with outside shower (&), marine pumpout station.
RECREATIONAL FACILITIES: 2 miles of hiking trails, tennis court, horseshoe pits, swimming beach, wading pool, dock with float (192 feet of float space), 2-lane boat ramp with boarding floats, 7 mooring buoys.
CONCESSIONS: Food, beverages, firewood.
CAR ACCESS: Take SR 304 southwest out of Bremerton to its junction with SR 3.

Continue west on SR 3 for 9 miles to Belfair. Just west of Belfair follow SR 106 southwest for 7.7 miles to the park.

BOAT ACCESS: The park is on the southeast shore of Hood Canal, 6 miles east of Union.

Twanoh State Park straddles SR 106 midway along the 10-mile-long "Great Bend" of Hood Canal. The campground and hiking trails are found in the forested area south of the road, while the beach and day-use facilities lie on the road's north side.

A launch ramp and parking space for cars and boat trailers occupy the west end of the beach. To the east, across Twanoh Creek, the main day-use area fills a lawn where huge old fir and cedar trees shade

The picnic area at Twanoh State Park is shaded by giant old evergreens.

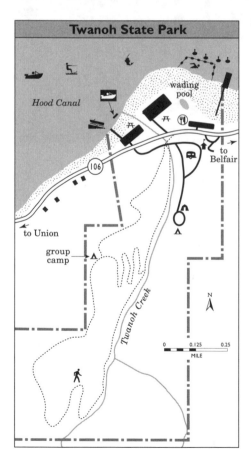

picnic tables, fire braziers, and kitchen shelters. East of here, a dock with floats that extends into Hood Canal is used both for fishing and boat access to the park; mooring buoys are near the float.

When summer sun warms the water to an inviting level, bathers flock to the park's broad sand and gravel beach. For small fry, a shallow wading pond lies in the gravel of the upper beach. A nearby bathhouse and a concession stand are open during summer months.

The camping area has a trailer hook-up loop around a small tree-shaded flat and a smaller tent-camping loop farther up the narrowing gulch that holds Twanoh Creek. The sturdy rustic restrooms here, as well as most of the buildings in the day-use area, were constructed between 1936 and 1937 by the Depression-era CCC. A display in the picnic area describes the park activities of the CCC.

The park extends far inland up the green gully of Twanoh Creek. Several miles of trails lace this wooded section; one leg of a trail loop follows the creek bank uphill, cutting through typical moist-forest growth of devil's club, moss, and wispy ferns. Near the park's southern boundary, the trail switchbacks upward to an open huckleberry-covered hilltop, skirts the western edge of the park, and then drops down a ridge through second-growth cedar to rejoin its start point. Halfway through the loop, a shortcut switchbacks steeply from hilltop to creek-bed through fir and hemlock forest. The park was logged in the 1890s; observant hikers might spot springboard notches in old cedar stumps.

BELFAIR STATE PARK

Camping, picnicking, swimming, kite flying, beach walking, crabbing, fishing

SEASON/HOURS: Year-round; campsite reservations accepted in summer.

AREA: 62.77 acres; 3,720 feet of saltwater shoreline on Hood Canal.

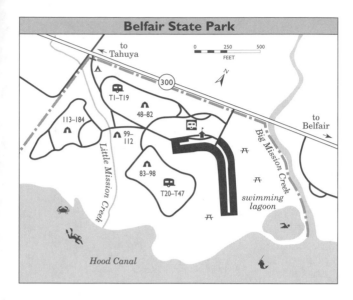

Belfair State Park

The lagoon at Belfair State Park has water warm enough for wading.

OVERNIGHT AND DAY-USE FACILITIES: 47 RV sites (2 ♿), 137 standard campsites (1 ♿), 3 primitive campsites, 205 picnic tables (2 ♿), picnic shelter, 4 restrooms (showers, 2 ♿), trailer dump station, children's play area, horseshoe pits, swimming beach, bathhouse (♿).
EDUCATIONAL FACILITIES: Interpretive display.
CAR ACCESS: Follow SR 304 southwest out of Bremerton to its junction with SR 3. Continue west on SR 3 to Belfair and SR 300. Follow SR 300 north, then southwest for 3 miles to the park.

When the Skokomish tribe of long ago chose this spot near the tip of the "hook" of Hood Canal as a campsite, they were undoubtedly drawn here by the shallow, clam-filled tideflats. Although today the clams and oysters are victims of pollution, and the shores are lined with homes, the site is still a magnet for people eager to enjoy the warm, placid water and pleasant camping it offers. Since the park's "beach" becomes a mudflat at the slightest hint of a low tide, a unique swimming area has been created: a gravel-rimmed pool, large enough for several dozen paddlers, that is separated from the canal by a rock dike. A tide-gate controls the water level of the lagoon.

The tough, wind-blown beach grass along the shore gives way to a manicured meadow. Three camping loops, two of which have trailer hookups, lie along the west side of the park. The newest of these sits in a grassy flat broken up with planted evergreen and deciduous trees. A more secluded loop for tent camping lies on the west side of Little Mission Creek, surrounded by a stand of Douglas-fir, red cedar, and alder, with a scattering of native rhododendrons.

The park and offshore waters are home or way station for squadrons of ducks, geese, and great blue herons. Eagles drop by occasionally. In mid-October to mid-November chum salmon spawn in both creeks. Crabs that are caught are safe for consumption, but pollution makes clams and oysters found on the mudflat unsafe to eat.

JARRELL COVE STATE PARK

Camping, picnicking, birdwatching, hiking, shellfish, fishing, boating, paddling

SEASON/HOURS: Year-round.
AREA: 42.62 acres; 3,506 feet of saltwater shoreline on Pickering Passage.
OVERNIGHT AND DAY-USE FACILITIES: 21 standard campsites (♿), group camp (64 persons), Cascadia Marine Trail campsite, 17 picnic sites, 2 reservable picnic shelters, restroom (showers), marine pumpout station.

RECREATIONAL FACILITIES: 1 mile of hiking trails, 2 docks with floats, 14 mooring buoys.
CAR ACCESS: From SR 3, 7 miles north of Shelton, take Pickering Road southeast to Harstine Island. After crossing the bridge onto the island, turn north on East North Island Drive, and in 3.5 miles, at East Wingert Road, bear north on a dirt road to reach the park in another 0.8 mile.
BOAT ACCESS: The park is at Jarrell Cove on the north side of Harstine Island, 2 miles southwest of Dougall Point. Nearest launch ramps are at Harstine Island Bridge, Fair Harbor, and Joemma Beach State Park.

Because of the remoteness of Harstine Island by road, boaters are the primary visitors to Jarrell Cove, and it is considered by the state to be a marine park. The park's natural attractions are best accessed from the water, and most of

111

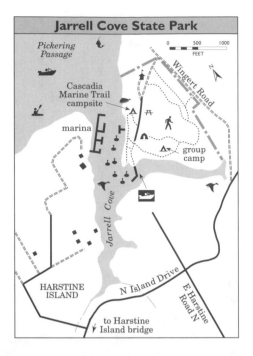

Jarrell Cove State Park

Pickering Passage

Cascadia Marine Trail campsite

marina

Wingert Road

group camp

Jarrell Cove

HARSTINE ISLAND

N Island Drive

E Harstine Road N

to Harstine Island bridge

its facilities are boater-oriented. The passage into this narrow inlet is squeezed between a private marina on the west and a park dock and float on the east. Exercise caution if using this float, as it rests on the mud at extreme minus tides. The remainder of the cove is filled with park mooring buoys; all have at least 10 feet of water below at lowest tide levels. Another longer dock with float is at the southwest tip of the park, filling most of the entrance to a smaller side inlet.

This side cove to the east is interesting for paddle exploration. At high tide trees, brush, and vines press to water's edge along many tiny fingers and coves, giving the place an Everglades feeling. Retreat with the water as the tide goes out, for this enchanting little water passage soon transforms to a gooey mudflat. Look for residents of a heron rookery in the vicinity. Short trails from the camp area push through the brush on the bank above the finger cove. Water access from them is

limited, and the beach is steep, slick, and muddy at low tide.

Campsites laid out along a short trail just above the entrance dock offer boaters the option of sleeping ashore. A Cascadia Marine Trail campsite is at the north of this trail. The main camping area in the center of the park is a large, open meadow with few well-defined campsites; pick a convenient chunk of grass and that becomes your turf.

HOPE ISLAND MARINE STATE PARK

Camping, picnicking, beach walking, hiking, boating, paddling, fishing

SEASON/HOURS: Year-round.
AREA: 106.11 acres; 8,541 feet of saltwater shoreline on Squaxin Passage.
OVERNIGHT AND DAY-USE FACILITIES: 4 standard campsites, Cascadia Marine Trail campsite, 4 picnic sites, 2 toilets (*not open to fires, no pets allowed on the island*).
RECREATIONAL FACILITIES: 1.5 miles of hiking trail, 5 mooring buoys.
BOAT ACCESS: Hope Island lies at the confluence of Totten Inlet, Hammersley Inlet, and Pickering Passage. Nearest launch ramps are at Arcadia and Boston Harbor.

This heavily forested island had been owned by a Tacoma family for 80 years, and was first sold by their estate to a developer who planned to divide it into housing lots. Just in time the state managed to buy the entire island, the last remaining undeveloped island in south Puget Sound. An information kiosk displays historic photos of the island's past, and describes old farm equipment that sits nearby. The caretaker's house and toilets have been designed to match the architecture of the historic cabins that once made up the farm.

This mooring dock at Jarrell Cove State Park is immediately across from the cove's commercial marina.

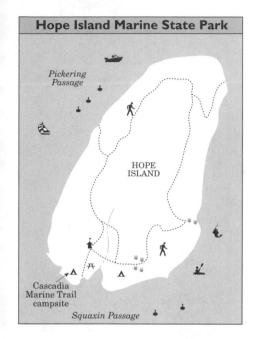

Hope Island Marine State Park

Developments include three mooring buoys on the northwest side of the island and two more on the southeast corner. Campsites on the south side of the island are near an old vineyard, where forearm-

thick grape vines twist around tree trunks. Picnic sites and a Cascadia Marine Trail site have been added on the southwest portion of the island near the old farm. More campsites and a group camp are planned.

An informal trail, beaten out years ago by two resident horses, circles the perimeter of the island at the top of the flat wooded bench forming the interior. Spurs from this trail reach the beach midway up the west side of the island, and at two spots on the eastern shoreline.

STRETCH POINT MARINE STATE PARK

Picnicking, beach walking, shellfish, fishing, boating

SEASON/HOURS: Year-round.
AREA: 4.2 acres; 610 feet of saltwater shoreline on Case Inlet.
RECREATIONAL FACILITIES: 5 mooring buoys (*no water, no toilets, no camping or open fires*).

BOAT ACCESS: On the northeast point of Stretch Island on the west side of Case Inlet. Nearest launch ramps are at Fair Harbor and Vaughn.

Although Stretch Island itself is accessible by a bridge from the mainland, private property blocks any upland approach to the state park at its northeast tip. For those who can reach the park via water, mooring buoys have been placed along the perimeter; the beach drops off so steeply that they seem only a step away from shore.

The beach is gloriously smooth sand, with possibilities for clams at low tide. There is no garbage pickup, so please be considerate of the visitors following you— keep it clean and pack out garbage.

HALEY PROPERTY

Picnicking, beach walking, shellfish, fishing, boating

AREA: 177.91 acres; 1,980 feet of saltwater shoreline on Case Inlet.
FACILITIES: Cascadia Marine Trail campsite, toilet.
BOAT ACCESS: The property is on Case Inlet north of Herron Island and due east of Dougall Point on Harstine Island. Nearest launch ramps are at Vaughn Bay, Grapeview, and Joemma Beach State Park.

This property, acquired from the Haley of Brown and Haley candy fame, was once the subject of elaborate park development plans, but objections from neighboring property owners and the inability to obtain a land access easement brought this effort to a halt. The only overnight use is at a Cascadia Marine Trail campsite. The property includes steep, forested hillsides inland that once surrounded a manmade lagoon created by damming a creek that runs through the north side of the property. An earthquake fractured

Kayakers land at Hope Island Marine State Park.

113

the dam and drained the lagoon. A flat, bare strip of land now separates the former lagoon from the shore of Case Inlet. At low tide clams can be harvested on a wide, gently sloping gravel beach that fronts the property on Case Inlet.

HARSTINE ISLAND STATE PARK

Hiking, beach walking, shellfish

SEASON/HOURS: Year-round.
AREA: 310 acres; 3,100 feet of saltwater shoreline on Case Inlet.
DAY-USE FACILITIES: 4 picnic tables (*no water, no toilets, no camping or open fires*).
RECREATIONAL FACILITIES: 1 mile of hiking trail.
CAR ACCESS: From the Harstine Island bridge, drive north on East North Island Drive for 3.2 miles to the intersection with East Harstine Island Road North. Here turn south, and in 1 mile turn east on East Yates Road. Follow this single-lane gravel road for 1 mile, and at a Y-intersection turn right to reach the trailhead parking in 0.3 mile.

At Harstine Island State Park, rustic railing edges the trail as it descends through forest to the beach.

With the exception of a small section of old-growth Douglas-fir, most of the uplands of this property was clearcut when it was owned by the DNR; however, alder and second-growth fir are starting to erase signs of the logging. The attraction here is not the uplands, but the nice hike down to the beach, and the beach itself.

Two trails lead from the gravel parking area. A graveled trail heads south from the parking area across a flat for 0.25 mile, passing picnic sites along the way, to the head of a canyonlike drainage. Here the trail drops steeply down the 100-foot-high forested bank, with steeper sections aided by log stairsteps. A few rustic benches are provided along the way for rest stops on the uphill drag.

A newer trail leaves the east side of the parking lot and wanders through thick second-growth fir, taking a longer and more gentle grade down the steep bank, then joins the old trail about 200 yards above the beach.

The trail breaks out onto the gravel beach on Case Inlet, between McMicken Island and the point north of it. The gently sloping beach has clams that may be harvested at low tide. An additional 3,100 feet of

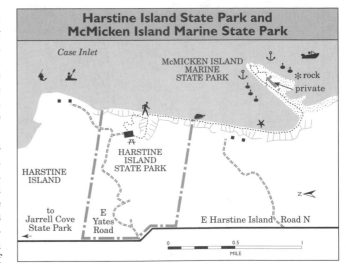

Harstine Island State Park and McMicken Island Marine State Park

DNR tidelands run south from the state park boundary, and at minus tides these muddy tideflats can be walked to a drying sandbar off the east side of McMicken Island for land access to that park.

McMICKEN ISLAND MARINE STATE PARK

Picnicking, beach walking, hiking, swimming, shellfish, fishing, boating, paddling

SEASON/HOURS: Year-round.
AREA: 11.45 acres; 1,661 feet of saltwater shoreline on Case Inlet.
RECREATIONAL FACILITIES: 2 toilets (*no water*), 5 mooring buoys (*no camping or open fires*).
CAR ACCESS: At minus tides walk the beach south 1 mile from Harstine Island State Park and cross on a sandbar.
BOAT ACCESS: McMicken Island is on Case Inlet off the east side of Harstine Island. Nearest launch ramps are at Joemma Beach State Park, Fair Harbor, and Johnson Point.

This small island is an excellent place to get off the boat and stretch your legs with a short hike around its perimeter. Trails lead through brush and second-growth forest (*and also poison oak—be careful!*). On the south end of the island, a fenced-in area with a cabin and sheds is private property.

The beaches along the north, east, and south sides of the island are cobble with boulders below vertical rocky banks. To the west a sandspit emerges at low tide to link McMicken to Harstine Island. When exposed, the sandy beach affords good clamming, and the shallow waters are warm enough for wading or swimming.

Mooring buoys lie on both the north and south sides of the island; nearby is ample additional room to anchor in good holding ground. Boaters should remember the drying spit and avoid passing west of the island, even at high tide. A large boulder on the southeast side of the island is barely covered at high tide.

JOEMMA BEACH STATE PARK

Camping, picnicking, beach walking, hiking, shellfish, crabbing, fishing, boating, paddling

SEASON/HOURS: Year-round.
AREA: 122 acres; 3,000 feet of saltwater shoreline on Case Inlet.
OVERNIGHT AND DAY-USE FACILITIES: 19 standard campsites, 2 primitive campsites, 2 Cascadia Marine Trail campsites, 7 picnic tables, picnic shelter (&), 5 toilets (&).
RECREATIONAL FACILITIES: 0.5 mile of hiking trail, boat ramp, dock (&) with floats (500 feet of float space, *removed in winter*), 5 mooring buoys.
CAR ACCESS: Follow the Key Peninsula Highway southwest from Key Center to a Y-intersection 1.5 miles south of Home. Here bear southwest

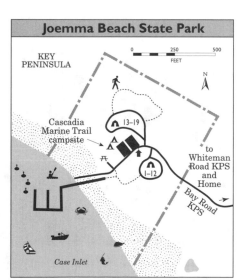

on Whiteman Road KPS, and follow it for 2.3 miles to Bay Road KPS, signed to the park. Head west on Bay Road to reach the park in 0.8 mile.
BOAT ACCESS: The park is on the east side of Case Inlet just north of Whiteman Cove.

A crab trap set at Joemma Beach State Park yields a tasty red rock crab.

Glacial till bluffs edging Case Inlet weather away to create the wide beach at Joemma Beach State Park. This property, which some may remember as the rustic DNR Robert F. Kennedy Recreational Area, was beautifully refurbished and then turned over to state parks. It was renamed for Joe and Emma Smith, who lived here from 1917 to 1932.

The park's two standard campground loops sit high on the hillside above the beach. One loop has sites around the perimeter of a small wooded knoll, while the second loop encloses a grass slope sprinkled with second-growth fir. A short hiking trail wends through second-growth above the lower campground.

Joemma Beach State Park

KEY PENINSULA

0   250   500
FEET

N

Cascadia Marine Trail campsite

13–19

1–12

to Whiteman Road KPS and Home

Bay Road KPS

Case Inlet

Below the parking area at the heart of the park, a grass embankment shaded by 100-foot-high trees slopes down to the bank above Case Inlet. Here are a pair of primitive campsites and a pair of Cascadia Marine Trail campsites. The bluff is breached by a single-lane concrete launch ramp that drops down to the cobble and gravel. A pier with small bays for fishing and crabbing stretches out to a ramp leading down to a series of floats. Buoys provide additional moorage space at the popular park.

PENROSE POINT STATE PARK

Camping, picnicking, beach walking, hiking, swimming, shellfish, fishing, boating, paddling

SEASON/HOURS: Closed October 1 through March 31; campsite reservations accepted in summer.

AREA: 152.1 acres; 11,751 feet of saltwater shoreline on Carr Inlet.

OVERNIGHT AND DAY-USE FACILITIES: 83 standard campsites, group camp with picnic shelter (50 persons), 90 picnic sites, 2 picnic shelters, 4 restrooms (2 with showers) (3 ♿), trailer dump station.

RECREATIONAL FACILITIES: 2.5 miles of hiking trails, nature trail, horseshoe pits, floats (304 feet of float space), 8 mooring buoys.

CAR ACCESS: From SR 16, 2.5 miles north of Gig Harbor, take the SR 302 exit, marked to Purdy and Key Peninsula. Follow SR 302 and the Key Peninsula Highway south for 14.7 miles (1.4 miles south of Home), then turn east on Cornwall Road KPS. In 0.4 mile, at Lakebay, turn south on Delano Road KPS, and in 1 mile, at its junction with 158th Avenue KPS, turn north to reach the park in 0.3 mile.

BOAT ACCESS: On the west shore of Carr

Inlet at Mayo Cove. The nearest launch ramps are at Mayo Cove and Von Geldern Cove.

Whether you arrive by land or water, this beautiful park on the south shore of tiny Mayo Cove will appeal to you. Penrose Point State Park provides a nice balance of wheel vs. rudder facilities, and its long, slender peninsular end gives it far more shoreline than land-based parks usually enjoy.

Camping is along a maze of timbered circles at the west side of the park above the dock area. The park entrance road Ts above the beach; the west arm goes to parking above the dock and picnic areas on the bluff above the beach; the east arm leads to the group camp and day-use areas. A large, open lawn with picnic tables along the perimeter was once a swamp that was filled and groomed to its present meadowy state.

Several short trails lace the timbered strip above the Mayo Cove beach. A 0.25-mile nature loop that leaves the day-use parking lot introduces walkers to maple, hemlock, fir, and ferns, as well as a variety of birds, insects, and other small forest critters. A longer trail, with several

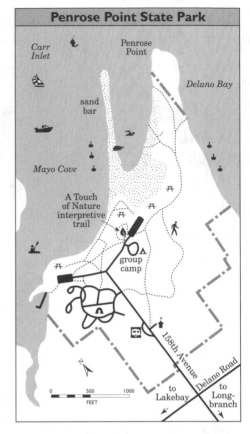

A long sandbar, revealed at low tide, offers good digging for butter and littleneck clams at Penrose Point State Park.

indistinct side spurs, heads through forest to the beach on the east side of the point; still another heads uphill from the day-use area, eventually splitting into forks leading to various points around the park.

At the west end of the park, near the head of the cove, a flat finger of land protects a small basin with a dock and a 90-foot float. Boaters need to enter the cove cautiously at low tide, as the entrance becomes choked between this protecting finger and a sandspit protruding from the north.

Mooring buoys are also provided off the north and east sides of Penrose Point. Those to the north seem far offshore, but the reason becomes readily apparent at low tide, when a long sand and cobble spit emerges from the water to form a shallow, horseshoe-shaped cove below the day-use area. The drying spit offers hardscrabble clamming at low tide.

EAGLE ISLAND MARINE STATE PARK

Beach walking, shellfish, fishing, boating, paddling

SEASON/HOURS: Year-round.
AREA: 10 acres; 2,600 feet of saltwater shoreline on Balch Passage.
RECREATIONAL FACILITIES: 3 mooring buoys (*no water, no toilets, no camping or open fires*).
BOAT ACCESS: Eagle Island lies in Balch Passage between Anderson and McNeil Islands. Nearest launch ramps are at Steilacoom and Drayton Passage.

This minuscule island was named not for the bird, but for Harry Eagle, one of the party members of the Wilkes Expedition of 1841. No one notes whether Harry was as small in stature as his namesake island.

The park has no shoreside facilities. Sporadic tags of toilet tissue attest, un-

fortunately, to the lack of formal sanitary facilities (and the boorishness of some visitors). Inland, the island has a primitive trail through thick brush and madrona; short spurs lead to the beach. *Be wary of poison oak.* The narrow beach is mostly gravel, with the exception of a pleasant point of sand on the south end of the island near Anderson Island—a nice spot for sunbathing or clamming.

Three mooring buoys are set off the south side of the island in 15 feet of water. Take care to avoid a submerged reef off the west side of the island that is marked by a navigation buoy at its north end. This, and the nearby island beach, are favorite haul-out sites for harbor seals.

KOPACHUCK STATE PARK

Camping, picnicking, birdwatching, swimming, waterskiing, scuba diving, beach walking, shellfish, fishing, boating, paddling

SEASON/HOURS: Year-round; campground closed October 1 through March 31.
AREA: 107.7 acres; 3,500 feet of saltwater shoreline on Carr Inlet.
OVERNIGHT AND DAY-USE FACILITIES: 41 standard campsites (占), 2 primitive group camps with picnic shelters, Cascadia Marine Trail campsite, 79 picnic sites, 3 picnic shelters, 3 restrooms (2 with showers) (占), outdoor shower, trailer dump station.
RECREATIONAL FACILITIES: Hiking trails, underwater marine park, 2 mooring buoys.
CAR ACCESS: From SR 16, 3.7 miles north of the Tacoma Narrows Bridge, take the exit marked Gig Harbor City Center, Rosedale, Kopachuck State Park. Head southwest on Wollochet Drive NW, and in 0.6 mile bear west on Hunt Street NW, then in 1 block turn north on 46th Avenue/Skansie Ave NW. Con-

tinue north for 1 mile, and turn west on Rosedale Street NW. In 2.4 miles turn south on Ray Nash Drive NW, and in 0.7 mile continue straight ahead on Kopachuck Drive NW, to reach the park in another 1.7 miles.
BOAT ACCESS: The park is on the east shore of Carr Inlet, 2 miles north of Fox Island and just north of Horsehead Bay. The nearest launch ramp is at Horsehead Bay.

Kopachuck State Park derives its name from two words in the Chinook trade jargon of the Northwest Indians, *kopa* meaning "at," and *chuck* meaning "water." This was certainly an apt description, as the Puyallup and Nisqually tribes used the shoreside site for seasonal fishing and clamming.

The park's blunt, nose-shaped beach curves outward into Carr Inlet. The south

In spring trilliums bloom in profusion at Kopachuck State Park.

117

end is covered with cobbles and driftwood, while the north end, nearest the heart of the park, is gently sloping sand. This shallow sandy beach bares well out into the inlet at low tide, exposing an extensive foreshore for clamming. Shallow water also means warmer water, and in summer this is a favorite swimming and wading spot.

An old barge that was sunk offshore to create a reeflike shelter for fish and marine invertebrates is designated an underwater marine park. Scuba divers regularly explore this relatively easy dive site. Two mooring buoys bob offshore for visiting boaters' use.

Picnic sites are sprinkled along the

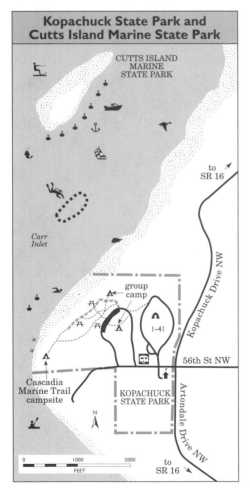

The bluffs of Cutts Island Marine State Park form a striking profile.

wooded hillside above the beach, as well as just above the shoreline where there are also two small picnic shelters. Trails to the beach lead down through the picnic area from either end of the parking lot. Cascadia Marine Trail campsites are found just above the beach at the extreme south end of the park. Car campsites lie in the upper wooded flat near the park entrance. Although heavy forest growth blocks all campsite views of the water and the Olympic Mountains, the greenery provides some privacy. Short, easy trails from the campground loop wend through salal, false Solomon's seal, and sword fern to the picnic area and beach.

CUTTS ISLAND MARINE STATE PARK

Beach walking, swimming, scuba diving, shellfish, fishing, boating, paddling

SEASON/HOURS: Year-round.
AREA: 5.5 acres; 2,100 feet of saltwater shoreline on Carr Inlet.
RECREATIONAL FACILITIES: Underwater marine park (shared with Kopachuck), 10 mooring buoys.
BOAT ACCESS: Cutts Island lies 0.2 mile west of Kopachuck State Park and is

a subsidiary of that park. Nearest launch ramps are at Horsehead Bay and Wauna; hand-carried boats can be launched from the beach at Kopachuck.

Cutts Island is a secluded "boaters-only" outpost of Kopachuck State Park. At low tide a sandbar nearly links it to nearby Raft Island. It is an easy paddle from the park, but use care in a heavily loaded boat or if the wind or tide is strong.

The island has enjoyed varied names. In 1792 it was named Crow Island by the Vancouver Expedition. The Wilkes Expedition of 1841 dubbed it Scotts Island after the expedition's quartermaster. Early settlers called it Deadmans Island, reflecting the native tribes' use of the island to inter their dead in canoes placed in trees. The source of its current name is a mystery.

At high tide the island has virtually no beach, and the barren clay cliffs at its north end rise 40 feet from the water's edge to a tuft of trees above, giving the island a unique appearance. Lower tide levels expose a cobble and boulder beach to the south and portions of the sandy bar to the north. Clams can be found here, but digging is pretty strenuous in the cobble areas. Ten mooring buoys lie around the island, but camping and fires are prohibited.

SALTWATER STATE PARK

Camping, picnicking, beach walking, hiking, swimming, scuba diving, fishing, boating, paddling

SEASON/HOURS: Year-round; campground closed September 30 to May 1.
AREA: 87.84 acres; 1,445 feet of saltwater shoreline on East Passage.
OVERNIGHT AND DAY-USE FACILITIES: 53 standard campsites (2 ♿), 2 primitive campsites, group camp with picnic shelter and fireplace (64 persons), 128 picnic tables, 2 picnic shelters (1 reservable) (♿), kitchen shelter, 30 barbecues, 4 restrooms (1 with showers) (3 ♿), 2 toilets, trailer dump station, outside shower.
RECREATIONAL FACILITIES: 2 miles of hiking trails, volleyball stanchions, horseshoe pits, children's play equipment, swimming beach, underwater marine park, 3 mooring buoys.
CONCESSIONS: (In summer) snacks, firewood, ice.
CAR ACCESS: Take Exit 149 (SR 516, Kent, Des Moines) west from I-5. At the first traffic light, turn south on Pacific Highway S, and in 0.6 mile turn west on S 240th Street. After 1.2 miles turn south on Marine View Drive (SR 509), and in 0.7 mile turn west on S 251st Street for 50 feet, then south on 8th Place S to reach the park in two blocks.
BOAT ACCESS: The park lies 2 miles south of the Des Moines Marina, the nearest launch site.

McSorley's Gulch might not be immediately recognized by its name, but most Puget Sound park-goers are quite familiar with the state park that surrounds this deep, forested ravine. Over three-quarters of a million people visit Saltwater every year, making it the most-used state park on Puget Sound. Most of the park activity centers on the beach, so hikers who seek out remote, shaded trails usually are still able to find some degree of solitude, even on busy weekends. On brisk winter days, visitors might find they are sharing the entire park with only a few other stalwart souls.

McSorley Creek trickles down the gulch to the shore. A road wends up the narrow gully past trailer camping spots to branch into two sets of tent camping sites, many fronting on the creek. The steep, wooded hillsides mask the noise of traffic on the bridge 200 feet above, giving the campground an unexpected degree of seclusion. A group camp sits high on the bluff at the northwest end of the park.

Just east of the park's concession stand,

A rock riprap bulkhead edges the path at Saltwater State Park.

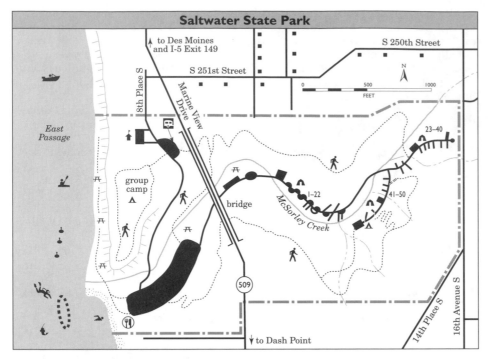

Saltwater State Park

The rock riprap bulkhead protecting the northern segment of the beach gives way to a tapering, sand-bottomed swimming beach, one of the best on all of Puget Sound. Little marine life remains on the heavily used beach; however, a sunken barge and old tires 50 feet offshore near the south edge of the park form an underwater reef that harbors marine life such as plumose anemone, nudibranchs, starfish, a plethora of fish, and even an occasional octopus. The site is a favorite for scuba divers. Mooring buoys north of the reef accommodate visiting boaters. Kayaks put in here can range north to Des Moines, south to Redondo and Dash Point, or shoot straight across East Passage to Maury Island, 5 miles away.

WEST HYLEBOS WETLANDS STATE PARK

Birdwatching, nature study, hiking

SEASON/HOURS: Year-round.
AREA: 58.36 acres.
DAY-USE FACILITIES: Picnic table, bicycle rack, informational kiosk, toilet.
RECREATIONAL FACILITIES: 1 mile of self-guided nature trail, mostly on boardwalks.
CAR ACCESS: From I-5, take Exit 142B (SR 299, Federal Way) 1.6 miles south of Federal Way, and head west on S 348th Street to Pacific Highway S, 0.2 mile. Continue west on S 348th for 0.8 mile, and watch for 4th Avenue S, a hard-to-spot, single-lane road to the south, just east of a power substation. Turn south onto 4th, and in 2 blocks turn east at a sign into a small gravel parking lot.

This small, natural enclave on the south edge of Federal Way contains one of the most thorough and enjoyable courses in botany, biology, and ecology to be found in the state. The creation of West

Sandy bottoms are not restricted to off-shore waters.

a 2-mile loop trail climbs a wooded ridge to the rim of the gulch. Bigleaf maple, Douglas-fir, hemlock, and cedar form a green canopy, and bright spatterings of wildflowers paint the trailside. The path continues high on the hill around the perimeter of the park, then drops down to the middle of the tent camping area. On the north side of the creek the path again climbs to the rim of the ravine and traces it westward to a branch; one leg heads uphill to the park entrance parking lot, while the other finally returns to the lower picnic meadow. The trails on the north side of the park are in better shape, receiving periodic maintenance from volunteer groups.

Picnic tables, restrooms, and a massive stone fire circle are scattered north along the grassy beach strip backed by a steep clay bluff. More picnic areas, including group shelters, are available in a meadow above the beach along the edge of McSorley Creek. Alcoholic beverages are prohibited in the day-use areas.

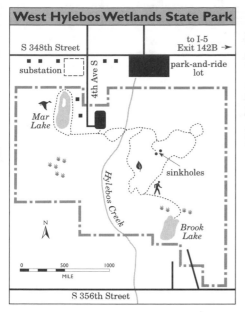

West Hylebos Wetlands State Park

S 348th Street

to I-5
Exit 142B →

substation

4th Ave S

park-and-ride lot

Mar Lake

Hylebos Creek

sinkholes

N

Brook Lake

0   500   1000
MILE

S 356th Street

The boardwalk detours around huge trees at West Hylebos State Park.

Hylebos Wetlands State Park and the 1-mile nature trail that it holds has been the ongoing project of Francis and Ilene Marckx, whose home adjoins it.

The nature trail leaves the parking lot and loops through a forest and bog at the headwaters of Hylebos Creek, most of it on a wood plank pathway. Signs on posts along the route identify the leaves and the fruit or flowers of more than 50 different plants. Other signposts explain natural phenomena such as wind-thrown trees and insect- and bird-ravaged logs. A trail spur leads to a brush-shrouded overlook of Brook Lake, and views of waterfowl that might be resting there.

Side platforms along the trail provide views of geological features: a pair of sink holes, a foot or so in diameter at the surface, but over 20 feet deep; glacial erratics; drumlins; and the sticky black sediments carried here by an ice sheet that covered the area more than 12,000 years ago. Along the trail, where tall trees have toppled, huge but shallow root systems tip up at right angles to the bog floor. In another section of the park are not only native flora, but "living fossils"— trees such as coast redwood, ginkgo, and

giant sequoia that have recently been planted here as examples of the forests that covered the region some 30 million years ago.

DASH POINT STATE PARK

Camping, picnicking, beach walking, hiking, swimming, scuba diving, marine life study, boating, paddling

SEASON/HOURS: Year-round; campsite reservations accepted in summer.

AREA: 397.63 acres; 3,251 feet of saltwater shoreline.

OVERNIGHT AND DAY-USE FACILITIES: 29 RV sites (EW), 109 standard campsites (♿), group camp (96 persons), 71 picnic sites, 2 picnic shelters (♿), fire pit, 5 restrooms (2 with showers) (2 ♿), outside shower, 4 toilets, trailer dump station.

RECREATIONAL FACILITIES: 7.4 miles of hiking trails.

CAR ACCESS: *From I-5 headed south,* take Exit 143 (Federal Way, S 320th

Street) and turn west on S 320th Street. In 4.8 miles turn north on 47th Avenue SW. After three blocks head west on SW Dash Point Road (SR 509) and follow it to the park entrance in 0.9 mile.

From I-5 headed north, take Exit 137 (Fife, Milton) and head north on 54th Avenue E (Valley Avenue), which becomes Taylor Way in 3.2 miles. Continue on Taylor Way to its intersection with 11th Street in 2.3 miles, then turn northeast on 11th Street. In 0.5 mile turn northwest on Marine View Drive (SR 509), which eventually becomes East Side Drive. Follow this road for 4 miles to the park.

The beach at Dash Point was a favorite with local beachcombers and fishermen long before 1958, when it and the first sections of forested upland were acquired for a state park. Key to the park's popularity is the gradual slope of the sandy beach, which at a minus tide bares out more than 2,000 feet, exposing some intertidal life for easy exploration. Check out a piece of seaweed for tiny mollusks and insects clinging to it, but leave all plants and sea creatures on the beach for the incoming tide. Gathering clams from the beach is unsafe due to pollution. The summer sun warms the shallow water, making it inviting for wading and swimming.

The park divides naturally into three distinct areas: the beach, a grassy, tree-shaded flat atop the bluff, and the wooded campground south of the highway. Picnic sites fill a hollow near the beach, and a group day-use area sits on the grassy plateau on top of the bluff. The group camp is separated from this upper picnic area by a slight ravine. The campground is in the south section of the park. One long camping loop holds some electric and water hookups; the remainder of this loop are standard campsites, as are those in a second loop. Most of the sites enjoy a good deal of individual seclusion amid second-growth forest and head-high brush.

A network of trails links all of the picnic areas and campsites to the beach. South of the campground, more than 6 additional miles of hiking trails meander

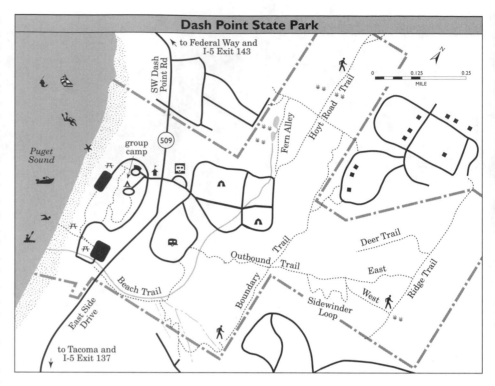

Dash Point State Park

through the dense forest of maple, fir, and alder, leading nowhere special but providing some intimate glimpses of woodland animals, plants, flowers, and fungi.

TOLMIE STATE PARK

Picnicking, nature displays, hiking, beach walking, scuba diving, shellfish, fishing, boating, historical displays

SEASON/HOURS: Year-round; closed Monday and Tuesday in winter.
AREA: 106.15 acres; 1,800 feet of saltwater shoreline on the Nisqually Reach.
DAY-USE FACILITIES: 42 picnic sites, 2 kitchen shelters, 2 restrooms (&), outside showers.
RECREATIONAL FACILITIES: 3.4 miles of

The wide beaches of Dash Point State Park are ideal for flying kites.

hiking trails, underwater park, 5 mooring buoys.

EDUCATIONAL FACILITIES: Interpretive stations.

CAR ACCESS: Take Exit 111 (Yelm, Marvin Road, SR 510) from I-5. Follow Marvin Road north for 3.8 miles to 56th NE; turn east on 56th, and in 0.5 mile turn north on Hill Road NE to reach the park entrance road in 0.3 mile.

BOAT ACCESS: The park is on the south side of Nisqually Reach, 0.5 mile west of the Nisqually delta. The nearest launch ramps are at Luhr Beach and Johnson Point.

At high tide the waters of south Puget Sound flood a small saltwater marsh hidden behind a beach-front gravel bar at Tolmie State Park. The freshwater flow from a creek and the twice-daily saline flux of the sound nurture plants such as eelgrass and pickleweed that thrive in this shallow, fragile habitat. Lugworms, ghost shrimp, and tiny, shrimplike amphipods burrow in the soft mud, feeding on detritus. Juvenile salmon hide from

Ferns edge the Tolmie State Park trail.

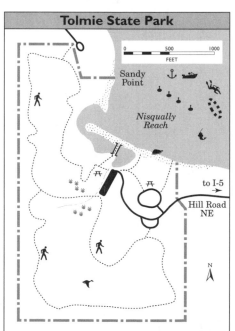

Tolmie State Park

Sandy Point

Nisqually Reach

to I-5 →

Hill Road NE

N

predators and bottom fish scavenge wastes that sink to the bottom. With the increasing press of urbanization in the Puget Sound area, unique saltwater marshes such as this are rapidly disappearing, much to the detriment of the region's ecology. Interpretive displays at the beach and the upper picnic area describe the evolution and ecology of the shoreline and the history of the park.

Day-use facilities offer pleasant spots for a family to spread the potato salad and fried chicken. One picnic area wraps around a circular road on the wooded bluff just inside the park entrance. A steep trail leads down a gully from here to the east end of the park beach. A second picnic area lies just above the beach. A scattering of trees offer shade.

A 2.5-mile-long loop trail that starts at the lower picnic area meanders through

the forest along the perimeter of the park. The trail rises and falls, but it is well maintained; marshy sections are bridged or planked over. Several log benches beside the trail invite a moment's rest and encourage one to stop and listen to the conversation of the forest: squirrels chattering, jays scolding, and unseen creatures chirping and rustling. Halfway through the loop a short-cut trail permits a quick return to the beach parking lot.

The beach tapers gently into Nisqually Reach, and minus tides reveal an expanse of sand for digging clams. Three wooden barges have been sunk below the lowest tide levels to form an artificial reef, attracting a variety of marine life including rockfish and cabezon. This underwater park is a favorite of novice scuba divers because the tidal current is minimal. West of the reef are a series of mooring buoys.

ILLAHEE STATE PARK

Camping, picnicking, hiking, swimming, waterskiing, scuba diving, beach walking, shellfish, crabbing, fishing, boating, paddling, historical display

SEASON/HOURS: Year-round.

AREA: 74.54 acres; 1,785 feet of saltwater shoreline on Port Orchard.

OVERNIGHT AND DAY-USE FACILITIES: 25 standard campsites (&), primitive group camp (40 persons), 88 picnic sites, fire braziers, 3 kitchen shelters, 2 reservable group day-use areas (50 and 75 persons), 4 restrooms (1 with showers) (&), outside shower, trailer dump station.

RECREATIONAL FACILITIES: Hiking trails, horseshoe pits, ball field, children's play equipment, boat ramp, dock with floats (356 feet of float space), 5 mooring buoys, historical naval guns.

CAR ACCESS: From Bremerton head north on SR 303 (Warren Avenue). Cross the Warren Avenue bridge, and in 0.8 mile turn east on SR 306 (NE Sylvan Way); reach the park in 1.6 miles.

BOAT ACCESS: The park is on the east side of Kitsap Peninsula on the south end of Port Orchard Bay.

Mooring buoys offshore from Illahee State Park provide a spot to tie up for a lunch break, a scuba diving exploration of underwater walls, or a visit to the park.

Although it sits in the backyard of Bremerton, Illahee State Park packs enough recreational goodies into its limited acreage that it can absorb the crowd from the nearby city and still have room for visiting folks. A steep, 250-foot-high bluff divides the park into two distinct areas: a wooded upland with camping and picnicking, and the beach with water and shore activities. Near the park entrance, kids enjoy clambering on two historic naval guns taken from World War I ships. A steep road takes several hairpin turns down the bluff between the two areas—this is not a road for large RVs or vehicles with trailers. For the strong-of-foot, a trail switchbacks through cedar, fir, and maple leading from the upland to the beach.

The tideland below the bluff becomes a wide, gently sloping sandy beach at low tide. A boat ramp dips steeply down to the water at the north end of the beach parking, although the steep road down the bluff doesn't encourage the hauling of large boat trailers. A dock with four floats, protected from northerly wind and waves by a concrete breakwater, is a popular fishing and sunbathing spot, as well as a park access point for boaters. Five mooring buoys offshore provide dock overflow capacity, and certainly a bit more solitude than the floats.

Port Orchard Bay extending from here north through Agate Passage is a favorite hangout for scuba divers. An enormous amount of marine life lives on the dock pilings and rocky walls of the channel. Divers must exercise care, due to the heavy boat traffic.

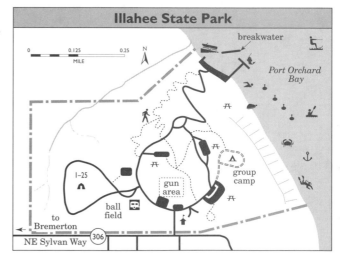

Illahee State Park

FAY-BAINBRIDGE STATE PARK

Camping, picnicking, hiking, scuba diving, beach walking, shellfish, fishing, boating, paddling, historical interpretation

SEASON/HOURS: Year-round, campground closed mid-October through April 1.

AREA: 16.84 acres; 1,420 feet of saltwater shoreline on Puget Sound.

OVERNIGHT AND DAY-USE FACILITIES: 26 standard campsites (&), 10 walk-in vehicle sites, Cascadia Marine Trail campsite, 80 picnic tables, 20 fireplaces, 4 beach fire rings, 3 kitchen shelters (one reservable), group day-use area (50 persons), 2 restrooms (1 with showers) (&), trailer dump station, children's play equipment, horseshoe pits, volleyball court, 2 mooring buoys.

EDUCATIONAL FACILITIES: Historical display, interpretive signs.

CAR ACCESS: From the Bainbridge Island ferry terminal, head northwest on SR 305 for 4.2 miles, then turn east on E Day Road, and in 1.2 miles north on Sunrise Drive. The park lies 1.8 miles to the north.

BOAT ACCESS: The park is immediately south of Point Monroe at the northeast tip of Bainbridge Island. Nearest boat ramps are at Shilshole Bay in Seattle and Suquamish.

A swath of sandy beach, cooling salt-air breezes, and a pleasant campground make Fay-Bainbridge State Park a hit with visitors. This is the only park on the island that has camping, so it is usually crowded in the summer. The park's hyphenated name commemorates both the original property owner, Dr. Temple S. Fay, and the park location, Bainbridge Island.

The large bell near the park entrance was purchased in San Francisco in 1883 by the citizens of the community of Port Madison, and was to be placed in the school belfry to ring out on important events. Plans went awry, however, and over time the bell was moved to a number of sites on the island, for various uses. Eventually the much-traveled bell found its current (and hopefully final) home here at the state park.

The grassy, tree-shaded uplands of the park, reserved for picnicking and tent camping, are not usually as crowded as the more popular beach strip. At the beach, campsites cram one side of the beach road elbow-to-elbow. Fire rings, horseshoe pits, volleyball posts, and a children's play area are scattered along the open sandy beachfront. A pair of tent pads and a picnic table near the driftwood line at the south end of the park mark a Cascadia Marine Trail site.

Two mooring buoys offshore, unprotected from the wind and waves of the sound, offer a bouncy stay for visiting boaters. Paddlers who put in at the park can roam north around Point Monroe and into the shallow tideflat created by the long, hooking sandspit.

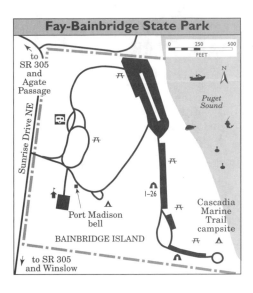

Two offshore buoys at Fay-Bainbridge State Park are handy for a quick stop, but are a bit unprotected for overnight stays.

FORT WARD STATE PARK

Primitive camping, picnicking, birdwatching, hiking, bicycling, scuba diving, beach walking, shellfish, crabbing, fishing, boating, historic Coast Artillery battery emplacements

SEASON/HOURS: Year-round, upper day-use area closed in winter.

AREA: 137.1 acres; 4,300 feet of saltwater shoreline on Rich Passage.

OVERNIGHT AND DAY-USE FACILITIES: Cascadia Marine Trail campsite, 17 picnic tables, 2 bird blinds, 6 toilets (&).

RECREATIONAL FACILITIES: 2.5 miles of hiking trails, underwater park, 2-lane boat ramp, 2 mooring buoys.

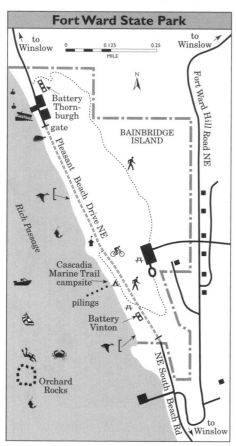

The remains of World War I Battery Vinton can be seen from the beach road at Fort Ward State Park.

EDUCATIONAL FACILITIES: Historic gun batteries, interpretive displays.

CAR ACCESS: From the Bainbridge Island ferry terminal, turn west on Winslow Way E, north on Madison Avenue, then west on Wyatt Way NW, and follow it to the west end of Eagle Harbor, where it becomes NE Eagle Harbor Road. At a Y-intersection in 0.2 mile, continue south on NE Blakely Avenue. At a Y-intersection in another 1.9 miles, each fork leads to a different entrance to the park.

To reach the south entrances, continue southeast on NE Blakely Avenue for 0.7 mile, then head southeast on NE Country Club Road. In another 0.2 mile turn south on Fort Ward Hill Road NE to reach the upper park entrance at 0.9 mile. For the south beach entrance, continue south on Fort Ward Hill Road NE for another 0.6 mile to NE South Beach Road, then head northwest on it for 0.2 mile to a residence turnaround loop at the park boundary.

To reach the northwest entrance, from the Y-intersection of NE Blakely Avenue and W Blakely Avenue NE, take the latter south for 0.4 mile to a T-intersection with Pleasant Beach Drive NE. Here head west to reach the park in 0.4 mile.

BOAT ACCESS: The park is on the north side of Rich Passage, just west of Beans Point.

Fort Ward and Manchester, its companion site across Rich Passage, are vestiges of a coastal defense system from the early 1900s designed to protect the Bremerton Naval Shipyard in the advent of war. The fort's armament consisted of an 8-inch gun battery, a 5-inch gun battery, and two 3-inch gun batteries. The guns were all removed in the 1920s. During World War II, the site controlled submarine nets that stretched across Rich Passage. After being deactivated, a portion of the old fort was acquired for a state park. The only evidence of its military legacy are the moldering remains of the batteries. Many of the old buildings from the fort are now private residences.

In the upland portion of the park, off Fort Ward Hill Road, wooded picnic sites surround a parking lot. Trails drop from here to the shore. The paved path at the south end of the parking area leads down to the beach-front road, emerging near the south end of the park beach by Battery Vinton. From the north end of the parking lot, a dirt trail wends along the park boundary through a greenwood of ferns, ivy, maple, and firs, before descending a small ridge to reach the beach road near the remains of Battery Thornburgh, at the north end of the park. *Do not wander off the trail, as there is poison oak in the undergrowth.*

The beach road running through the park is open only to foot traffic and bicycles; parking is available at the northwest beach entrance to the park. A paved launch ramp and two mooring buoys are found here. Because the buoys are exposed to wind, tide, and the wakes of passing boats and ferries, they tend to be bouncy moorages. The area offshore is designated as an underwater park. Scuba divers explore the steep walls along Rich Passage and the undersea crannies of Orchard Rocks, just to the south. It is a long swim from shore to Orchard Rocks, so boat transportation is recommended. Dive with care, as boat traffic is heavy in the area and the current is strong.

Picnic sites and a Cascadia Marine Trail campsite are found near the south end of the beach, adjacent to Battery Vinton. Elsewhere along the road, short tracks penetrate the dense cover of nettles, brush, and Scotch broom, leading to bird blinds overlooking the beach. Watch for ducks, geese, coots, cormorants, and other waterfowl.

MANCHESTER STATE PARK

Camping, picnicking, hiking, swimming, scuba diving, fishing, boating, paddling, historic displays

SEASON/HOURS: Year-round; campsite reservations accepted in summer.

AREA: 111.17 acres; 3,400 feet of saltwater shoreline on Rich Passage.

OVERNIGHT AND DAY-USE FACILITIES: 15 RV sites (EW; ♿), 35 standard campsites (♿), group camp with 12 RV sites (EW) and a picnic shelter (130 persons), 3 primitive campsites, 2 Cascadia Marine Trail campsites, 30 picnic sites, 2 picnic shelters, group day-use area (150 persons), 3 restrooms with showers (♿), bathhouse (♿), trailer dump station.

RECREATIONAL FACILITIES: Hiking trails, nature trail, horseshoe pits, volleyball court.

EDUCATIONAL FACILITIES: Historic Coast Artillery mine control, torpedo warehouse, and gun battery emplacement.

CAR ACCESS: *From Bremerton,* follow SR 304 west until it joins SR 3 southwest of the city, then continue on SR 3 to its junction with SR 16. Follow SR 16 and then SR 160 to Port Orchard. Turn onto Bay Avenue, which becomes N Bay Street, then Beach Drive E. Turn north on E Hilldale Road 5.2 miles from Port Orchard, and reach the park in 0.3 mile.

From the Southworth ferry landing, head west on SR 160, and in 3.7 miles turn north on SE Colchester Drive. In 1.7 miles, at the community of Manchester, continue north on Beach Drive E to reach E Hilldale in another 0.8 mile.

Manchester, along with Fort Ward, was a 1900s Coast Artillery fortification intended to protect the entrance to Rich Passage and the Bremerton Naval Ship-

yard. Manchester was to serve as a control center for remotely fired "torpedoes" (as underwater mines were called in those days) when enemy ships were spotted. The torpedoes were to be placed in the passage only in the event of imminent hostilities; such a threat never occurred, and eventually the defense system was abandoned.

Today the park's most unusual attraction is a large brick structure just above the beach that once served as a warehouse for storing the torpedoes, but has been converted to an enormous picnic shelter. A smaller, gutted concrete building nearby served as the "mining casemate," or fire control center, where cables leading to the underwater torpedoes were connected to electrical firing triggers. On the northernmost point of the park is Battery Mitchell, a large concrete gun emplacement, built to mount two 3-inch guns that were to prevent small boats from disarming the minefield. The guns were never installed.

The park sits on a small, shallow cove, which warms enough for wading in summer months. Scuba divers put in here to explore underwater rocks off the point. The inviting lawn between the torpedo

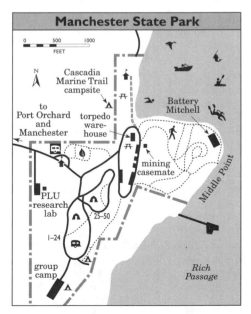

Manchester State Park

The World War I torpedo warehouse at Manchester now serves as a state park picnic shelter.

warehouse and the beach hosts several sunny picnic spots.

Trails lead along the beach to the gun battery site and circle the hillside above. Walk quietly, and perhaps spot squirrels, deer, and foxes, that make the park home. *Stay on the trails to avoid poison oak and stinging nettles.* A short nature trail that loops through the woods opposite the park entry-station describes local trees and plants.

Two Cascadia Marine Trail campsites are tucked in the brush above the day-use area, and two campground loops are upland, near the park entrance. Heavy undergrowth and timber provide some seclusion to the campsites that rim the loops. A large, modern group camp, complete with RV hookup sites, a picnic shelter, and restrooms with showers, lies in the center of a large grass field just south of the campground loops.

SQUARE LAKE STATE PARK

Picnicking, hiking, swimming, fishing, boating, paddling

SEASON/HOURS: Closed September 15 through April 30.
AREA: 237 acres; 2,700 feet of freshwater shoreline on Square Lake.
DAY-USE FACILITIES: 5 picnic sites, toilet (&), swimming beach, 1-lane gravel boat ramp (*no gasoline motors*).
CAR ACCESS: From SR 16, 4.3 miles south of Gorst, take the SR 16, Sedgwick Road exit. Head southwest on SE Sedgwick Road for 0.8 mile, then continue southwest on Glenwood Road for 1.1 miles to SW Lake Flora Road. Follow Lake Flora Road southwest for 0.9 mile to Square Lake Road, and turn north on it to arrive at the park entrance in 0.3 mile.

Square Lake has a small day-use park on a 60-acre lake southwest of Port Orchard. Although state park property surrounds the lake, only the southeast corner of the lake has been developed for recreational use. A grass strip along the lakeshore holds picnic sites, shaded by ancient firs. The shallow shoreline offers summer swimming (unguarded). A boat launch at the south end of the park leads to a lily pad-choked access to the lake for small boats. Undeveloped park property extends northwest from the lake, and to the southeast across Lake Flora Road.

HARPER STATE PARK

Fishing, boating

SEASON/HOURS: Year-round.
AREA: 3.03 acres; 777 feet of saltwater shoreline on Puget Sound.
RECREATIONAL FACILITIES: Boat ramp.

CAR ACCESS: From the ferry landing at Southworth, head west on SR 160. Reach the park in 1.2 miles, at the intersection of SR 160 and Olympiad Road.

This park consists of a short stretch of beach and a wide gravel boat launch ramp that drops into Colvos Passage. The ramp is only usable at high tide; at lower tide levels, the mudflat below might offer up a few clams. Boats launched here have ready access to Blake Island, lying just a mile to the northeast.

BLAKE ISLAND MARINE STATE PARK

Camping, picnicking, birdwatching, hiking, swimming, scuba diving, beach walking, shellfish, fishing, boating, paddling, Native American dances

SEASON/HOURS: Year-round.
AREA: 475.5 acres; 17,307 feet of saltwater shoreline on Puget Sound.
OVERNIGHT AND DAY-USE FACILITIES: 54 standard campsites, group camp (80 persons), adirondack shelter, Cascadia Marine Trail campsites, 54 picnic sites, 3 picnic shelters, 12 barbecues, 3 fire rings, 2 group day-use area (50 persons each), 2 restrooms with showers, 3 toilets, marine pumpout station, 2 portable toilet dump stations.
RECREATIONAL FACILITIES: 12 miles of hiking trails, 0.75-mile nature trail, 2 volleyball courts, horseshoe pits, underwater park, docks with 12 floats (1,744 feet of float space), 20 mooring buoys, 200-foot-long linear moorage system.
EDUCATIONAL FACILITIES: Remnants of an historic estate, Northwest Native American dances.
CONCESSIONS: Restaurant, tour boat service from the Seattle waterfront.

BOAT ACCESS: Blake Island lies off the east side of the Kitsap Peninsula, south of Bainbridge Island. For private boats, the nearest launch facilities are at Don Armeni Park in West Seattle, and at Manchester and Des Moines. It can be reached from the Seattle waterfront via a Tillicum Tours boat (*fee*).

Blake Island is by far the most popular of all of the state's marine parks, lying but an hour or so from Puget Sound's most populous cities. At night the island offers spectacular views of the brilliantly lit skyline of Seattle and nearby communities, glow-worm ferries, and overhead beads of light from the airport's jet traffic. The distant city lights fail to dull the expanses of stars sparkling brightly in the evening sky. During the early 1900s, the island was the private estate of William Pitt Trimble, a Seattle lawyer. The foundations of the home, some now-wild plants from the extensive garden, and a few other meager remnants of the estate can still be seen.

The boat-in state park is not limited to those people who have a boat—transportation is also available via a regularly scheduled commercial tour boat from the

A replica of a Northwest Indian longhouse overlooks the boat basin at Blake Island Marine State Park.

Seattle waterfront. The tour boat ride includes a traditional Northwest Indian salmon dinner and authentic native dances in a longhouse. Contact the management of Tillicum Tours regarding cost and availability of space if wanting only the ride and not planning to partake of the dinner, or if wanting to stay on the island and catch a later boat.

The well-protected pier and floats in the moorage basin on the island's northeast tip is the heart of activity. Summer weekends find the floats jam-packed; boaters should respect the demand for float space, and take up only the minimum they need. Space is on a first-come, first-served basis. Above the basin are the Indian longhouse and a broad lawn with picnic shelters, fire rings, and ample room for ball games and Frisbee tossing. Tent-camping spots line a road to the east. The beach below these sites is shallow and sandy—one of the best on the island for wading, sunbathing, or perhaps even building a sand castle.

To avoid the crowded moorage basin, mooring buoys are set outside the jetty on both sides of the point, off the northwest tip of the island and along the middle of the south shoreline, and good

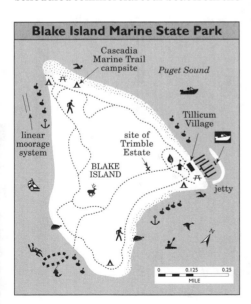

Blake Island Marine State Park

Cascadia
Marine Trail
campsite

Puget Sound

linear
moorage
system

Tillicum
Village

site of
Trimble
Estate

BLAKE
ISLAND

jetty

0   0.125   0.25
MILE

You might encounter one of the resident deer at Blake Island Marine State Park.

anchorages are nearby. These last two locations also have tenting sites on shore. The northwest tip of the island also has a linear moorage system, where boaters can tie into either of two parallel, 200-foot lines strung between spars.

Hiking trails on the island are mostly old service roads that are wide and reasonably flat. The least strenuous is a short nature trail just behind the longhouse; signs along this trail point out traces of early logging activities, identify various plants, and tell how local Native Americans used those plants. The longest trail traces the perimeter of the island on the bluffs above the beach, dropping down to the beach at the campgrounds on the sandy northwest tip and the south shore. At lower tides the rocky beach can be walked. Other trail segments wander through the timbered core of the island. On any of the trails expect encounters with deer. Due to overpopulation, they are quite small and tend to mooch from humans; appealing as they are, don't feed them—it makes them more dependent on humans for survival.

A buoy-marked artificial reef lying off the south side of the island provides excellent fishing from boats for lingcod and rockfish. Experienced scuba divers familiar with diving in strong tidal currents can explore the reef. Check current local regulations before taking fish with spears.

ST. EDWARD STATE PARK

Picnicking, birdwatching, hiking, tennis, soccer, handball, racquetball, softball, orienteering, bicycling, horseback riding, fishing, paddling

SEASON/HOURS: Year-round.
AREA: 316 acres; 3,000 feet of freshwater shoreline on Lake Washington.
DAY-USE FACILITIES: 85 picnic sites, group day-use areas (20, 25, 50, 75, and 100 persons), restrooms, primitive toilets.
RECREATIONAL FACILITIES: 8 miles of hiking trails (some open to bicycles), 1 mile of equestrian trail, fitness trail, ball fields, tennis courts, handball courts, gymnasium with stage.
CAR ACCESS: *From the north,* 2 miles west of Bothell, take 68th Avenue NE south from Bothell Way NE (SR 522). 68th becomes Juanita Drive NE, and the park entrance is 1.5 miles south of Bothell Way.

From the south, take Market Street (which becomes 98th Avenue NE) north out of Kirkland to its junction with NE Juanita Drive, which becomes Juanita Drive NE as it turns north. The park is reached 3.5 miles from the 98th Avenue intersection.

These quiet wooded grounds on a bluff above the northeast shore of Lake Washington were operated as a Catholic seminary from 1931 to 1977. When it was sold to the state for recreational use, instead of the usual primitive land of many new parks, the state received fully developed property that included athletic facilities and a seminary building. Today the seminary building is mothballed, but the remainder of the grounds are open for public use.

Signs for the park and the St. Thomas Center mark the entrance on Juanita Drive NE. The athletic facilities, picnic sites, and seminary complex are on a flat bluff. Below it a forested 275-foot-high hillside drops steeply down to the lake.

Redflower currant blooms in May at St. Edward State Park.

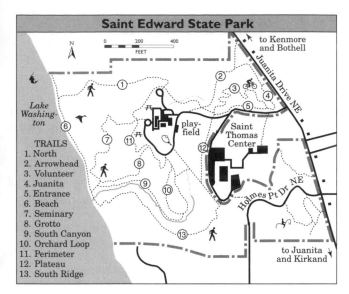

Saint Edward State Park

Lake Washington

TRAILS
1. North
2. Arrowhead
3. Volunteer
4. Juanita
5. Entrance
6. Beach
7. Seminary
8. Grotto
9. South Canyon
10. Orchard Loop
11. Perimeter
12. Plateau
13. South Ridge

to Kenmore and Bothell

Juanita Drive NE

Saint Thomas Center

play-field

Holmes Pt Dr NE

to Juanita and Kirkand

The remainder of the park is trail-laced forest. Several paths lead down the hillside, all eventually joining at a small grassy terrace above a boulder bulkhead and a sandy pocket beach. Cool your feet by wading; swimming is not advised, as the shoreline drops away steeply about 30 feet out.

The northernmost trail, 0.6 mile in length, is appropriately named North Trail. It starts at the gymnasium parking lot and heads to the rim of a deep ravine along the north side of the park. The trail drops quickly down the ravine, and on reaching the low bank of the lake, runs north and south along the shore. There is precious little lake access, however, as the trees run right down to the water's edge.

Seminary Trail (0.6 mile) leaves the west side of the seminary building as a service road, weaving gently down a broad ridge to the lakeshore. The much steeper Grotto Trail (0.3 mile) begins at the southwest corner of the grounds and drops precipitously down the side of another ravine to join the Seminary Trail near the water.

A deep ravine hooks uphill south of the seminary building. South Canyon Trail (0.6 mile) follows the floor of the ravine, while South Ridge Trail (1.1 miles) climbs steeply up the backbone of the ridge to the south of the ravine before swinging back to the southeast side of the seminary complex. For a gentler walk, take the Orchard Loop Trail (0.6 mile), which wanders around a small knoll south of the seminary.

The Arrowhead Trail leaves the playfield and runs to the northeast corner of the park, emerging at Juanita Drive across from a grocery. One can almost visualize the trail being pounded out by furtive seminarians sneaking out for evening snacks. A 3-mile-long multipurpose trail designed to accommodate mountain bikes is also on this wooded flat at the northeast corner of the park. Horseback riding is permitted in the southeast corner of the park, south of Holmes Point Drive NE.

BRIDLE TRAILS STATE PARK

Picnicking, birdwatching, jogging, walking, hiking, orienteering, horseback riding, horse shows

SEASON/HOURS: Year-round.
AREA: 481.52 acres.
DAY-USE FACILITIES: 30 picnic tables, 2 stoves, 4 barbecues, grandstand, judge's stand, water, restroom.
RECREATIONAL FACILITIES: 28 miles of hiking/equestrian trails, horse arena (with grandstand, paddock, 2 warm-up rings), small horse-schooling ring (*no bicycles*).
CONCESSIONS: Snacks (only during horse shows).
CAR ACCESS: The park, which is immediately west of SR 405 at the Bellevue/Kirkland city limits, is bounded on the west by 116th Avenue NE, on the north by NE 60th Street, and on the east by 132nd Avenue NE. The arena and grandstands are on the southwest side of the park off 116th Avenue NE at NE 53rd Street.

Twenty years ago Bridle Trails State Park was a remote enclave in the hinterlands of Bellevue devoted to the use of riders from numerous nearby stables and farms. Like a camel, suburbia got its nose in the tent, and now it has nearly taken

Bridle Trails State Park provides excellent trails for equestrians and hikers.

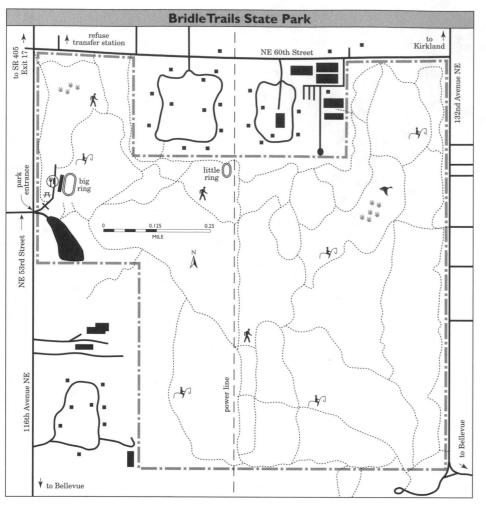

Bridle Trails State Park

es have the right-of-way. When approached by a rider, move to the side of the trail and stand quietly. Dogs must be on a leash and under control. Horses must be ridden in a manner that does not endanger the life and limb of any person, and must not be left unattended.

The mazelike trails are unmarked, and their meandering routes are confusing. The only wide-open trail in the park is an arrow-straight service road under a power transmission line that splits the middle of the park. The remainder of the trails wind in profusion through the forest. The trails more popular with equestrians are reasonably wide and well maintained, with occasional muddy spots in marshy areas or during the wet winter months. Narrower paths and a web of interconnecting footpaths are also taken by venturesome equestrians, but are more often used by hikers.

Whether on foot or horseback, if one leaves the main paths getting lost is almost a certainty, although staying lost is highly improbable. Aids to orientation are glimpses of surrounding roads from trails that are near the outer edge of the park, the drone of traffic on I-405 to the west, and the crash and clatter of a refuse transfer station at the northwest edge of the park. However, in the thick woods at the center of the east half of the park, clues to your location disappear. A map of the park created by the Sammamish Orienteering Club is an asset.

The park is an example of the lowland forest that once covered the Puget Sound region. In some sections huge, decaying stumps testify to past logging. The most common trees are Douglas-fir, western hemlock, and some western red cedar. A few small groves hold moss-clad bigleaf maple, and in places tall stands of thin fir are packed tightly together like toothpicks in a box. An impenetrable growth of alder, vine maple, and devil's club surrounds a sizable marsh in the heart of the east section of the park and a smaller one in the northwest corner. Coyotes and small mammals, as well as a wide variety of forest birds, live in the park.

over; only a few of the equestrian facilities still exist, although many nearby homes have backyard paddocks. The park remains a magnet for equestrians and as many people ride the trails today as did years ago; however, some must come from farther afield, guiding their mounts along road shoulders or on the 2-mile-long bridle path that comes up from Marymoor County Park in Redmond; many even tote their horses in trailers to use the trails or compete in shows held at the park.

The arena and grandstands on the west side of the park are used by horse clubs who hold both English and western riding shows here virtually every weekend from spring through fall. Competitions, which are usually small practice-type "schooling shows," include events such as hunt seat and stock seat equitation, western trail, barrel racing, dressage, jumping, and in-hand showing. There is no charge to spectators.

One does not have to ride a horse, however, to enjoy the state park; hikers frequent the trails, and it is used for orienteering competitions. Trails are so numerous that one might spend several hours in the park and not see a rider at all. Walkers should remember that hors-

LAKE SAMMAMISH STATE PARK

Picnicking, birdwatching, softball, soccer, jogging, orienteering, swimming, waterskiing, windsurfing, fishing, boating, paddling, sailing

SEASON/HOURS: Year-round.
AREA: 509.65 acres; 6,858 feet of fresh-water shoreline on Lake Sammamish.
DAY-USE FACILITIES: Primitive group youth camp (200 persons) with 36 picnic sites and 4 toilets, 475 picnic tables, 4 kitchen shelters (3 reservable), 80 barbecues, group day-use areas (100, 200, and 300 persons), 3 restrooms (♿), trailer dump station.
RECREATIONAL FACILITIES: Hiking trails, jogging path, 5 volleyball courts, 2 children's play areas, sports field, horseshoe pits, 2 swimming beaches, 2 bathhouses (♿), 2 waterski floats, 9-lane boat ramp.
CONCESSIONS: Snacks, kayak rentals.
CAR ACCESS: At Issaquah, take Exit 15 (Lake Sammamish State Park, Renton, SR 900) from I-90, cross north over the highway on 17th Ave NW, then turn west on NW Sammamish Road to reach the park in 0.4 mile. The launch ramps and youth camp area are in the northeast section of the park, reached by turning east from 17th Ave NW onto SE 56th Street; in 1.2 miles drive northwest on E Lake Sammamish Parkway SE for 1 mile.

Lake Sammamish State Park, a water playground that boasts one of the largest freshwater beaches in the greater Seattle area, becomes a summertime magnet for crowds bent on boating, waterskiing, windsurfing, swimming, kayaking, or sunbathing—or for watching those who do. With more than 1.5 million visitors each year, escape from the masses would seem impossible, yet surprisingly enough, just a few feet from the frenetic beach and picnic areas are quiet paths through woods and shrubs to secluded shorefronts and to wide, untrammeled meadows. Over half of the park's acreage is preserved as natural area where more than 100 species of birds, as well as coyote, fox, opossum, raccoon, beaver, weasel, porcupine, muskrat, and deer exist only a Frisbee-toss from the sunburned throngs.

The heart of the park (aside from two huge parking lots) is divided into three day-use areas. The one to the north is a spacious grass flat, shaded by large old poplar, maple, willow, and birch. Here a snack

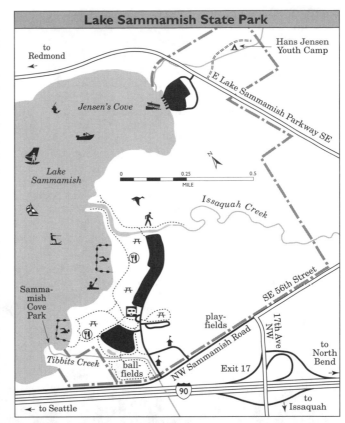

Polliwogs congregate in shallow Lake Sammamish water.

stand, bathhouse, a pair of picnic shelters, and sports areas complement the usual collection of picnic tables and fire braziers. The lawn tapers down to a wide sandy beach with roped-off swimming areas and waterski floats. To the southwest, rolling grass hummocks shaded by trees front another roped-off swimming beach; here is another bathhouse with a concession stand that sells snacks in summer months. A large, distinctive, octagonal group kitchen shelter lies at the entrance to the parking lot for this area. A smaller group day-use area is between the beachfront sites on the opposite side of the entrance road. No waterfront here, just a broad level grass field and a picnic shelter. A field at the entrance to the park has space for organized games of softball and soccer; a jogging path winds through trees along its east side.

A wide, marshy natural area separates the beach from the boat and group camps.

A wooden bridge at the north corner of the parking lot crosses placid Issaquah Creek and leads to the center of a trail on the perimeter of the natural area. The east leg shortly arrives at a large, open field of pasture grass and thistles, while the wooded west leg parallels the creek and eventually arrives at a shaded grass thumb at the beach where the creek meets the lake. A narrow spur leads northeast from this trail through blackberry brambles and a canopy of dense brush to a tiny pocket cove amid encircling marshland.

The entrance to the large, heavily used boat launch area is on the north side of the park, some 2 miles beyond the main park entrance. Across the road from the launch area is the Hans Jensen Youth Group Camp, named for the man who donated much of the park property. The group camp, which is available to youth groups only, requires advance reservations.

SQUAK MOUNTAIN STATE PARK

Nature study, birdwatching, hiking

SEASON/HOURS: Year-round.
AREA: 1,645.77 acres.
DAY-USE FACILITIES: Parking, toilets.
RECREATIONAL FACILITIES: Natural area, 7 to 10 miles of hiking trails (some open to horses), (*no water*), horse loading ramp (&), hitching posts.
CAR ACCESS: The park lies south of the Issaquah city limits, between SE Renton–Issaquah Road (SR 900), SE Issaquah–Hobart Road, and SE May Valley Road. Two major trailheads, and other unmarked ones, lead into the park.

South trailhead: The official, developed trailhead is off SE May Valley Road 2.6 miles west of SR 900, or 1.5 miles east of SE Issaquah–Hobart Road.

North trailhead: The second major trailhead, on the north side of the park, is reached by taking NW Newport Way west from SR 900. In 1.5 miles turn southeast on Mountain Park Boulevard SW, which winds steeply uphill. In 0.9 mile, turn left on Mountainside Drive SW. At a hairpin turn in 0.4 mile, an unmarked trail leaves the end of a paved pulloff with parking for five or six cars.

Northwest access: An access trail at the northwest corner of the park leaves SR 900 at a gated gravel road 1.8 miles south of NW Newport Way. There is no parking available outside the gate, and only limited roadside parking on the opposite shoulder of SR 900.

In Issaquah, residential development has crept its way up the steep north side of Squak Mountain in a quest for the grandest and highest home with the most far-reaching views. At the uppermost limit

A kayaking class at Lake Sammamish State Park teaches safe boat handling.

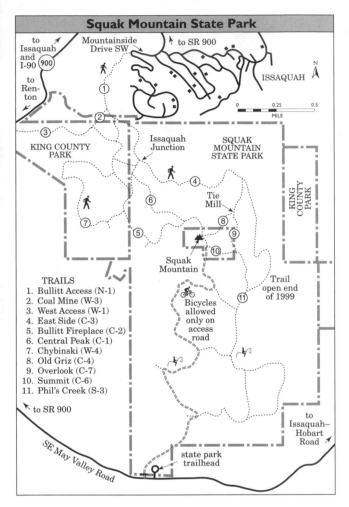

Squak Mountain State Park

to Issaquah and I-90 ⑨⑩⑩

to Renton

Mountainside Drive SW

to SR 900

ISSAQUAH

N

0   0.25   0.5
MILE

KING COUNTY PARK

Issaquah Junction

SQUAK MOUNTAIN STATE PARK

KING COUNTY PARK

Tie Mill

Squak Mountain

Trail open end of 1999

TRAILS
1. Bullitt Access (N-1)
2. Coal Mine (W-3)
3. West Access (W-1)
4. East Side (C-3)
5. Bullitt Fireplace (C-2)
6. Central Peak (C-1)
7. Chybinski (W-4)
8. Old Griz (C-4)
9. Overlook (C-7)
10. Summit (C-6)
11. Phil's Creek (S-3)

to SR 900

Bicycles allowed only on access road

SE May Valley Road

state park trailhead

to Issaquah–Hobart Road

of the city, these homes bump up against the boundary of Squak Mountain State Park. The Bullitt family donated the original 600-acre section of land, encompassing the upper portions of the mountain, to the State Parks Commission with the provision that it would remain natural. Additional acquisitions over the years have expanded the park to its present size. Only the mountain summit, where an inholding of King County property holds communication antennas, is excluded from the park. Trails on the north side of the park are restricted to foot traffic. Those on the south side of the summit are open to equestrians as well as hik-

ers. Bicycles and motorized vehicles are not permitted on any trails.

Roads once laced the upper reaches of the mountain; however they are now mostly overgrown. The lack of trail maintenance, the scarcity of signs, inadequate maps, and the confusion of unmarked paths make the park an orienteering challenge not to be taken lightly. Several trails leave the park to wander through King County Park property on both the east and west sides of the park; boundaries are poorly marked. If nature and exercise excite you, the park can fulfill your desires, but don't come here for scenic views—they are masked by the dense forest growth.

The park's developed trail access off SE May Valley Road has a horse loading ramp, hitching posts, parking space, and toilets. A short spur trail leads to the gated gravel road to the west that climbs 2.5 miles to the King County inholding at the top of the mountain. Equestrian trails branch from the east side of this road.

The best access to the north side of the park is from Mountainside Drive. The trail enters the park as N-1, the Bullitt Access Trail. Moss-encrusted maple, cedar, and a few Douglas-fir make up the forest. A few unmarked paths wander in from housing developments to the east. Just before you enter the park, an unmarked path to the southwest joins other trails in the King County Parks property west of the park. At 1 mile is Issaquah Junction; here C-3, the East Side Trail,

heads southeast, traversing the hillside through brush that gives way to stands of alder along creek drainages, becoming progressively more primitive. Only once does the thick forest part enough to permit views of the Issaquah Creek valley and Tiger Mountain rising above. This trail may eventually be extended through Thrush Gap to connect with trails on the south side of the mountain.

The trail south beyond Issaquah Junction becomes the Bullitt Fireplace Trail, C-2; shortly another trail junction is reached. To the southeast is the Central Peak Trail, C-1, which climbs steeply and most directly to the summit and its antenna towers. The branch to the south, which continues as C-2, shortly arrives at a junction with the West Access Trail, W-1. The West Access Trail heads west out of the park, descending to the unmarked, gated trailhead on SR 900. About 0.25 mile farther up the Bullitt Fireplace Trail, another branch to the west, the Chybinski Trail, W-4, wanders into King County property and eventually joins the West Access Trail. C-2 continues its relentless climb, levels at a saddle, then climbs again past unmarked spurs and

Delicate white fringecups edge the Squak Mountain trail.

the Bullitt fireplace, the last remnant of the family house. It finally reaches a junction with the Central Peak Trail a short distance below the summit.

An array of semi-obscure trails northeast of the summit, among them Old Griz, Summit, and Overlook, wander among the ridges to the northeast. Old Griz and the Overlook meet at a huge sawdust pile, the Tie Mill, where a portable saw mill once carved out railroad ties for logging tracks into the lumber-covered hills between Issaquah and North Bend. Getting lost in this part of the mountain can be a distinct possibility. Use care.

OLALLIE STATE PARK

Hiking, fishing, interpretive signs, views of Twin Falls

SEASON/HOURS: Year-round.
AREA: 539.10 acres (including the Twin Falls Natural Area, Garcia area, and Snoqualmie Pass Wagon Road Heritage area); 21,588 feet of freshwater shoreline on the South Fork of the Snoqualmie River.
DAY-USE FACILITIES: 9 picnic tables, sports field, 6 toilets (2 &).
RECREATIONAL FACILITIES: 3.5 miles of hiking trails.
EDUCATIONAL FACILITIES: 0.5-mile interpretive trail, viewing platforms overlooking Twin Falls.
CAR ACCESS: *To reach the west trailhead to Twin Falls,* take Exit 34 (468th Ave SE) from I-90, 4.5 miles east of North Bend. Turn south on SE Edgewick Road, and in 0.6 mile, just before the bridge over the South Fork of the Snoqualmie River, turn east on SE 159th Street, reaching the Twin Falls parking lot in 0.6 mile.

To reach the east trailhead to Twin Falls, take Exit 38 (Fire Training Center) from I-90. The exit from the eastbound lanes is 7.3 miles east of North Bend, and the exit from the

The lower falls at Twin Falls Natural Area roars over a 150-foot-high cliff.

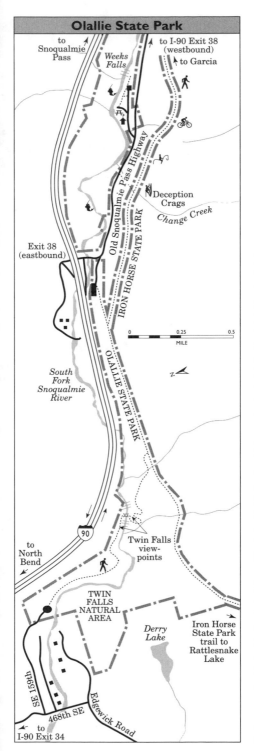

Olallie State Park

to Snoqualmie Pass

to I-90 Exit 38 (westbound)

to Garcia

Weeks Falls

Old Snoqualmie Pass Highway

Deception Crags

Change Creek

Exit 38 (eastbound)

IRON HORSE STATE PARK

OLALLIE STATE PARK

South Fork Snoqualmie River

0   0.25   0.5
MILE

to North Bend

Twin Falls viewpoints

TWIN FALLS NATURAL AREA

Derry Lake

Iron Horse State Park trail to Rattlesnake Lake

SE 159th

468th SE

Edgewick Road

to I-90 Exit 34

westbound lanes is 2 miles farther east; the old Snoqualmie Pass Highway runs along the south side of the river, connecting the two ends of the exit. At the eastbound exit, just south of the bridge over the Snoqualmie River, turn west on a gravel road leading into the Twin Falls parking area. From the westbound exit, follow the Snoqualmie Pass Highway west 1.9 miles to the Twin Falls parking area. The entrance to the picnic area is 0.6 mile east of the Twin Falls parking lot.

Olallie State Park spans a 3.5-mile-long section of the Snoqualmie River. The historic Snoqualmie Pass Wagon Road, which was completed in 1869, once passed through here, and traces of logs from its roadbed can be found. The section of present-day road between the east and west ends of Exit 38 is a portion of the now-becoming-historic Sunset Highway (old Snoqualmie Pass Highway). The park lies north of the old highway, between the two ends of this exit, then extends west, encompassing the Twin Falls Natural Area.

The east end of the road through the park ends just below Weeks Falls, where there is a power plant that balances power needs with the ecological requirements of the river's fish. Upstream from the falls, an adjustable weir diverts water into the power generators only when the amount of water is adequate to assure that the remaining river flow will support the needs of fish inhabiting the river.

A large grass sports field with a few picnic tables sits inside the park entrance. A gravel road to the north ends at another small riverside picnic area. Anglers can take advantage of access trails to the river to try their luck at luring rainbow and cutthroat trout. A short self-guided nature trail also loops through this area.

Twin Falls Natural Area

At Twin Falls, the South Fork of the Snoqualmie River drops more than 300 feet through a rocky gorge in a series of

Weeks Falls is a pleasant companion to the dramatic Twin Falls.

glistening cascades. Trails provide breathtaking viewpoints of the falls. From the east end of the park, the path starts on a barricaded access road that shares a short segment of the Iron Horse Trail, then gives way to a foot trail in 0.7 mile. Total distance to the falls is 1.6 miles, with an elevation loss of 500 feet, which must be regained on the return hike from the falls. From the west, the trail distance to the falls is also 1.6 miles. The first 0.5 mile is flat along the riverbank, then switchbacks up over a finger ridge, drops down near river level, then climbs again to the falls viewpoints; a total elevation gain of 230 feet.

From a viewing platform at the upper falls, look directly into the throat of a narrow gorge that boils with a series of 20- to 50-foot cataracts. From here a wooden stairway leads down to a bridge just above the lower falls and further views of the upper cascades. A short length of trail and stairs on the north bank lead down to an eagle's aerie platform with a view of the river as it roars over a sheer 150-foot cliff at the lower falls and drapes adjoining rock walls with wispy veils of water.

IRON HORSE STATE PARK (WEST)

Hiking, rock climbing, mountain biking, horseback riding, wagon-train riding, cross-country skiing, snowshoeing

SEASON/HOURS: Year-round.
AREA: 613.10 acres.
OVERNIGHT AND DAY-USE FACILITIES: Primitive campsites at Alice Creek and Carter Creek; 4 toilets (2 ♿) and 2 picnic sites (♿) at Cedar Falls trailhead.
RECREATIONAL FACILITIES: 18.1 miles of trail, 4 trestles, 1-mile tunnel (*motorized vehicles prohibited*).
CAR ACCESS:

Annette Lake. Take Exit 47 (Tinkham Road, Denny Creek, Asahel Curtis) from I-90. After crossing the South Fork of the Snoqualmie River, head east for 0.7 mile to the Annette Lake trailhead (USFS trailhead parking pass required). Take the trail uphill, crossing under power transmission lines, and in 1 mile intersect Iron Horse Trail.

McClellan Butte. Take Exit 42 (Tinkham Road, West Entrance) from I-90 and park at the gauging station just south of the South Fork of the Snoqualmie River (USFS trailhead parking pass required). Follow the McClellan Butte trail uphill. The trail crosses under a power line right-of-way and intersects Iron Horse Trail in 0.7 mile.

Olallie. Take Exit 38 (Fire Training Center) from I-90. The eastbound end of this exit is 7.3 miles east of North Bend, and the westbound exit is 9.3 miles east of North Bend; the old Snoqualmie Pass Highway runs along the south side of the river between these two exits. At the western end of Exit 38, just south of the bridge over the South Fork of the Snoqualmie River, turn west on a gravel road into the Twin Falls Natural Area parking lot. Hike or

Tinkham Peak, on the right in the distance, is one of many Cascade summits seen from the Iron Horse State Park trail.

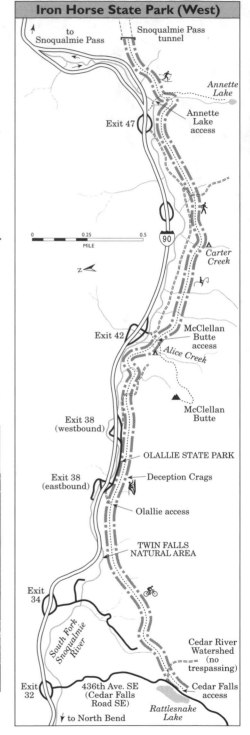

Iron Horse State Park (West)

to Snoqualmie Pass

Snoqualmie Pass tunnel

Annette Lake

Exit 47

Annette Lake access

Carter Creek

Exit 42

McClellan Butte access

Alice Creek

McClellan Butte

Exit 38 (westbound)

OLALLIE STATE PARK

Exit 38 (eastbound)

Deception Crags

Olallie access

TWIN FALLS NATURAL AREA

Exit 34

South Fork Snoqualmie River

Cedar River Watershed (no trespassing)

Cedar Falls access

Exit 32

436th Ave. SE (Cedar Falls Road SE)

Rattlesnake Lake

to North Bend

0   0.25   0.5
MILE

bike the service road headed uphill to the west to intersect Iron Horse Trail in 0.2 mile.

Cedar Falls. Take Exit 32 (436th Avenue SE) from I-90, 4.5 miles east of North Bend, and head south for 2.9 miles on 436th SE, which becomes Cedar Falls Road SE, to arrive at a park and trailhead, jointly developed by state parks and the Seattle Public Utilities.

A park 110 miles long and a mere 100 feet wide must rank as one of the most unusual in the state—if not in the country. Its unique dimensions make it ideal for some unique recreation: In addition to the to-be-expected hiking, mountain bike riding, and cross-country skiing, the trail is used for equestrian trail rides, old-time wagon train treks, and horse-drawn sledge rides. Dogsled competitions are staged at the Easton trailhead every January. Four accesses that are plowed in winter provide parking for snowshoers and cross-country skiers (snowmobiles prohibited). The groomed trail that leaves the Crystal Springs Sno-Park (Exit 62) offers level, easy skiing along the edge of Lake Keechelus.

The park had its beginning in 1909 when the Chicago, Milwaukee, St. Paul, and Pacific Railroad laid tracks across Snoqualmie Pass for its iron horses. After 70 years of service, the railroad was forced into bankruptcy by competition and changing modes of transportation. Since that time, additional parcels of the right-of-way between North Bend and the Idaho border have been purchased. The section between Rattlesnake Lake and the Columbia River is designated as Iron Horse State Park. The old iron tracks have been removed, and throughout much of its length the trail is a 20-foot-wide gravel path with a maximum 2-percent grade. In some places a few remaining deteriorated railroad ties protrude through the surface.

Two primitive campsites allow camping along this part of the trail; each has tent pads, picnic tables, and a toilet. One is at Carter Creek, 5.5 miles west of the summit tunnel entrance, and the second is at Alice Creek, 3 miles farther west. Only at the Cedar Falls access can this western segment of the park be reached directly by roads; the other accesses must be reached via short Forest Service trails. Trailhead parking passes, available from the Forest Service, are needed at these access points. The park is described in two parts: Chapter 8 covers the 92-mile-long portion that begins at Snoqualmie Pass and runs east to the Columbia River; here we describe the 18-mile-long section that begins at Rattlesnake Lake near North Bend and runs east to the Snoqualmie summit.

Snoqualmie Pass Tunnel to McClellan Butte Trail

The upper end of the trail begins at the west entrance to the 2.3-mile-long Snoqualmie Pass tunnel. Blasts of moist, frigid air roll from the tunnel mouth, even on warm days. The tunnel entrance is gated from November to May, but access is permitted in summer. There is no lighting, so flashlights are needed—the tunnel is not recommended for claustrophobics!

West from the tunnel, the way traverses an open hillside with spectacular views to peaks north of the pass: Snoqualmie, Guye, Denny, the Tooth, Hemlock, Bryant, and Chair. To the west the view down Snoqualmie Valley is terminated by the serrated ridge leading south from the snag tooth of McClellan Butte.

The trail heads into the woods along Humpback Creek near the Annette Lake access. Here a collapsing snowshed west of the creek is bypassed by a dirt road along its outer edge. Trees again block views until the airy trestle over Hansen Creek, where the Snoqualmie valley, Bandera Mountain, and Mount Defiance to the north side of the valley are visible. Slopes west of the Hansen Creek trestle are prone to avalanche, so cross-country skiers coming up from McClellan Butte should not venture beyond here.

McClellan Butte Trail to Rattlesnake Lake

The next access is another 5 miles west at the McClellan Butte Trail. From here the Iron Horse Trail loops below steep cliffs, with more views north to the steep forested ridges west of Mount Defiance. In another mile the trail crosses the forest road at the old Garcia station. To the west a high trestle crosses the expanse of Mine Creek, and a newly reconstructed trestle crosses a gaping gully at Hall Creek (the center of the original span was washed away by floods caused by extensive clearcutting on the upstream slopes). Another 1.25 miles to the west, at the east side of the Change Creek trestle, is a popular rock climbing area known as Deception Crags. It can be reached more directly by hiking a bootpath along the west side of the creek from roadside parking

The west end of the Snoqualmie Pass tunnel is open to hikers and bikers in summer.

0.2 mile west of the entrance to the main portion of Olallie State Park.

Two miles farther west is an access from a spur trail uphill from the Twin Falls parking lot. A large gravel pit scars the face of the hillside to the north. After passing a power substation above Twin Falls, the trail swings southwest from the Snoqualmie River past an abandoned gravel pit at the old Ragnar Station, then descends gradually through the thickly forested hillside above Boxley Creek to the Cedar Falls trailhead. Here are toilets and a few picnic tables. More extensive recreational facilities are available at the Seattle Public Utilities' companion park on the shore of Rattlesnake Lake. Connections can be made here to other King County bike paths on former railroad beds.

GREEN RIVER GORGE CONSERVATION AREA

Nature study, hiking, fishing, paddling, rafting, historical interpretation

SEASON/HOURS: Year-round.
AREA: 2,008 acres; 18 miles of freshwater shoreline on the Green River.
RECREATIONAL FACILITIES: 6 miles of hiking trails.
EDUCATIONAL FACILITIES: Abandoned mines, interpretive display, historic platted townsite, historic cemetery.
CAR ACCESS:
Walter A. Jellum Site. From the center of Black Diamond take SE Green River Gorge Road (Lawson Street) east and cross the Franklin Bridge in 4.2 miles. In 0.4 mile, at the junction of SE Green River Gorge Road and the Enumclaw–Franklin Road, head northeast on SE Green River Gorge Road for 0.5 mile to a gated logging road that leads northwest through Plum Creek Timber property to the Walter A. Jellum Site.
Old Town of Franklin Site. West of the Franklin Bridge, 4.1 miles from Black Diamond, look for any legal roadside parking. Walk the road to the west to a gate at unmarked SE 336th Street; this county road heads west for a few hundred feet, past no trespassing signs, to the park gate.
Hanging Gardens Site. On the south side of the Green River, from SR 169, 1.5 miles south of the Kummer Bridge, turn northeast on the Enumclaw–Franklin Road. In 2.4 miles, at a rusty gate, an unmarked logging road heads northwest into the park property. This gate is 1.6 miles south of the junction of SE Green River Gorge Road and the Enumclaw–Franklin Road. On the north side of the Green River, follow directions to the Old Town of Franklin Site. Take the road/trail southwest from the park gate for 0.6 mile to reach the adjoining Hanging Gardens Site.

The Green River Gorge is an exquisite "hanging garden," with miniature waterfalls wisping down vertical walls, rock grottos draped in ferns and moss, frothing whitewater rapids, and cold, crystal pools. The river slices through layers of sandstone and shale—300 feet deep in places—for 14 twisting miles. Historically, the Green River area was exploited for its coal, clay, and cinnabar (from which mercury is derived). As the mineral resources were depleted, the gorge was recognized anew for its natural beauty and

Moss- and fern-encrusted rock walls of the Hanging Gardens are preserved in the Green River Gorge Conservation Area.

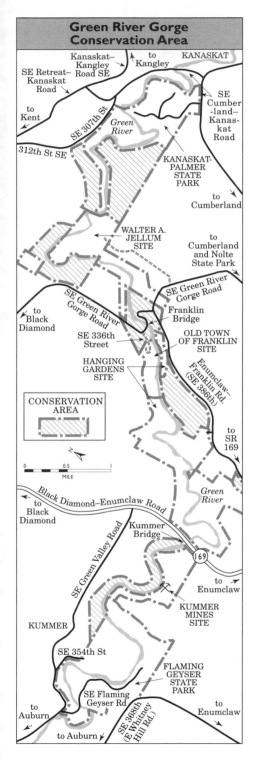

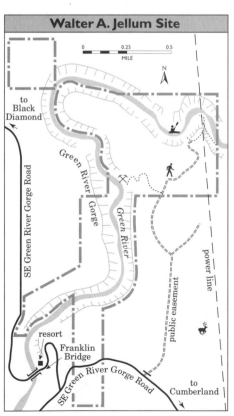

recreation potential. In 1969 the state legislature established boundaries for the Green River Gorge Conservation Area and directed State Parks to protect the unique natural and geological features of the area.

State Parks acquired property, developmental rights, timber-cutting rights, and trail easements in the area, and is in the process of acquiring more. Unfortunately, some of the land on the rim of the gorge already has been residentially developed. In some places the best that can be hoped for is acquisition and protection of the gorge walls, so that at least from river level the visual appearance of a serene, unblemished wilderness will be protected.

Undeveloped state property includes the three sites described here. The only access to a fourth location, the Kummer Mines Site, that doesn't cross private land

is along the highway just southwest of the Kummer Bridge; however, there is no parking in the vicinity, and there are no access trails into the property.

Developed state parks, described later, are Flaming Geyser, Nolte (which does not lie on the Green River, but is nearby), and Kanaskat-Palmer, although only the latter has camping facilities. A strip of property connecting Nolte State Park to the Green River Conservation Area at the Hanging Gardens Site is on the parks' acquisition list.

WALTER A. JELLUM SITE. This area of the Green River Gorge includes all of a broad thumb of property that pokes northwest into a bend of the river, as well as strips of land south from it along the river and inland across the Franklin–Cumberland Road. Walk the gated logging road described above for 0.6 mile (a public easement permits hiking the road). At a Y-intersection, continue on the northwest branch of the road to the park boundary, obvious by the line of 90-year-old timber, compared to the clearcut to the south. In a short distance a road spur to the east twists downhill to a shelf about 150 feet above the river; here a faint and difficult footpath cuts down the steep bank to the tailings and collapsed entrance of an old cinnabar mine. One wonders if the grizzled miner who tried to eke out his livelihood here was aware of the natural treasures that surrounded him. Use caution around all old mines.

The trail going straight ahead from the above spur continues north for 0.25 mile, then descends to another flat, possibly once a cabin site, but now a crude hunter's camp. From here an old road and various deteriorating footpaths thread north, eventually leading to more long-closed mining sites and difficult scramble routes or precipitous drops of 100 feet or more to the riverbank.

OLD TOWN OF FRANKLIN SITE. Park along the shoulder of SE Green River Gorge Road about 0.2 mile north of the Franklin Bridge, and walk Green River Gorge

Trees coated with green velvet moss are seen along Green River trails.

Road to the county road, SE 336th Street. Follow it to the gated road at the park boundary. Head southwest past the site of the former coal mining town of Franklin. At a switchback in 0.5 mile, this road crosses the roadbed of the Franklin–Black Diamond Railroad, long since nothing but a memory. One can follow the level railroad grade, now an unmaintained trail, as it continues west; but

difficult scrambling is required where a creek has washed out a trestle. In about a mile the trail improves as it intersects an access road to the Black Diamond watershed pump station.

For an alternate route, at the railroad grade continue uphill to a Y. The road to the northeast leads past foundations of old mine wheelhouses and shortly reaches the park boundary. The fork to the west climbs gradually to the gated mouth of the 1,300-foot-deep Franklin #2 coal mine shaft, and an interpretive sign telling of the coal mine at the height of its glory. From here a trail traverses west to the Hanging Gardens Site and the overgrown Franklin Cemetery adjacent to the Black Diamond watershed road. Respect this historic burial ground.

HANGING GARDENS SITE. At the south access point, park at the gated road end and hike north along the logging road. In a short distance, this route heads northwest along the fence of the Black Diamond watershed, and then continues atop a wooded ridgeline leading toward the river. At the lip of the gorge, the trail drops steeply down the ridge on a poorly maintained trail and descends to a cobble beach at a sharp bend in the river. The vertical, fern-draped wall of the hanging gardens, a classic photo shot depicting the reason for naming of the area, soars upward on the opposite side of the river.

To approach the area from the north, follow the trail described above to the Franklin Cemetery. A few hundred feet west, the watershed road switchbacks some 400 feet down the north side of the gorge to the river's edge, where a suspension bridge supports a water pipeline that crosses the river. Here are views of river rapids and possibly of kayakers attempting this section of the river. Back atop the rim of the gorge, the railroad grade/road continues west for another 0.5 mile before reaching the park boundary. By carefully tracing mapped road connections it is possible to follow unimproved roads west to SR 169.

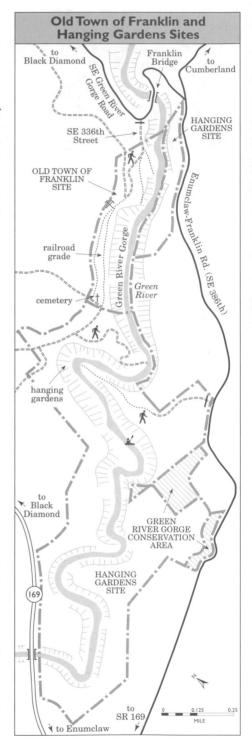

KANASKAT-PALMER STATE PARK

Camping, picnicking, nature study, hiking, fishing, paddling, rafting

SEASON/HOURS: Year-round; campsite reservations accepted in summer.
AREA: 397.79 acres; 19,900 feet of fresh-water shoreline on the Green River.
OVERNIGHT AND DAY-USE FACILITIES: 17 RV sites (E) (2 &) 33 standard campsites (2 &) group camp with 2 adirondack shelters (80 persons), 65 picnic sites, 3 picnic shelters, group day-use area with kitchen shelter (50 persons), 5 restrooms (3 with showers) (&), 3 toilets, trailer dump station.
RECREATIONAL FACILITIES: 3 miles of hiking trails, kayak/raft launch sites.
CAR ACCESS: *From the north,* take SR 169 south from Renton, and 1.7 miles south of Maple Valley turn east on SE Kent–Kangley Road. At an intersection in 3.6 miles, turn south on SE Retreat–Kanaskat Road, which joins SE Cumberland–Kanaskat Road in another 3.2 miles. Head south 1.9 miles to the park entrance.

From the south, at a flashing yellow light 2.8 miles north of Enumclaw, turn east from SR 169 onto SE 400th Street, which becomes SE 400th Way in 0.4 mile, joins SE 392nd Street in another 0.7 mile, and then Ts into Veazie–Cumberland Road in 0.8 mile more.

Just as it begins its tortuous descent through the gorge, the Green River sweeps around a small, low plateau that holds Kanaskat-Palmer State Park. The park's location makes it the prime spot for those planning to run the river, as well as for those who come to fish, play in its pools, or enjoy the surrounding lush forest.

In the center of the park, two campground loops have sites rimmed by trees and undergrowth; a group camp is secluded in trees near the northeast side of the park. Along the park's western edge, the day-use areas have ample space for games and gamboling. Trails lead to the riverbank and follow its edge, providing access for fishing. Trout catches are good in the summer, but it is in winter, when steelhead run, that fishing begins in earnest and hardy anglers flock to the river. A steelhead-rearing pond is directly across the river from the park.

Three boat launch/retrieval sites are provided in the park. *Anyone attempting to run the river should have proper equipment and knowledge of whitewater techniques, and be familiar with river conditions.* Between the upstream and middle launch sites, the rafting is Class II+, requiring intermediate skills. At the middle launch site, where the river takes a right-angle turn and heads due south, it becomes Class IV and demands expert skill in handling the boiling rapids, powerful waves, and dangerous rocks.

Although seasonal weather changes affect river conditions, the water level is largely controlled upstream at Howard Hansen Dam. River-runners can call the Army Corps of Engineers office number listed in Appendix A for information on the current water level. The river is at its most diffi-cult from late fall to mid-June, but even in summer rafters and kayakers must exercise care. When the river is high enough, experienced boaters equipped with the proper gear can run the river for 14 miles from here through the gorge to Flaming Geyser State Park.

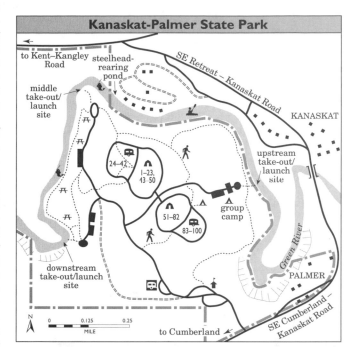

Worn river rocks are a kayaking challenge at Kanaskat-Palmer State Park.

FLAMING GEYSER STATE PARK

Picnicking, birdwatching, hiking, swimming, fishing, rafting, paddling, horseback riding, model airplane flying, interpretive displays

SEASON/HOURS: Year-round.

AREA: 519.94 acres; 22,345 feet of fresh-water shoreline on the Green River.

DAY-USE FACILITIES: 172 picnic tables, 7 fire pits, 30 barbecues, 6 group day-use areas with picnic shelters (150 persons each; 2 may be combined for 350 persons), 3 restrooms (♿).

RECREATIONAL FACILITIES: 4 miles of hiking trails, 6 sets of volleyball standards, horseshoe pits, fields for equestrian use, remote-control model airplane fields.

EDUCATIONAL FACILITIES: Steelhead imprint ponds.

ELC: Sleeping quarters, meeting room, kitchen, dining area, volleyball standards (25 persons overnight, 50 persons day-use).

CAR ACCESS: From SR 169, 1.4 miles south of Black Diamond, turn west on SE Green Valley Road. In 2.9 miles turn south on SE Flaming Geyser Road and enter the park. To reach the north side of the river, turn south on SE 354th Street, 0.6 mile east of the bridge to the main part of the park.

Although "flaming geyser" conjures up the image of a fire-breathing natural dragon, the state park's namesake is presently less dramatic. In 1911 miners drilled a coal test-hole at the edge of Christy Creek, and in a coal seam over 1,000 feet down hit pockets of methane gas and salty water. For many years fire from the ignited gas roared as much as 25 feet into the air, and up to 20 gallons of water a minute flowed from the hole. Today the gas is largely depleted, the flame is a modest 6 to 10 inches high, and the water flow is reduced to a dribble. Several hundred yards farther up the creek, Bubbling Geyser, which resulted from exploratory drilling for methane gas, is marked by a small pool of bubbling gray mud.

The flaming geyser is now merely an interesting attraction in the lovely park that sits at the end of the Green River Gorge. The heart of the park, on the south side of the meandering river, is a series of meadows rimmed by cottonwood, yellow cedar, and 100-foot-high maples. The section enclosed by the western river bend holds large grass fields designated as remote-control model airplane flight zones. A large circular clipboard serves as a control station for posting radio frequencies to avoid conflicts.

The burger-and-chips crowd gather at the middle of the park, where picnicking and other day-use facilities are stretched along the outward-curving bend of the river. A pair of shallow concrete ponds next to the ELC holds up to 5,000 steelhead smolt each spring. The smolt spend about 8 weeks becoming "imprinted" with the water of Christy Creek to prepare them to return to the spot for spawning—a bit like training homing pigeons.

Several trails weave through the park. The longest, about 1 mile, follows the forested hilltop above the heart of the state park. Others explore farther reaches of the park, occasionally reaching the river. Four distinct types of park habitat—marsh, riverbank, meadow, and woodland —make the trails heaven for birdwatchers; in the forest look for the parrot-bright red, yellow, and black flash of the western tanager. Large rectangular holes in conifers are evidence of pileated woodpeckers. Other park residents include deer, raccoon, black bear, beaver, and otter.

The Green River is relatively placid at this end of the gorge and becomes even calmer as it continues west through farmland. During the low water levels of summer, this section of the river is popular for floating on small inflatables, inner tubes, and air mattresses. When water is higher, however, even this part of the river requires some skill, as well as the

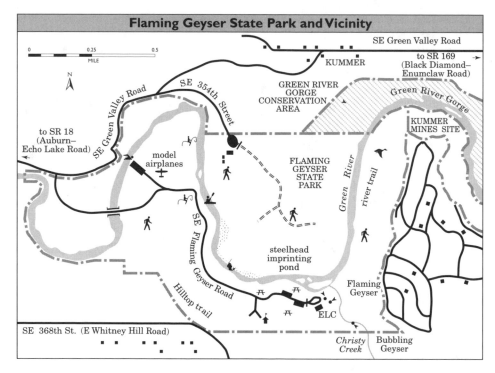

Flaming Geyser State Park and Vicinity

Flaming Geyser is but a whisper of its former glory, but it is still interesting.

and barbecues sit in grass above the beach. Two large picnic shelters on the southwest side of the park may be reserved for groups.

In spite of its rather modest 39 acres, at some points the lake is over 100 feet deep, thus its name. Two fishing docks give youngsters a chance to catch catfish, perch, and crappie, while experienced anglers can try for more canny trout. A road spur and short trail 0.2 mile north of the main entrance permit easy launching of cartop boats; cars, however, must be parked in the main lot.

A wide, 1.4-mile-long trail circles the lake, with frequent spurs down to fishing spots along the shore. A secluded lagoon, rimmed with fallen dead trees, marks the north end of the lake. Midway along the east side of the lake a bridge crosses Deep Creek, which feeds the lake. Perhaps you might spot some of the local deer or small creatures such as squirrels and skunks. Migratory waterfowl drop by for a brief stay in spring and fall. A short interpretive trail circles through the woods on the southeast side of the park.

proper safety equipment. The state park is the take-out point for whitewater boaters who have bested the more tumultuous sections higher in the gorge.

Most of the flat, broad thumb of land on the north side of the river also is park property. It's a nice spot to explore but has no facilities, and paths are primitive. Follow old roads or beat a route through grass to the river.

NOLTE STATE PARK

Picnicking, birdwatching, nature study, hiking, bicycling, jogging, swimming, fishing, paddling

SEASON/HOURS: Closed September 30 through mid-April.
AREA: 117.23 acres; 7,174 feet of fresh-water shoreline on Deep Lake.
DAY-USE FACILITIES: 60 picnic sites, 20 barbecues, 2 group day-use areas with picnic shelters (50 persons each), restrooms (&).
RECREATIONAL FACILITIES: 1.4 miles of hiking/bicycling trails, self-guided nature trail, sports field, horseshoe pits, swimming beach, 2 fishing docks, hand-carried boat launch (*no gasoline motors*).
CAR ACCESS: See directions to Kanaskat-Palmer State Park. Nolte is 3.8 miles south of Kanaskat-Palmer on the Veaze–Cumberland Road.

Deep Lake has been a favorite family retreat since the early 1900s, when the Nolte family developed and operated a private resort along its shore. With the death of matriarch Minnie Nolte in 1972, the property was willed to the state for use as a park so future generations could continue to enjoy the scenic retreat.

The parking area adjoins a lawn that sweeps down to the sandy swimming beach. Concrete pads with picnic tables

FEDERATION FOREST STATE PARK

Picnicking, guided nature walks (by appointment), hiking, fishing, cross-country skiing, interpretive center

SEASON/HOURS: Day-use year-round; Catherine Montgomery Interpretive Center open May through September, Wednesday through Sunday, 10:00 A.M. to 5:00 P.M., other times by appointment only.
AREA: 618.9 acres; 19,800 feet of fresh-water shoreline on the White River.
DAY-USE FACILITIES: 35 picnic sites, 2 picnic shelters, amphitheater, 2 rest-rooms (&), 2 toilets (&).
RECREATIONAL FACILITIES: 2 miles of interpretive trails, 9.5 miles of hiking

trails.
EDUCATIONAL FACILITIES: Interpretive
center, interpretive displays.
CAR ACCESS: 15.8 miles southeast of
Enumclaw on SR 410.

While many of Washington's state parks have recreation as a focus, Federation Forest is a showcase for ecosystems, with humans present only as guests. The park includes the Catherine Montgom-

An enormous old Douglas-fir carries a thick coat of moss at Federation Forest State Park.

ery Interpretive Center, which holds displays designed to acquaint visitors with the plant and animal life in the seven different biotic zones found in the state. Adjoining five of the displays are windows with views of small outdoor plots that are living dioramas of plants of particular zones. Other panels describe the geological evolution of the White River valley and the history of the Naches Trail, one of the first pioneer trails from eastern Washington to Puget Sound. Vestiges of that trail can be found in the park.

Visitors can enjoy the park's richness of flora and fauna from the network of trails and self-guided nature loops. Guidebooks are available; a separate pamphlet has a checklist of some 94 different birds that you might see. Just west of the interpretive center a kiosk marks the start of the two Fred Cleator interpretive trails. West Trail, 0.9 mile long, and East Trail, 0.4 mile long, together wind through five different major forest communities. River Trail, a 0.75-mile branch of East Trail, parallels the bank of the White River, following a portion of the old Naches Trail. Gape upward at virgin trees that our pioneer forefathers saw in 1853 on their brutal trek across the Cascades. A second kiosk, adjacent to the highway 0.6 mile east of the main park entrance, marks the start of a shorter nature trail that describes the devastating effect of a 1983 windstorm. The park's level trails are popular cross-country skiing routes in the winter.

A short road spur leads east from the interpretive center parking lot to a loop of tree-shaded picnic tables. From here a long, elevated boardwalk crosses a creek and marsh to emerge from the trees at another picnic area where tables and fire braziers line the edge of a grassy flat that overlooks the braided riverbed. A third picnic area is at a pulloff loop north of the highway, about 0.5 mile east of the main park entrance.

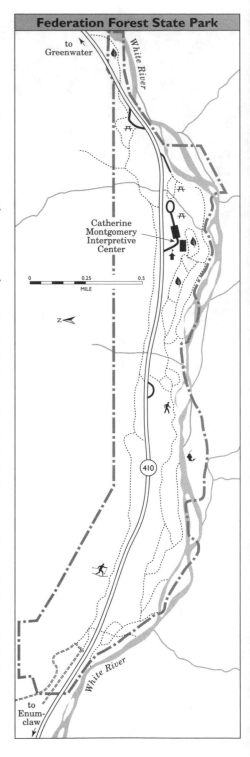

CHAPTER SIX

SOUTHWEST CASCADES

MILLERSYL-VANIA STATE PARK

Camping, picnicking, fitness trail, hiking, bicycling, swimming, fishing, boating

SEASON/HOURS: Year-round; campsite reservations accepted in summer.

AREA: 843.56 acres; 3,300 feet of fresh-water shoreline on Deep Lake.

OVERNIGHT AND DAY-USE FACILITIES: 48 RV sites (2 &), 118 standard camp-sites (3 &), 4 primitive campsites, group camp (40 persons), 216 picnic sites, 4 reservable kitchen shelters, group day-use area (300 persons), 4 restrooms (3 with showers) (2 &), trailer dump station.

RECREATIONAL FACILITIES: 6.6 miles of hiking/bicycling trails, 1.5-mile fit-ness trail, 2 swimming beaches, 2 bathhouses (&), hand-carry boat launch, dock.

ELC: (70–158 persons summer, 40–158 persons winter), kitchen/dining hall, 3 staff cabins, 16 squad huts, 2 rest-rooms with showers, 2 teaching/pic-nic shelters, horseshoe pits, volleyball court, basketball hoop, baseball backstop, canoes, trails.

Rolling hills create a scenic backdrop for an old wagon at Dalles Mountain Ranch.

CAR ACCESS: At Exit 95 (SR 121 N, Little Rock, Maytown) from I-5, take Maytown Road SW east for 2.6 miles, then turn north on Tilley Road SW, and reach the park in another 0.7 mile.

Millersylvania could actually be named "Mueller's Woods." This site was settled in 1881 by Johann Mueller (not known to be a relative of the authors). Mueller was a general in the Austrian army who married the daughter of Emperor Franz Josef I without benefit of official permission. For this transgression the couple was exiled to the U.S.; at some point their name was anglicized to Miller. Their homestead was deeded to the state upon the death of the last remaining family member. During the early 1930s the Depression-era CCC set up an area headquarters here; most of the sturdy rock-and-log structures of the park reflect that time.

Northeast of the park's main road, numerous campground roads circle among enormous Douglas-fir. The heavy shade of the forest canopy makes ground cover sparse, but the cathedral-like stand of cedar and fir provide a degree of privacy to the campsites. Hookup loops line one side of a grassy playfield near the campground entrance. At the west end of the field, a massive stone fireplace is all that remains of a onetime maintenance building.

South of the road lies Deep Lake, ringed by pleasant woods. Parking loops lead to picnic areas and several massive log-and-stone picnic shelters and bathhouses. Picnic sites are scattered amid the trees along the shore; whatever grass was once here has long since been ground to dirt by the tread of thousands of visitors. Tall firs bathe the area in shade, even during the hottest days of summer. Two swimming beaches are near-twins, although the one on the east is larger. These beaches are the only spots where the shoreline is readily accessible; elsewhere the shore is held by trees and marsh growth.

A fishing pier and boat launch mark the west end of the main park area, next to a small section of private land within the park boundaries. "Boat launch" here means cartop or hand-carried boats only; a log barrier at water's edge prevents trailered boat launching. The popular 66-acre lake, which is regularly planted with rainbow trout, provides good fishing from April through July. Motors are permitted; the speed limit is 5 mph. A commercial resort is on the east end of the lake.

The road continues west to the ELC. Here is another swimming beach, a dock, sports areas, and ELC buildings, with cabins clustered around patches of lawn separated by trees and brush.

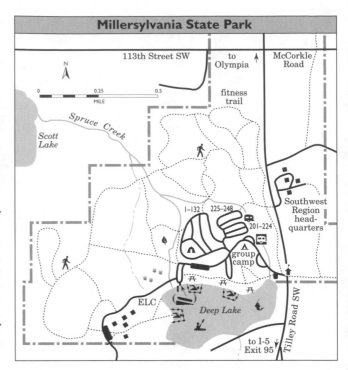

Stately fir and cedar trees shade the campsites at Millersylvania State Park.

Trails weave through ferns, Scotch broom, an old orchard, and ancient timber north of the ELC. Watchful hikers might spot remnants of an old narrow-gauge railroad, several skid roads, and springboard notches in stumps, all evidence of logging activity dating to the early 1800s. Additional trails penetrate the wooded sections of the park north of the campground area. Some paths connect to a 1.5-mile fitness trail northeast from there.

NISQUALLY-MASHEL PROPERTY

Birdwatching, hiking, mountain biking, fishing

AREA: 742 acres; 21,000 feet of freshwater shoreline on the Nisqually and Mashel Rivers.
FACILITIES: None.
CAR ACCESS: No driveable road access into the property. To reach a gated road into the heart of the property, which can be hiked, at I-5 Exit 133 (Eatonville, Mount Rainier) in Tacoma, take SR 7 south. In 22 miles, pass the intersection with SR 702 to Yelm. Continue south for another 3.2 miles, then turn south on Medical Springs Road (unmarked, except as "Dead End"). In one mile take a dirt road to the east, which is soon gated. Park on the road shoulder and hike east on the road.

For several years the state has been acquiring property adjoining the confluence of the Mashel and Nisqually Rivers, 1.5 miles southwest of Eatonville. More than 160 acres lie on the south bank of the Nisqually. However, the old bridge across the Nisqually near the confluence of the two rivers was destroyed by floods, and only gated, private Weyerhauser logging roads reach the property. The access from the north, described

here, is an old abandoned logging road, which can be hiked to the site of the old Nisqually bridge, a distance of about 1.3 miles, one way.

The hike begins in an old forest clearcut. On clear days enjoy knock-out views of the west face of Mount Rainier from here. In about 0.5 mile the road makes a switchbacking descent across the wooded cliff on the west side of the Mashel River drainage, then reaches a bridge across the river. The property between the east side of the river and the north bank of the Nisqually is part of the University of Washington's Pack Forest, but is open to public travel.

The confluence of the two rivers, once a village site of the Nisqually tribe, was also the location of the "Mashel Massacre." In 1856, during the short-lived Puget Sound Indian Wars, all white settlers in the vicinity were killed.

The sandy riverbank at the confluence of the rivers is framed by impressive 100- to 250-foot-high walls of the Nisqually Canyon and Mashel Gorge. Cliff faces are laced with bird nests, and at this point the rivers are important steelhead and salmon spawning grounds.

State Parks hopes to have the funds to develop this beautiful and historic site in the future.

MATILDA N. JACKSON STATE PARK AND JOHN R. JACKSON HOUSE HERITAGE AREA

Picnicking, historical display, historic building

SEASON/HOURS: Year-round. John R. Jackson House open by appointment only.
AREA: Park 5 acres, John R. Jackson House 1.38 acres.
DAY-USE FACILITIES: 3 picnic tables, picnic shelter, toilet.
EDUCATIONAL FACILITIES: Historical cabin and monument.
CAR ACCESS: From Exit 68 (US 12 E, Morton, Yakima) from I-5, head east on US 12 and in 3 miles, at Mary's

The John R. Jackson House, on the South Fork of the Newaukum River, was the first American pioneer home north of the Columbia River.

Corner, the intersection of US 12 and Jackson Highway, drive north for 0.3 mile; the park is on the west side of the highway. The John R. Jackson house is on the east side of the road 0.1 mile south of the intersection.

John R. Jackson headed west to Oregon Territory from Illinois and settled on the banks of the South Fork of the Newaukum River. Two small portions of his extensive holdings have been donated to state parks. One is the site of the John R. Jackson House; the second is a small plot that is now a day-use park named for his wife, Matilda. The park is shaded by the only remaining Douglas-fir in the immediate vicinity. A monument placed by the Daughters of the American Revolution commemorates the Cowlitz Trail, a northern extension of the Oregon Trail that ran past the site.

Jackson's one-room log cabin, built in 1848, was the first American pioneer home north of the Columbia River. Since it was on the Cowlitz Trail, the home was a favorite stop for travelers. Jackson served on various occasions as sheriff, assessor, tax collector, justice of the peace, and territorial representative. The house had an equally diverse history; it was used at times as a post office, grocery store, tavern, voting place, and in 1850 as a courtroom for the U.S. district court. In later years the dwelling was enlarged and additional buildings were constructed to accommodate the increasing number of visitors. Among these were Ulysses S. Grant and Isaac T. Stevens, Washington's first governor.

Age took its toll on the property, and after John and Matilda died, all of the buildings except the original Jackson home were torn down. The house itself had partially collapsed when the property was acquired by Augustine Donohoe in 1911. When he donated it to the state in 1915, it became one of the first two state park properties. Over the next seven years local historical societies worked at restoring the house, and repairs were completed by the CCC in 1935. Most of the furniture and tools displayed belonged to the Jackson family. An interpretive panel on the lawn tells the history of the Jacksons and the house, and has a map of the Cowlitz Trail. The house is open by appointment; contact Lewis and Clark State Park to schedule a visit.

LEWIS AND CLARK STATE PARK

Camping, picnicking, wading, hiking, horseback riding, juvenile fishing

SEASON/HOURS: Closed October 1 through March 31.
AREA: 621.28 acres.
OVERNIGHT AND DAY-USE FACILITIES: 25 standard campsites (&), group camp with picnic shelter (50 persons), group camp with a 3,500-square-foot rental building (100 persons), 62 picnic sites, picnic shelter, 2 kitchen shelters, group day-use area (100 persons), 2 restrooms (1 with showers), 3 toilets.
RECREATIONAL FACILITIES: 3.5 miles of hiking/equestrian trails, interpretive displays, amphitheater, horseshoe pits, wading pool, horse corral, hitching posts, horse loading ramps.
EDUCATIONAL FACILITIES: 1.25-mile interpretive trail.
ELC: (12–50 persons day-use), bunkhouse (24 persons), kitchen, 2 restrooms (1 with showers).
CAR ACCESS: From Exit 68 (US 12 E, Morton, Yakima) off I-5, head east on US 12 for 2.6 miles to Mary's Corner, then drive south on the Jackson Highway to reach the main park entrance in 1.8 miles. The entrance to the equestrian area is east of Jackson Highway another 0.2 mile south of the main park entrance.

Have you ever wondered what the forests in this area were like when the first pioneers saw them? Most of the forests

Mount St. Helens can be seen from Lewis and Clark State Park. The park housed the first St. Helens interpretive center after the volcano's devastating eruption.

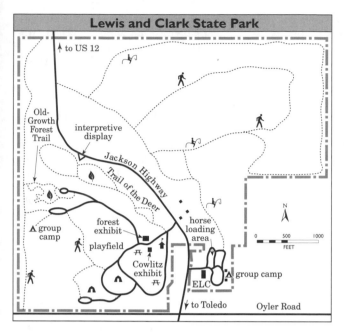

Lewis and Clark State Park

[Map labels: to US 12; Old-Growth Forest Trail; interpretive display; Jackson Highway; Trail of the Deer; group camp; forest exhibit; playfield; Cowlitz exhibit; horse loading area; ELC; group camp; to Toledo; Oyler Road; N; 0 500 1000 FEET]

we see today are second- or third-growth, and the predominant species are those that provide the most profitable timber harvests. At Lewis and Clark State Park one of the last major stands of old-growth forest remaining in the Puget Sound lowlands is preserved for us to see. A pair of platforms along the west side of the Jackson Highway near the north park boundary overlook prime examples of old-growth Douglas-fir and western red cedar, and invite you to visit the park's trails. A kiosk at the day-use area and a nearby pavilion tell the human and ecological history of the region.

The park's 0.5-mile Old-Growth Forest Interpretive Trail loops through the west side of the park. Stop at benches along the trail to look at trees and consult the descriptive park brochure. Spectacular Douglas-fir, grand fir, western hemlock, and western red cedar form a green canopy hundreds of feet overhead, and the faint whisper of wind through their upper branches is the only sound to be heard. A second interpretive loop, the Trail of the Deer, leads past a series of stations, also described in a brochure,

that depict the various life cycles in the forest ecosystem. More hiking trails through equally spectacular timber lace the remainder of the park. As magnificent as the forest is, not long ago it was even greater. The devastating Columbus Day storm of 1962 blew down over half of the park's trees; some 8.5 million board feet were lost, and a more recent storm in 1995 caused further damage.

The park's small campground has sites pressing back into timber and brush so dense that one feels like the only camper in the area. A small creek that runs through the day-use area near the entrance has been dammed to create a natural wading pool. An amphitheater in the area is used for presentations on the park's history on Friday and Saturday evenings in summer. The remainder of the picnic area and the adjoining playfield are grassy plots carved out of the thick surrounding woods. Evident throughout the park is CCC construction, in the sturdy rock and log picnic shelters, restrooms, and ranger residences.

A second section of the park east of the Jackson Highway is devoted to equestrian use, a group camp, and the park's ELC. The entrance to this section is 0.2 mile south of the main park entrance, on the opposite side of the road. Horse unloading facilities are along a pair of short loop roads. An equestrian trail leads northwest through the woods to the park boundary, then traces the north, east, and south perimeter of the park before returning. Total loop distance is a little over 2 miles. A 1.75-mile-long hiking loop circles through the same area, inside the equestrian trail.

Ike Kinswa State Park

Camping, picnicking, hiking, bicycling, swimming, waterskiing, fishing, boating, paddling

SEASON/HOURS: Year-round, reduced campsites in winter; campsite reservations accepted in summer.

AREA: 457.32 acres; 46,000 feet of freshwater shoreline on Mayfield Lake and the Tilton and Cowlitz Rivers.

OVERNIGHT AND DAY-USE FACILITIES: 41 RV sites (占), 60 standard campsites (2 占), 2 primitive campsites, 51 picnic sites, 4 restrooms (3 with showers, 占), bathhouse, trailer dump station.

RECREATIONAL FACILITIES: 3.1 miles of hiking trails (占), children's play equipment, unguarded swimming beach, 2-lane paved boat ramp with boarding float.

CONCESSIONS: Food, beverages, groceries, fishing tackle.

CAR ACCESS: From Exit 68 (US 12E, Morton, Yakima) off I-5, head east on US 12 for 14 miles, then turn north on SR 122 (Silver Creek Road). At a Y-intersection in 1.9 miles, take SR 122 (Harmony Road) east 1.6 miles to the park.

When electric companies construct dams for hydroelectric power, recreationists often benefit too, as they gain lakes for all sorts of water-oriented activities. This is the case with Ike Kinswa State Park, which was acquired from Tacoma City Light after the construction of the Mayfield Dam. The dam creates a 14-mile-long, 2,200-acre reservoir at the point where the Tilton River joins the Cowlitz; the state park stretches along the northeast corner of Mayfield Lake and extends 4 miles up the flooded arm of the Tilton. The spacious reservoir easily accommodates boating, paddling, fishing, waterskiing, and swimming without crowding. As a result, the state park is extremely

151

popular during the summer, and its campgrounds are popular all season long.

The rivers bountifully provided fish for the Cowlitz Indians, who once had villages along the banks. With the building of the dam, most of the ancient sites were flooded; a pair of graves within the park, marked for historic preservation, are the only vestige of this heritage. To acknowledge the history of the Cowlitz tribe in the area, in 1971 the name of the park was changed from Mayfield to Ike Kinswa. He was a member of the tribe that lived here in the 1880s.

At the south end of the bridge over the mouth of the Tilton River, a single-lane boat ramp drops from a parking lot to the water. The remainder of the park lies north of the bridge. Three camping loops are laid out on a triangular-shaped peninsula southeast of the road. The first loop, equipped with hookups, has some sites fronting on the low-bank rocky beach of Mayfield Lake. The other two loops lie in woods, closer to the bank of the Cowlitz. At the beach between them a small grassy slope flows down to the water's edge, permitting easy beaching of boats. A trail circles the peninsula between the water and the campsites.

The day-use area is west of the highway. Here a small arm of the Tilton River loops around a wooded islet. The shallow channel behind the island is roped off for summertime swimming and paddling. A broad swimming beach is roped off at the northwest end of the channel, and above it a grassy slope leads up to a bathhouse, concession stand, and playground equipment. A second side lawn tapers down to the west to the shore of the Tilton. Picnic tables are scattered throughout both of these areas.

A segment of trail parallels the west side of the entrance road from the gate to the channel behind the island. A second trail, a one-time logging road that has gracefully deteriorated into a wide flat path, heads north from the day-use area along a low bench between the lake and the adjoining hillside. Spur trails lead inland and down to the edge of the mouth of the Tilton River, now an arm of the lake. Moss-covered alder, some as much as 120 feet high, arch over the trail, and huge cedar stumps with loggers' springboard notches remind the visitor of the immense forest that once grew here.

From boatside, keep an eye out for tall, bare fir snags along the shoreline. Eagles nest here in winter months, and osprey "sublet" the sites when the eagles migrate during the summer.

An osprey nest can be seen atop a tall snag at Ike Kinswa State Park.

Ike Kinswa State Park

(map: 0 — 2000 — 4000 FEET; N; Tilton River; to Mossy Rock; Mayfield Lake; Cowlitz River; Harmony Road; to US 12; I-41; 42-101)

PACKWOOD PROPERTY

Nature study, hiking, fishing

AREA: 174.6 acres; 1,000 feet of freshwater shoreline on Skate Creek and the Cowlitz River.

CAR ACCESS: From US 12 at Packwood, just west of the Packwood Ranger Station, take Skate Creek Road northwest from town across the Cowlitz River. The park property lies west of this road, and south and east of Craig Road.

This undeveloped state park property straddling Skate Creek is bounded on the west, north, and east by county roads. Most of the property has been logged at one time, and is now covered by second-growth Douglas-fir, pine, and alder. Although there are no developed facilities at present, the property is accessible for short hikes on overgrown roads carpeted by green mats of moss, or for fishing in Skate Creek.

SEAQUEST STATE PARK

Camping, picnicking, hiking, bicycling, interpretive displays and programs at adjacent Mount St. Helens National Volcanic Monument Interpretive Center

SEASON/HOURS: Year-round; campsite and reservations accepted in summer.

AREA: 475.13 acres; 3,000 feet of fresh-water shoreline on Silver Lake.

OVERNIGHT AND DAY-USE FACILITIES: 34 RV sites (18 EW) (&), 54 standard campsites (2 &), 4 primitive campsites, group camp with 3 adirondack shelters and a picnic shelter (50 persons), 113 picnic sites, picnic shelter, group day-use area with kitchen shelter (150 persons), campfire ring, 5 restrooms (3 with showers) (4 &), trailer dump station.

RECREATIONAL FACILITIES: 8 miles of hiking trails, children's play equipment, horseshoe pits, sports field, boat launch nearby.

CAR ACCESS: At Exit 49 (SR 504 E, Toutle, Castle Rock) from I-5, head east on SR 504, and in 5.6 miles arrive at the park entrance.

A splendid stand of timber near the shore of Silver Lake shelters Seaquest State Park. Gape in awe at the enormous old-growth trees, some over 7 feet in diameter, that have been preserved in the park.

The campground is split into three segments: The two loops to the northwest lie in a wooded area of tall fir and hemlock;

Adirondack shelters provide cozy accommodations for groups at Seaquest State Park and several other Washington State Parks.

in a second loop to the west, hookup sites sit side by side in an open field; the third loop, to the south near the highway, lies amid alder and maple, with thick brush undercover providing seclusion. A walk-in bicycle camp is west of the entrance to this loop.

The picnic area has a kitchen shelter in a large meadow at the center, with individual sites along the edge, in the woods. A second small picnic shelter sits in the woods at the east edge of the day-use area. Picnic in seclusion or communal conviviality, whichever you choose. A trail leads from the

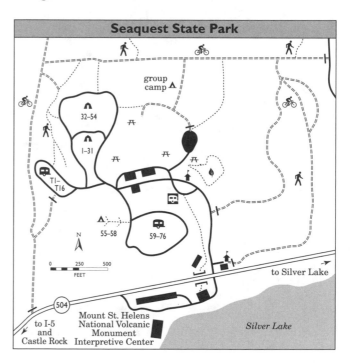

Seaquest State Park

32–54

1–31

T1–T16

55–58

59–76

group camp

N

0   250   500
FEET

504

to I-5 and Castle Rock

Mount St. Helens National Volcanic Monument Interpretive Center

to Silver Lake

Silver Lake

picnic area down through a huge conduit under the highway to the interpretive center. East of the picnic area, a short self-guided nature trail loops through the woods. Other trails wander along service roads and link paths through the forest at the north and east ends of the park. You might see deer, owls, or any of a variety of other birds that live here.

Although the park includes frontage on Silver Lake, the shoreline here is a wide marsh, and no water access is available at the park. A public boat launch is 3 miles to the east. The 2,000-acre lake offers some of the best fishing in the state for bass, crappie, and other spiny rays.

The state park property is host to the U.S. Forest Service's Mount St. Helens National Volcanic Monument Interpretive Center—and quite a center it is! Outside the building, telescopes focus on the distant truncated rim of the volcano. In-

side, displays, a short movie, and a geographical scale model tell the volcanic story. Most impressive, however, is the 20-foot-diameter model of the mountain, with stairs descending into it. Walls along the staircase show the strata below the surface of the mountain; at its heart a red magma tube flows up from a hole that creates the illusion of looking deep into the molten core of the earth.

PARADISE POINT STATE PARK

Camping, picnicking, hiking, fishing, boating, paddling

SEASON/HOURS: Some facilities closed October 1 through April 1; campsite

reservations accepted in summer.

AREA: 91.57 acres; 6,180 feet of freshwater shoreline on the East Fork of the Lewis River.

OVERNIGHT AND DAY-USE FACILITIES: 70 standard campsites, 9 primitive campsites, 29 picnic sites, 2 restrooms with showers (&), 3 toilets, trailer dump station.

RECREATIONAL FACILITIES: 2.5 miles of hiking trails, primitive 1-lane unpaved boat ramp.

CAR ACCESS: At Exit 16 (NW 319th Street, La Center) from I-5, head east on NW La Center Road for 0.2 mile, then turn north on NW Paradise Park Road and reach the park entrance in 0.9 mile.

Paradise Point was perhaps aptly named when it was established some 35 years ago, before I-5 was built and thousands of cars daily roared along the thoroughfare. The campsites are immediately east of the northbound lanes of I-5, and the day-use area extends under it. As a consequence, traffic noise pervades all but the wooded hiking trails of the park. Although quiet and solitude are not its strong points today, the park does offer easy access to some fine boating and fishing on the East Fork of the Lewis River. The stream flows wide and smooth for a mile down to its junction with the main branch of the Lewis River, and then in 3 more miles meets the Columbia.

The campground is on top of a steep wooded bluff that drops down to the banks of the Lewis River. Some sites are shaded by timber; a few are in the meadow of an old orchard. At the northwest corner of the campground loops a trail leads into the woods to primitive walk-in sites. Some parks stick primitive campsites into a back parking lot, but here they are scattered along a lovely wooded trail, truly secluded from the developed campground. The first few are close to water and a toilet, but the remainder are some distance from these amenities, and consequently are seldom used.

The road to the day-use area drops

Tables on the bank of the Lewis River at Paradise Point State Park work well for a game of checkers, as well as for picnicking.

steeply downhill, then just under the freeway ends in a turn-around loop and an unpaved launch ramp. Picnic tables are scattered among the trees. A sandy beach below the freeway invites wading or swimming in the quiet water. Additional picnic sites are west of the freeway along the south shore. In late summer, dessert is provided by thick clusters of blackberry bushes.

A trail heads southeast along the bank of the river to the eastern end of the park. This trail is joined by two steep paths down the hillside from the camp area, one starting at the entrance to the campground loops, and the second descending a ravine at the east end of the string of primitive campsites. A short spur from this latter trail leads over to views of the creek that flows down the ravine, and to what, during the run-offs of spring and early summer, is a pretty, 25-foot-high waterfall.

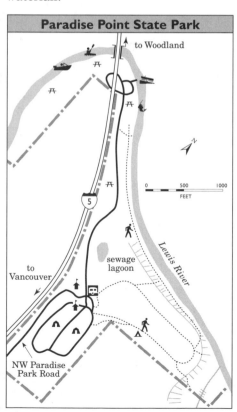

BATTLE GROUND LAKE STATE PARK

Camping, picnicking, nature study, organized sports, hiking, bicycling, horseback riding, swimming, scuba diving, fishing, boating, paddling

SEASON/HOURS: Year-round; campsite reservations accepted in summer.

AREA: 276.5 acres; 4,100 feet of freshwater shoreline on Battle Ground Lake.

OVERNIGHT AND DAY-USE FACILITIES: 35 standard campsites (&), 15 primitive campsites, group camp with 4 adirondack shelters (32 persons), 89 picnic sites, 2 picnic shelters, group day-use area with kitchen shelter (150 persons), primitive equestrian camping area with 2 corrals, 2 restrooms with showers (&), 7 toilets, trailer dump station.

RECREATIONAL FACILITIES: 2 miles of hiking/bicycling trails, 5 miles of equestrian trails, self-guided nature walk, children's play area, horseshoe pits, swimming beach, 1-lane paved boat ramp with adjoining dock (*no gasoline motors*).

CONCESSIONS: Food, firewood.

CAR ACCESS: From I-5 Exit 9 (SR 502, Battle Ground) take SR 502 north, then east for 8 miles to Battle Ground, where it becomes E Main Street. Turn north on NE Grace Avenue, which becomes NE 142nd Avenue in 0.3 mile. In another 0.2 mile turn east on NE 229th Street. Continue east for 2.5 miles on this road, which at various corners successively becomes NE Heisson Road, NE 244th Street, and NE Palmer Road. The park entrance is at the intersection of NE Palmer Road and NE 249th Street. To reach the group and equestrian camps, continue north on NE 182nd Avenue (which NE Palmer becomes at the park entrance) for 0.5 mile, then turn

Fishing interests park-goers at Battle Ground Lake State Park, but resident mallards are more interested in mooching treats from the photographer.

west on NE 259th Street. The group camp entrance is on the south side of the road in 0.3 mile, and the equestrian camp entrance (unmarked) is another 0.4 mile.

What do Battle Ground Lake State Park and Crater Lake National Park have in common? Both lakes are believed to have been created by the collapse of a

Battle Ground Lake State Park

Battle Ground Lake offers excellent fishing year-round.

volcanic cone to form a caldera, which later filled with water. Dimensions are different, of course, with Battle Ground Lake a modest 28 acres, while Crater Lake is 22 square miles in size, but the geological events that created the two are similar.

The park's main camping and day-use areas are on the south side of the park. A campground loop through second-growth timber has gravel pulloffs and enough brush to provide some site isolation. A string of walk-in campsites, shaded by towering Douglas-firs, runs around the south and east sides of the lake. From the park entrance, paths lead downhill to the shore and a sandy beach above a roped-off swimming area. At the south end of this beach is a boat ramp with dock. The spring-fed lake is stocked annually with rainbow trout, cutthroat, small-mouth bass, and catfish eager to take an angler's hook. Fishing is open year-round.

In the 1940s Battle Ground Lake was a private resort, complete with an elaborate swimming beach and a dance floor in the main resort building. After the resort closed, the buildings were bulldozed into the lake, where portions of them remain today. Scuba divers visit the old submerged dance floor and explore for coins and other artifacts from the resort's heydays.

Trails trace the perimeter of the lake. One stays close to the water's edge, with periodic brush-free points that permit shoreside fishing; another path follows the forested rim of the crater above the lake. Rest stops at log benches along the way might once have offered scenic views of the lake, but forest growth now hides all but glimpses of the water. Occasional spurs link the trails. The upper trail accesses the walk-in campsites. The segment of the shoreline trail below the campground is a self-guided nature trail.

Battle Ground is one of the few state parks that has facilities for equestrians. A primitive campground at the northwest corner of the park has been set aside exclusively for their use. See the park ranger to get the gate unlocked. A small meadow can be used for parking horse trailers and staking out horses; another meadow a short distance away has picnic tables, fire grates, and a toilet. The several miles of service roads around the perimeter of the park are open to horses. Equestrian trails may be used for hiking, but walkers must yield the right-of-way to horses and avoid spooking them.

REED ISLAND MARINE STATE PARK

Camping, picnicking, birdwatching, nature study, hiking, waterskiing, fishing, boating, paddling

SEASON/HOURS: Year-round.
AREA: 508.35 acres; 30,400 feet of freshwater shoreline on the Columbia River.
OVERNIGHT AND DAY-USE FACILITIES: 10 primitive campsites, toilet.
RECREATIONAL FACILITIES: 0.5 mile of hiking trail.

BOAT ACCESS: In the Columbia River, 1 mile east of Washougal. Nearest boat ramp is at the Port of Camas/Washougal.

It was on Reed Island that, in November of 1792, Lieutenant William Broughton, captain of the *Chatham*, claimed the Columbia River for Great Britain. Broughton was a member of the Vancouver Expedition, which was returning from its epic exploration of Puget Sound and the waters around Vancouver Island. Although both the *Chatham* and Captain Vancouver's *Discovery* had intended to explore the Columbia, only Broughton's ship was able to make it over the bar at its mouth. Two of Broughton's small boats rowed 80 miles upstream before stopping at Reed Island, laying claim to the river, and also naming Mount Hood for the Lord of the Admiralty.

Today Reed Island is a marine state park, accessible only by boat, although the channel on its north side is nearly shallow enough to wade across during low water. Ten primitive campsites and a toilet are on the southwest side of the island; a sketchy trail leads from here through tall canary grass to the north shore. A heron rookery is on the west end of the island, and the Stigerwald Wildlife Refuge is to the north on the mainland, making the park an excellent place for spotting and photographing birds. The wooded island interior also hosts deer and other wildlife.

BEACON ROCK STATE PARK

Camping, picnicking, hiking, rock climbing, mountain biking, horseback riding, fishing, boating, paddling

SEASON/HOURS: Year-round; campground closed November 1 through April 1.

AREA: 4,675 acres; 9,500 feet of fresh-

Beacon Rock, with its striking form, holds a place in early Northwest history, as well as Native American legend.

water shoreline on the Columbia River.

OVERNIGHT AND DAY-USE FACILITIES: 60 RV sites (&), 33 standard campsites, 2 primitive campsites, group camp with 2 adirondack shelters (200 persons), 101 picnic sites, 5 kitchen shelters, group day-use area (50 persons), 9 restrooms (3 with showers) (5 &), trailer dump station, equestrian camp area.

RECREATIONAL FACILITIES: 9.5 miles of hiking trails, 13 miles of fire roads for hiking/biking/equestrian, 1.25-mile nature trail, children's play equipment, 2-lane paved boat ramp with boarding float, hand-carried boat launch, mooring floats, fishing float.

EDUCATIONAL FACILITIES: Interpretive sites.

CAR ACCESS: On SR 14, drive 3 miles east of Skamania or 6.9 miles west of the Bridge of the Gods.

The dramatic monolith that is the focal point of Beacon Rock State Park has captured the imagination of people since earliest times. For local Native Americans the rock, known by them as *Che-che-op-tin*, marked the lower end of the Columbia River rapids, below which the river flowed obstruction-free to the Pacific Ocean (dams have since flooded the rapids). Legend has it that the rock was first climbed by a princess, Wahatpolitan, in an attempt to save her baby son from the anger of her father, who disapproved of her marriage. The pair died atop the rock, and the wailing of her spirit is said to be still heard when warm chinook winds whip over the summit.

The Lewis and Clark Expedition camped near the base of the rock and named it Beacon Rock, although for many years it was called Castle Rock. The original name was restored in 1916. It is an olivine basalt plug—the 848-foot-high heart of a volcano that has long since eroded away. In 1915 Henry Biddle purchased the rock and started construction on the present, 4,000-foot-long trail.

The trail, which is used by thousands of casual hikers each year, begins at the northwest corner of the rock, adjacent to the highway. From here it threads through 53 switchbacks up the south side of the rock before reaching the small, flat summit. A railing protects the trail's outer edge. Be aware that leaving the trail at any point is dangerous, and hikers should be careful not to dislodge rocks or other debris that could be hazardous (or fatal) to rock climbers on the cliffs below. Views from the top are breathtaking in every direction. The vast Columbia River Gorge stretches east and west; to the north is the sheer 900-foot-high basalt face of Hamilton Mountain; to the south ribbons of delicate waterfalls plummet down the walls on the Oregon side of the river.

Vertical cliffs at the lower part of the south side of the rock provide challenging rock climbing routes. Only properly

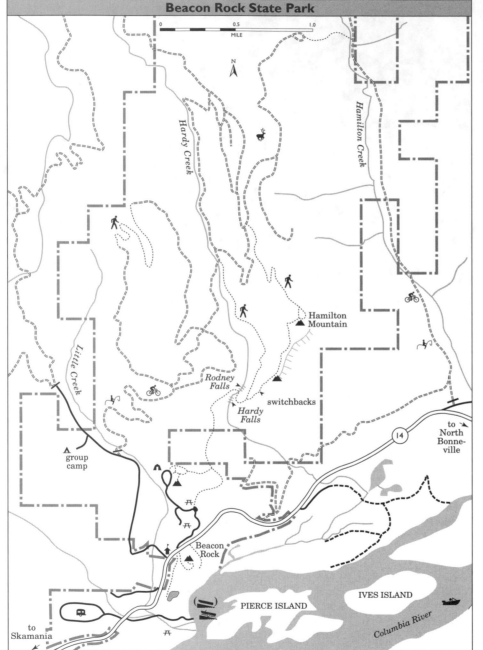

Beacon Rock State Park

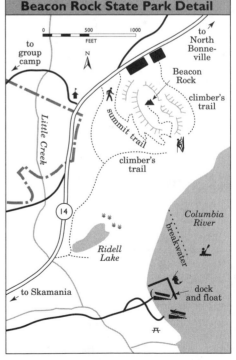

Beacon Rock State Park Detail

equipped rock climbers with advanced skills should attempt these routes; all must sign in and out at the park climbing register. The rock is closed to climbing for two months in the spring during the nesting season for peregrine falcons. Climbing hazards here include poison oak below and rockfall from above.

The older picnicking and camping areas, with vintage 1930s CCC-built structures, sit in the wooded uplands across the highway from Beacon Rock in huge old-growth Douglas-fir with dense ground cover. Newer campsites with full hookups are at the east side of the park on a bluff north of the highway. These sites have excellent views out over the Columbia River.

The largest portion of the park lies inland and north of the highway, encompassing Hamilton Mountain and the Hardy Creek drainage. A gated service road 0.3 mile southeast of the group camp serves as an equestrian loading/unloading site and the start point for a string of more than 13 miles of narrow fire roads that climb through the forest to the steep ridgelines at the north and west sides of the park. These roads are open for equestrian and mountain bike use, as well as hiking.

From trailheads at both the campground and the east picnic area, foot trails join to climb uphill 1 mile to Hardy Creek. Follow short trail spurs to views upward to picturesque Rodney Falls and downward to Hardy Falls. From here the trail continues uphill with a vengeance, gaining nearly 1,200 feet of elevation in a never-ending series of switchbacks to reach the summit of Hamilton Mountain. The route follows the ridgeline north before joining one of the fire roads that then loops back down, meeting the uphill trail about 0.5 mile above the Hardy Creek crossing.

West from the ranger station 0.3 mile, a road marked only by a Recreation Area sign leads east to the park's marine facilities and a large day-use area on the Columbia River. A nearby pasture now serves as a picnic area, with trails along

Fifty-three switchbacks thread up the side of Beacon Rock to the summit.

the river and signs explaining the geology, natural resources, and Native American history of the area. From here enjoy views of the south and west faces of Beacon Rock.

SPRING CREEK FISH HATCHERY

Sunbathing, windsurfing, kayaking, fishing

SEASON/HOURS: Year-round, day-use only.
AREA: 15 acres; 500 feet of freshwater shoreline on the Columbia River.
DAY-USE FACILITIES: Picnic tables, restroom (&), information kiosk.
CAR ACCESS: On the south side of SR 14, 3.8 miles west of Bingen, or 16.7 miles east of Stevenson.

The mid-section of the Columbia River Gorge has some of the most exciting windsurfing available in the world. Steady, strong, 30-mph winds are channeled by basalt cliffs bordering the river, and westerlies that oppose the direction of the river current raise challenging whitecaps along its course. Large swells, chop, and boat traffic in the river make this an area to be used only by expert windsurfers.

Doug's Beach, described following, has long been the popular access for windsurfers. The recent addition of the Spring Creek Fish Hatchery to the parks system takes some of the load off that busy site, fulfilling the basic requirements of windsurfers: good river access and plenty of parking. Winds here are equally strong and steady, although the beach area is narrower than Doug's Beach. The site was once part of the adjoining national fish hatchery, but all of the waterfront not necessary to the hatchery operations has been acquired by State Parks.

DOUG'S BEACH STATE PARK

Sunbathing, windsurfing, kayaking, fishing

SEASON/HOURS: Year-round, day-use only.
AREA: 31 acres; 240 feet of freshwater shoreline on the Columbia River.
DAY-USE FACILITIES: 10 picnic tables, toilets in summer (*no water*).
CAR ACCESS: On the south side of SR 14, 4.6 miles west of the junction of SR 14 and US 197, or 2.5 miles east of Lyle.

When the wind is up (which is nearly all the time) and weather is good, the 0.25-mile-long parking area on the south shoulder of the highway by Doug's Beach is lined with roof-racked vehicles, and the beach and river are a sea of gaudy chartreuse, pink, teal, and purple as sailboards guided by lycra-clad bodies scamper deftly back and forth across the river. A summer weekend with good winds will find hundreds of sailboards on the river, like flocks of multicolored mayflies.

As a park, Doug's Beach is little more than a river access point. A parking area lines the south shoulder of the highway, between it and the railroad tracks. Since this is an active rail line, crossing gates have been installed to block the path to the beach when trains are approaching. A few picnic tables and toilets that serve the hordes are the sole facilities. A swatch of sandy beach grass beside the river functions as a board assembly point, impromptu picnic site, and rest and recreation area for board-sailors and their retinue. Watching the activity can be as much fun as taking part in it.

The park is also a put-in point for kayakers, who experience the same hazards as windsurfers—as well as similar thrills. Gear must be carried some 100 feet from car to launch site.

DALLES MOUNTAIN RANCH

Nature study, hiking

AREA: 3,154.39 acres.
FACILITIES: None.
CAR ACCESS: From SR 14, 0.8 mile east of its junction with US 197, or 0.7 mile west of Horsethief Lake State Park, turn north on Dalles Mountain Road, first paved, then gravel. In 3.5 miles arrive at the ranch site.

This lovely old ranch on the golden, rolling hills above the Columbia River holds promise of a marvelous park. The slopes of the ranch sweep gradually down to SR 14, then drop to the deep channel cut by the Columbia River. Mount Hood can be seen on the horizon. At present, the 6,000-acre property has only the original ranch buildings, which sit unoccupied and ghostly; the lands are leased for cattle grazing and for growing its hay

Doug's Beach State Park and nearby Spring Creek Fish Hatchery offer access to superb windsurfing in the Columbia River Gorge.

fields. Springtime flower walks are conducted by a volunteer naturalist and the previous owner, and the property is open at other times for hikes across the broad expanses, but there is no other formal recreation.

HORSETHIEF LAKE STATE PARK

Camping, picnicking, hiking, rock climbing, boating, paddling, fishing, historic interpretation

SEASON/HOURS: Closed November 1 through April 1.

AREA: 343.81 acres; 7,500 feet of freshwater shoreline on Horsethief Lake and the Columbia River.

OVERNIGHT AND DAY-USE FACILITIES: 12 standard campsites, 2 primitive campsites, 35 picnic sites, restroom with changing room, trailer dump station.

RECREATIONAL FACILITIES: 2 miles of hiking trails, 2 boat ramps.

EDUCATIONAL FACILITIES: Indian petroglyphs.

NEARBY: The Dalles Dam.

CAR ACCESS: On the south side of SR 14, 1.5 miles east of the junction of SR 14 and US 197, or 7.9 miles west of Wishram.

When the railroad was built along the Columbia River, in numerous spots causeways were laid over low, marshy areas. With the building of dams and raising of the water level, many of these marshes flooded and became backwater lakes enclosed by the causeway. The largest of these is 90-acre Horsethief Lake, just above The Dalles Dam.

Although the horsethief who gave the lake its name is not known, other history of the area is well documented. This section of river was a gathering site for canoe Indians from the ocean and lower Columbia River, and nomadic plateau Indians,

who met here to fish, barter, and socialize. A permanent settlement was at Wakemap, the present location of Horsethief Lake State Park. When Lewis and Clark stopped here they described it as a great emporium, where neighboring nations assembled. Today a small Indian cemetery lies inside the park entrance, and a trail along the south edge of the park leads to Indian pictographs painted on rock—believed to be some of the oldest found in the Northwest.

Most of the park lies along the west shore of the lake, where irrigation creates emerald lawns, in stark contrast to surrounding parched desert landscape. Lines of tall Lombardy poplar partition the day-use area and provide windbreaks and shade to the semicircular picnic area. The camping area is unshaded, however, with just a windbreak line of trees behind it.

Two separate launch ramps provide boat access to both Horsethief Lake and the Columbia River. The ramp into the Columbia is steep and gravel, making it a challenge for launching. The paved ramp into Horsethief Lake is less venturesome. The lake is planted with rainbow trout, and because it is joined to the river by a culvert, expect to find most of the same fish here that are found in the river itself. Winds that whip up the river are deflected somewhat from the lake, making it a slightly more protected spot for novice windsurfers to practice the tricks of boardsailing, although winds are erratic, due to its nearness to land.

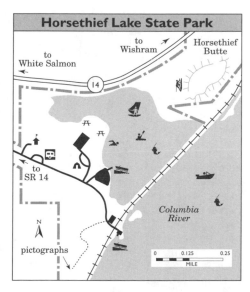

Tsa gag lal all *(She Who Watches) is a combination pictograph (drawing painted on rock) and petroglyph (drawing inscribed on rock).*

MARYHILL STATE PARK

Camping, picnicking, nature study, hiking, swimming, waterskiing, windsurfing, fishing, boating, kayaking

SEASON/HOURS: Year-round; campsite reservations accepted in summer.

AREA: 98.44 acres; 4,700 feet of freshwater shoreline on the Columbia River.

OVERNIGHT AND DAY-USE FACILITIES: 50 RV sites (&), 20 standard campsites (2 &), 3 primitive campsites, group camp with kitchen shelter (192 persons), fire ring, horseshoe pits, 50 picnic sites, 2 picnic shelters, 2 restrooms with showers (&), trailer dump station, swimming beach, bathhouse (&), 2-lane paved boat ramp with boarding float.

NEARBY: Maryhill Museum and the Stonehenge Memorial, John Day Dam.

CAR ACCESS: On the east side of US 97, just north of the bridge across the Columbia River, 1.6 miles south of the junction of SR 14 and US 97 (12.9 miles south of Goldendale).

The Sam Hill Bridge, just west of Maryhill State Park, links the major highways that run along the Washington and Oregon sides of the Columbia River. This location, and its proximity to both the Maryhill Museum and the Stonehenge Memorial, make the park an ideal stopover for visitors. In addition, the park's excellent river access draws swimmers, boaters, fishermen, waterskiers, and windsurfers.

A group camp and two campground loops fill the level, tree-shaded lawns at the west end of the developed park. Lines of trees provide windbreaks for the flat green lawns of the camping loops and the day-use area. Below a bathhouse two rock breakwaters frame a gravel swimming beach, protecting it from river currents. The breakwaters also serve as fishing

The trail to the Indian pictographs starts at the Columbia launch ramp parking lot and leads westward along the base of low basalt cliffs. Unfortunately, in recent years vandalism has caused the path to be closed to the public, and its wonderful rock paintings, including the famous *Tsa gag lal all* (She Who Watches), may now be seen only on ranger-conducted tours, available by reservation on Friday and Saturday at 10:00 A.M. Contact the park for information.

Horsethief Butte rises dramatically above the lake. The 500-foot-high basalt mesa is a striking reminder of the lava flows that once spread across this area. A hiking trail to the butte leaves from the highway, 1.25 miles east of the park entrance. Some limited parking can be found along the road or at a road-marker wayside. The short trail leads straight to the mesa, then climbs some 200 feet up a cleft to the top. Rock climbers use the area for bouldering and short, roped climbs.

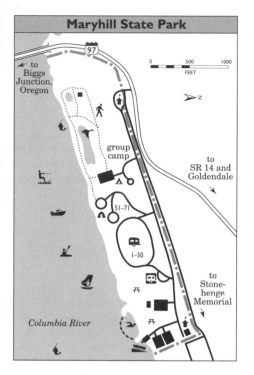

Maryhill State Park

Most of the recreation at Maryhill State Park is focused on the Columbia River.

piers for casting a line well out into the river. East of the swimming beach two launch ramp lanes flank a wooden boarding float. The grassy day-use area serves as space for rigging sailboards. Windsurfing is prohibited in the vicinity of the swimming area, so you should launch downstream. The heavy winds, strong current, and rough water usually present here demand expert boardsailing skills.

Ponds enhance a wetland at the west edge of the park where primitive firebreak roads form foot-trails through a natural area; over 4,300 native plants and shrubs have been planted here as mitigation for wetland destruction elsewhere in the Gorge. Look for eagles, hawks, plovers, seagulls, red-wing blackbirds, and other birds and wildlife.

The state park is 5 miles east of Maryhill Museum, a mansion built in the 1920s by railroad entrepreneur Sam Hill. The museum contains a fascinatingly eclectic collection, ranging from Rodin sculptures to nineteenth-century Russian icons, Native American artifacts, and chess sets.

Another of Hill's creations, Stonehenge Memorial, lies on a bluff just east of the park. It is a full-sized replica (in concrete) of England's prehistoric monument.

GOLDENDALE OBSERVATORY STATE PARK

Astronomy, interpretive lectures, scientific displays

SEASON/HOURS: *Summer hours*, April through September, Wednesday through Sunday, 2:00 P.M. to 5:00 P.M. and 8:00 P.M. to midnight. *Winter hours,* October through March, Saturday 1:00 P.M. to 5:00 P.M. and 7:00 P.M. to 9:00 P.M., Sunday 1:00 P.M. to 5:00 P.M., or by appointment.

AREA: 5 acres.

DAY-USE FACILITIES: Restrooms.

EDUCATIONAL FACILITIES: Lecture room, library, observatories with 24.5-inch reflecting telescope and 8-inch Celestron telescope, six portable telescopes with camera accessories (available to the public), astronomical displays.

CAR ACCESS: At the flashing light on SR 142 (Broadway Street) at the center of Goldendale, turn north on N Columbus Avenue. At the Y-intersection in 1.7 miles, follow the road signed to the park uphill to the right, and reach the observatory in 0.7 mile.

An astronomical observatory is without a doubt unique among all state parks. The dry cloudless nights typical of the Klickitat Valley and minimal light pollution from the small community of Goldendale combine to provide optimal viewing conditions here.

The observatory didn't start out as a state park. It began with astronomers John Marshall, M. W. McConnell, Don Conner, and O. W. VanderVelden, who built the large telescope in 1970 at Clark

The 24.5-inch Cassegrain reflector telescope at Goldendale State Park is open for public viewing daily.

televised worldwide. When the city budget could no longer support the observatory, it was purchased by State Parks.

The main telescope, a 24.5-inch Cassegrain reflector, is one of the largest of its kind in the nation that is available for public use. In addition to the main telescope, an 8-inch Celestron telescope and six portable telescopes with camera attachments (you provide the camera) are available. Tours and very informative lectures are provided to the general public.

The observatory building and exhibits are open to the public in the afternoons of scheduled visiting days. The short trip to the wooded hilltop where the observatory sits offers spectacular views of Mount Adams and Mount Hood. In the afternoon public lectures begin with a view of the rim of the sun through the Celestron, which is equipped with special filters to make this possible. An early evening viewing of seasonally bright celestial objects is followed by an entertaining, informative talk that is geared to making stargazing understandable for the uninitiated and keeping even young visitors interested. When the sky has darkened, visitors are taken to an outside amphitheater and led through identification of constellations and major stars. Later the main telescope is used to view whatever is most interesting or prominent in the evening sky. Smaller telescopes outside the building offer more variety. With the observatory dome open, the evening air can be chilly; warm clothing is advised.

College in Vancouver, Washington, then selected this hilltop north of Goldendale for its location. The city, aided by a federal grant, constructed the facilities to house the telescope, and operated the observatory from 1973 until 1979. Over 15,000 people came here to observe a February 1979 total eclipse of the sun, and it was

CHAPTER SEVEN

NORTHEAST WASHINGTON

PEARRYGIN LAKE STATE PARK

Camping, picnicking, hiking, swimming, waterskiing, fishing, boating, cross-country skiing, snowmobiling

SEASON/HOURS: Closed November 1 through April 1; campsite reservations accepted in summer.

AREA: 578.17 acres; 8,200 feet of freshwater shoreline on Pearrygin Lake.

OVERNIGHT AND DAY-USE FACILITIES: 30 RV sites, 53 standard campsites (&), 2 primitive campsites, group camp with toilet (48 persons), 30 picnic sites, fireplaces, 3 restrooms (&), trailer dump station.

RECREATIONAL FACILITIES: Swimming beach, bathhouse, fishing pier (&), boat ramp (paved, fee), boarding float.

CONCESSIONS: Food, snacks, ice cream, paddleboat rentals (all nearby).

CAR ACCESS: From SR 20 at the center of Winthrop, head north out of town on Bluff Street, which becomes Chewuch River Road. In 1.7 miles

Dry Falls Lake lies below Dry Falls. The ancient waterfall that boiled over the 200-foot-high cliff was more than 4 miles wide—larger than renowned Victoria Falls in Zimbabwe-Rhodesia.

turn east on Bear Creek Road, signed to the park. At a Y-intersection in another 1.8 miles, the paved road makes a sharp turn to the south, reaching the park boundary in 0.2 mile and the contact station in 0.5 mile.

Some 15,000 years ago, during the last Ice Age, an enormous glacier flowed south from Canada, gouging out the Methow Valley in its course. As it retreated, gravelly till left behind by the melting ice sheet blocked some of the drainages, leaving lakes scattered among the scoured hills. Spring-fed Pearrygin Lake is a result of this glacial handiwork.

Viewed from the bluff inside the park entrance, the turquoise lake provides bright contrast to the surrounding hillsides that are parched brown in summer, or in spring painted yellow, blue, and pink with balsamroot, sunflowers, lupine, larkspur, and wild rose. Red-winged and yellow-headed blackbirds flit among the trees, and marmots pop up from nooks and crannies.

Pearrygin Lake is typical of central Washington state parks—a flat, green oasis of lawn where enormous old willows and ash provide respite from the sun. A sandy beach below the day-use area tapers to a roped-off swimming area. Campground loops flank three sides of the day-use area and a lawn that backs

Pearrygin Lake State Park boasts beautiful green campsites edging the lake.

up against the surrounding hillside, while a few edge the brushy lakeshore where bushes provide a modicum of privacy between sites. Short trails leave the easternmost camp loop to circle around the east shore of the lake or to wander a short distance through brush toward the park boundary.

A boat ramp at the west end of the park provides water access for boating, waterskiing, and fishing. The lake is stocked annually with rainbow trout, and a fishing pier offers anglers a chance to land a pan-fry for the evening meal. Probing near-shore shallows might also yield some crawfish. Nearby, outside the park boundary, a small store handles fishing supplies and boat rentals, as well as ice, groceries, and sandwiches.

When winter snow makes swimming, fishing, and waterskiing just a fond memory, cross-country skiers and snowmobilers frequent the park's rolling hills.

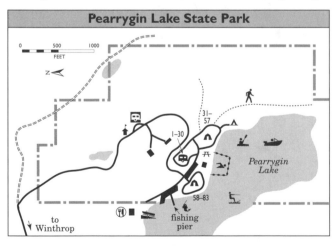

Pearrygin Lake State Park

0   500   1000
FEET

N

31–57

I–30

58–83

Pearrygin Lake

to Winthrop

fishing pier

RUBY TOWNSITE HERITAGE AREA

Sightseeing, historical interpretation

SEASON/HOURS: Day-use, ranger talks by appointment.
AREA: 6.64 acres.
EDUCATIONAL FACILITIES: Historic mining town site.
CAR ACCESS: From US 97/SR 20 in either Omak or Okanogan, follow signs for the road to Conconully. At 7.4 miles northwest of the intersection with the Riverside Cutoff Road (3.1 miles southeast of Conconully), turn uphill to the southwest on Salmon Creek/Ruby Road. Follow this narrow dirt road for 2.8 miles to the historic marker at the old townsite.

A narrow, dusty, out-of-the-way road and a few hidden, weed-shrouded rock foundations are all that remain of what once was the 0.25-mile-long main street of the infamous, roistering city of Ruby. The town, born in 1886 following a rich silver strike in the ridges to the west, became one of the major mining camps in the northwest. Miners and speculators pouring into town slaked their thirst with cheap, free-flowing whiskey. The growing population caused Ruby to be named the first county seat. The origin of the town's name is uncertain. Ruby silver was a particular type of ore; the name also could stem from some miner's love.

Fortune was fickle, however, and in 1893, when the price dropped out of the silver market due to the nationwide economic depression, the town of Ruby was abandoned virtually overnight. Now only a historical signboard and plaque mark the site. When exploring the area, beware of rattlesnakes.

CONCONULLY STATE PARK

Camping, picnicking, swimming, fishing, boating, cross-country skiing

SEASON/HOURS: Closed November 1 through mid-April except weekends and holidays, ranger talks by appointment.

AREA: 80.85 acres; 5,400 feet of freshwater shoreline on Conconully Reservoir.

OVERNIGHT AND DAY-USE FACILITIES: 82 standard campsites (7 with water hookups), 2 primitive campsites, 80 picnic sites, kitchen shelter, group day-use area (350 persons), 4 restrooms (2 with showers) (&), trailer dump station.

RECREATIONAL FACILITIES: 0.5-mile nature trail, children's play area, horseshoe pits, wading pool, unpaved boat launch on Conconully Reservoir; hand-carried boat launch; 2-lane paved boat launch (fee) on Conconully Lake, with boarding float.

EDUCATIONAL FACILITIES: School bell, historical cabin.

CAR ACCESS: From US 97/SR 20 in either Omak or Okanogan, follow signs for the road to the town of Conconully; or continue 5.2 miles north from Omak to Riverside Cutoff Road, turn west onto it, and at a junction in 5.4 miles head northwest on Conconully Road to reach Conconully in another 10.1 miles. The park is on the west side of the highway just inside the town, along the south side of Broadway Street. *To reach the boat launch on Lake Conconully,* continue north into town on the county road for 0.3 mile. Here, at an intersection inconspicuously marked to Conconully Lake and Loomis, turn east and follow the road up the sidehill above the earthen dam and its lake for 0.9 mile to the state park boat ramp.

When the Bureau of Reclamation created Conconully Reservoir in the early 1900s as part of an irrigation project, it also provided the local community with a picnic grounds, a schoolhouse, and a baseball field. Even though the property became a state park in 1945, along with several adjoining parcels, it still has the flavor of a community gathering spot.

The wide grassy field that spreads around the north end of the reservoir is divided into large spaces by huge, venerable willow, pine, and cottonwood trees. Each section provides visitors with an ample picnic ground or playfield. The area to the east offers non-hookup campsites. Another area at the opposite end of the park has water hookups.

Because it is a reservoir, the level of the lake fluctuates widely. When it is at its fullest, the beachfront is marshy and not particularly suited for swimming; however, tots can frolic

Pretty, gently rolling hills surround Conconully Reservoir.

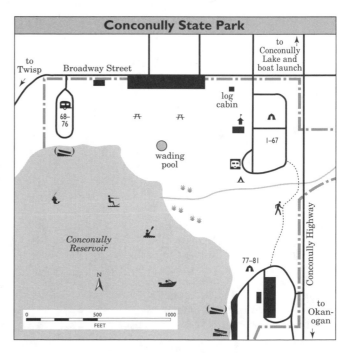

in a wading pool at the center of the park near the beach. Rainbow trout, stocked annually, provide fishing opportunities.

Area history is recounted at a sod-roofed cabin and a school bell near the park entrance. The bell is from the old Conconully Schoolhouse, built in 1890, that stood for many years in the heart of what is now the park. The cabin is a replica of one used as a courthouse when Okanogan County was organized in 1888.

A second camping area lies along the lakeshore south of the main park area. This campground offers lakeside sites and a restroom with showers, although the dirt-surfaced areas make camping here a bit spartan compared to that in the grassy field of the main area. The gradually sloping shoreline and sandy bottom provide a nice, natural swimming beach. The main park area can be reached by a 0.4-mile-long trail that leads north across a footbridge over the creek that flows between the reservoir and Conconully Lake. A dirt ramp for launching cartop boats has been carved from marsh grass that chokes the shore. A better boat launch is east of town on Conconully Lake, as described in the driving directions.

OSOYOOS LAKE STATE VETERAN'S MEMORIAL PARK

Camping, picnicking, volleyball, birdwatching, swimming, waterskiing, fishing, ice fishing, boating, sledding, ice skating

SEASON/HOURS: Closed November 1 through mid-March, except for weekends and holidays; campsite reservations accepted in summer.

AREA: 47.22 acres; 7,306 feet of freshwater shoreline on Osoyoos Lake.

OVERNIGHT AND DAY-USE FACILITIES: 79 standard campsites (2 &), 6 primi-

tive campsites, 58 picnic sites (2 &), picnic shelter, fireplaces, restroom with showers (&), trailer dump station.

RECREATIONAL FACILITIES: Swimming beach, bathhouse, 2-lane paved boat ramp with boarding float (&), mooring float.

CONCESSIONS: Groceries, snacks, recreational equipment, board games.

CAR ACCESS: On the east side of US 97, immediately north of the Oroville city limits.

As the Okanogan River reaches the international border on its southward journey from the Canadian Rockies, it briefly widens into Osoyoos Lake. Although the bulk of the 14-mile-long lake lies in British Columbia, enough extends into Washington to provide a spacious year-round playground.

Early Native Americans called the south end of the lake *soyoos,* meaning "the narrows." The story goes that an Irishman named O'Sullivan added the "O," having little truck with names not beginning in this fashion. The broad flat on the southeast side of the lake was originally used

A young picnicker enjoys a cool drink.

as a campsite by the Okanogan tribe, who also held horse races here. During the mid-1850s the site was used by miners and cattle drivers who followed what was known as the Cariboo Trail north to gold fields on Canada's Fraser River.

From the park entrance a wide lawn drops down the hillside to the flat, shaded campground loops. The lush grass continues on to the sandy lakeshore, interrupted only by a parking lot between the camping and day-use areas. A bathhouse, a host of picnic sites, and a kitchen shelter serve this area. The concession stand in the bathhouse offers more than usual snacks and fast food; you can also rent volleyball equipment, and board games such as Scrabble and Monopoly. A roped-off swimming area provides relief from the summer's blazing heat.

A boat ramp drops into the Okanogan River at the point where it exits from the lake. An adjacent mooring float can also be used for angling for the small-mouth

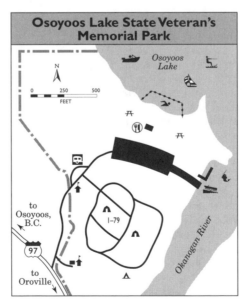

Osoyoos Lake State Veteran's Memorial Park

Osoyoos Lake

to Osoyoos, B.C.

I-79

97

to Oroville

Okanogan River

bass, rainbow trout, kokanee, crappie, and perch found in the lake.

In this region winters are as cold as summers are hot, and snow and freezing temperatures change the recreational focus of the park from swimming and boating to sledding, ice skating, and ice fishing.

RANALD MacDONALD'S GRAVE HERITAGE AREA

Historical marker

SEASON/HOURS: Day-use only.
AREA: 0.1 acre.
FACILITIES: None.
CAR ACCESS: At Curlew, take the West Kettle River Road west from its intersection with SR 21. In 9.5 miles turn east, cross the Kettle River, and follow the highway 1.1 miles north to where a single-lane dirt road heads steeply uphill to the east

Ranald MacDonald, whose grave is in a cemetery near the Kettle River, was the son of a Scotsman and a Native American princess.

for 500 feet to the cemetery. There is a sign on the hillside on the east side of the road, just below the graveyard. If you reach the Midway border crossing, which takes you into Canada, you have gone too far.

A simple, tiny country cemetery sits on a bluff overlooking the rich bottom-land of the Kettle River. Headstones date back to the 1800s, and many graves are marked only by a plain cross. The largest stone in the cemetery commemorates Ranald MacDonald (1824–1894), the son of a pioneer Scotsman and Princess Raven, daughter of Chinook Chief Comcomly.

MacDonald was an adventurer who learned Japanese from two sailors at Fort Vancouver, then later deliberately had himself shipwrecked on the shores of Japan, which was closed to all foreigners. Although at that time Western sailors were usually executed, he succeeded in working his way across the country, teaching the English language and promoting more open and friendly relations between Japan and the U.S. MacDonald was instrumental in helping bridge the gap between Japan and the United States. The men who helped translate at Admiral Perry's negotiations with Japanese officials had been taught English by MacDonald. His birthplace in Astoria, Oregon, is marked by a monument.

Other ventures took MacDonald to Europe, Australia, and Alaska before he returned to live in a small Washington town near where he is now buried.

CURLEW LAKE STATE PARK

Camping, picnicking, swimming, waterskiing, fishing, ice fishing, boating, cross-country skiing, flying

SEASON/HOURS: Closed November 1 through April 1; campsite reservations accepted in summer.

AREA: 123.3 acres; 4,540 feet of freshwater shoreline on Curlew Lake.
OVERNIGHT AND DAY-USE FACILITIES: 25 RV sites (7 EW), 57 standard campsites, 10 picnic sites, fireplaces, 2 restrooms with showers, trailer dump station.
NEARBY: 5 primitive fly-in sites with tie-downs.
RECREATIONAL FACILITIES: 1 mile of hiking trail, swimming beach, 2-lane trailered boat ramp, dock.
CAR ACCESS: The park is on the east shore of Curlew Lake off SR 21, 7.9 miles north of Republic, and 13 miles south of Curlew.

Campers searching for a respite from the civilized, pancake-flat lawns and carbon-copy sites of numerous other state parks in this part of Washington will love Curlew Lake. Although the main campground loop is an RV-crowded flat, many

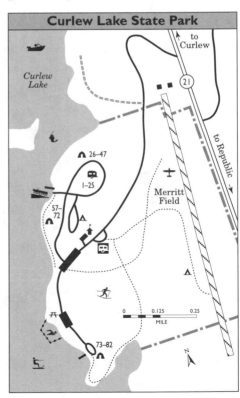

of the park campsites that edge the lake are on grassy hummocks and terraces framed by Douglas-fir. With some, gear must be carried 30 or 40 feet uphill from the car.

Near the entrance to the main camp area, a two-lane boat ramp and adjoining dock provide lake access for boating or fishing. At the day-use area, farther south along the lakeshore, large ponderosa pines shade picnic tables scattered along a grass slope. Below, a swimming beach has been roped off at a small bay. Beyond the picnic area a second snug camping area lies at the road end; individual sites are nicely divided by the natural contours of the hillside. This area also has a dock below it on the lake.

Merritt Field (Ferry County Airport), whose north end lies within the park boundary, has tie-downs for visitors who fly to the park. A trail leads downhill from the airport, or when possible the park will provide transportation for fly-in visitors with camping gear.

In summer the grassy hillsides above the camping area burst with color—blue-purple blossoms of phacelia and lupine, yellow splashes of mule-ears, and white clusters of yarrow. Killdeer skitter through the grass, and at dusk deer emerge. With winter's snow and freezing temperatures, the park attracts ice fishermen and cross-country skiers; restrooms are closed in winter, but the gate usually is left open.

CRYSTAL FALLS STATE PARK

Scenic views

SEASON/HOURS: Year-round, day-use only.
AREA: 156.25 acres.

RECREATIONAL FACILITIES: Primitive trails.
CAR ACCESS: On the south side of SR 20, 14.2 miles east of Colville. The park is not conspicuously marked; look for a gravel roadside pulloff on the south side of the road at this point.

A roadside pulloff on the south side of SR 20 offers pine-framed views down to the Little Pend Oreille River as it drops about 80 feet in a series of white-foamed terraces that form Crystal Falls. Future plans call for day-use facilities and short hiking trails through forest north of the highway.

CRAWFORD STATE PARK (GARDNER CAVE)

Picnicking, guided cave tours

SEASON/HOURS: May to mid-September, Thursday through Monday, tours at 10:00 A.M., noon, 2:00 P.M., and 4:00 P.M.; closed mid-September to May.
AREA: 48.57 acres.
DAY-USE FACILITIES: 8 picnic sites, picnic shelter, water, restroom (&).
RECREATIONAL FACILITIES: Interpretive trail, limestone cave.
CAR ACCESS: From SR 31, 0.3 mile north of Metaline, turn west on Boundary Road (Boundary Dam, Crawford State Park). Follow the road north for 12 miles to reach the park entrance.

Although it is tucked away in the far northeast corner of the state, and not along the route to anywhere, Crawford State Park and Gardner Cave are well worth a special trip. This unique park holds the longest (second longest, according to some figures) limestone cave in the state of Washington. Guided tours explore the upper 494 feet of the 1,055-foot-long cave; at the lower end of the

Fishing is a favorite activity at Curlew Lake State Park, both in summer and winter.

cave three rooms and a narrow passage leading to them are not open to the public.

The cave is said to have been discovered around 1899 by Ed Gardner, a bootlegger who had stills in the area. Legend has it that Gardner lost the cave in a poker game with William Crawford, a Metaline merchant, who gave the property to State Parks in 1921. Early visitors to the park did not understand the delicate nature of the formations, or didn't care about them, and the cave has unfortunately been vandalized. Fine stalactite pipes along the ceiling, which rang like chimes when hit, were broken off by blows from picks, stones, and rifle butts. Initials and dates carved in the limestone indicate that graffiti was as much a problem in the 1920s as it is today.

In the 1950s the State Parks Commission installed wooden ladders, planking, and a crude lighting system and opened the caves to formal public tours. Increased visitation led to the discovery that the oil from human skin stopped the growth of the calcite formations. The 90,000-year-old formations, which grow only in the winter, at a rate of half an inch every 100 years, were being killed by the touch of visitors. To minimize physical contact with the delicate formations and prevent further deterioration of the cave, the park put in the present steel walkways, staircases, and platforms.

Guided tours leave every two hours from the parking and picnic area. Since the temperature inside the cave is 41 degrees year-round, a sweater or jacket is advisable. Once inside, the imagination takes hold, and a flowstone formation transforms itself into a Christmas tree, decorated with a walrus, bumblebee, mountain goat, and alligator. Other formations bear names such as the Wedding Cake, Queen's Throne, and Fried Eggs. When the tour guide briefly turns off the lights at the lower platform, you can actually hear the cave grow as the calcite-laden water drips from the ceiling into the rimstone pools bordering the walkway.

A guide leads a tour through Gardner Cave.

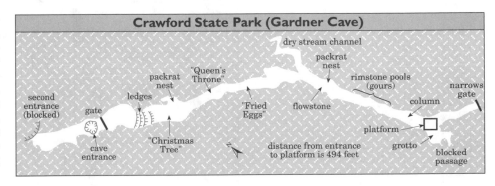

LAKE WENATCHEE STATE PARK

Camping, picnicking, hiking, horseback riding, swimming, waterskiing, windsurfing, fishing, sailing, boating, paddling, cross-country skiing, snowshoeing, sledding

SEASON/HOURS: Year-round, campground closed November 1 through mid-April; Sno-Park permit required for winter activities; campsite reservations accepted in summer.

AREA: 484 acres; 12,623 feet of freshwater shoreline on Lake Wenatchee.

OVERNIGHT AND DAY-USE FACILITIES: 197 standard campsites, group camp (80 persons), 60 picnic sites, 3 picnic shelters, group day-use area (100 persons), 7 restrooms (5 with showers) (&), trailer dump station.

RECREATIONAL FACILITIES: 7.7 miles of hiking/biking trails, 3.5 miles of equestrian trails (some outside park property), children's play equipment, 25 km–35 km of cross-country ski trails (Sno-Park permit required), swimming beach, bathhouse, 1-lane boat ramp (fee).

EDUCATIONAL FACILITIES: Amphitheater (programs Saturday evenings and Sunday mornings, July through September).

CONCESSIONS: Snacks, groceries, firewood, riding stable.

CAR ACCESS: From US 2, 20.5 miles east of Stevens Pass or 10.8 miles northwest of Leavenworth, turn north on SR 207 (signed to Lake Wenatchee State Park, Nason Creek Campground, Fish Lake, Plain) and follow it 3.6 miles to Cedar Brae Road. Here turn west and reach the main park area in 0.2 mile. The north campground is 1.2 miles farther north on SR 207 and the Lake Wenatchee Highway.

The first state park east of Stevens Pass marks the transition from the dense rain-drenched woodlands of western Washington to the more open Douglas-fir and ponderosa pine forests of the Cascades' dry side. Lake Wenatchee stretches for more than 5 miles, filling the valley floor between the steep forested sides of the massive Chiwawa and Nason Ridges. Wenatchee Ridge rises above the far end of the lake, and beyond are glimpses of the Glacier Peak Wilderness.

The park lies on the lake's southeast corner, spanning its outlet at the Wenatchee River. In the heart of the day-use area a gravel beach tapers gently into the water. Just beyond, a tiny tree-studded island is mirrored on the surface of the lake. The woods above the beach contain a group camp and an amphitheater where, on summer weekend evenings, visitors can see interpretive programs on the local geology, history, and wildlife. A few trails thread through this section of the woods,

Lake Wenatchee State Park

North Shore Drive
to White River
207
to Fish Lake
0 500 1000 FEET
N
149–197 LP2
101–148 LP1
Lake Wenatchee
Emerald Island
Wenatchee River
amphitheater
group camp
207
Nason Creek
1–100
stable
South Shore Road
to SR 207
to US 2

Trail rides beginning at Lake Wenatchee State Park explore trails in the park and nearby Forest Service lands.

offering sample views of the native flora and a dash of color from lupine and other seasonal wildflowers.

A single-lane boat ramp, with an adjoining dock and float, is found around the corner from the beach at the Wenatchee River headwater. From boat or bank, anglers can fish the lake for rainbow trout, Dolly Varden, and kokanee salmon. Launch canoes or rafts here for float trips down the placid upper reaches of the river, with chances of spotting osprey nests and riverside wildlife.

Campground loops amid Douglas-fir and ponderosa pine fill the south portion of this section of the park. Signs remind campers that this is bear country; food and coolers cannot be left out, and garbage must be put in bear-proof dumpsters. Mosquitoes are another park pest from April to July, and in recent years concerns over environmental safety and personal health have ended a control program using pesticides—be forewarned and bring your own protection.

A stable inside the entrance offers horseback rides that begin in the park and continue onto adjoining National Forest land. Day rides of one to two hours are available, subject to demand, during summer; wrangler-led overnight pack trips for camping, fishing, or hunting can be scheduled in summer and fall.

A second section of the park lies on the lakeshore north of the Wenatchee River. Here two campground loops in a pine and fir forest are ringed by sites. Trails lace the woods surrounding the campground and follow the river and lake shorelines to the park boundaries.

When winter brings up to four feet of snow, the area is a mecca for snowmobilers and cross-country skiers. Some 35 kilometers of groomed trails are available in the park and on adjoining private and national forest land. Snowmobiles are prohibited on these trails.

Sno-Park permits can be purchased at a store just outside the park on SR 207. Food and other services are also available there.

TWENTY-FIVE MILE CREEK STATE PARK

Camping, picnicking, swimming, wading, fishing, boating

SEASON/HOURS: Closed October 1 through March 31; campsite reservations accepted in summer.
AREA: 235 acres; 1,500 feet of freshwater shoreline on Lake Chelan.
OVERNIGHT AND DAY-USE FACILITIES: 23 RV sites, 63 standard campsites, group camp (48 persons), 6 picnic sites, 2 restrooms with showers (&), trailer dump station.
RECREATIONAL FACILITIES: Wading area, 1-lane boat ramp with boarding float.
CONCESSIONS: Groceries, snacks, marina with 10 public small-boat moorages, boat fuel.
CAR ACCESS: From the north, 1.6 miles south of Chelan, turn north from US 97A onto SR 971 (South Lakeshore Drive) and reach the park in 16.6 miles. From the south, 8 miles north of Entiat on US 97A, turn north onto SR 971 (Navarre Coulee Road) and follow it 9.4 miles to Lake Chelan State Park. Twenty-five Mile Creek State Park is 10.3 miles to the north on South Lakeshore Drive.

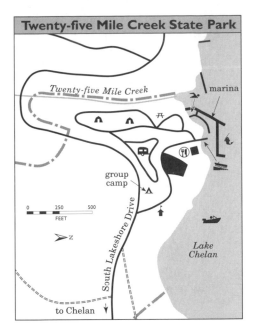

South Lakeshore Drive concludes its meandering, water's-edge route at Twenty-five Mile Creek. The resort that was located here was one of the oldest in the Chelan Valley, enjoyed by millions of recreationists. In 1975 state parks, which planned a major addition of the campground, purchased the resort. Although lack of funding has prevented expansion, all the nice original amenities are maintained.

Tops on the list is the marina, with its wood-faced piling breakwater protecting a gas float and moorage for about 35 boats. Some slips are leased seasonally, but 10 always remain available for visiting boats. If you've hauled your boat all this distance, a launch ramp gives trailered boat access to Lake Chelan. Above the ramp a small store carries essential supplies for

Fishing is a great way to spend a sunny afternoon at Twenty-five Mile Creek State Park.

camping and fishing. The shallow end of the marina basin, inside a footbridge to the breakwater, is great for wading and paddling. The bridge leads to a fishing pier that extends from the north side of the breakwater.

The campsites are a rustic relief from the landscaped lawns found at many state parks east of the Cascades. Here are gravel pulloffs into dirt or grass sites amid a natural second-growth forest of cottonwood, ponderosa pine, and birch. Rushing, burbling Twenty-five Mile Creek creates nature's version of "white noise"— a pleasant, continuous background sound that reaches many of the campsites. The creek offers good fishing for rainbow trout.

Because it is surrounded by Wenatchee National Forest, the park is frequently a take-off point for backpacking or hunting treks in the area. Deer, bear, and grouse live in the nearby mountains.

LAKE CHELAN STATE PARK

Camping, picnicking, swimming, waterskiing, scuba diving, fishing, boating, paddling, sailing, skiing, sledding

SEASON/HOURS: Closed November 1 through mid-March, except weekends and holidays; campsite reservations accepted in summer.
AREA: 127.01 acres; 6,454 feet of freshwater shoreline on Lake Chelan.
OVERNIGHT AND DAY-USE FACILITIES: 25 RV sites (18 EW), 109 standard campsites, 52 picnic sites, picnic shelter, 5 restrooms (with showers), trailer dump station.
RECREATIONAL FACILITIES: Children's play area, swimming beach, bathhouse, waterski floats, 1-lane paved launch ramp (fee), boarding float, 6 moorage floats.
CONCESSIONS: Groceries, deli, snacks, equipment rentals, camping supplies.

CAR ACCESS: From the north, 1.6 miles south of Chelan, turn north from US 97A onto SR 971 (South Lakeshore Drive), and reach the park in 6.1 miles. From the south, 8 miles north of Entiat on US 97A, turn north onto SR 971 (Navarre Coulee Road) and follow it 9.4 miles to Lake Chelan State Park.

Ice Age glaciers that carved a deep, 55-mile-long cleft through the Cascades created Lake Chelan. The lake links the high ragged peaks of North Cascades National Park, on its northwestern tip, above Stehekin, to the arid plateau east of Chelan, at its southeastern end. Although the ribbonlike lake is scarcely 0.25 mile wide in places, the water plunges to depths of nearly 1,500 feet, while adjoining mountains rise more than 4,000 feet within a couple of horizontal miles. For over half its length the shoreline is inaccessible except by boat; the only commercial access to the lake is via the passenger ferry *Lady of the Lake,* which makes regular day-long excursion trips from Chelan to Stehekin and back.

Lake Chelan State Park, scenically situated on the southwest shore of the lake, provides access to this magnificent inland fjord. This largest and most popular public campground in the area lies 7.5 miles west of the busy tourist town of Chelan. The park's many water activities, along with its camping and picnicking attractions, keep it filled throughout the summer.

Campground hookup sites are tightly packed along the perimeter of the circular grassy picnic area, shaded by elm, maple, sycamore, black walnut, and a few ponderosa pine. The road east from here traverses the hillside above the lake, with tent campsites lining both sides of the road. All sites require

At Lake Chelan State Park, several short floats provide boat tie-ups for nearby campers.

174

short carries of camping gear. Those below the road have views of the lake and easy access to a series of short docks spotted along the shore. Two more campground loops lie at the west end of the park, with sites in a grassy, tree-shaded flat lined by elderberry, wild rose, and snowberry.

Open grassy terraces below the bathhouse/concession stand have picnic tables overlooking the swimming beach. The concession stand has a deli, groceries, camping supplies, and water sport rentals. At the west end of the park shoreline a launch ramp drops into the lake next to a 120-foot-long float. A second shorter float is to the east.

ICE CAVES HERITAGE AREA

Sightseeing

SEASON/HOURS: Day-use only.
AREA: 160 acres.
FACILITIES: None.
CAR ACCESS: From the south, take US 97 north from Chelan, and in 2.8 miles turn north on Airport Drive/Apple Acres Road. In another 3.7 miles a blocked dirt road at a roadside pulloff on the west side of Apple Acres Road marks the park property. From the north, 11 miles south of Pateros, turn west on Antione Creek Road, and in 2.1 miles turn south on Apple Acres Road. The pulloff is 1 mile to the south.

Some years ago, before the days of modern refrigeration, local orchardists dug caves in talus slopes where water that had collected and frozen during the winter remained as ice until late summer. These caves, off a back road, were used to preserve fruit from nearby orchards during the hot fall days that followed the harvest. Refrigerated warehouse storage has long since replaced this use of the caves; entrances are now covered by rock slides, leaving only their memory preserved in the history of this small, obscure spot.

The story is more interesting than the site itself now is; however, the barricaded road can be hiked from roadside parking south for 0.25 mile to minuscule Green Lake at the foot of the rock slide that now buries the caves.

ALTA LAKE STATE PARK

Camping, picnicking, birdwatching, hiking, swimming, waterskiing, scuba diving, fishing, boating, paddling

SEASON/HOURS: Closed from November 1 through April 1.
AREA: 182 acres; 3,996 feet of freshwater shoreline on Alta Lake.

OVERNIGHT AND DAY-USE FACILITIES: 32 RV sites (E) (&), 157 standard campsites (&), group camp (88 persons), 20 picnic sites, 2 kitchen shelters, 4 restrooms with showers (&), trailer dump station.
RECREATIONAL FACILITIES: 1.5 miles of hiking trails, swimming beach, bathhouse, 2-lane boat ramp, dock.
CONCESSIONS: Groceries, snacks, equipment rentals, camping supplies, ice.
CAR ACCESS: Take SR 153 west, 0.2 mile south of Pateros. In 1.8 miles an asphalt road, signed to the park, heads south, reaching the entrance in another 2 miles.

The azure jewel of Alta Lake nestles in a side canyon of the Methow Valley. The parched, sagebrush-covered hills give way to rimrock cliffs that line the east side of the lake and steep, pine-edged talus slopes that frame the west. Portions of

Alta Lake lies between steep canyon walls.

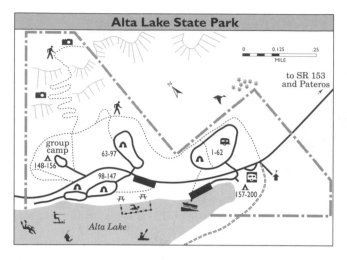

Alta Lake State Park

group camp

148-156

63-97

98-147

I-62

157-200

to SR 153 and Pateros

Alta Lake

Okanogan National Forest touch the east and west shores of the lake. At the lake's south end, a meadow marks two small resorts.

Just inside the state park entrance at the north end of the lake is a boat launch. The 187-acre lake is planted annually with rainbow trout, and fishing generally is fine, especially early in the season. The flat sun-baked field north of the boat launch, nominally a random camping area, offers scattered picnic tables, campstoves, and portable toilets, but no shade.

The first formal camping area lies on the north side of the road. One loop has sites that have full hookups, while sites along a second loop are for tenting. A stand of lodgepole and ponderosa pine offers sparse shade, and undergrowth of sumac and serviceberry provides some separation of sites.

Greener, shaded campsites are found at the west end of the park, just above the beach. The lawn sloping down to the roped-off swimming beach holds picnic shelters, tables, and a bathhouse. The concession stand in the bathhouse offers not only snacks and fast food, but also toys, groceries, propane, some camping gear, and rentals of water and sports equipment. Paths in this day-use area are barrier-free.

At the northwest corner of the park, a gated road marks the entry to a group camp, which is set in a meadow bracketed by small pines. The park's hiking trails begin here. One trail follows a wide service road, climbs a gentle ridge, then contours north at the base of the steep sidehill along the west side of the park before returning to the main road near the park entrance. Charred tree snags along the road stand as sad memorials to a 30-acre forest fire that burned through here in 1990.

The second trail does not delay in going uphill. After crossing the service road, it heads up the steep talus slope in a relentless succession of switchbacks, occasionally ducking back into the forest cover. After a climb of more than 900 vertical feet in about half a mile, the path ends at a small forested plateau. Views here are enormous: The deeply carved cleft of the Columbia River lies beyond the forest-topped cliffs to the east; north, the brown, lumpy hills of the Okanogan pile endlessly against the Washington sky, while below, boat wakes trace patterns on Alta Lake.

FORT OKANOGAN HERITAGE AREA

Picnicking, historical displays, views

SEASON/HOURS: Day-use, Wednesday through Sunday in summer, otherwise by appointment only.

AREA: 44.73 acres; 1,000 feet of freshwater shoreline on Lake Pateros (Columbia River).

DAY-USE FACILITIES: 3 picnic sites, picnic shelter, restroom.

EDUCATIONAL FACILITIES: Interpretive displays.

CAR ACCESS: On SR 17, 8.2 miles north of Bridgeport, or 0.5 mile east of the junction of US 97 and SR 17.

In the early 1800s competition between British, American, and Canadian factions to control the valuable fur trade in the Pacific Northwest led to the establishment of Fort Okanogan as a trading post at the confluence of the Columbia and Okanogan Rivers. Although the fort was built in 1811 by American John Jacob Astor, it was sold in 1813 to the Canadian North West Company, which later merged with the British-owned Hudson's Bay Company. It wasn't until the advent of the Oregon Treaty of 1846 that it was once again in American hands.

The Fort Okanogan Interpretive Center details the fascinating story of the fort, the local Native Americans, and settlement of the Okanogan area. Dioramas recreate early history; a display of artifacts includes tools, fur traps, and

Fort Okanogan once sat here, at the confluence of the Okanogan and Columbia Rivers.

trading items recovered during excavations of the fort, which, over time, was at two separate locations nearby. Archeologists identified remains of the buildings and walls of the forts before the backwater of Wells Dam began lapping at the sites.

The bluff on which the interpretive center stands provides sweeping vistas of Lake Pateros, the river confluence, and the fort sites. Adjoining the center's parking lot is a small picnic shelter and a few Indian petroglyphs.

CHIEF JOSEPH STATE PARK

Hiking, fishing, boating

SEASON/HOURS: Day-use only, no vehicle access.
AREA: 297.6 acres; 25,000 feet of freshwater shoreline on Lake Pateros (Columbia River).
FACILITIES: Causeway, primitive boat launch, 4.5 miles of 1-lane primitive road.
CAR ACCESS: From the east, take SR 173 north from Bridgeport. In 4 miles, where the highway makes a sharp turn to the west, continue north on Moe Road. In 0.2 mile, just before Moe Road angles to the northwest, a gated dirt spur road leads east across the causeway to the park. From the west, Moe Road is 6.5 miles east of Brewster via SR 173.

North of Bridgeport, Lake Pateros bends sharply south around an elbow of land that has been turned into an island by a narrow water channel cutting along its west side. A dirt road crosses a causeway onto the island from the west and links into dirt roads that lace the brush-and-tree-covered island. The site is closed to vehicles; walk-in day-use is permitted.

The state park master plan for this area calls for a large campground, a swimming beach, and a boat launch. Rows of trees that will shade the future campground are in place and irrigated, so the only elements lacking are development and maintenance dollars—prod your legislators!

BRIDGEPORT STATE PARK

Camping, picnicking, swimming, waterskiing, fishing, boating, golfing

SEASON/HOURS: Closed from November 1 through April 1.
AREA: 673.08 acres; 7,500 feet of freshwater shoreline on Rufus Woods Lake (Columbia River).
OVERNIGHT AND DAY-USE FACILITIES: 20 RV sites (&), 10 standard campsites, 4 primitive campsites, group camp with picnic shelter (75 persons), 20 picnic sites, picnic shelter, 2 restrooms with showers (&), trailer dump station.
RECREATIONAL FACILITIES: 0.25-mile hiking trail to a viewpoint, children's play area, swimming beach, bathhouse, 2-lane paved boat launch with boarding floats.
CONCESSIONS: Restaurant, golf course.
CAR ACCESS: Turn east from SR 17, 0.4 mile north of Bridgeport, onto a road signed to the park and Chief Joseph Dam, and reach the park entrance in another 2.4 miles.

Bridgeport State Park sits on the north shore of Rufus Woods Lake, just a short distance upstream from Chief Joseph Dam. The road to the park provides views of the dam, one of the largest in the nation, and its massive powerhouse and row of 27 generator penstocks pouring frothy water into the river below.

The park was nursed out of the surrounding desert, after the 1955 completion of the dam, by the determined labor of Army Corps of Engineers retiree Ralph Van Slyke, who tackled the project with

"Haystack" boulders at Bridgeport State Park were deposited here by ancient glaciers that once flowed over this region.

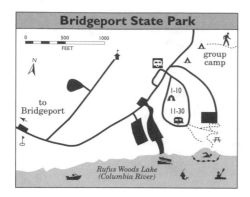

Bridgeport State Park

FEET

N

to
Bridgeport

group
camp

I-10

II-30

*Rufus Woods Lake
(Columbia River)*

little more than garden tools. Today the manicured lawns of the park and the fairways of the adjoining Lakewood Golf Course (on park property and open to the public) prove what irrigation can wrest from a barren landscape.

Cottonwood and aspen shade the green campground loop; scattered outcroppings of rough basalt intrude through the groomed turf. The day-use area is a broad bowl anchored at both ends by unique tile-roofed stucco picnic shelters, fronted

by the swimming beach. Ramps provide disabled access to one of the shelters and to the beach. A community of marmots that lives near the east side of the swimming area often can be spotted playing in the rocks and quizzically watching park activity.

At the north end of the park another grassy flat, this one with an amphitheater, holds a group camp. Boats can be launched into the 50-mile-long reservoir via a paved ramp in a small boat basin. Anglers report catches of rainbow trout and sturgeon.

One step from the irrigated oasis of the park the desert again dominates. Scattered about the parched landscape are fascinating, unusual 30-foot-high basalt "haystack" boulders, which were plucked from the lava flows at the north edge of the Columbia Plateau and deposited here by the massive glacier that flowed over this region some 15,000 years ago. The harsh terrain is habitat for rabbits, coyotes, quail, chukars, partridges, owls, and snakes (including rattlers).

Marmots live in rocks near the swimming area at Bridgeport State Park.

CROWN POINT STATE HERITAGE AREA

Sightseeing, views of Grand Coulee Dam

SEASON/HOURS: Year-round.
AREA: 13 acres.
EDUCATIONAL FACILITIES: Viewpoint vista dome, interpretive display.
CAR ACCESS: From SR 174, 1.1 miles north of Grand Coulee, turn northeast on a paved road signed to Crown Point Vista and reach the park in 1.4 miles.

Grand Coulee Dam is so stupendous that it is hard to grasp from up close. People who tour the dam might well want to see an overall view of the project. At Crown Point an open concrete pavilion sits atop a bluff, with an expansive view far below to the imposing concrete spillways and powerhouses of the dam, proclaimed as one of the wonders of the modern world.

The adjacent communities of Grand Coulee, Coulee Dam, Electric City, and Elmer City, along with the manmade channel of the Columbia below the dam, complete the scene in the valley below.

The viewpoint is a prime spot to watch the spectacular, 35-minute laser light show that is shown on the face of the dam nightly from Memorial Day through September 30. The narrative portion of the light show is broadcast on the local radio station. An interpretive sign describes the dam construction.

Although the dam, which was completed in 1941, originally was intended as part of the Columbia River Irrigation Project, it played a critical role in supplying electricity for the manufacture of aluminum airplanes in World War II. Today it continues to be a major source of power for the state. A visitor center is just northwest of the dam on SR 155, and tours of the dam are conducted year-round.

BANKS LAKE RECREATION AREA

Camping, hiking, birdwatching, horseback riding, waterskiing, fishing, ice fishing, boating, cross-country skiing, snowshoeing, flying, hunting (shotgun only in some areas)

SEASON/HOURS: Year-round.

AREA: 17,700 acres; 81,840 feet of fresh-water shoreline on Banks Lake.

OVERNIGHT AND DAY-USE FACILITIES: 44 primitive campsites on Jones Bay, 36 primitive campsites on Osborn Bay, 5 toilets on Jones Bay, toilet on Osborn Bay.

RECREATIONAL FACILITIES: 5 miles of trail, 10 miles of dirt road, boat ramp at Osborn Bay, and Department of Fish and Wildlife accesses with ramps at Barker Canyon and two sites along SR 155 south of Steamboat Rock State Park.

CAR ACCESS: *Osborn Bay* is on the northeast shore of Banks Lake, 0.5 mile south of Electric City on SR 155.

Jones Bay is on the northeast shore of Banks Lake, 3.2 miles south of Electric City on SR 155.

To reach Barker Canyon, take SR 174 northwest out of Grand Coulee, and in 8.7 miles turn south on Barker Canyon Road and reach the lakeshore in another 5.3 miles.

Surprisingly, Grand Coulee Dam is not located on Grand Coulee, but adjacent to the head of it. It is North and Dry Falls Dams, both earthfill dams, that enclose the ends of Upper Grand Coulee, preventing the water from spilling over Dry Falls, thus keeping Dry Falls dry. Banks Lake fills the enormous gash of the canyon—some 27 miles long and 4 miles wide in places. The lake, which serves as an equalizing reservoir used in maintaining a consistent flow of irrigation water for the Columbia Basin Reclamation Project, is filled with water transferred by pumps from Franklin D. Roosevelt Lake behind Grand Coulee dam.

The State Department of Fish and Wildlife and State Parks jointly administer all land surrounding Banks Lake. Bird and deer hunting is permitted in season outside the developed park area. The major developed recreation areas on the lake are formally part of Steamboat Rock State Park; however, several primitive camping areas and boat launches scattered along the edge of the lake are also administered by the park or the Department of Fish and Wildlife.

Just south of Electric City, after crossing the bridge over Osborn Bay, head west on a gravel road (57.1E) that follows the shoreline, and in 0.5 mile arrive at a paved launch ramp with parking shaded by a few trees. The site, which has toilets and a self-registration station, is used by boaters and fishermen with RVs as a primitive camp spot. Rough dirt roads thread through the adjoining sagebrush-covered desert.

Two additional primitive campgrounds can be found on the east side of the lake at Jones Bay, north of Castle Rock, 3.2 miles south of Electric City. Both have a self-administered pay station at the head of the dirt roads leading to them, level campsites under sparse trees near the marshy shore, and toilets.

Another launch ramp and primitive camping area (15 day limit) is on the west shore of the lake at the base of Barker Canyon, although it's a long haul from civilization by car, and the last 6 miles are on a rough, single-lane gravel road. The ramp, parking, and toilet that have been provided here are administered by the Department of Fish and Wildlife. Two other Department of Fish and Wildlife access areas with ramps,

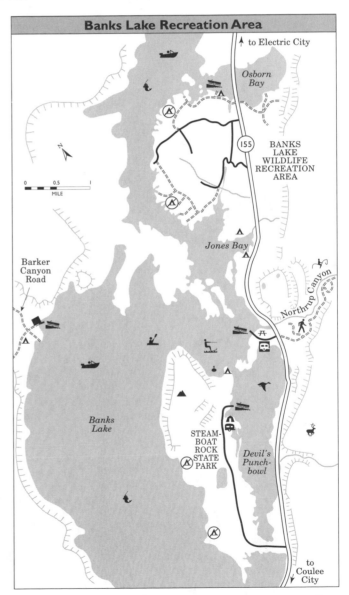

Banks Lake Recreation Area

to Electric City

Osborn Bay

BANKS LAKE WILDLIFE RECREATION AREA

155

0   0.5   1
MILE

Barker Canyon Road

Jones Bay

Northrup Canyon

Banks Lake

STEAMBOAT ROCK STATE PARK

Devil's Punchbowl

to Coulee City

The view from the north end of Steamboat Rock overlooks Banks Lake and, behind, Northrup Canyon. Peninsulas hold the state park's boat-in campground and the day-use boat launch area.

parking, and toilets, but no camping, are found off SR 155, at 9 and 13.5 miles south of the entrance to Steamboat Rock State Park.

All launch sites on the lake warn of submerged and dangerous obstructions barely covered by water. Wind vanes are found at various sites on the lake; when intermittent high winds sweep the lake, the vanes' flashing yellow lights warn that boaters should immediately seek protection in a safe cove.

For fishermen, Banks Lake is close to heaven, as its many rock-walled coves are home to both smallmouth and largemouth bass. The lake is stocked annually with kokanee salmon and rainbow trout; it holds walleye, crappie, perch, blue gill, and whitefish as well. Winter ice fishing yields perch.

The lake serves as a migratory stopover and nesting grounds for shore and waterbirds. Gulls and grebes that are more normally found along the coast are regularly seen here in fall and winter. Surrounding sage and grasslands host hawks and a regiment of perching birds ranging from shy wrens to bold magpies and ravens.

Even for those not interested in fishing, the scenic grandeur of the lake entices. Fingers and arms of the lake, and dozens of small islets, are framed by imposing, 700-foot-high basalt cliffs. For more than a century, trails used by Native Americans, fur traders, and settlers have threaded along the base of the cliffs where roads and highways now run. A major Native American trail followed the eastern shoreline; it later became the American Trail used by the military traveling between Camp Chelan and Fort Walla Walla. A route down the west side of the canyon was known as the Okanogan Trail.

STEAMBOAT ROCK STATE PARK

Camping, picnicking, sightseeing, kite flying, nature preserve, hiking, birdwatching, swimming, waterskiing, windsurfing, scuba diving, fishing, ice fishing, boating, paddling, cross-country skiing, snowshoeing, hunting on adjacent Department of Fish and Wildlife lands (shotgun only in some areas)

SEASON/HOURS: Year-round; campsite reservations accepted in summer.
AREA: 3522.8 acres; 50,000 feet of freshwater shoreline on Banks Lake.
OVERNIGHT AND DAY-USE FACILITIES: 100 RV sites (1 ♿), 26 standard campsites (2 ♿), 12 primitive campsites (boat access), 56 picnic sites, 4 restrooms with showers (2 ♿), 2 toilets, trailer dump station (at Northrup Creek).
RECREATIONAL FACILITIES: 34 miles of hiking/equestrian trails, 3 miles of unimproved road, children's play area, swimming beach, bathhouse, 2 two-lane boat ramps with boarding floats, 2 fish-cleaning stations, 5 mooring buoys.
CONCESSIONS: Snacks, hot foods, beverages, limited camping groceries.
CAR ACCESS: West of SR 155, 9.3 miles south of Electric City or 26.5 miles north of Coulee City.

The dominating natural feature in the north end of Banks Lake is Steamboat Rock, whose 700-foot-high basalt cliffs once bounded an enormous island in the middle of the lip of an ancient waterfall. With shifts in the course of the Columbia River over time, the rock fortress now stands guard over the northwest end of a peninsula in Banks Lake. Although from some views the rock wall seems impregnable, a cleft at the center of its east side breaches the band of cliffs. A short, steep trail, reached from roads starting at the campground and day-use areas, gains 800 feet of elevation in 1 mile before reaching the plateau atop the rock. Once there, rough paths lead around the rim and crisscross its broad, flat, 640-acre summit. No drinking water is available along the route. Horses are not permitted on any of the trails or roads on the peninsula where the developed park is located.

The two campground areas and the day-use area that occupy flat, emerald-green lawns edging Banks Lake are protected against the omnipresent wind by rows of tall Lombardy poplar. Campsites are laid out around the perimeter of asphalt access loops. The sandy-shored swimming beach lies in a narrow channel behind a small island. A triangular section of the channel, with the island at its apex, has been roped off to form the swimming area. A two-lane paved launch ramp is on a small cove to the north. The peninsula north of the boat ramp holds a dozen primitive boat-in campsites above a pleasant, shaded sandy beach. Mooring buoys sit in the cove on the north side of the peninsula.

A second boat launch with an adjacent picnic area is found at Northrup Creek on the west side of SR 155, 3.4 miles north of the main park entrance road. The ramp is well protected by the low rock walls of a small cove. A shaded grassy picnic area adjoins the uphill side of the ramp parking lot.

Immediately across the highway from the entrance to the Northrup Creek boat launch, a single-lane gravel road that climbs up Northrup Canyon is a remnant of a stagecoach and freight wagon road that at one time connected Almira to Bridgeport. Today the road is gated 0.7 mile from the highway. The edge of

the flat-topped butte to the north is the Castle Rock Natural Area Preserve. From the gate several miles of informal hiking and horse trails are open for day-use, including a trail into Northrup Lake, the only natural forest area found in Grant County. The surrounding countryside has deliberately been left natural; in spring and early summer wildflowers are profuse, tingeing the gray-green scablands with hues of yellow, blue, and pink.

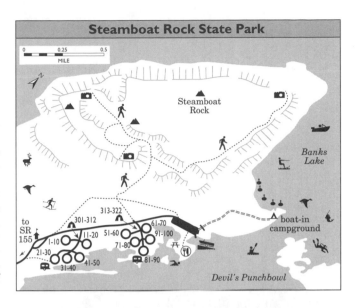

Steamboat Rock provides a scenic backdrop for the State Park's campground.

SUN LAKES–DRY FALLS STATE PARK

Camping, picnicking, golf, hiking, swimming, fishing, boating, paddling, interpretive displays

SEASON/HOURS: Year-round; Visitor Center and Deep Lake open from May through September; Dry Falls Lake open from May through November; campsite reservations accepted in summer.

AREA: 4,023.71 acres; 73,640 feet of freshwater shoreline on Park, Deep, Perch, Mirror, Vic Meyer, and Dry Falls Lakes and several other small unnamed lakes.

OVERNIGHT AND DAY-USE FACILITIES: 18 RV sites, 174 standard campsites (&), group camp (40 persons), 90 picnic sites, 7 restrooms (3 with showers) (&), trailer dump station.

RECREATIONAL FACILITIES: 15.5 miles of hiking trails, 27.5 miles of road, swimming beach, paved boat launch with boarding float (Deep Lake), hand-carried boat launch (Park Lake).

EDUCATIONAL FACILITIES: Visitor center.

CONCESSIONS: Golf course, cafe, general store, 50 cabins, 10 mobile homes, 112 RV sites, laundromat, marina, boat launch, boat rentals, boat fuel.

CAMP DELANY ELC: (84 persons), air-conditioned cabins, kitchen, dining hall, recreation room, volleyball court, quarter basketball court.

CAR ACCESS: Just east of SR 17, 5.9 miles southwest of Coulee City or 16.9 miles north of Soap Lake. Dry Falls Interpretive Center is on SR 17, 1 mile north of the main park entrance.

The sheer immensity of the geological forces that sculpted this area of the state defies imagination, despite the impressive evidence of their action. Mammoth ice sheets from the Pleistocene epoch,

Sun Lakes–Dry Falls State Park

which began about a million years ago, pushed south from Canada and blocked the northbound flow of the ancient Columbia River, forcing it to carve a new channel through the lava-layered plateau to the south. By the time the glaciers began to retreat, an enormous lake covering large portions of present-day western Montana had built up behind an ice dam. Scientists believe this dam initially gave way some 16,000 years ago, releasing a vast surge of water, over 300 feet deep, that swept through eastern Montana, northern Idaho, and eastern Washington, almost instantly enlarging existing river channels. Huge, roaring waterfalls were created that shook the ground and could be heard for miles, but that lasted for only a few weeks. The alternate damming and flooding occurred numerous times over the following centuries—some think as many as 40 times—each time sweeping away more of the layered basalt and excavating deep canyons. The coulees that scar the eastern Washington landscape are the remnants of the

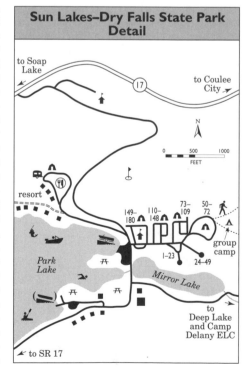

Sun Lakes–Dry Falls State Park Detail

flood channels, and the Grand Coulee is the largest and most impressive of them all.

One of the waterfalls in the Grand Coulee began near present-day Soap Lake, but the torrents of water rushing over it rapidly eroded the lip, and by the time the floods subsided, the face of the falls had moved 20 miles upstream to the present site of Dry Falls. Today the dry skeleton of that monstrous falls is a sheer cliff stretching across the coulee, 3.5 miles wide and 400 feet high—some 10 times larger than present-day Niagara Falls. The remnants of plunge pools at its base now form a series of placid lakes at the northeast end of Sun Lakes State Park.

At a breathtaking overlook on the northwest rim of Dry Falls, a visitor center houses displays telling the area's geological history and describing archeological digs that provide evidence of early man's use of the area.

Sun Lakes State Park, lying in the Lower Grand Coulee, encompasses the northeast end of Park Lake as well as a jumble of smaller lakes in the chasm below Dry Falls. The park facilities are primarily on Park Lake, where a concession provides extensive resort-type amenities. State Park-maintained campgrounds, picnic areas, and swimming beaches are found east and south of the resort area. The lakes in the park, which are planted with rainbow trout, offer good fishing in spring and summer; however, Dry Falls Lake is a selective fishing area: only barbless hooks permitted, one-fish limit, boat motors prohibited.

A narrow paved road heads east up the coulee to a fork. The right fork eventually leads to Deep Lake, a long, narrow former waterfall plunge-pool at the southeast base of Dry Falls, where there is a boat launch, picnic area, and primitive campsites. In another 0.25 mile from the fork, a second road to the right leads to Camp Delany, an ELC.

The left fork of the road deteriorates quickly to a one-lane dirt road, rough, rutted, steep, and studded with sharp lava rocks, most suitable for four-wheel-drive vehicles. The route passes Perch

The cool water of Deep Lake and warm eastern Washington sunshine make for a perfect day.

Lake and ends at 3 miles in a primitive hand-carry launch area on the shore of Dry Falls Lake. Its convoluted shore and the immense basalt walls that surround it make Dry Falls Lake ideal for canoe or kayak exploration. The saddle trails that wend through the desert landscape linking this area to the main part of the park are suitable for hikers, but are not recommended for bicyclists.

LAKE LENORE CAVES STATE PARK

Hiking, geological and historical interpretation

SEASON/HOURS: Year-round.
AREA: 213.7 acres.
RECREATIONAL FACILITIES: 0.75 mile of gravel roads, 0.25 mile of hiking trails.

EDUCATIONAL FACILITIES: Interpretive sign, historic caves.
CAR ACCESS: On the east side of SR 17, 13.9 miles south of Coulee City or 8.9 miles north of Soap Lake.

A chain of slender lakes leads south, down the floor of the Lower Grand Coulee, from Sun Lakes–Dry Falls State Park to Soap Lake. Along the eastern rim of Lake Lenore, a glance up at the basalt cliffs reveals a series of caves that pock the walls of the upper layer of lava flow. These caverns were formed naturally when ancient floods plucked loose basalt from the coulee walls, and they were later enlarged by freezing and thawing in the cracks of the columnar basalt walls. Archaeological evidence shows that prehistoric hunters used these caves for temporary residence during their migrations through the area. Such caves can be found in other places in the Grand Coulee as well.

Turn off SR 17 onto a gravel road that

Caves in basalt layers above Lake Lenore were used for shelter by prehistoric nomadic hunters.

ends in a small parking area. From here an asphalt path leads up the talus slope to a stairway breaching the lower band of cliffs. Above, a dirt path leads along the bench between the lava layers for 0.25 mile past several of the caves. Not all are easily accessible. At the south end of the trail, the biggest cave is at the base of a 100-foot-wide, 30-foot-deep pit that was bored out by the swirling waters of the ancient floods. Swifts and swallows nest in the cliffs. Watch the trailside brush for gray-and-white northern shrikes.

SUMMER FALLS STATE PARK

Picnicking, fishing, view of Summer Falls

SEASON/HOURS: Closed October 1 through April 30.
AREA: 260 acres; 5 miles of freshwater

shoreline on Billy Clap Lake.
DAY-USE FACILITIES: 9 picnic sites, 2 picnic shelters, fire braziers, restroom.
CAR ACCESS: *From the north,* turn south off US 2 in Coulee City on 4th Street. In 0.2 mile turn east on Main Street, and in 0.2 mile turn south on McEntee Street, which becomes Pinto Ridge Road as it leaves town. South of Coulee City 8.6 miles a gravel road leads east down a draw to reach the park in 1.3 miles more.

From the south, 8.3 miles east of Soap Lake, turn north from SR 28 onto Pinto Ridge Road and reach the road into the park in 6.2 miles.

Summer Falls State Park provides an oasis of green amid the arid gray coulees of central Washington. The small grassy picnic area on the shores of Billy Clapp Lake sits near the base of a stunning waterfall that pours over the rimrock wall into the lake below. The nearby irrigation canals spill surplus water over

the falls only during summer months, thus the name. *Do not swim in the lake here*—whirlpools and undertow make the water treacherous.

The surrounding scrub and a nearby marsh provide habitat for an army of birds, including red-winged blackbirds, Say's phoebes, kingbirds, vireos, warblers, and chats. Red-tailed hawks nest in nearby cliffs.

PESHASTIN PINNACLES STATE PARK

Picnicking, hiking, rock climbing

SEASON/HOURS: Closed November 1 through mid-March.
AREA: 28 acres.
DAY-USE FACILITIES: 6 picnic tables, 2 toilets.
RECREATIONAL FACILITIES: 1.5 miles of trails.
CAR ACCESS: From US 2/US 97, 8.3 miles southeast of Leavenworth and 10.7 miles northwest of Wenatchee, turn north on North Dryden Road to reach the park in 0.6 mile.

For years these unique, near-vertical sandstone outcroppings rising abruptly from a small ridge above an apple orchard were a popular informal rock-climbing area. The low elevation and dry climate made the pinnacles accessible most of the year, even when other rock-climbing areas in the state were either buried in snow or drenched by rain.

Unfortunately, the owners of the property had to make the area off limits to the public to save the adjoining orchards from climbers who were not always considerate, and to avoid potential financial liability for injuries. Responding to requests from the climbing community and outdoor clubs, State Parks purchased the property and reopened it.

Facilities are meager, but adequate for the purpose—just a large parking lot,

now only in memory and old photos; it snapped off at the "knuckle" in 1978.

The pinnacles remain an excellent practice spot, challenging a wide spectrum of skill levels. Less experienced climbers can gain confidence on Donald Duck Rock or stem a crack to the top of Orchard Rock and experience a vertical rappel. Intermediate-to-difficult routes exist on Martian Slab and Sunset Slab. The west faces of Grand Central Tower and Austrian Slab offer routes requiring advanced skills. Enjoy the thrill of climbing here safely, but avoid placing any new unnecessary "iron" and help preserve the rock for the generations of climbers to follow. Drilling and bolting is strictly prohibited, unless authorized by park staff.

Nonclimbing visitors might enjoy picnicking and watching with binoculars as climbers dangle from spider webs or creep lizardlike up rock faces.

WENATCHEE CONFLUENCE STATE PARK

Camping, picnicking, competitive sports, birdwatching, hiking, bicycling, swimming, waterskiing, windsurfing, fishing, boating, paddling, sailing, interpretive walks

SEASON/HOURS: Year-round; campsite reservations accepted in summer, 1 picnic shelter reservable, group day-use area reservable.

AREA: 196.99 acres; 8,625 feet of fresh-water shoreline on the Wenatchee and Columbia Rivers.

OVERNIGHT AND DAY-USE FACILITIES: 51 RV sites (&), 8 standard campsites, group camp (300 persons), 111 picnic sites (5 &), 2 picnic shelters, group day-use area (500 persons), 5 restrooms (3 with showers) (&), trailer dump station.

RECREATIONAL FACILITIES: 2 miles of paved trail (&), children's play equipment, multi-use playfield,

Climbers practice on Dinosaur Tower in the Peshastin Pinnacles.

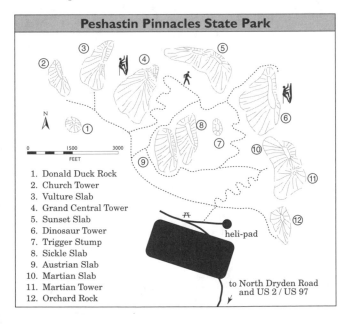

Peshastin Pinnacles State Park

1. Donald Duck Rock
2. Church Tower
3. Vulture Slab
4. Grand Central Tower
5. Sunset Slab
6. Dinosaur Tower
7. Trigger Stump
8. Sickle Slab
9. Austrian Slab
10. Martian Slab
11. Martian Tower
12. Orchard Rock

heli-pad

to North Dryden Road and US 2 / US 97

toilets, a kiosk with a map, and a few picnic tables. For safety, the park has replaced old rappel and belay anchors with new solidly placed ones, but beyond that the rock climbing routes are unchanged. Unfortunately, the pinnacles have suffered wear; cracks in the soft sandstone have flaked away from too many years of piton placement, and indiscriminate and overuse of expansion bolts has marred or fractured friable rock faces. The classic eye-catching pinnacle "Trigger Finger" exists

185

2 tennis courts, volleyball court, 2 basketball courts, cross-country ski trail, swimming beach (&), bathhouse (&), 2-lane boat ramp (fee) with boarding float.

EDUCATIONAL FACILITIES: 1.33-mile nature trail.

CAR ACCESS: *From US 2 / US 97 west of Wenatchee,* head northeast on US 97A (signed to Chelan, State Patrol, SR 28, US 2E, US 97N). In 0.3 mile take the exit marked for Olds Station, State Patrol, and Washington Apple Visitor Center.

From US 97A north of Wenatchee, take the Olds Station exit. Either of these exits leads to Euclid Avenue. Follow this road south for 0.8 mile, where it turns west and becomes Olds Station Road. Reach the park in 0.3 mile.

Wenatchee Confluence State Park offers fine boating on both the Wenatchee and Columbia Rivers.

Confluence: a flowing together. Wenatchee Confluence State Park lies at the flowing together (or junction) of the Wenatchee and the Columbia Rivers. The park nicely fulfills the desires of campers wanting an outdoor experience in a comfortable urban setting that provides a variety of amenities—a rustic hotel that's not too primitive.

Park campsites are on a flat, shaded grassy field. An assortment of sports fields, as well as picnic areas, makes the park popular for local church gatherings, company picnics, and youth group outings. A semicircle of concrete steps on the bank of the Columbia River leads down to a roped-off swimming and wading area, protected from river currents by its cupped design. A nearby boat ramp offers river access for trailered and hand-carried boats.

Despite the civilized nature of the main park area, known as the North Confluence, the South Confluence, a section on the opposite side of the Wenatchee River, retains a nature-oriented role. A bicycle/pedestrian path crosses a bridge over the Wenatchee River to the Horan Natural Area and an interpretive kiosk. Footpaths (no bicycles permitted) lead through the heart of the natural area and along the riverbank. Several path-side interpretive signs describe the ecology and inhabitants of the wetlands. Residents include eagles, osprey, hawks, great blue heron, and a variety of ducks, as well as muskrats, river otter, raccoons, and beavers—all only a wingtip from downtown Wenatchee. Sections of the trail close in the winter when eagles and other birds are roosting.

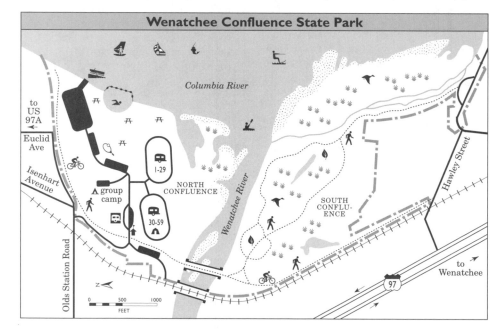

SQUILCHUCK STATE PARK

Group camping, picnicking, hiking, tubing, sledding, cross-country skiing

SEASON/HOURS: Open to groups, by reservation, from April through September.
AREA: 287.17 acres.
OVERNIGHT AND DAY-USE FACILITIES: Group camp (160 persons), 20 standard campsites, 14 picnic sites, group day-use area (100 persons), lodge, fire circle, restroom with showers.
RECREATIONAL FACILITIES: 14 miles of fire roads in park and on adjoining USFS and Department of Fish and Wildlife land for hiking/biking/cross-country skiing.
CAR ACCESS: Take Wenatchee Avenue (SR 285) southeast through Wenatchee to Ferry Street, then turn southwest for one block to Mission Street. Follow Mission south to the city limits where it becomes Squilchuck Road, and in 7.7 miles arrives at the park entrance.

The bone-dry coulees south of Wenatchee begin to green as the road climbs into the Wenatchee Mountains near Mission Ridge. By the time Squilchuck State Park is reached, surrounding hillsides are covered by a cool coat of evergreen forest. Due to limited state park funds, this former campground operates as a reservation-only group camp. This is a mixed blessing—unfortunate for the casual camper, but a treasure for the family or youth group that, for a nominal fee, can secure private use of this forest retreat.

The road beyond the lodge leads to the campground, which has 20 sites and a restroom with showers. For reservations contact Wenatchee Confluence State Park at the number listed in Appendix A.

Because none of the recreation facilities typical of developed state parks are provided, the area offers a real wilderness experience. You can hike or bike over 14 miles of fire roads along the forested ridges above the campground while enjoying the sounds and scents of the forest. In winter some of the trails are marked for cross-country skiing.

DAROGA STATE PARK

Camping, picnicking, basketball, baseball, tennis, soccer, birdwatching, hiking, bicycling, swimming, waterskiing, windsurfing, fishing, boating, sailing

SEASON/HOURS: Closed mid-October through mid-March.
AREA: 185.79 acres; 8,775 feet of freshwater shoreline on Lake Entiat (Columbia River).
OVERNIGHT AND DAY-USE FACILITIES: 28 RV sites (EW) (&), 17 primitive campsites, 2 group camps (100 persons each), 33 picnic sites (&), 3 picnic shelters (2 in group camps), group day-use area (75 persons), 3 restrooms (2 with showers) (&), 2 toilets, portable toilet dump station, trailer dump station.
RECREATIONAL FACILITIES: 2.1 miles of paved trail, children's play equipment, baseball/soccer field, 2 tennis/basketball courts, swimming beach, bathhouse, 2-lane paved boat ramp with boarding float, 2 mooring docks (576 feet of moorage space).
CAR ACCESS: On US 97 on the east side of the Columbia River, 6.6 miles north of the junction with US 2, and 15.3 miles south of the Bebee Bridge.

The manicured, emerald green lawns of Daroga State Park stand in sharp contrast to the surrounding rolling brown hills of the Columbia Basin. The layout of the park is unique: An incursion of private land and a small lagoon break it into three sections. A slender tree-lined causeway separates the lagoon from Lake Entiat (the Columbia River); only the outer shore of the lagoon lies within the park boundary. Midway, on a widened section of the causeway, is a primitive walk-in campground, ideal for bicyclists or other campers unburdened with heavy loads of gear. The park provides carts to lessen the work of hauling what gear you have to the camp. A small dock in a tiny cove at the river's edge permits boaters to take advantage of this isolated site, yet keep their craft close at hand.

To the south, the group camp is a grassy pocket on the shore, virtually isolated from the main section of the park except for a narrow lakeshore trail along the

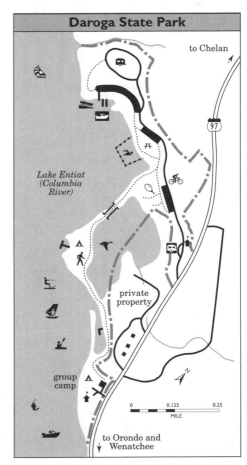

Daroga State Park

to Chelan

Lake Entiat (Columbia River)

private property

group camp

to Orondo and Wenatchee

0   0.125   0.25
MILE

Rows of tents march across the group camp at Daroga State Park.

causeway that links it to the remainder of the park.

The main portion of the park lies to the north, where a wide grass bowl has been laid out with sports fields. Beyond these, a grassy picnic area stretching along the riverbank includes a bathhouse and picnic shelter set above a tree-shaded swimming beach. The lawn sweeps northward, where a small peninsula divides the shoreline into two tiny coves. Above, a huge parking lot for boat trailers fronts a boat ramp and boarding float. A second long float nearby provides short-term moorage.

The extreme end of the park is capped by a campground loop on a small bluff above the river. Cottonwood and poplar stands form a windbreak along the riverside. Signs warn against kite flying because high-voltage transmission lines pass high above the campsites.

LINCOLN ROCK STATE PARK

Camping, picnicking, basketball, soccer, softball, tennis, volleyball, swimming, waterskiing, windsurfing, fishing, boating, sailing

SEASON/HOURS: Closed mid-October through mid-March; campsite reservations accepted in summer.

AREA: 80 acres; 2,300 feet of freshwater shoreline on Lake Entiat (Columbia River).

OVERNIGHT AND DAY-USE FACILITIES: 67 RV sites (35 EW) (2 ♿), 27 standard campsites, 80 picnic sites (♿), 3 picnic shelters (2 reservable), group day-use area (100 persons), amphitheater, 4 restrooms with showers (♿), trailer dump station.

RECREATIONAL FACILITIES: 1.3-mile paved trail, children's play equipment, sports field, 2 tennis courts, 2 volleyball courts, paddleball/handball/basketball court, horseshoe pits, swimming beach, bathhouse, 3-lane paved boat ramp (fee) with boarding floats, 6 boat docks (1,240 feet of moorage space).

CAR ACCESS: On US 2/US 97, on the east side of the Columbia River, 4.9 miles north of the junction of US 2/US 97 and SR 28.

Rocky Reach Dam blocks the flow of the Columbia River north of Wenatchee, creating the placid, 31-mile-long thread of Lake Entiat. On the east shore of the lake, just above the dam, Lincoln Rock State Park utilizes the lake's quiet water and broad, open reaches for activities ranging from swimming to water- and jet-skiing.

The park's namesake, Lincoln Rock, is a basalt cliff on the opposite shore where a nature-sculpted rock resembles the profile of Abraham Lincoln. A view-finder pointing at the rock is located in the park's day-use area. The Rocky Reach Dam Interpretive Center, on the west shore, can only be reached by traveling up- or downriver to the nearest bridge crossing at Chelan or Wenatchee.

The park is typical of those in this part of the state, where a green tree-shaded lawn offers a welcome respite from the parched brown scabland, broken only by irrigated swatches of apple orchards. Unique to this park, however, is the wide border of white river rock used to edge trails and parking lots, making it one of the prettiest parks around.

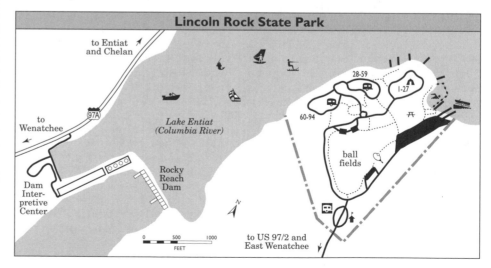

Floats at Lincoln Rock State Park are the starting point for a day of water fun.

True to its water orientation, Lincoln provides extensive aquatic facilities. Two single-lane launch ramps each have boarding floats alongside, and another nearby float is available for docking boats. Five more small floats, placed along the shoreline below the lower camping loop, are available to overnight campers on a first-come, first-served basis. A swimming beach with a shallower wading area occupies an indentation in the northern shoreline at the edge of the picnic area.

The broad field of the day-use area, which stretches from the park entrance to the swimming beach, is for your sport of choice: softball, soccer, volleyball, tennis, basketball, or horseshoe pitching. Large trees offer shade and wind protection for the day-use area and lower campground loop. Two newer camping loops on a slight bluff above the river on the west side of the park have more expansive views of the lake and dam, but the trees here are also younger and have a few years to go before they will shield campers from the elements.

SPOKANE PLAINS BATTLEFIELD STATE HERITAGE AREA

Historic site

AREA: 1 acre.
EDUCATIONAL FACILITIES: Rock pyramid with plaque.
CAR ACCESS: Take US 2 west from Spokane for 9 miles. The monument is on the north side of the highway on Dover Road, west of the entrance to Fairchild Air Force Base and immediately east of a nearby railroad overpass.

At this road wayside a stone pyramid bears a plaque commemorating the battle of Spokane Plains, which was fought near here on September 5, 1858. It was here that U.S. troops under the command of Colonel George Wright defeated a combined force of Coeur d'Alene, Palouse, and Spokane tribes.

RIVERSIDE STATE PARK

Camping, picnicking, nature study, hiking, orienteering, fishing, boating, paddling, cross-country skiing, bicycling, motorcycle and ORV riding, snowmobiling, horseback riding, historic sites, Native American petroglyphs

SEASON/HOURS: Year-round; Spokane House: 10:00 A.M. to 6:00 P.M., Wednesday through Sunday, June through September.
AREA: 7,922.37 acres; 105,550 feet of freshwater shoreline on the Spokane and Little Spokane Rivers.
OVERNIGHT AND DAY-USE FACILITIES:
  Bowl and Pitcher area: 90 picnic sites, 2 kitchen shelters (1 reservable), 2 group day-use areas (30 and 100 persons), 3 restrooms (1 with showers), 2 toilets, 101 standard campsites (2 &).
  Equestrian and hiking area: 6 toilets.
  ORV area: 10 picnic sites, picnic shelter, restrooms.
  Little Spokane River area: Group camp (50 and 198 persons), 9 toilets, restrooms in interpretive center.
RECREATIONAL FACILITIES:
  Bowl and Pitcher area: 1.7 miles of foot trail, suspension bridge.
  Equestrian and hiking area: 28.8 miles of multi-use trails, 47.3 miles of road, 7.2 km of groomed cross-country ski trail (Centennial Trail).
  ORV area: 600-acre ORV/snowmobile area.
  Little Spokane River area: 5.6 miles of hiking trail, boat launch, paddler's put-in and take-out sites.
CONCESSIONS: Stable, horse rentals.
EDUCATIONAL FACILITIES: Spokane House Interpretive Center, Indian petroglyphs.
CAR ACCESS: To reach the Bowl and

Pitcher area from Division Street, the major north/south arterial through downtown Spokane, take Francis Avenue (SR 291) west from Division Street for 3.2 miles to its intersection with Nine Mile Road. In 0.9 mile turn southwest on Rifle Club Road, then in 0.4 mile turn south on A. L. White Parkway. Reach the park entrance in another 1.7 miles. Refer to the map for access to other parts of the park.

Riverside State Park and the Little Spokane Natural Area follow the convoluted courses of the Spokane and Little Spokane Rivers as they meander for over 9 miles along Spokane's west side. The numerous sections of land that comprise the park make it confusing to grasp, but at the same time give it a remarkable diversity. Even though surrounded by urban communities, the size and shape of the park permit it to be a habitat for over 150 different species of birds and mammals, including some rare and endangered ones.

The Bowl and Pitcher Area

Campsites, most of the picnic sites, and the park headquarters on the river's east shore are on a small peninsula, edged by a large oxbow of the river, known as the Bowl and Pitcher area. The name comes from a group of unique basalt monoliths, remnants of ancient lava flows, found along the riverbank. The road into this section of the park skirts the top of a sheer bluff that drops nearly 200 feet to river's edge. This bluff continues to a rock promontory inside the park, accessible by paths from a parking lot. Here are views down into the river gorge with its rapids, to the Bowl and Pitcher formations, and upstream to a suspension footbridge spanning the turbulent river.

The road then descends to the picnic areas and park offices. Ponderosa and jack pine offer shade, but the sparse grass ground cover is worn to dirt in most places by many years of hard use. Sturdy rustic stone restrooms are of

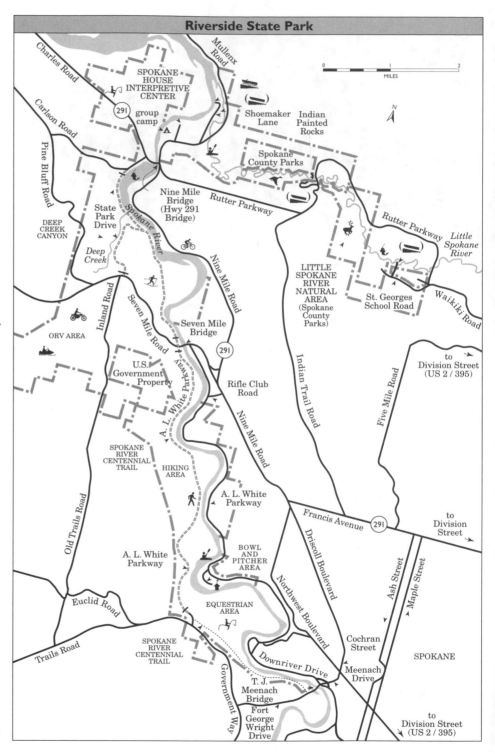

Riverside State Park

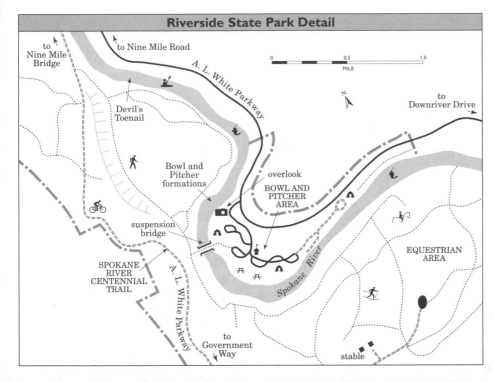

Riverside State Park Detail

CCC-vintage construction. At the south side of the peninsula the road drops down to a strip of campsites near river's edge. Here the brushy riverbank is accessible in places, but swimming is prohibited due to dangerous undercurrents. Short trails lace the riverbank and the heart of the peninsula. A path leading from the picnic area to the suspension bridge connects to trails on the west side of the river.

As the name of the rapids called the "Devil's Toenail" implies, this section of the river is a challenge for kayakers; although the rapids are not exceptionally difficult, the huge volume of water makes this a run only for those with advanced skills. Putting in boats at the park is prohibited, in order to discourage unskilled boaters from attempting to run the rapids.

Equestrian and Hiking Area

The west bank of the river between Seven Mile Bridge and the T. J. Meenach Bridge is a spider's web of jogging, hiking, and equestrian trails through scrub grass and stands of ponderosa pine. One popular hike begins at the suspension bridge and follows the scenic west side of the river opposite the Bowl and Pitcher area for 2.5 miles. Hikers can return via the same route or follow spurs up to A. L. White Parkway or to inland horse trails. The Centennial Trail follows sections of now-closed State Park Drive and A. L. White Parkway along the bluff above the west side of the river. The accompanying maps show other major trails.

Just off the parkway, at the south end of the park, a concessionaire manages a stable where guided horseback trips leave hourly for 5-mile or longer rides. The stable and associated facilities hold forth in some false-front, "Old West" buildings beside the horse paddocks. At the north end of this section of the park, an equestrian trail system with 10- and 25-mile loops is available to riders with their own mounts or those who rent them here.

During winter months with adequate snow, the 7.2-kilometer section of the Centennial Trail through this portion of

Paddlers set out to explore the Little Spokane River.

191

Dramatic rock formations, remnants of the area's volcanic past, give the Riverside State Park's Bowl and Pitcher Area its name.

the park is groomed for cross-country skiers. Motorized vehicles are prohibited on the trail, so skiers here don't have to compete with snowmobiles.

Near the north end of the park, Deep Creek and Coulee Creek meet in a narrow 200-foot-deep gorge that threads 0.5 mile north to the Spokane River. The trail up the canyon passes fossil beds with imprints of a 7-million-year-old forest that once grew in the area. The start of the trail can be reached by walking the Centennial Trail south for 0.8 mile from Carlson Road, or north for 2.2 miles from Seven Mile Road.

Off-Road Vehicle (ORV) Area

A section of the state park dedicated to ORVs lies at the head of the Deep Creek drainage, where steep banks bound a 600-acre open, dry bowl. A moonscape of sandy hillocks within the bowl has been stripped to barren soil by the treads of motorcycles. Trails thread the few wooded sections within the area. Any type of ORV, such as dirt bikes, 3- and 4-wheelers, four-by-fours, or snowmobiles, may use this area, provided that licensing, spark arrester, and muffler regulations are met. The large parking lot has a convenient loading ramp.

Little Spokane River

The Little Spokane River is a slender thread that meanders its way through marshlands before joining the Spokane River. Its final 7-mile leg (4 miles as the crow flies) is designated as the Little Spokane River Natural Area. Marshes along the serpentine path of the river teem with songbirds, woodpeckers, ducks, and grebes, and a blue heron rookery is in cottonwood trees along the shore. The river might be closed during the heron's nesting season. Woodlands along the riverbank and above it are home to beaver, muskrat, porcupines, coyotes, deer, raccoons, bobcat, cougar, and black bear. Visitors may enjoy the natural attractions of the area either on foot or by water. Since this is a natural area, removing plants or disturbing wildlife is prohibited.

From the parking lot off St. Georges School Road, a short path leads to the upriver canoe or kayak put-in site. From here drift or paddle quietly along the undulations of the river to see what creatures or sights might lie around the next bend. An intermediate put-in/take-out site is at the Indian Painted Rocks site, where Rutter Parkway crosses the Little Spokane River. Near the mouth of the Little Spokane, 7.3 miles downstream and just beyond the SR 291 bridge, is a second parking lot and canoe take-out site.

At a trailhead a short distance east of the put-in site, a path heads into the forest south of the river and quickly switchbacks 500 feet up the steep ridgeline before joining an overgrown service road that traverses the wooded, brushy hillside west to the park boundary. The path continues across a steep open hillside high above the St. Georges School before reentering the park and dropping down from the bluff and eventually joining Rutter Parkway on the south side of the bridge near the Indian Painted Rocks.

A second trail follows along the north bank of the river between the Rutter Parkway bridge and the SR 291 bridge for about 2 miles. The route has views of the many oxbows in the river channel, beaver-cut trees, a heron rookery, and meadows frequented by white-tail and mule deer. Because this trail stays close to the marshy riverbank, mosquitoes can be a problem during the summer.

Just above the parking lot at the middle trailhead off Rutter Parkway, a rock face contains the Indian Painted Rocks, colored traces of petroglyphs. Painted symbols of this type are found throughout the West, but their origin and meaning have been lost over time. Some think they record hunting successes, tribal meetings, or religious experiences, but no one knows for sure.

North of Nine Mile Bridge

The Spokane House Interpretive Center, on the bank of the Spokane River, is the site of a fur trading post that was the first permanent white settlement in eastern Washington. The post was established by explorer David Thompson in 1810, but because it proved too far from the main artery of trade, the Columbia River, it was relocated to Kettle Falls in 1826. The interpretive center tells the story of the Spokane House and its rivalry with competing fur companies, and displays artifacts from archaeological digs conducted here. A diorama portrays activities at Spokane House about 1819.

Dirt roads into the woods just west from Spokane House lead to two primitive group camps along the riverbank. Each consists of a string of picnic tables at river's edge and a single toilet. During summer when fire danger is high, open fires are not permitted here. The riverbank is low at this point, so it is easy to launch a hand-carried watercraft and float downstream to the boat launch area. Keep an eye out for osprey in tree snags.

On Shoemaker Lane, a short distance north of the take-out site on the Little Spokane River, is a one-lane boat ramp that provides access to Long Lake (the Spokane River). A short trail from the parking lot leads to the site of the original Pacific Fur Company trading post, a competitor of the nearby Spokane House trading post.

SPOKANE RIVER CENTENNIAL TRAIL

Hiking, jogging, bicycling

SEASON/HOURS: Year-round.
AREA: 376.17 acres; 95,040 feet of freshwater shoreline on the Spokane River.
DAY-USE FACILITIES: Benches and restrooms at the Spokane River Visitor Center (&), Sullivan Park, Riverfront Park (&), Sontag Park, and Mirabeau Park; toilets at Barker Road (&), Donkey Islands (&), John H. Shields Park (&), Deep Creek, and McClellan trailhead.

RECREATIONAL FACILITIES: 39 miles of multi-use trail (*no motorized vehicles*), 3 footbridges.
EDUCATIONAL FACILITIES: Interpretive sign at Plantes Ferry.
CAR ACCESS: The trail runs east from Riverfront Park in downtown Spokane to the Idaho border, and west from Riverfront Park to Carson Road, just west of the Nine Mile Bridge. The trail can be accessed wherever it parallels or crosses city streets, or from the points shown on the maps.

Walk, jog, bicycle, or in-line skate—no matter how you propel yourself, the Spokane River Centennial Trail is a delight. The heavily used trail honors the 1989 Washington State Centennial. As of 1999, the route has been completed from the Idaho border to near the Nine Mile Bridge west of the city; however, the section from Riverfront Park, in the heart of Spokane, to Riverside State Park, at the southeast end of the T. J. Meenach Bridge, currently follows a road-shoulder bicycle path not well-suited to walking. Plans for this section call for a dedicated hiking trail running from the north end of the Post Street Bridge at Riverfront Park to the T. J. Meenach Bridge.

Reaching Riverside State Park, the trail continues as both a bicycling and hiking route, following the west side of the river to Nine Mile Bridge. Trail extensions to the Spokane House Interpretive Center and to Columbia Plateau State Park at Cheney are under consideration. Only those trail sections that exist as of 1999 are detailed here. The trail is described going east from downtown Riverfront Park to the Idaho border, and then headed west from that park through Riverside State Park to Nine Mile Bridge.

East from Riverfront Park to the Denny Ashlock Footbridge

The eastern portion of the trail starts in Spokane near the Opera House in Riverfront Park where parking, restrooms,

Spokane River Centennial Trail

Spokane River Centennial Trail

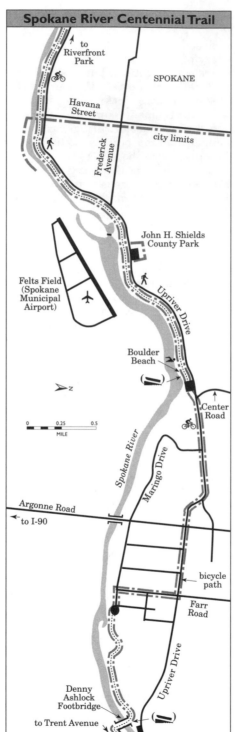

Spokane River Centennial Trail

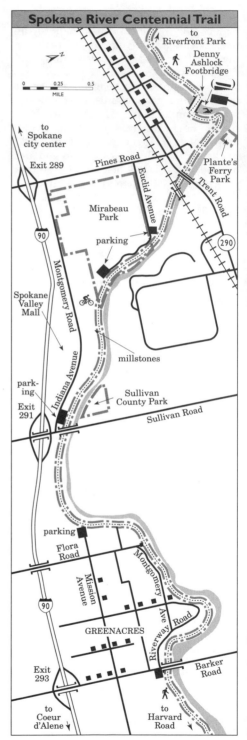

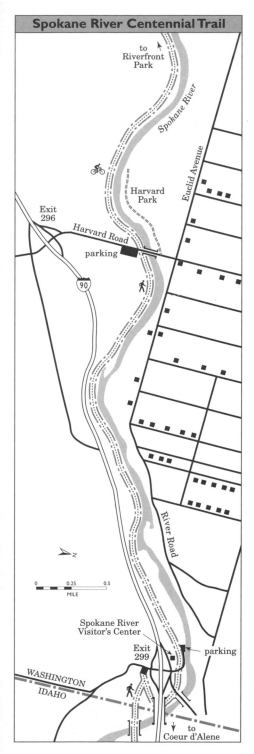

Spokane River Centennial Trail

to Riverfront Park

Spokane River

Euclid Avenue

Harvard Park

Exit 296

Harvard Road

parking

90

River Road

N

0   0.25   0.5
MILE

Spokane River Visitor's Center

Exit 299

parking

WASHINGTON
IDAHO

to Coeur d'Alene

and water are available. The paved path heads east and crosses the Kardong Burlington Northern Bridge over the Spokane River, named for Don Kardong, a local runner who initiated an annual race here, claimed to be the second largest foot race in the country. Originally a railroad bridge, this structure has been redecked and reconstructed with viewing platforms, tables, and benches on its north side and painted in multihued pastels.

From the Don Kardong Bridge the trail passes the Gonzaga University campus, crosses the Hamilton Street overpass, then swings north along the river through Mission Park. From here separate jogging and bicycle paths edge Upriver Drive for nearly 5 miles. Although they merge in places, the jogging path generally follows close to the riverbank, while the bicycle path stays near the road shoulder. Beyond the city limits 0.5 mile is John H. Shields County Park, which holds Minnehaha Rocks.

Another 1.2 miles eastward along Upriver Drive is Boulder Beach, where a grassy slope tapers to a boulder-studded riverbank. Launch hand-carried boats here, swim, or spread a picnic blanket (or all of the above). The formal trails end here. Bicyclists may continue east on city streets, following the shoulder of Upriver Drive, which is designated as a part of the Centennial Trail. The road-shoulder bike path crosses Argonne Road, and three blocks beyond turns south onto Farr Road, then east onto Maringo Drive. At the end of Maringo Drive, another 1-mile-long foot and bike trail section leads east to the Donkey Islands trailhead (also known as Plantes Ferry). Here is a large paved parking lot, a toilet, and an information kiosk that tells the natural and human history of the river. An Indian trail once forded the river at this spot, and in the 1850s a Canadian trapper, Antoine Plante, operated a river current-powered barge ferry at the site.

The Centennial Trail crosses the river here on a footbridge dedicated to Denny Ashlock, who conceived the trail and supported its creation. Hand-carried boats can be launched at a river access point just west of the south end of the bridge.

East from the Denny Ashlock Footbridge to the Idaho Border

From the footbridge the trail follows the south bank of the river, and at Trent Avenue crosses under this major arterial and a railroad bridge, then skirts Mirabeau Park. As the route continues east, it again picks up the Burlington Northern right-of-way. Near the railroad trestle in about a mile, note old millstones alongside the trail; they were once used by the Inland Empire Paper Company to turn wood into pulp for paper. In another mile the trail ducks under the Sullivan Road

The Centennial Trail crosses the Spokane River on the Kardong Burlington Northern Bridge.

195

An attractive bridge at Mirabeau Park spans a gully by the Spokane River.

bridge, where both a spur path and stairs lead up to a parking lot at the southwest corner of the bridge. On the opposite side of the river, at the northwest corner of the bridge, is Sullivan County Park, where there are picnic tables and shelters, restrooms, and water. Short scrambles down the rocky bank on either side of the river lead to fishing and impromptu picnic sites.

The trail continues to hug the south riverbank as it continues west through the Greenacres district. Edging the river, the route goes under Barker Road, the major north/south arterial in Greenacres. For the next two miles the trail parallels the river slightly inland from the bank. At the Harvard Road bridge, scramble down a dirt and gravel slope to cool your feet in the Spokane River or to launch a paddlecraft for a down-river tour. East from here the trail follows the riverbank for about 2 miles, then swings close to I-90 just west of the Spokane River Visitor Center near the Idaho border. The trail continues west for a short way, ducks under the freeway at the bridge that crosses over the Spokane River, then at the border joins a companion trail that continues east in Idaho.

West from Riverfront Park to Riverside State Park

West from the start point at Riverfront Park, the Centennial Trail currently follows a city bicycle route across the Howard Street Bridge, then west on Maxwell Avenue to Pettit Drive, which it follows to T. J. Meenach Drive. Plans call for this section of the trail to be relocated to Summit Boulevard in the future.

At a trailhead just south of the T. J. Meenach Bridge the paved path runs along the river to the boundary of Riverside State Park, then heads inland along the west edge of the park's equestrian area. At the entrance to this area the route uses the west side of the old A. L. White Parkway (closed to vehicles) as it continues north to Seven Mile Bridge. The old State Park Drive between Seven Mile Bridge and Carlson Road, just west of the Nine Mile Bridge, which also is closed to vehicles, forms the final, northern end of the trail.

MOUNT SPOKANE STATE PARK

Camping, picnicking, scenic views, huckleberry picking, hiking, mountain biking, horseback riding, downhill skiing, cross-country skiing, snowmobiling

SEASON/HOURS: Year-round, campground closed October 1 through May 31.
AREA: 13,820.77 acres.
OVERNIGHT AND DAY-USE FACILITIES: 12 standard campsites, group camp (90 persons), 3 cabins, 85 picnic sites, 3 picnic shelters, Vista House, 2 restrooms (&), 16 toilets.
RECREATIONAL FACILITIES: 50 miles of hiking/equestrian/snowmobiling trails in the park and on adjacent lands, 20 kilometers of groomed cross-country ski trails, 2 horse feeding stations.
CONCESSIONS: 5 ski lifts, 2 ski lodges, 32 ski runs.
CAR ACCESS: *To reach the park entrance, take US 2 from its junction with US 395 north of Spokane, and in 4.5 miles turn east on SR 206, signed to Mount Spokane State Park. The park is reached in another 15.5 miles. Ski areas are 5 miles beyond the entrance; the summit is 7.5 miles from the entrance.*

To reach the paved west end of the Day–Mount Spokane Road, drive US 2 to a marked intersection 5.5 miles from the intersection with US 395 north of Spokane. Follow the road as it weaves its way northeast to reach the park boundary in 13.5 miles.

If the summit views of the Selkirk and Bitterroot Mountains were all that Mount Spokane State Park had to offer, that would be enough. However, as a bonus the park contains miles of summer trails for hikers, mountain bikers, and equestrians, as well as snow trails for cross-country skiers and snowmobilers and slopes for alpine skiers.

Inside the park entrance the road climbs through timber for some 1,500 feet to an intersection midway up the mountain in 3 miles. Here the left branch heads to the summit, while the center branch leads to the ski area. The road to the right ends at a large Sno-Park area and Selkirk Lodge, open in winter for cross-country skiers and snowmobilers. The steep, winding road to the summit is nerve-wrackingly narrow, with no guard rail protection on its precipitous outer edge—not the place for the nervous, or large RVs.

At a bend in the summit road in 0.6 mile is the Big Springs picnic area; only nominal parking and a few picnic tables in a wooded hillside above the road. At Bald Knob, 1.2 miles above the junction, a grassy picnic area with restrooms, water, and a picnic shelter presents broad scenic views to the west over the ski area condos below. An adjacent campground loop has a dozen campsites, water, and toilets.

Continuing on, the 5,881-foot top of Mount Spokane is reached. Crowning the summit, surrounded by granite slabs and boulder fields, is Vista House, which was once used as a fire lookout. The sturdy, weathered rock and shingle structure is typical of 1930s CCC construction. The upper station of one of the area's ski lifts, a fire lookout tower, and a forest of radio and microwave antennas also share the mountaintop. Views spread north into Canada, northeast to the lofty summits of the Selkirks, east over azure lakes of the Idaho Panhandle to the distant rugged peaks of Montana's Bitterroot Range, south to the Spokane plains, and west to the softly rolling plateau of the Columbia Basin.

Using the Park Trails, Summer and Winter

In summer, the park's trail system accommodates both hikers and horse riders; a horse unloading dock is 0.25 mile inside the park entrance. Several marked trailheads leave the road between the entrance and the ski area junction. At a sharp turn 1.9 miles from the entrance, the gated lower end of the unpaved Mount Kit Carson Loop Road leads to the northwest. Picnic areas are found along the lower end of this road loop at Deep Creek, and also at the trailheads at Burping Brook, Smith Gap, and Deer Creek.

Another dirt road, the Day–Mount Spokane Road, joins the Mount Kit Carson Loop Road 1.6 miles west of its lower end, offering trail access to the park from

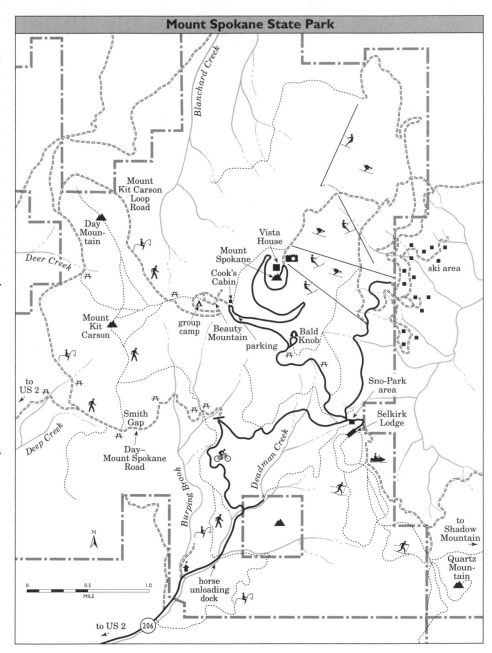

Mount Spokane State Park

Hikers survey the hills spreading below Mount Spokane.

the west side of the mountain. Both the Day–Mount Spokane Road and the Mount Kit Carson Loop Road are closed to vehicular traffic, but are open to hikers and equestrians during summer months. At the hairpin turn at Cook's Cabin, 0.7 mile below the summit, is the gated upper end of the Mount Kit Carson Loop Road. Limited parking is available in a flat just below the gate. The gated dirt road heads northwest and in 0.3 mile reaches a picnicking, group camp, and horse camping area. Trails from this area lead to the Mount Spokane summit, to Mount Kit Carson, to Day Mountain, and down to Smith Gap on the lower end of the loop road. These trails run through a forest of ponderosa pine broken by open mountain meadows, decorated with bear grass, and laced with bushes bearing succulent huckleberries in season.

The park attracts even more visitors in the winter than in the summer, as it is the premier ski area of Washington's Inland Empire. Chair lifts carry skiers, feeding downhill ski runs ranging from beginner to expert. A private development that includes condominiums and a restaurant lies just outside the park, below the lifts.

The park also caters to cross-country skiing with a day-lodge and over 13 miles of groomed trails originating on the hillside above Selkirk Lodge. Trails, ranging from easy to extremely difficult, cut through the wooded hills to the west of the lodge; the more challenging ones loop around Shadow Mountain. Snow-covered service roads are open for use by snowmobilers.

CHAPTER EIGHT
SOUTHEAST WASHINGTON

Green wheatfields and purple hills spread for miles below Steptoe Butte State Park.

HYAK LODGE STATE PARK

Hiking, skiing, mountain biking, equipment rentals, horseback riding, fishing, boating, conference center

SEASON/HOURS: Year-round; reservations accepted in summer.
AREA: 8 acres.
FACILITIES: 32 dormitory rooms (72 persons), kitchen, dining room, restrooms with showers, meeting room with audio-visual facilities.
CAR ACCESS: Take Exit 54 (Hyak, Gold Creek) from I-90 at Snoqualmie Summit. Where the exit ramp Ts into a road parallel to the freeway, head east, and in 0.4 mile turn south on a road marked to Iron Horse Trail and Keechelus Lake boat launch. In 0.3 mile turn north and cross a bridge to the conference center parking lot.

This remodeled bunkhouse, formerly used by Department of Transportation crews that keep I-90 open during winter months, now serves as a scenic conference center with overnight accommodations. Scenery is not the only attraction; groups can leave their meetings to fish or boat on Lake Keechelus, or hike or bicycle nearby trails. The Hyak trailhead for Iron Horse Trail State Park is about 500 yards west of the center, and Snoqualmie Summit is the starting point for trails into the surrounding scenic backcountry. Winter brings cross-country skiing on nearby groomed trails, or downhill skiing and snowboarding at any of four major Snoqualmie Summit ski areas.

The 16 private sleeping rooms are available for rental. Duplicate facilities are planned for the second floor, and each floor will be reservable separately. The kitchen and dining room are run by a concessionaire.

LAKE EASTON STATE PARK

Camping, picnicking, hiking, bicycling, swimming, fishing, boating, paddling, mushrooming, birdwatching, cross-country skiing, snowshoeing, snowmobiling

SEASON/HOURS: Year-round, campground and launch ramp closed mid-October through mid-April; campsite reservations accepted in summer.

AREA: 270.86 acres; 24,000 feet of freshwater shoreline on Lake Easton (Reservoir), and 2,000 feet on the Yakima River.

OVERNIGHT AND DAY-USE FACILITIES: 45 RV(&), 92 standard campsites (&), 2 primitive campsites, 3 weather ports (4 persons each), group camp (50 persons), 40 picnic sites, 4 restrooms with showers (&), trailer dump station.

RECREATIONAL FACILITIES: 2 miles of hiking trails, 30 kilometers of groomed cross-country ski trails and 9.5 miles of multi-use cross-country ski/snowmobile trails on state park and adjacent private and U.S. Forest Service land, swimming beach, children's play equipment, boat ramp with boarding float.

CONCESSIONS: Canoe and paddleboard rentals.

CAR ACCESS: From I-90 16 miles east of Snoqualmie Pass and 1 mile west of Easton, take Exit 70 (Lake Easton State Park, Easton, Sparks Road) and follow signs to the park. In winter park in the designated Sno-Park at the boat launch area (*parking permit required*).

L ying in the Cascade Mountains near the Snoqualmie summit, Lake Easton gives more of a deep forest experience than most other state parks, although it still offers amenities such as RV hookups and restrooms with showers. When snow coats the countryside, the park serves as a prime base for snowmobiling and cross-country skiing on park trails and on nearby private and forest service lands stretching along the I-90 corridor. Because the 237-acre lake is a U.S. Bureau of Reclamation reservoir, the water level varies. During summer months lake water laps at the thick shoreline vegetation, leaving only a thread of a beach in a few spots; in winter the water is drawn down, drastically changing the nature of the lake and making boat launching difficult, or impossible.

Park facilities are found in a narrow, 2-mile-long forested strip along the shore. At the southeast end of the park, near the entrance, two standard camping loops are sheltered by a stand of fir and pine. The boat launch, day-use area, and RV camping loop are found near the northwest end. A small sandy beach at the heart of the day-use area fronts a roped-off swimming beach. The RV sites at the northwest campground are more jammed together than sites in the standard campground loops, but about half of them have glimpses of the lake through trees. Because the park is immediately adjacent to the I-90 freeway, some sections, such as the northwest camping area, are subjected to the steady drone of traffic.

For a unique experience, campers can rent one of the park's three weather ports, wood-floored Quonset-like units that accommodate four persons each. Each building has a table, chairs, refrigerator, bunk beds, futon, and electric heat and lights. The shelters, which in summer are located

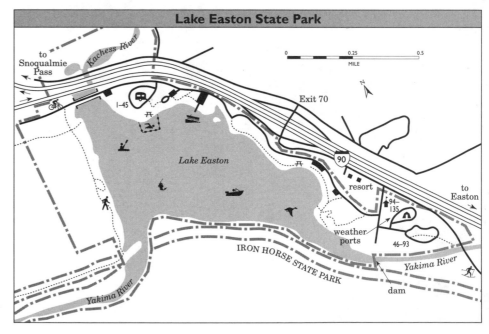
Lake Easton State Park

Picnickers find a sunny spot among the trees at Lake Easton State Park.

on one of the southeast camping loops, are moved to the day-use area in winter and heated with propane stoves.

Trails along the north shore lead past open spots on the bank where land-bound anglers can compete with boat-based trollers to lure rainbow trout, cutthroat, and Dolly Varden trout. At the west end of the park, the old concrete bridge, which carried traffic before the freeway was built, is a prime spot for bicycling, fishing, or boat watching. A foot trail leaving the end of the bridge follows the wooded west shore, occasionally touching the lake. Jays, woodpeckers, owls, and osprey inhabit the timber, and migratory waterfowl use the lake as a stopover.

IRON HORSE STATE PARK (EAST)

Hiking, bicycling, horseback riding, wagon trains, cross-country skiing, dog sledding

SEASON/HOURS: Year-round, Hyak tunnel closed from November 1 to May 1.

AREA: 1,766.9 acres.

FACILITIES: 92-mile multipurpose trail, 16 trestles, 5 tunnels, 2 primitive campsites with toilets at Cold Creek and Roaring Creek. *Motorized vehicles prohibited.* **Exit 54:** Restroom with showers (&), hitching rails, information kiosk. **Exits 62, 71, and 84:** Toilets.

CAR ACCESS: Official accesses are listed following. Refer to the map for additional, unofficial accesses.

Hyak, Gold Creek. Take Exit 54 (Hyak, Gold Creek) from I-90 at Snoqualmie Summit. Where the exit ramp Ts into a road parallel to the freeway, head east, and in 0.4 mile turn south on a road marked to Iron Horse Trail and Lake Keechelus boat launch. In 0.2 mile is a designated Sno-Park on the west side of the road; parking permit required.

Stampede Pass, Lake Kachess. Take exit 62 from I-90 and head southwest on Forest Road 54 for 1.1 miles to a Y-intersection with Forest Road 5480 to Lost Lake. Continue on Forest Road 54 for 0.2 mile to intersect the trail at a parking lot next to a telephone company regeneration station. Forest Road 5480 runs west, par-

allel to the trail, and intersects it again in 1.5 miles at the south end of Lake Keechelus. The Crystal Springs Sno-Park is at the Y in the road 1 mile from the exit; parking permit required.

Easton. Take exit 71 from I-90, and head south on Cabin Creek Road to reach the trail in 0.3 mile.

Roslyn, Salmon La Sac. Take Exit 80 from I-90. At a T-intersection 0.1 mile south of the freeway, head west on Scale House Road to intersect the trail in 0.8 mile. Limited parking is just beyond the trail.

Cle Elum, South Cle Elum. Take exit 84 rom I-90. In 1 mile turn south on Rossetti Street and cross the river to South Cle Elum. Follow South Cle Elum Way (4th Street) to Madison Avenue, turn west, and in two blocks turn south on 6th Street. In one block turn west on N Milwaukee Street. The old railroad station is next to the trail. This parking area is cleared in winter.

Thorp Highway, Thorp. Take Exit 101. Thorp Highway crosses the trail 0.3 mile north of the off-ramp. Just beyond, turn west on West Depot Road, and in 0.3 mile reach a signed parking area.

Canyon Road, Ellensburg. Take Exit 109 from I-90, and follow Canyon Road, which becomes Main Street, north to 8th Avenue, where it becomes A Street. There is a short break in the trail as it crosses the campus of Central Washington University. To access the section of trail that heads west, continue north on A Street to 14th, and park at Kiwanis Park at this intersection. The trailhead is on the north side of 14th. To access the section of trail that heads east, turn east on 8th Street and continue through the campus. At 8th and Euclid Way, stay on 8th for two blocks, then turn north on Maple Street to intersect the trail in one block.

Kittitas. Take Exit 109 from I-90. In 0.7 mile intersect the trail at the old railroad station on the south side of Kittitas.

Beverly Junction. Take Exit 136 (Vantage, Huntzinger Road) from I-90, and 7.3 miles south on Huntzinger Road, intersect the trail. Another short spur leads to the trail in another 0.2 mile.

This is a continuation of the ribbonlike state park that formerly was the roadbed of the Chicago, Milwaukee, St. Paul, and Pacific Railroad, once the longest electrically-powered railway in the world. Trains ran along the route between the 1920s and the 1970s. The western portion of Iron Horse State Park, and its history, were described in Chapter 5.

The abandoned railroad station at Cle Elum sits next to the Iron Horse Trail.

Only a few access points have facilities—and those are minimal, such as parking, toilets, and a restroom at Hyak. Camping is permitted at two sites on the trail along the shore of Keechelus Lake at Cold Creek and Roaring Creek; each site has toilets, tent pads, and picnic tables. At some points there are hazards, such as trestles without decking. A few short segments of the right-of-way remain in private hands, and the portion between Boylston and Beverly is part of the Army's Yakima Firing Center.

Snoqualmie Pass to Cle Elum

This eastern portion of the park starts at Hyak, at the east end of the old 2.3-mile-long tunnel, Tunnel 50, which runs under Snoqualmie Pass. When first constructed, the railroad went over the pass; the tunnel was built between 1912 and 1914. Tunnel 50 is open to the public from May 1 to November 1, and State Parks has improved the tread and drainage; however, no lighting is provided, so it is very dark; carry a flashlight. Clouds of moisture often belch from the black entrance hole, much like smoke from the mouth of a dark dragon, making it an excitingly eerie experience. In winter, when ice on the floor and icicles hanging from the ceiling create a hazard, the tunnel is barricaded by metal gates at the west end and heavy wooden doors at the east end.

Just outside the Hyak entrance is a trail access and Sno-Park. Snow sheds once stood to the east along the Lake Keechelus lakeshore to protect trains from snowslides, but they became unsafe and were removed. When it was operating, the Milwaukee Road was the longest electric railway in the world. An information kiosk tells the story of the trains and their use of electricity, which was at first very controversial.

From the east end of the Hyak tunnel, the trail proceeds around the south shore of Lake Keechelus. North are spectacular views of ragged peaks at the head of Gold Creek. The trail contours the forested hillside above the Yakima River, passes through a short tunnel, and is soon

paralleled by a companion track, the active Burlington Northern rails from Stampede Pass. There is a temporary gap in the trail between the west end of Lake Easton State Park and Easton, where State Parks has not yet acquired all the right-of-way, and a bridge is missing. Until these problems are resolved, trail users are diverted from the park along local roads to the Easton trailhead. From Easton, the right-of-way runs along the south side of I-90 to Cle Elum.

Cle Elum to Kittitas

At Cle Elum the Iron Horse Trail passes the boarded-up ghost of the powerhouse that once provided the electric current to overhead power lines that enabled the engines to pull their loads over the summit. Electric engines were preferred over coal-fired engines for the summit climb because they were cheaper and more efficient to operate, and smoke in the long tunnels would be hazardous to train crews and passengers. State Parks has acquired the powerhouse, the adjacent railroad station, and the switchyard to the south, and plans to eventually convert it to a National Historic District with a railroad interpretive center.

East from Cle Elum, the roadbed follows the south bank of the Yakima River, descending through the thick riparian woodlands below steep bluffs cut by the river valley. A few miles west of Thorp, the track skirts the foot of a sheer cliff, and the river's undulations are interrupted by two short tunnels through the adjoining hillsides. This section of the trail is subject to slides when there is water in a canal along the crest of the bluffs, so it might be closed during irrigation season.

From here east to Ellensburg the landscape flattens. Trestles bridge several roads, creeks, and finally the Yakima River as the Iron Horse Trail cuts through open farmland. The campus of Central Washington University interrupts the route briefly in Ellensburg, but from the east side of the campus, the track runs straight and true through farm and field from Ellensburg to Kittitas.

Iron Horse State Park (East)

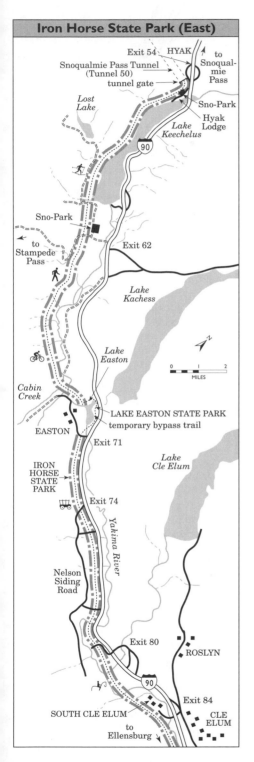

Exit 54   HYAK
to Snoqual-mie Pass
Snoqualmie Pass Tunnel (Tunnel 50)
tunnel gate
Sno-Park
Hyak Lodge
Lost Lake
Lake Keechelus
90
Sno-Park
to Stampede Pass
Exit 62
Lake Kachess
Lake Easton
N
Cabin Creek
LAKE EASTON STATE PARK
temporary bypass trail
EASTON
Exit 71
IRON HORSE STATE PARK
Exit 74
Lake Cle Elum
Yakima River
Nelson Siding Road
Exit 80
ROSLYN
90
SOUTH CLE ELUM
Exit 84
CLE ELUM
to Ellensburg

Iron Horse State Park (East)

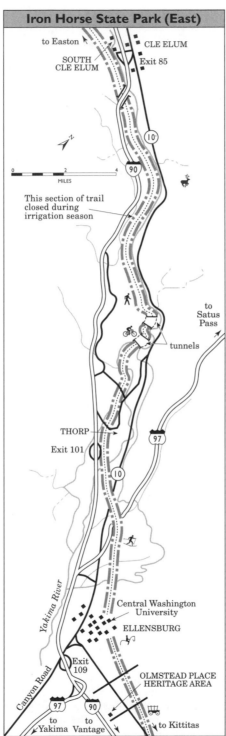

to Easton
CLE ELUM
SOUTH CLE ELUM
Exit 85
10
N
0 2 4
MILES
90
This section of trail closed during irrigation season
to Satus Pass
tunnels
THORP
Exit 101
97
10
Yakima River
Central Washington University
ELLENSBURG
Exit 109
OLMSTEAD PLACE HERITAGE AREA
Canyon Road
97 90
to Yakima   to Vantage
to Kittitas

Iron Horse State Park (East)

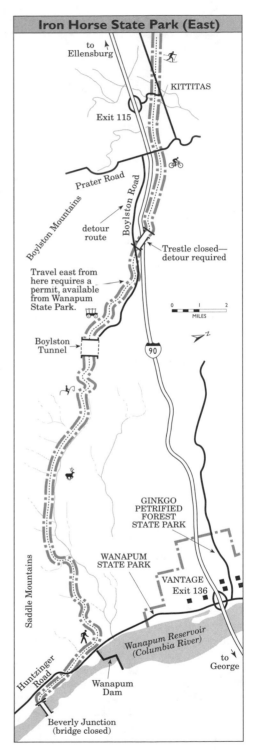

to Ellensburg
KITTITAS
Exit 115
Boylston Mountains
Prater Road
Boylston Road
detour route
Trestle closed—detour required
Travel east from here requires a permit, available from Wanapum State Park.
Boylston Tunnel
0 1 2
MILES
N
90
GINKGO PETRIFIED FOREST STATE PARK
WANAPUM STATE PARK
VANTAGE
Exit 136
Saddle Mountains
Wanapum Reservoir (Columbia River)
to George
Huntzinger Road
Wanapum Dam
Beverly Junction (bridge closed)

A baggage cart sitting at the old railroad station along the Iron Horse Trail at Kittitas evokes memories of the time when trains stopped here.

Kittitas to the Columbia River

From the relic railroad station at Kittitas, the trail and a parallel road leave the lush farmlands and head into the encroaching gray sagebrush of the central Washington steppes. The trestle over I-90 is unsafe to cross and is barricaded, so the trail has been diverted to local roads at Prater Road, which crosses a freeway overpass 2.5 miles to the west, and then Boylston Road, which parallels the freeway until it rejoins the old right-of-way.

Once south of the freeway, the track slowly climbs the parched scrub of the Boylston Mountains and passes through 1,980-foot-long Boylston Tunnel. This unique tunnel has walls near the middle that are natural rock, rather than the concrete used in other tunnels. The dark roof serves as lair for owls and bats; occasionally rattlesnakes slither into the cool of the tunnel to escape the outside heat.

East from Boylston the roadbed ignores the natural contours of the land and runs straight through a seemingly endless series of land cuts and fills. Underlying layers of basalt that are exposed in the cuts offer insights into local geology. This less-used section of trail offers an excellent chance of seeing deer, coyote, hawks, jackrabbits, snakes (including rattlers), and other dry-land inhabitants. The track winds down the east end of the Saddle Mountains and then runs below the steep wall of Sentinel Gap, which sweeps up to a series of spectacular basalt towers cut by the Columbia River.

In 1994 the Army acquired large portions of the property south of Boylston for an addition to the Yakima Firing Center. *This section of trail is subject to closure during military maneuvers; a permit, obtained at kiosks near both trailheads, is required while using it.* Although, when they acquired the property, the Army agreed to keep the trail open, it later contended that the general signing the agreement didn't have the authority to do so, and it is not bound by it. The matter is still unresolved. The state park ends as it meets the Columbia River at the barricaded Beverly Junction Bridge. Railroad right-of-way continuing east of the river is owned by the State Department of Natural Resources.

GINKGO PETRIFIED FOREST STATE PARK

Picnicking, sightseeing, hiking, interpretive information

SEASON/HOURS: Year-round; Interpretive Center Wednesday through Sunday, 10:00 A.M. to 6:00 P.M. mid-June to mid-September; weekends only, 10:00 A.M. to 6:00 P.M., or by appointment in winter.

AREA: 7,007.88 acres; 8,260 feet of freshwater shoreline on the Columbia River (Wanapum Reservoir).

DAY-USE FACILITIES: 10 picnic sites, 2 restrooms.

RECREATIONAL FACILITIES: 3 miles of hiking trails, 1-mile interpretive trail.

EDUCATIONAL FACILITIES: Interpretive center (&), Indian petroglyphs, viewing telescopes.

CAR ACCESS: From I-90 take Exit 136 (Vantage, Huntzinger Road) to Vantage. North of Vantage 0.2 mile, turn west on Ginkgo Avenue, and in 0.4 mile reach the Ginkgo Petrified Forest Interpretive Center. To reach the interpretive trail, drive northeast from Vantage 2.3 miles to the parking lot at the trailhead.

What on earth is a ginkgo, you ask? Well, it's a tree that in its living form is currently found only as cultivated specimens—a "living fossil," unchanged for more than a million years, and the sole survivor of a group of plants that were abundant during the Triassic period, 230 to 160 million years ago. This park is one of the few places on earth where petrified wood of the ginkgo

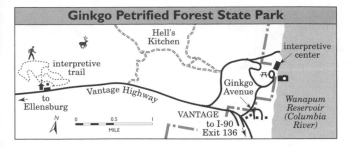

Ginkgo Petrified Forest State Park

tree has been found, proving its ancient lineage.

Over 200 species of trees, including Douglas-fir, spruce, walnut, and elm, as well as the very rare ginkgo, once grew in the area's lush, moist forest—hard to imagine today when scanning the park's parched desert landscape. Lava that later flowed across eastern Washington decimated these forests, and log-littered lake bottoms were sealed under thick layers of volcanic basalt. Over time the organic material of the logs was replaced by silica-based minerals that faithfully duplicated the structure of the original wood. Floods that followed the Ice Age uncovered the basalt layers in places, exposing the fossilized stone logs. This petrified forest was discovered in the 1930s, and the initial park facilities were developed by the Depression-era CCC.

The park interpretive center sits on a bluff just north of Vantage, at the rim of cliffs that edge the Columbia River. The grounds outside the center are scattered with fossilized logs, while inside interesting displays and a short slide program tell about petrified wood, ginkgo trees, and local geology. Samples of cut and polished petrified wood show beautiful colors and patterns. Telescopes on an outside deck offer expansive views of the Columbia.

Drive 2 miles farther west from Vantage to find an interpretive trail that loops through the desert past a score of sites where fossils have been uncovered. Unfortunately, the logs here are enclosed in cages to preserve them from destructive humans. Beyond the interpretive trail, a 2.5-mile-long hiking trail wanders across the barren sage-covered desert. The hot, dry trail's main appeal is the blush of color from wildflowers in spring and early summer; there's also the possibility of sighting rattlesnakes, lizards, deer, coyote, or a variety of birds.

Native American petroglyphs can be seen near the interpretive center at Ginkgo Petrified Forest State Park.

WANAPUM STATE PARK

Camping, picnicking, swimming, waterskiing, fishing, boating

SEASON/HOURS: Park closed November 1 through April 1, except weekends and holidays, launch ramp open year-round; campsite reservations accepted in summer.

AREA: 462 acres; 5,700 feet of freshwater shoreline on the Columbia River (Wanapum Reservoir).

OVERNIGHT AND DAY-USE FACILITIES: 50 RV sites (&), 47 picnic sites, 3 restrooms with showers (&).

RECREATIONAL FACILITIES: Swimming beach, bathhouse, 2-lane paved boat ramp with boarding float.

CONCESSIONS: Snacks, beverages, groceries, and camping supplies.

CAR ACCESS: Take Exit 136 (Vantage, Huntzinger Road) from I-90. Drive 3 miles south on Huntzinger Road to reach the park.

Although Ginkgo Petrified Forest has hosted interested visitors since 1935, no camping facilities were provided in early years. Wanapum State Park, which was created after the reservoir behind Wanapum Dam came into being, now fills that need, and also provides fine boating and swimming on the Columbia River. Green lawns have been wrenched from a

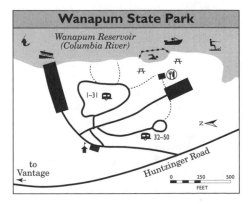

Wanapum State Park

grudging desert, and persistent irrigation prevents their regression into sagebrush. Two campground loops have swatches of grass at each site, with a type of olive trees providing some shade; parched sagebrush marks the outer perimeter of each site. Trails lead from both camping loops to the brushy lakeshore and day-use area.

The day-use area and the boat launch bracket the camping loops at the water's edge. To the north, below a spacious parking lot, two lanes of a launch ramp share a boarding float. South, on another island of green lawn, the picnic area and the bathhouse with a concession stand look down to broad sand beach and a roped-off swimming area. Trails through the sagebrush link all of the sites. The popular park is crowded on weekends during the summer.

The Olmstead Cabin at Olmstead Place Heritage Area boasts the finest furnishings of the time.

OLMSTEAD PLACE HERITAGE AREA

Picnicking, historic interpretation

SEASON/HOURS: Year-round; tours Memorial Day to Labor Day, Saturday and Sunday, noon to 4:00 P.M., and by appointment year-round.
AREA: 217.8 acres.
DAY-USE FACILITIES: 17 picnic sites, group day-use area (300 persons), restrooms at the Seaton site (&), 2 toilets at the Olmstead site.
RECREATIONAL FACILITIES: 0.75-mile interpretive trail.
EDUCATIONAL FACILITIES: Display sheds with farm equipment and tools, dairy barn, homestead cabin, Olmstead residence, farm buildings, Seaton schoolhouse.
CAR ACCESS: Take Exit 115 (Kittitas) north from I-90. Drive Main Street through Kittitas, then turn west on Patrick Avenue, which becomes the Kittitas Highway at the city limits. In 2.4 miles, at an intersection signed N Ferguson Road, turn

south, and in 0.4 mile reach the Seaton cabin; the red barn and Olmstead cabin are 0.5 mile farther south.

Olmstead Place, in addition to being a historical museum, is a functioning 200-acre farm that still produces wheat, oats, and hay, and has dairy cattle and chickens. This has been an active farm since it was homesteaded in 1875 by Samuel Bedient Olmstead. The original cozy log cabin, considered quite comfortable for its day, still stands at the south end of the park. It has been restored and furnished with the Olmsteads' belongings and articles typical of the time gleaned from other farms of similar age. During summer months the park provides interpretive talks on the farm and local history at the cabin. Olmstead's later residence, which is adjacent, is also open for tours on summer weekends. Visitors can lunch at picnic tables scattered around the lawn by the cabin.

Behind the house to the west are farm buildings—chicken coops, a wagon shed, tool shed, granary, milkhouse, and dairy barn. North of the house, farm implements of varying vintages sit alongside a large red barn that was built in 1908. Altapes Creek meanders along the west boundary of the property, and a 0.75-mile-long, self-guided nature trail follows the creek bank from the red barn to the Seaton Schoolhouse. A brochure available from the park describes sights along

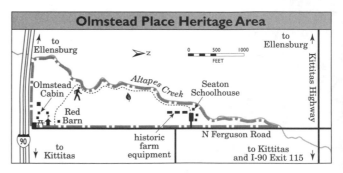

the way, such as red osier dogwood (a strong flexible wood used by the Native Americans for hunting bows and baskets) and trees felled by beavers for food and creating dams.

North of the Olmstead residences, near the creek, is the Seaton Schoolhouse. Here children can see what it was like to learn their lessons long ago. In 1876 the single-room log cabin became home to the Terry family. The Terrys used part of the cabin as a small private school for valley children. One corner is fitted out as a schoolroom, with benches, a desk, and a few books typical of the time, while the rest of the cabin has a bed and kitchen equipment for the Terrys' everyday life.

Sheds near the schoolhouse contain more farm implements and machinery collected over the years by a local historical society. A pair of covered wagon replicas are used for scheduled wagon train rides. School field trips are available, for a fee.

Helen McCabe State Park

Fishing

SEASON/HOURS: Year-round.
AREA: 64 acres; 2,640 feet of freshwater shoreline on Wilson Creek, including a 7.4-acre unnamed pond.
FACILITIES: Toilet.
CAR ACCESS: Take Exit 110 (Yakima, US 82E, US 97S) south from I-90, 1 mile east of Ellensburg. In 2.1 miles take Exit 3 (SR 821S, Thrall Road) and go west on Thrall Road for 0.7 mile to its intersection with Canyon Road. The park lies southeast of this intersection.

This property was acquired as a part of a plan for recreational development along the Yakima Canyon Recreational and Scenic Highway, which runs south from here through the picturesque canyon to Yakima.

Funding for the development of the park has never been approved, so it is currently managed in cooperation with the Department of Fish and Wildlife and the Kittitas County Field and Stream Club. Its only facilities are a dirt parking lot and a toilet near the pond that comprises the heart of the park. The tree-edged pond has a rough footpath around its perimeter; breaks in the shoreline foliage permit access for fishing. The lake and Wilson Creek contain rainbow trout.

Indian Painted Rocks State Heritage Area

Indian petroglyphs

AREA: 0.1 acre.
EDUCATIONAL FACILITIES: Pictographs, interpretive sign.
CAR ACCESS: From US 12, 4.2 miles west of its junction with I-82 and US 97, and just east of the bridges over the Naches River, turn southwest onto Ackley Road, and in a block, turn northwest onto W Powerhouse Road. The site is at the base of basalt cliffs above a gravel pulloff in about 2 blocks.

History passed by here. A 100-foot-high basalt cliff towers above what once was an Indian trail leading from the Wenas Mountains, to the northwest, to the territory of the Ahtanum band of the Yakamas to the southeast. Later, miners heading for the British Columbia goldfields used the trail, and later yet a stagecoach route passed this point. It's not hard to imagine all these people trekking through this spot.

Concrete steps lead to a path along the base of the cliff where faint and fading figures can be seen painted on the rocks. Most appear to be stylized faces with an arc of rays surrounding the head. The origin of the paintings, and their meaning, is unknown in the folklore of the present tribes. However, they are a fragile and important heritage of local Native Americans, as well as of the state—treat them with respect and don't deface them.

Yakima Sportsman State Park

Camping, picnicking, birdwatching, hiking, horseback riding, fishing

SEASON/HOURS: Year-round; campsite reservations accepted in summer.
AREA: 246.65 acres; 19,116 feet of freshwater shoreline on the Yakima River and several small ponds.
OVERNIGHT AND DAY-USE FACILITIES: 37 RV sites (&), 28 standard campsites (1 &), 4 primitive campsites, 120 picnic sites, 3 reservable picnic shelters, group day-use area with kitchen shelter (200 persons), 2 restrooms with showers (&), trailer dump station.
RECREATIONAL FACILITIES: 3 miles of hiking trails, 1 mile of equestrian trails, children's play equipment.
EDUCATIONAL FACILITIES: Nature trail (&).
CAR ACCESS: From I-82/US 97/US 12 on the east side of Yakima, take Exit 34 (SR 24E, Moxee, Yakima State Park). Head east on SR 24 for 0.8 mile and after crossing the Yakima River turn north on Keys Road. The park entrance is in 1 mile at the intersection of Keys and Gun Club Roads.

Yakima Sportsman State Park is a shaded glen with a trickling creek and ponds along the east side of the Yakima River. The Yakima Sportsmans Association created it in 1940 to promote game management and the preservation and protection of natural resources. Because the ponds and small lakes within the park are stocked, fishing is limited to youngsters under 15 years old. The Yakima River, which has great fishing for all ages,

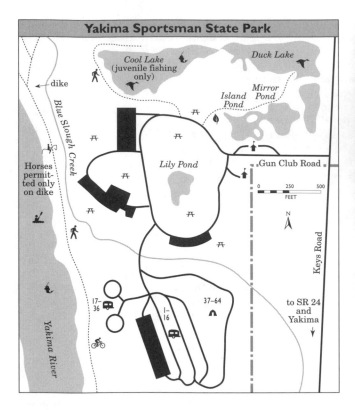

Yakima Sportsman State Park

A mixture of wild and domestic ducks and geese enjoy the good life on Cool Lake at Yakima Sportsman State Park.

is known for its excellent catches of large trout and bass.

A pond lying in the heart of the broad grassy expanse of the park's day-use area flaunts brilliant pink water lilies in summer. A remarkable variety of beautiful, mature deciduous trees, including elm, ash, willow, catalpa, and maple shade picnic tables. The north side of the park is framed by more ponds—home not only for fish, but also for both domestic and wild ducks and geese. A nature trail leads to an observation platform overlooking the pond. Blue Slough Creek flows through a profusion of brush along the south and west sides of the day-use area. A bridge across the creek leads to the campground on the south side of the park.

For riverbank fishing, a scramble through brush west of the campground leads to a dike edging the Yakima River. It can also be reached from the day-use area at a few spots where fallen trees

bridge Blue Slough Creek. By walking quietly along the service road that tops the dike you might spot swallows, hawks, owls, red-winged blackbirds, or other of the 140 species of birds that have been identified here.

FORT SIMCOE STATE PARK

Historical interpretation, picnicking

SEASON/HOURS: Open April through October (buildings open Wednesday through Sunday, 9:30 A.M. to 4:30 P.M.); October through April, open weekends and holidays (buildings open only by request).

AREA: 200 acres.

DAY-USE FACILITIES: 52 picnic sites, 8 fire braziers, picnic shelter, 2 restrooms.

RECREATIONAL FACILITIES: 0.8-mile interpretive trail, children's play equipment.

EDUCATIONAL FACILITIES: 10 historic buildings, interpretive center, interpretive displays.

CAR ACCESS: From US 97 at Toppenish, take SR 220 (White Swan, Fort Simcoe) west for 27.5 miles to arrive at the park.

Fort Simcoe State Park is not for casual drive-by visitors; after a 27-mile trek through hop and grape fields of the Yakama Nation west of Toppenish, the road dead-ends at the park. However, the fort is well worth the trip because of its view into the state's military and Native American history. Here the abundant spring water of *Mool Mool* (bubbling waters) nourished a surrounding forest and lush grassland that stood in stark contrast to the otherwise parched countryside. The area had long been used as a campsite by Yakama tribes, and in 1855, when Indian hostilities mandated an advanced military post in Washington Territory, it was selected as the site for a new fort.

In the summer of 1856, during the renewed Indian wars, troops from Fort Simcoe engaged bands from the Coeur d'Alene, Spokane, and Palouse tribes. The end of hostilities led to the abandonment of the fort in 1859. It was turned over to the Bureau of Indian Affairs, and until 1923 served as Indian Agency headquarters. The agency-run school at the fort taught reservation Indians reading and writing and trained them in trades such as carpentry, blacksmithing, and farming.

Today the broad grass parade field of the fort has been restored, and the corner blockhouses that protected it have been reconstructed. One of the barracks that housed enlisted men was also rebuilt, and the prim white clapboard homes for

Rough-hewn timbers and dove-tail construction can be seen in some of the buildings at Fort Simcoe State Park.

the officers and commandant have been restored to their original condition and decorated with period furnishings. The remainder of the fort buildings, including other barracks, junior officers' quarters, warehouses, laundry, hospital, and servants' buildings, are now remembered only by concrete markers.

The old Indian Agency commissary has been converted into an interpretive center where displays tell the story of the Native Americans who lived in this region, and the history of the fort.

BROOKS MEMORIAL STATE PARK

Camping, picnicking, nature talks, hiking, mountain biking, fishing, cross-country skiing, snowshoeing, snowmobiling (nearby)

SEASON/HOURS: Year-round.
AREA: 700.8 acres.
OVERNIGHT AND DAY-USE FACILITIES: 23 RV sites, 22 standard campsites, 2 primitive campsites, group camp (50 persons), 40 picnic sites, 2 kitchen shelters, 2 restrooms (1 with showers), 3 toilets, trailer dump station.
RECREATIONAL FACILITIES: 9 miles of hiking/bicycle trails, sports field, horseshoe pits, children's play equipment.
ELC: Dining hall, kitchen, 2 restrooms with showers, 7 cabins (40–104 persons), 1 or 2 teepees, campfire circle, sports field, volleyball court, quarter basketball court, horseshoe pits,
CAR ACCESS: The park straddles US 97, 12.7 miles north of Goldendale, and 2.5 miles south of Satus Pass.

Satus Pass marks the transition between the barren hills at the south side of the Yakima Valley and the lodgepole pine forest of the Simcoe Mountains. Brooks Memorial State Park lies in the forested region just south of the 3,149-foot pass. In addition to the usual picnicking and

Campers using the Environmental Learning Center at Brooks Memorial State Park may stay in a teepee.

camping, the park, with its group camp and ELC, is heavily oriented toward group recreation.

The park's picnic area and individual campsites are on the northwest side of US 97. Here, beneath a hillside stand of ponderosa pine, are standard campsites holding tables and fire braziers; hookup sites are paved diagonal strips on two swatches of lawn. The larger part of the park, with its group camp and ELC, lies southeast of the highway. The extensive facilities of the ELC make it ideal for scout troops, church camps, and family reunions, while the dry climate of eastern Washington virtually guarantees good weather for a summer gathering.

Trails lead from the ELC to two different environmental experiences: riparian and meadow. A short trail enters the brush below the playfield and soon reaches the

Little Klickitat River. Trailside mud and dust reveal tracks of beaver, deer, fox, and other visiting wildlife. A road near the ELC entrance heads out to a forest-rimmed meadow on a long extension of the park. Ponderosa pine, Douglas-fir, white pine, and Oregon oak dominate the timber, and seasonal wildflowers such as lady's slipper, balsam root, and lupine add color to the open forest floor. The glacier-clad summit of Mount Hood rises over the southwest horizon. Forest inhabitants include deer, raccoons, porcupines, wild turkeys, black bear, coyotes, and bobcats, and raptors such as owls, hawks, and eagles.

Cold, snowy winters and open timber make the park ideal for cross-country skiing and snowshoeing, however the park does not groom any trails, and only limited park facilities are available during the winter.

CROW BUTTE STATE PARK

Camping, picnicking, birdwatching, hiking, swimming, waterskiing, fishing, boating

SEASON/HOURS: Park closed mid-October to mid-March, except weekends and holidays, launch ramps open year-round; campsite reservations accepted in summer.
AREA: 1,311.75 acres; 33,910 feet of freshwater shoreline on the Columbia River (Lake Umatilla).
OVERNIGHT AND DAY-USE FACILITIES: 50 RV sites (&), group camp (60 persons), 26 picnic sites, 3 picnic shelters, restroom with showers (&), trailer dump station.
RECREATIONAL FACILITIES: 4 miles of hiking trails, 0.8-mile sand-dune beach trail, swimming beach, bathhouse with showers (&), 2-lane paved boat ramp with boarding floats, 1-lane paved boat ramp, boat basin, dock with 10 moorage floats, 4 mooring buoys.
CONCESSIONS: Snacks and beverages.
NEARBY: Umatilla National Wildlife Refuge.
CAR ACCESS: The park is on an island in the Columbia River (Lake Umatilla) reached by a causeway on the south side of SR 14, 12.2 miles west of Paterson, and 21.6 miles east of Roosevelt. Tall trailers should be aware of a low-clearance (14' 9") underpass under Highway 14.

Folks in eastern Washington who are surrounded by the tough green-brown rolling hills of the Columbia plateau like

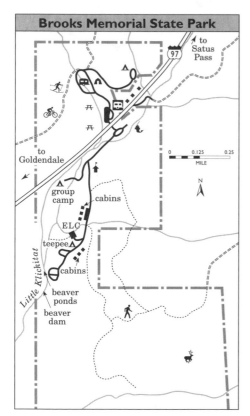

Swimmers and paddlers trek to the beach at Crow Butte State Park.

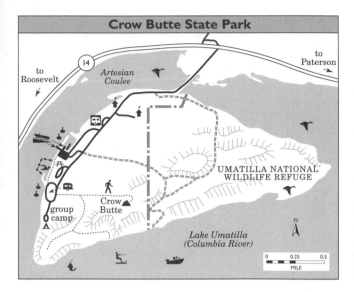

beetles, deer, and other desert inhabitants (but hopefully, no rattlesnakes).

Crow Butte is the top of a hill that became an island when the reservoir backed up behind John Day Dam, flooding this stretch of the Columbia River and creating 76-mile-long Lake Umatilla. The east end of the island is a portion of the Umatilla National Wildlife Refuge, which extends east on both sides of the river for over 15 miles.

Huge numbers of waterfowl wintered on islands in this stretch of the Columbia before the John Day Dam was built. The wildlife refuge was established to mitigate the loss of islands drowned by the construction of the dam. With the irrigation the dam brought, the birds now have a larger food source from newly created wheat fields, and they flock here in even greater numbers than before. White pelicans and long-billed curlews nest in the region. From fall through spring this is also a "bed and breakfast" for hundreds of thousands of migratory ducks and Canada geese as they wend their way north or south with the seasons.

their park getaways soft and shady. Crow Butte State Park meets their expectations nicely, with its neatly groomed grassy crescent on the shore of Artesian Coulee. Yet nature is only a stroll from the campground.

A small boat basin, protected on the north by a breakwater, provides a launch ramp and tie-up floats. A roped-off swimming beach is adjacent. A second ramp and mooring buoys are nearby in Artesian Coulee. The tree-rimmed green lawn above the swimming area holds a bathhouse and day-use picnic shelters; in the campground to the south, shade trees and windbreak fences shield campsites.

On the east side of the campground, a wide sandy trail enters the desert. (*Be careful venturing off the path: Signs warn of rattlesnakes.*) In 0.25 mile the east fork heads to the top of 671-foot-high Crow Butte. The west fork climbs to another Y; the east branch leads over a ridge and down a gully to the dune-edged Columbia River, while the right branch continues west to a viewpoint of the river and campground. Weather allowing, Mount Hood can be seen. Although the trail might seem a tedium of gray-green sagebrush, hikers with a vigilant eye will spot tiny colorful wildflowers, cactus, grasshoppers,

MOSES LAKE STATE PARK

Picnicking, swimming, waterskiing, scuba diving, fishing, ice fishing, boating, sailing, paddling, ice skating

SEASON/HOURS: Closed October 1 through April 1, except weekends and holidays.

AREA: 78 acres; 862 feet of freshwater shoreline on Moses Lake.

A moth and bee share an interest in a thistle blossom.

DAY-USE FACILITIES: 77 picnic sites, 3 group day-use areas with picnic shelters (100 persons each), 2 restrooms, toilet (&).

RECREATIONAL FACILITIES: Swimming beach , bathhouse, 2-lane boat ramp with boarding dock, 2 volleyball courts.

CAR ACCESS: From I-90 westbound, take Exit 175 (Moses Lake State Park, Mae Valley, Westshore Drive), and turn north on Westshore Drive. Continue to the park entrance in 0.2 mile. From I-90 eastbound, take Exit 174 (Moses Lake State Park), cross the overpass over I-90, and take the road parallel to the north side of the freeway for 1 mile to the park.

Moses Lake State Park resembles a typical city park, with lots of picnic sites scattered throughout a rolling, tree-shaded lawn, and three spacious picnic shelters for family or community group gatherings. Because the park lies on the west shore of Moses Lake, it also provides water-oriented facilities: a bathhouse and roped-off swimming beach, and a boat ramp with boarding float.

The many narrow arms of the 6,815-acre lake offer water recreation to everyone's taste. Fishing is the big attraction, but the cool lake also offers a summer respite to swimmers, waterskiers, and boaters who just enjoy a day on the water.

The park is immediately north of the westbound lanes of I-90, so it's an inviting place to stop for a leg stretch and picnic to break the tedious drive across the central Washington plateau. In winter the shallow lake freezes over, and on weekends the swimming area becomes a community ice-skating rink.

POTHOLES STATE PARK

Camping, picnicking, hiking, waterskiing, fishing, ice fishing, boating, paddling

SEASON/HOURS: Year-round; campsite reservations accepted in summer.
AREA: 640 acres; 6,000 feet of freshwater shoreline on Potholes Reservoir.
OVERNIGHT AND DAY-USE FACILITIES: 60

RV sites (2 ♿), 61 standard campsites, group camp (50 persons), 33 picnic sites (2 ♿), 4 restrooms with showers (2 ♿), 4 toilets, trailer dump station.
RECREATIONAL FACILITIES: 2 children's play areas, 4-lane paved boat ramp with boarding floats (♿), hand-carry boat launch.
NEARBY: Potholes Wildlife Recreation Area, Goose Lake Wildlife Recreation Area.
CAR ACCESS: *From the west,* at Exit 164 (Dodson Road) from I-90, head south on Dodson Road for 10.1 miles, then turn east on Frenchman Hills Road, signed to Potholes State Park, to reach the park in 11 miles. *From the east,* at Exit 179 (SR 17, Othello, Moses Lake, Ephrata) from I-90, head southeast on SR 17 for 9.3 miles, then turn west on O'Sullivan Dam Road, and reach the park in another 12 miles.

When O'Sullivan Dam was completed in 1949, raising the water table south of Moses Lake, sand-filled depressions that had been carved by Ice Age glaciers

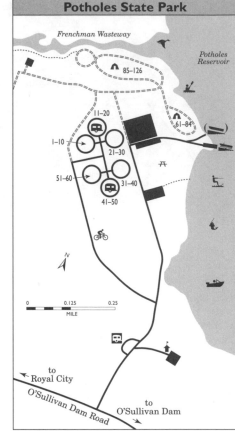

Potholes State Park

filled with water and created one enormous lake (28,200-acre Potholes Reservoir) and a network of interconnecting shallow lakes, ponds, and marshes that covers thousands of acres of scabland. The tops of old sand dunes protrude from the water of the reservoir, creating a maze of over a hundred low islands at its north end, and making this a boating and paddling paradise.

Potholes State Park lies on the southwest shore of the reservoir. Its day-use and RV camping areas are an oasis of green amid the surrounding drab desert landscape. Tall rows of Lombardy poplar interspersed with shorter evergreens protect the sites from high winds that occasionally whip the area. Tent campers need to be a hardier lot, however, as

A huge expanse of sparkling, fish-filled water attracts boaters and waterfowl to Potholes State Park.

tent sites, rimming two loops on the north end of the park, consist only of a meager gravel pad, table, and fire pit nestled into the surrounding sagebrush and sand.

As would be expected, most recreation involves water: boating, paddling, fishing, and waterskiing. To support these activities, the park has a paved two-lane boat launch, a separate gravel cartop launch ramp, and two huge lots for parking cars and boat trailers. Although the day-use area fronts on the reservoir, no defined swimming beach is roped off.

The lakes, which are planted with rainbow trout, also hold perch, crappie, largemouth and smallmouth bass, and walleye. The open water, marshes, and willow thickets of the potholes provide migratory stopovers and nesting spots for thousands of waterfowl and other birds, ranging from big, heavy-bodied white pelicans, to graceful black-crowned night herons, and delicate little American avocets. Yellow-headed and red-winged blackbirds add splashes of color to cattails. Quiet boaters and anglers might see muskrats and beavers, while campers enjoy the evening serenade of coyotes.

SACAJAWEA STATE PARK

Picnicking, birdwatching, swimming, waterskiing, fishing, boating, interpretive displays

SEASON/HOURS: Closed October 1 through April 1.
AREA: 283.72 acres; 9,100 feet of freshwater shoreline on the Snake and Columbia Rivers.
DAY-USE FACILITIES: 125 picnic tables, gazebo, group day-use area with kitchen shelter (200 persons), 3 restrooms (1 &).
RECREATIONAL FACILITIES: Children's play equipment, swimming beach, 2-lane paved boat ramp with floats, 3 mooring floats, 3 mooring buoys.
EDUCATIONAL FACILITIES: Interpretive

At Sacajawea State Park the launch ramp and boarding floats are in the protection of a small oval basin.

center (call the park for hours).
NEARBY: McNary National Wildlife Refuge.
CAR ACCESS: From US 12, 4.4 miles southeast of Pasco and just west of the bridge across the Snake River, turn southwest on Tank Farm Road. At a Y-intersection in 1 mile, bear east and reach the park entrance in another 0.9 mile.

Nearly every grade-schooler can identify Sacajawea as the Shoshoni woman who accompanied Lewis and Clark on their westward trek from Missouri to the Pacific Ocean and served as their interpreter. Sacajawea State Park and its interpretive center are named for this brave woman. The park, at the confluence of two major rivers, the Snake and Columbia, is at one of the party's campsites. It was here, in 1805, that Lewis and Clark first sighted the mighty Columbia River that was to provide their final access to the ocean.

During pioneer times this site lay on a route used by hunters and trappers seeking their fortune in the Northwest. The

park property includes the former site of Ainsworth, a rough-and-tumble railroad town that sprang to life during the construction of the Northern Pacific Railroad bridge across the Snake in the 1880s. The initial parcels of land were deeded to the state in 1931; huge old trees throughout the flat lawn testify to the park's age.

A swimming beach is roped off along the Columbia River side of the park. The Snake River shoreline supports the boat-oriented facilities: three docks with 40-foot-long mooring floats, a small oval basin enclosing a two-lane launch ramp with boarding floats, and three mooring buoys just outside the launch basin.

The Sacajawea Interpretive Center sits at the heart of the park. Sadly, hours are unpredictable because the park must rely on volunteer staffing; call in advance for the schedule if you plan to visit the center. One of the center's rooms tells of the competing claims to the Northwest that prompted Thomas Jefferson to send the Lewis and Clark Expedition west, and traces their route to the Pacific with montages of photos, maps, journal reproductions, and a video. A second room houses arrowheads, mortars, pestles, awls, bowls, and other artifacts used by the Native Americans of the Columbia Basin plateau. Display boards describe facets of the Native American culture, and tell how the tools and implements were made and used.

COLUMBIA PLATEAU TRAIL

Hiking, bicycling, horseback riding, nature and wildlife watching

SEASON/HOURS: Year-round.
AREA: 3,900.62 acres.
RECREATIONAL FACILITIES: 130-mile multi-use rail/trail conversion, 5 tunnels, 6 trestles (4 are historic landmarks). *Motorized vehicles prohibited.* **Ice Harbor Dam Road:** 12 miles of crushed gravel trail. **Myers Park Road:** 2 toilets, picnic shelter, information kiosk, 16 miles of improved trail (4 miles paved and 12 miles of crushed gravel).
CAR ACCESS: The only fully developed access to the trail is at the northeast end, four miles north of Cheney. Drive Cheney–Spokane Road 3.2 miles northwest of Cheney to Meyers Park, on the south side of the road. The trail access is on the east side of the park. Refer to the map for informal accesses.

The Columbia Plateau Trail traces the roadbed of the Spokane, Portland, and Seattle Railroad, which was built in 1908. The 130-mile-long route is steeped in history, both geological and human. Lava flows originating near the Washington–Idaho border between 17 million and 12 million years ago covered central Washington with layer upon layer of basalt. The northern portion of the state was then covered by immense continental glaciers, beginning a million years ago during the Pleistocene epoch, and continuing until about 16,000 years ago. Massive

floods from glacial Lake Missoula, an enormous lake that backed up into what is now western Montana, followed the final retreat of these ice sheets. The water torrent ate into the basalt base and gouged out the present washes, gullies, and canyons that are known as the channeled scablands.

When pioneers sought routes through this country, the easiest trails followed the paths of the ancient floods. In the late 1850s, Captain John Mullan laid out a wagon road joining the Missouri River drainage with the Columbia River; 40 years later the first railroads followed much of this original Mullan Road. Imprints of the geological forces that formed the area are still readily visible along the route of the old railbed, and many towns and structures along the way have changed little since the early 1900s. State Parks acquired the land in 1991 when it was abandoned by the Burlington Northern Railroad. The trail is described here from southwest to northeast.

Martindale to Kahlotus

From the southwest end of the trail near Pasco, at the small community of Martindale, the route follows the northwest side of the Snake River upstream from Ice Harbor Dam to Lower Monumental Dam. The 15 miles between Ice Harbor Dam and Snake River Junction have been improved to hiking/biking/equestrian quality with a layer of crushed gravel. Side roads from the Pasco–Kahlotus Road run down canyons at Murphy Road, McClenny/Votaw Road, McCoy Canyon Road, and Devils Canyon Road to the Snake River, some passing beneath the tall trestles of the old railroad. Four of these old trestles are on the National Register of Historic Places because of their age and unique design.

When these bridges are decked and open for travel, equestrians would be wise to dismount and lead their horses across, since side barriers will be less than 5 feet high, and bridge decks are up to 100 feet or more above the canyon floor. Other side roads cross at grade level, offering

access to the trail. Near the dam the trail leaves the Snake, swings north through a 0.5-mile-long tunnel, cuts along the middle of the west wall of steep-faced Devils Canyon, and passes through another 2,000-foot-long tunnel just south of Kahlotus before reaching that small town.

Kahlotus to Amber Lake

From Kahlotus the route heads northeast along the shore of Lake Kahlotus, then down along the floor of the wide, shallow Washtucna Coulee to arrive at the town of Washtucna. After crossing a trestle over the active Union Pacific line, the trail follows the general route of the Mullan Trail north up the canyon drainage of Cow Creek, once again crossing the Union Pacific line on a long, high trestle

An old water tower at Benge, along the Columbia Plateau Trail, was used in the days when trains ran through here.

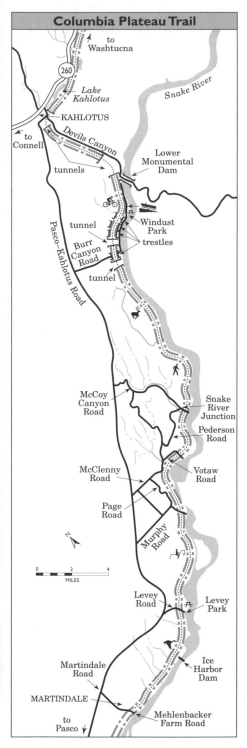

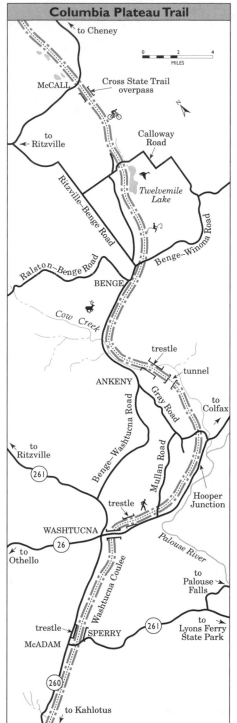

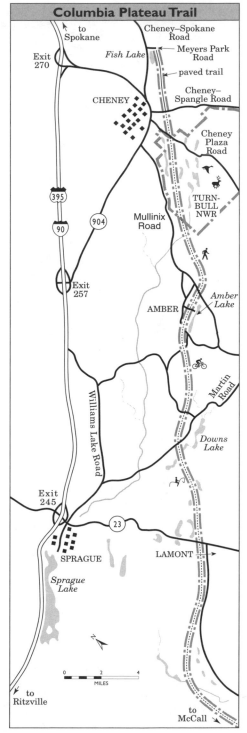

Columbia Plateau Trail

to Washtucna

260

Lake Kahlotus

Snake River

KAHLOTUS

Devils Canyon

to Connell

tunnels

Lower Monumental Dam

tunnel

Windust Park

Burr Canyon Road

trestles

tunnel

Pasco–Kahlotus Road

McCoy Canyon Road

Snake River Junction

Pederson Road

McClenny Road

Votaw Road

Page Road

Murphy Road

0 2 4
MILES

Levey Road

Levey Park

Martindale Road

Ice Harbor Dam

MARTINDALE

to Pasco

Mehlenbacker Farm Road

Columbia Plateau Trail

to Cheney

0 2 4
MILES

McCALL

Cross State Trail overpass

to Ritzville

Calloway Road

Ritzville–Benge Road

Twelvemile Lake

Benge–Winona Road

Ralston–Benge Road

BENGE

Cow Creek

trestle

ANKENY

tunnel

Benge–Washtucna Road

Gray Road

to Colfax

to Ritzville

261

trestle

Mullan Road

WASHTUCNA

26

Hooper Junction

Palouse River

to Othello

Washtucna Coulee

to Palouse Falls

trestle

SPERRY

261

McADAM

to Lyons Ferry State Park

260

to Kahlotus

Columbia Plateau Trail

to Spokane

Cheney–Spokane Road

Exit 270

Fish Lake

Meyers Park Road

paved trail

CHENEY

Cheney–Spangle Road

Cheney Plaza Road

395

90

904

TURN-BULL NWR

Mullinix Road

Exit 257

AMBER

Amber Lake

Williams Lake Road

Downs Lake

Exit 245

23

LAMONT

SPRAGUE

Sprague Lake

0 2 4
MILES

to Ritzville

to McCall

The Columbia Plateau Trail runs through the Turnbull National Wildlife Refuge, where birds and other wildlife might be seen.

that extends from one rim of the canyon to the other. The trail then climbs out of the deep coulees and reaches the eastern Washington plateau at the town of Benge.

Desolation is the byword for the next 23 miles, as the trail winds through endless dry washes with little trace of human habitation until it arrives at the community of Lamont. The next access point is in another 6 miles, near Downs Lake, east of Sprague, where the roadbed crosses an immense mile-long fill across the coulee just west of Martin Road. In the next 7 miles, the trail passes through a moonscape of basalt postpiles before reaching Amber Lake, the next access point.

Amber Lake to Fish Lake

Finally there is a respite from the arid, barren landscape as the trail reaches the forested Turnbull National Wildlife Refuge with its many small lakes, ponds, and sloughs. From Amber Lake to Cheney

the rough basalt road bed has been overlaid with crushed gravel that permits comfortable hiking and biking. Leaving the trail within the refuge is prohibited, so binoculars and telephoto camera lenses are advised for those who come to birdwatch. The varied habitat houses a startling array and abundance of birds. Open lakes attract migratory waterfowl such as ruddy ducks, blue wing and cinnamon teals, and whistling swans. The only breeding populations of trumpeter swans in Washington are found here. Marsh birds include Virginia rails, grebes, snipes, and red-winged blackbirds. Land birds in the dry, ponderosa pine forest include hairy woodpeckers, red crossbills, mountain chickadee, and pygmy nuthatches, while ruffed grouse and passerines such as red-eyed vireos and American redstarts might be spotted in aspen groves. Look also for squirrels, chipmunks, badgers, weasels, coyotes, and white-tailed deer.

North from Turnbull the trail passes

within 0.5 mile of Cheney as it cuts beneath Cheney–Spangle Road, then continues another 4 miles to its northeast terminus at the north end of Fish Lake. This paved trail between Cheney and Fish Lake is presently the only fully developed portion of the trail; however, a plan has been approved by State Parks that calls for a multi-phase development with 10 formal access points and several intermediate rest stops and primitive campsites between them. Only with time and dollars will this plan become reality.

LAKE COLVILLE SHORELANDS

Fishing, birdwatching

SEASON/HOURS: Year-round.
AREA: 4,422 feet of freshwater shoreline on Lake Colville (Sprague Lake).
DAY-USE FACILITIES: Toilet.
RECREATIONAL FACILITIES: 1-lane launch ramp (parking fee).
CAR ACCESS: Take Exit 245 (SR 23, Harrington, Sprague) from I-90, and at the east side of Sprague follow the truck route signed to Sprague Lake (Danekas Road) through town. Southeast of Sprague 6.4 miles a dirt road provides access to the shorelands.

Near the southwest corner of Lake Colville (Sprague Lake), a large thumb of land protrudes into the lake. All of the peninsula shoreline as well as the small cove on its east side is state park property; however, all the uplands are privately owned. The Sprague Lake Recreation Association maintains an access point with parking and a boat ramp here. A fee is charged for parking. Anglers can find perch, rainbow trout, largemouth bass, catfish, and crappie in the lake. The latter also are caught by ice fishing during the winter. The lake and its marshy shore provide nesting and migratory resting spots for waterfowl and other birds.

PALOUSE FALLS STATE PARK

Camping, picnicking, hiking, scenic views

SEASON/HOURS: Year-round; campground closed October 1 through mid-March.
AREA: 83 acres; 8,750 feet of freshwater shoreline on the Palouse River.
OVERNIGHT AND DAY-USE FACILITIES: 10

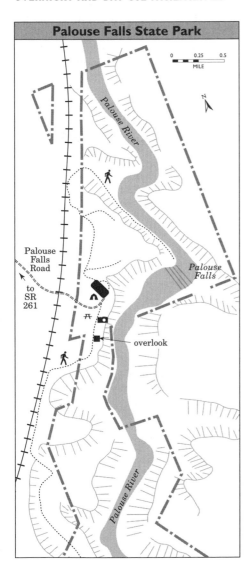

standard campsites (&), 9 picnic sites, picnic shelter (&), 2 toilets (&).
RECREATIONAL FACILITIES: 0.25 mile of hiking trail (&).
EDUCATIONAL FACILITIES: Observation shelter, historical display.
CAR ACCESS: From SR 261, 13.5 miles west of Starbuck, or 14.4 miles southwest of the junction with SR 261 and SR 260, take Palouse Falls Road to the east, reaching the park in 2.2 miles.

At the heart of a rock-rimmed amphitheater, the Palouse River takes a precipitous, 198-foot plunge into a deep green pool, creating one of the most spectacular natural sights in the state. When the sun strikes spray at the base of the falls, a rainbow can often be seen. The falls itself is breathtaking, but its beauty is enhanced by the surrounding rock formations. Just above the lip of the falls, a serrated rib of basalt spires mimics the turrets of a medieval castle, with defenses often manned by stalwart seagulls.

From the falls the river continues down the narrow gorge that it has carved over time, en route to the Snake River. The towering walls of the river channel are columnar basalt, layered in 100-foot-thick lava flows separated by narrow shelves holding meager dried grass and brush. This, and other similar vertical slices in basalt walls found in the channeled scablands, was created when the floodwaters of glacial Lake Missoula swept across the area from 17,000 to 12,000 years ago and plucked the rock columns out of the lower portions of the old basalt flows.

Above the parking lot, tent camping is permitted on a small tree-shaded lawn with picnic tables and fire braziers. A day-use picnic area with tables and a shelter lies on the opposite side of the road. Uphill from the picnic area, an overlook with an interpretive display perches at the canyon rim, with views to the falls.

The 0.25-mile path to the overlook is the only maintained trail in the park. Hiking any of the other impromptu routes is at your own risk; rockfall, rattlesnakes,

Palouse Falls plunges over a 198-foot basalt cliff.

and exposure can all be problems. The trails should not be undertaken lightly, and are definitely not for young children or people affected by vertigo. A dirt road/trail north from the parking lot follows the lip of the gorge, descends abruptly down to a railroad track, then drops to the river's edge and follows it to the top of the falls. A second beaten-out trail heads south from the parking lot, where again there is a short, steep descent to the railroad tracks. Several hundred yards south along the tracks, a steep path leads to a shelf between the lava layers. This shelf can be followed south for about 0.5 mile to a natural terrace with views of the canyon and falls.

217

LYONS FERRY STATE PARK

Camping, picnicking, hiking, swimming, waterskiing, fishing, boating

SEASON/HOURS: Closed mid-October through mid-March.

AREA: 1,282.42 acres (including Marmes Rock Shelter Heritage Area); 52,000 feet of freshwater shoreline on the Snake and Palouse Rivers (Lake Herbert G. West).

OVERNIGHT AND DAY-USE FACILITIES: 50 standard campsites, 2 primitive campsites, 21 picnic sites, 6 picnic shelters (1 reservable), 3 restrooms (2 with showers), 2 toilets, trailer dump station.

RECREATIONAL FACILITIES: 0.75-mile hiking trail, swimming beach, bathhouse with showers, 2-lane paved boat ramp with boarding pier, hand-carried boat launch, 6 mooring buoys.

EDUCATIONAL FACILITIES: Historical display, historic ferry, viewing shelter.

CONCESSIONS: Snacks, beverages, fast food, ice, limited camping supplies.

CAR ACCESS: On SR 261, 7.2 miles northwest of Starbuck, or 14.2 miles southeast of the junction of SR 261 and 260.

One of the most important archeological finds in the country was discovered in 1968 at what is now Lyons Ferry State Park. A professor from Washington State University found a rock shelter containing prehistoric fire-charred human bones. Some of these remains, named the "Marmes Man," were carbon-dated at 10,000 years old, far older than any other documented human remains in the Western Hemisphere. The discovery proved that humans were in the area much earlier than previously believed. Other remains collected here were established to be 4,000 and 6,000 years old; also found were artifacts and a variety of animal bones, leading scientists to conclude that this confluence of the Palouse and Snake Rivers was on a trail used by nomadic hunters. The construction of Lower Monumental Dam across the Snake flooded the cave, as well as a sacred Palouse tribe burial ground.

For most people now visiting the spot, the purpose is recreational. Building of the dam broadened the river and created a lengthy shoreline ideal for water play. A big, quiet basin fronting the state park's day-use area is enclosed by a long, curving rock breakwater that reaches out to a tiny island in the river. Lawns with picnic tables facing on the shore let parents enjoy sun and sandwiches while keeping an eye on small kids in the roped-off swimming area.

The old open-deck Lyons Ferry is tethered to the shore at the north end of the basin. Attached to it is a replica of the cable-and-pulley arrangement that permitted the ferry to use river current to power its crossings. Captain John Mullan constructed one of the first wagon roads through the region in the 1850s and it has remained a major travel route.

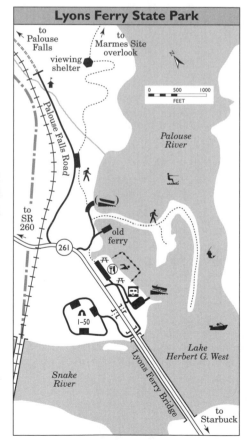

Lyons Ferry State Park

What could be grander than splashing in the water on a hot summer day at Lyons Ferry State Park?

Between 1949 and 1968 the wooden ferry was the primary means of crossing the Snake River just downstream from here. It now serves as a quaint fishing dock.

North of the breakwater, a dirt road ends at a cartop boat launch. Here also is the trailhead for a 0.75-mile gravel trail to the overlook, which has interpretive plaques describing the flooding of the area by the dam, the Marmes Rock Shelter, the Native Americans and their burial site, and the spectacular Joso railway bridge nearby. A trail leads a short distance north to an overview of the historic Marmes site.

The campground lies on the opposite side of SR 261, connected to the day-use area by a culvert under the highway. Campsites are rather spartan gravel pulloffs and pads, elbow-to-elbow in places, some with small swatches of grass. Trees provide some shade.

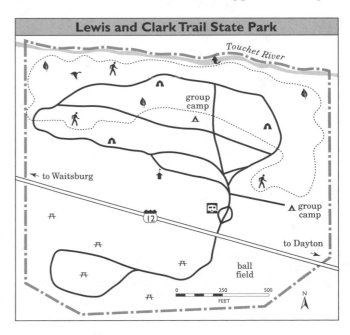

You might meet an old-time trapper during one of the scheduled interpretive programs at historic Lewis and Clark State Park.

LEWIS AND CLARK TRAIL STATE PARK

Camping, picnicking, birdwatching, hiking, fishing

SEASON/HOURS: Camping only in day-use area until further notice.

AREA: 36 acres; 1,333 feet of freshwater shoreline on the Touchet River.

OVERNIGHT AND DAY-USE FACILITIES: 25 standard campsites (&), 4 primitive campsites, 2 group camps (50 persons each), 50 picnic sites, kitchen shelter, 2 group day-use areas (50 and 100 persons), 2 restrooms with showers (&), trailer dump station.

RECREATIONAL FACILITIES: 1-mile interpretive trail, 0.75-mile birdwatching trail.

EDUCATIONAL FACILITIES: Interpretive kiosk, ranger-led interpretive programs.

CAR ACCESS: The park straddles US 12, 3.7 miles east of Waitsburg and 4.4 miles west of Dayton.

Lewis and Clark Trail State Park provides a lush green respite from the surrounding rolling, amber wheatlands. In summer the cool shallows of the Touchet River entice adults and kids alike to wade and wallow. The river is planted with rainbow trout and also provides good fishing for German brown trout and steelhead. Kids delight in finding crawfish lurking under rocks.

The camping area north of the highway lies along the bank of the Touchet River. The rich, moist river bottom supports vegetation so heavy it is an impenetrable tangle except where trails have been carved through it. One group camp lies immediately inside and east of the entrance, and a second is in the heart of the campground loop.

The remainder of the area is a double loop of tent camping sites. In 1995 a flood devastated the park's campground, causing nearly a million dollars in damage. Plans are for the campground to reopen

Lewis and Clark Trail State Park

Touchet River

group camp

to Waitsburg

to Dayton

group camp

ball field

12

0   250   500
FEET

N

in 1999. Until it is reopened, the day-use area will be used for camping.

A nature trail begins at the restrooms and roams west through the campground loops, circles back near the river, and returns to its start. Numbered stops along the trail correspond to a park brochure that identifies plants seen and tells of their use by Native Americans for food, fire fuel, and medicine.

The day-use area on the south side of US 12 has a grass baseball field and a wide lawn with sky-scraping old ponderosa pine. Just after the Civil War the Bateman family settled here, retaining ownership of the property until the Depression, when it was sold to the state. The Batemans wisely resisted cutting the stand of pine, although the trees were a tempting source of lumber for building homes. The nearby communities shared the family's devotion to the site, known as Shilo, and in a common effort helped develop the park, hauling over 10,000 stones from the river to construct the unique restroom that still stands here.

The park marks the site of a stop by the Lewis and Clark Corps of Discovery in May of 1806 on their return from the Pacific Ocean to St. Louis. Although their journal remarks that the area reminded them of the Missouri plains, it provided them with little forage, and the party of 33 had to make do with a meal of a single duck. In August of every year the park staff schedules weekend interpretive programs commemorating Lewis and Clark. These programs cover a range of fascinating subjects such as the history of the area before the expedition, how early-day trappers and hunters lived and worked (the arrowhead-making demonstration is very popular), and how the natives used plants found here. Costumed local residents and scout troops assume the roles of historic characters to reenact the activities of the Corps of Discovery. Contact the park for specific dates and programs.

CENTRAL FERRY STATE PARK

Camping, picnicking, birdwatching, swimming, waterskiing, fishing, boating

SEASON/HOURS: Closed mid-November to mid-March; campsite reservations accepted in summer.

AREA: 185 acres; 6,500 feet of freshwater shoreline on the Snake River (Lake Bryan).

OVERNIGHT AND DAY-USE FACILITIES: 60 RV sites (2 ♿), 8 primitive campsites, group camp (150 persons), 48 picnic sites, picnic shelters, 6 cabanas, 2 campfire circles, 2 restrooms (♿, with showers), portable toilet and trailer dump stations.

RECREATIONAL FACILITIES: 4 horseshoe pits, 2 volleyball courts, swimming beach, bathhouse (♿), 2 water-ski docks, 4 paved boat ramps with boarding floats, 3 sets of mooring floats.

CAR ACCESS: On the west side of SR 127, 17.3 miles south of Dusty and 10.4 miles north of Dodge.

In the late 1960s and early 1970s, four dams were built on the Snake River: Ice Harbor, Lower Monumental, Little Goose, and Lower Granite. These dams, which included locks for boats, formed a series of slack-water lakes the entire length of the river to the Idaho border, making it navigable all the way to Clarkston and Lewiston, even for good-sized barges. The backwaters of Little Goose Dam formed Lake Bryan and created

The swimming area at Central Ferry State Park lies next to the soaring bridge that crosses the Snake River.

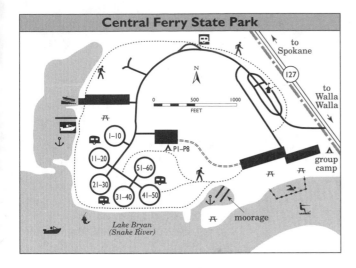

Central Ferry State Park

to Spokane

to Walla Walla

group camp

moorage

Lake Bryan (Snake River)

N

FEET
0   500   1000

the present shoreline of Central Ferry State Park.

Boaters, anglers, and waterskiers flock to the broad river in summer, when temperatures in the area can be 100 degrees at noon, and top out at 114, only cooling into the 80s at night. With its marine attractions in mind, the state park features two small boat basins that provide protected moorages. This protection is sometimes warranted, as winds up to 35 mph or greater can come up suddenly along the river gorge, making the open water rough and dangerous. At the west end of the park the larger of the boat basins lies behind a pair of overlapping entrance berms. This basin holds a four-lane launch ramp with boarding float, and a 100-foot mooring float. A second, smaller oval boat basin, with two floats sheltered by a tiny peninsula, indents the shore between the camping and day-use areas.

A large flat lawn spreads between the main boat basin and the camping area. Here campsites line six circular loops; in most, individual sites are nicely shaded by trees, and short sections of fence and brush provide some privacy. A low embankment leads to the rocky beach below. Primitive tent-camping sites, with a row of large poplars as a windbreak, are scattered about the grass flat at the northeast side of the campground.

The day-use area, separated from the camping area by an open field, has a roped-off swimming beach with a bathhouse and two fire circles. A number of beach-side cabanas provide welcome respite from the hot sun. The group camp is found at the east end of this day-use area.

In very early times, as its name suggests, a ferry that operated at this point in the Snake River linked Whitman and Garfield Counties; a distinctive bridge has long since replaced the ferry.

STEPTOE BATTLEFIELD STATE HERITAGE AREA

Historic site, informative display

SEASON/HOURS: Year-round.
AREA: 3.9 acres.
DAY-USE FACILITIES: Picnic table.
EDUCATIONAL FACILITIES: Interpretive marker, stone obelisk.
CAR ACCESS: From US 195, 32 miles south of Spokane, take either of the two Rosalia exits (Business 195). From the main street through Rosalia, Whitman Street, turn east on 7th Street; in a block head uphill to the south on 8th Street, which turns east in another block. In two blocks turn south on Summit Avenue, signed to the monument and the high school football field. Reach the park in 0.3 mile.

At this site of Steptoe Battlefield, a combined force of Spokane, Coeur d'Alene, and Palouse Indians decisively defeated U.S. troops commanded by Colonel E. J. Steptoe. After a day-long running battle drove them to defensive positions on a hill near Rosalia, Steptoe's troops conceded their route and buried their howitzers, muffled their horses' hooves, and retreated under cover of darkness to Fort Walla Walla. The Indian victory was short-lived, however, as it brought even more army forces to the Washington Territory and led to a ruthless, full-scale campaign to suppress them. The spot is now on the National Register of Historic Places.

A 20-foot obelisk commemorates members of the 1st Dragoons who were killed in the battle, and the friendly Nez Perce Indians under Chief Tam-Mu-Tsa who helped rescue the Steptoe expedition.

STEPTOE BUTTE STATE PARK

Picnicking, birdwatching, hang-gliding, scenic views

SEASON/HOURS: Year-round; the road to the summit may be impassable in winter due to snow.
AREA: 153.40 acres.
DAY-USE FACILITIES: 5 picnic sites with stoves (*no water*), 2 toilets.
EDUCATIONAL FACILITIES: Interpretive displays, scenic views.
CAR ACCESS: From US 195, 6 miles north of Colfax, turn east on Scholz Road, signed to Steptoe Butte and Oakesdale. At a Y-intersection in 1.2 miles, continue north on Hume Road, and in another 4 miles a small sign points west to a paved road to the park.
Alternatively, from SR 27 just south of Oakesdale, turn south on Hume Road, signed to the park, and reach the entrance road in 7.4 miles.

The promontory of Steptoe Butte rises 1,000 feet above the nearby rolling wheatland, and the summit commands views more than 50 miles north to Mica Peak, 100 miles east to Idaho's Bitterroot

Steptoe Butte is a striking landmark among the eastern Washington wheatfields. The road to the summit winds around it three times.

Range, 75 miles south to Oregon's Blue Mountains, and endless miles west across the Columbia plateau. Around the compass, acre upon acre of grain fields paint the fertile Palouse soil with geometric patterns. The butte itself is the tip of a granite peak that was high enough to escape immersion in the lava flows that engulfed the area between 18 and 10 million years ago, and the post–Ice Age blanket of wind-blown soil (loess) that created the surrounding Palouse hills.

The butte is the prototype for such a geological formation, known by scientists worldwide as a steptoe. The 3,616-foot-high butte was used as a reconnaissance point by the troops of Colonel E. J. Steptoe. In May of 1858 his troops were defeated nearby in an engagement with bands of Spokane, Palouse, and Coeur d'Alene Indians. It is ironic that a defeat led to the colonel's name being forever identified with a unique geological formation. (Custer should have been so lucky.)

The entrance road heads arrow-straight through wheatfields to the foot of the butte where an apple orchard offers the park's only amenities, a small picnic area and toilets. From here the road winds around the butte three times on its 3.4-mile ascent to the summit. The narrow road has no shoulders, and no guard rails on its steep outer side—not the place for the squeamish or a large RV. An interpretive sign placed on top amid microwave antennae describes the geological forces that formed the butte and the surrounding countryside. The unobstructed height of the butte and the constant breezes that blow across the summit make this a favorite take-off point for hang-gliders. Hawks, too, take advantage of the updrafts around the butte for long, soaring flights.

The mountain was once the site of a hotel and observation point, which burned in 1911 and was not rebuilt. Part of the old foundation is still in evidence.

CHIEF TIMOTHY STATE PARK

Camping, picnicking, sightseeing, hiking, swimming, waterskiing, fishing, boating, historical displays

SEASON/HOURS: Launch ramps open year-round, remainder of the park closed December 1 through February 28, except weekends and holidays; campsite reservations accepted in summer. Alpowai Interpretive Center open Wednesday through Sunday, 1:00 P.M. to 5:00 P.M.

AREA: 282 acres; 12,575 feet of freshwater shoreline on the Snake River (Lower Granite Lake).

OVERNIGHT AND DAY-USE FACILITIES: 33 RV sites (6 E only), 33 standard campsites (&), 2 primitive campsites, 24 picnic sites, 8 cabanas, 3 restrooms with showers (&), bathhouse (&), trailer dump station, marine pumpout station.

RECREATIONAL FACILITIES: Fire road around the perimeter of the park for hiking and bicycling, swimming beach, children's play equipment, 4 paved boat ramps with boarding floats, 5 mooring floats, 7 mooring buoys.

EDUCATIONAL FACILITIES: Alpowai Interpretive Center.

CONCESSIONS: Snacks, beverages, groceries, ice, firewood, fishing supplies.

CAR ACCESS: From US 12, 6.8 miles west of Clarkston, turn north on Silcott Road and cross a bridge to reach the park, on an island in Lower Granite Lake.

The steep basalt cliffs and sharply folded strata that form the Snake River canyon create a scenic backdrop for Chief Timothy State Park. The island on which the park sits was once a hill above the pioneer community of Silcott; a ferry ran from here to the opposite bank of the river. The island was created in 1975 when the waters of the Snake River behind the newly built Lower Granite Dam flooded the area. The park lies along the south shore of Silcott Island, which hugs the south shoreline of the lake, forming a protected channel for the water-oriented activities at the park.

Day-use areas with large tree-shaded lawns, picnic tables, fire braziers, and sun-shading shelters bound both sides of the entrance road. The area to the east emphasizes boating, with four launch ramps and boarding floats, a day-use mooring float, and ample parking for vehicles and boat trailers. To the west, the park is people oriented, with a roped-off swim area below a sandy beach, a bathhouse and concession stand, and a children's play area.

A long string of campsites with hookups stretches through the grass strip above the beach east of the day-use area; a couple of primitive campsites are spotted at the east end of the campground. A second and newer tent camping area lies uphill from the RV campground. Five mooring floats and seven mooring buoys are distributed along the water's edge below the campground strip, providing boating campers convenient access to their craft.

The Alpowai Interpretive Center, on the mainland near the park entrance, is a squat stone building buttressed with banks of basalt boulders. Windows look out over the Snake River Canyon. Displays at the center describe the geological formation of the landscape, the history of the Nez Perce Indians who inhabited the village of Alpowai at the site, and the story of the pioneer community of Silcott, which was located here between the 1880s and the 1920s. Showcased are artifacts from the archaeological excavations at Silcott prior to

Chief Timothy State Park offers sun, water, scenery, and one of the nicest campgrounds of any Washington state park.

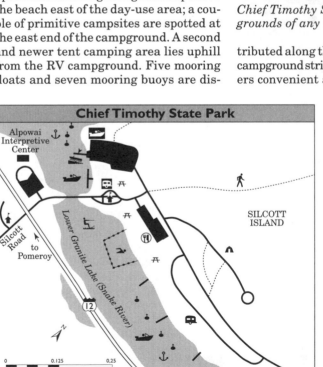

the flooding by waters behind the dam. Other displays tell of the Lewis and Clark Corps of Discovery, which passed through the area.

CAMP WILLIAM T. WOOTEN STATE PARK

Nature study, field sports, hiking, swimming, horseback riding, fishing, paddling

SEASON/HOURS: March through October, group use only, by reservation; limited availability at other times, subject to manager approval.

AREA: 40 acres; 4,100 feet of freshwater shoreline on the Tucannon River and a small pond.

ELC: 17 sleeping and 4 administrative cabins (100–240 persons; above 205 requires user-provided tent or RV sleeping accommodations), 3 RV

group use, by prior reservation. The park, which is a favorite spot for youth and church groups or large family reunions, has housing and recreational facilities; groups need only to provide their own food, play equipment, medical support, camp supervision, and recreational and educational programs. Cabins are scattered in groups around the perimeter of the park.

At the south end of the park, Donnie Lake, a shallow manmade pond, has canoes. A short tree-identification trail loops through the forest to the northeast. At the east side of the lake, a 0.75-mile nature trail climbs quickly uphill through forest before breaking out on a high grass-covered knob with views down to the lake and camp, and beyond to the Tucannon River valley. Because a nearby hatchery stocks the Tucannon River, the trout fishing is excellent.

The park accepts a few groups in the off-season, with manager approval; however, most of the facilities are unavailable in winter, and weather-caused power outages can leave those facilities that are open without heat.

At Camp William T. Wooten State Park groups can enjoy all sorts of activities.

sites with electricity and water, campfire circle, mess hall.

RECREATIONAL FACILITIES: Multipurpose sports field, tennis/basketball courts, archery range, 0.75-mile interpretive trail, 0.5-mile hiking trail, indoor swimming pool (guarded), manmade lake with 6 canoes, horse corral.

OTHER: Chapel, dispensary, meeting rooms, 2 interpretive shelters.

CAR ACCESS: Tucannon Road, a paved two-lane road signed to Camp Wooten, intersects US 12 from the southeast 12.8 miles north of Dayton. Follow this road south for 28.8 miles, then take a spur heading a short distance east through the USFS Tucannon Campground to Camp Wooten. Other secondary roads shown on road maps that appear to offer shorter routes are all partly gravel, narrow, steep, and winding washboards, and are not recommended for large vehicles or low-slung cars.

As it runs south into the heart of the Blue Mountains, the Tucannon River valley narrows, and high, dry, sagebrush-clad sidehills take on a green mantle of ponderosa pine and Douglas-fir. Camp William T. Wooten State Park is here, tucked between the Tucannon River on the west and a steep, forested ridge to the east in the Umatilla National Forest, not far from the Wenaha-Tucannon Wilderness. Some of the buildings of the scenic park are remnants of Camp Tucannon, a 1930s CCC camp.

Wooten is not your "drop-in" state park; the entire facility is an ELC, restricted to

FIELDS SPRING STATE PARK

Camping, picnicking, baseball, hiking, backpacking, wildflower viewing, birdwatching, cross-country skiing, sledding

SEASON/HOURS: Year-round.

AREA: 792.92 acres.

OVERNIGHT AND DAY-USE FACILITIES: 20 standard campsites, 2 primitive campsites, 14 picnic sites, 2 picnic shelters/warming huts, 2 ski lodges with fireplace, campfire circle, 2 restrooms with showers (&), trailer dump station.

RECREATIONAL FACILITIES: 7 miles of hiking trails, volleyball stanchions, archery range, softball field, children's play equipment, lighted sledding and tubing hill, 7.5 miles of cross-country skiing trails.

ELCS: 6 cabins (25–80 persons summer, 12–50 persons winter) at Puffer Butte; lodge (12–20 persons), 3 tee-pees (7 persons each) at Wo-He-Lo.

CAR ACCESS: On the east side of SR 129, 3.7 miles south of Anatone and 28.4 miles south of Clarkston.

The monotony of the flat wheatland plateau south of Clarkston changes abruptly at Rattlesnake Summit, just south of Fields Spring State Park, with the sudden rise of hillsides covered by ponderosa pine, western larch, Douglas-fir, and grand fir. Because of its location, this gem of a park supports a unique combination of plains and mountain flowers that attract hundreds of visitors in May and June when trails through the forest, interspersed with meadows of waist-high wild grass, are a riot of more than 30 species of wildflowers. Yarrow, cat's ear lily, calypso orchids, coral root, camas, skyrocket, and several varieties of paintbrush all add color to hikes. Nearly 50 species of birds, including owls, hawks, grouse, quail, pheasants, woodpeckers, jays, waxwings, chickadees, warblers, finches, and even wild turkeys are also commonly seen in the park, while four-legged forest dwellers include deer, elk, black bear, and porcupine.

The park's central day-use area is modest in size, but it includes a grassy softball field a short distance away to the east. Campsites surrounding a loop just south of the day-use area have gravel pullouts, tables, fireplaces, and a snug tent space, with each site surrounded by trees and dense brush.

Two ELCs, Puffer Butte on the southeast side of the park and Wo-He-Lo on the northeast, are reservable by groups. On request, rangers will provide interpretive programs and guided walks. A unique feature of Wo-He-Lo is an adjoining camp with three large, wood-floored teepees with seven bunks in each. Here also, framed by a concrete wall with wooden lids, you can find the slowly dripping spring that gave the park its name.

A steady 1-mile climb through forest leads to the top of Puffer Butte. Trailheads for this scenic hike are found at the day-use area and near both ELCs. A longer but gentler service road from south of the Puffer Butte ELC reaches the summit in 1.5 miles. At the top of the bluff,

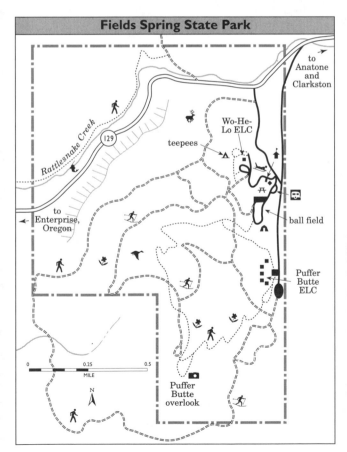

Large, seven-person teepees at Fields Spring State Park can be reserved for a unique group camping adventure.

Puffer Butte, with its nice lodge and open play areas, is one of two Environmental Learning Centers at Fields Spring State Park.

forest gives way to a broad grass-covered ridge line dropping away to the south. Catch glimpses of the Snake River, deep within the gorge to the east along the Washington-Idaho border, and distant snow-covered peaks of Lost River Range farther south in Idaho. Directly south, the 3,000-foot-deep Grand Ronde River Canyon carves into the landscape just north of the Oregon border. Southwest, the smoke-hued summits of the Blue Mountains dominate. Several other forested service roads in the park provide longer hikes, but none can match the Puffer Butte view.

WiFnter brings new park activities. A lighted slope near the Wo-He-Lo ELC has sledding and tubing runs, and two of the picnic shelters are heated to serve as warming huts. Most of the park's service roads become groomed, well-marked cross-country ski trails, with routes for every level of skier.

APPENDICES

A. ADDRESSES, TELEPHONE NUMBERS, AND CONTACTS

Army Corps of Engineers (for information on the water level of the Green River): (206)764-6702

Marine V.H.F: Coast Guard distress and hailing: Channel 16; Coast Guard liaison: Channel 22A; Marine Operator, Bellingham: Channels 28 and 85; Marine Operator, Victoria, B.C.: Channel 27 Red Tide Hotline: 1-800-562-5632

U.S. Coast Guard (for marine and air emergency): 1-800-592-9911

Washington State Ferries Information: 1-800-843-3779; Website: http://www.wadot.wa.gov; Seattle terminal: (206)464-6400; Anacortes terminal: (360)293-8166; Lopez terminal: (360)468-2252; Orcas terminal: (360)376-2134; Friday Harbor terminal: (360)378-4777

Washington Water Trails Association: 4649 Sunnyside Avenue North, Suite 305, Seattle, WA 98103-6900. Phone: (206)545-9161; e-mail: wwta@eskimo.com; website: http://www.eskimo.com/~wwta

Whale Hotline (to report whale sightings): 1-800-562-8832

State Parks

Washington State Parks, Headquarters: 7150 Cleanwater Lane, Box 42650, Olympia, WA 98504-2650; (360)902-8500. Website: http://www.parks.wa.gov

State Parks, Southwest Region: 11838 Tilley Road S, Olympia, WA 98512; (360)753-7143

State Parks, Northwest Region: 220 Walnut Street, Box 487, Burlington, WA 98233; (360)755-9231

State Parks, Eastern Region: 2201 N Duncan Drive, Wenatchee, WA 98801-1007; (509)662-0420

State Parks, Puget Sound Region: 1602 29th SE, Auburn, WA 98002; (253)931-3907

State Parks ELC Reservation Office: 7150 Cleanwater Lane, Box 42664, Olympia, WA 98504-2664; (360)902-8600. Telecommunications Device for the Deaf; (360)664-3133. Reservations Northwest (campsite reservations at all reservation parks); 1-800-452-5687

State Parks Addresses

A

Alta Lake State Park: 191A Alta Lake Road, Pateros, WA 98846. (509)923-2473

Anderson Lake State Park: contact Fort Flagler State Park

B

Banks Lake Recreation Area: contact Steamboat Rock State Park

Battle Ground Lake State Park: 18002 NE 239th, Battle Ground, WA 98604. (360)687-4621

Bay View State Park: 10905 Bay View–Edison Road, Mount Vernon, WA 98273. (360)757-0227

Beacon Rock State Park: 34841 State Road 14, Skamania, WA 98648. (509)427-8265

Belfair State Park: 410 NE Beck Road, Belfair, WA 98528. (360)275-0668

Big Eddy Access: contact Wallace Falls State Park

Birch Bay State Park: 5105 Helweg Road, Blaine, WA 98230. (360)371-2800

Blake Island Marine State Park: P.O. Box 277, Manchester WA 98353. (360)731-8330

Blind Island Marine State Park: contact Sucia Island Marine State Park

Bogachiel State Park: 185983 Highway 101, Forks, WA 98331. (360)374-6356

Bottle Beach State Park: contact Twin Harbors Beach State Park

Bridal Trails State Park: contact Lake Sammamish State Park. (425)649-4276

Bridgeport State Park: contact Alta Lake State Park. (509)686-7231

Brooks Memorial State Park: 2465 Highway 97, Goldendale, WA 98620. (509)773-4611

Burrows Island: contact Sucia Island Marine State Park

C

Cama Beach State Park: 1880 W Camano Drive S, Camano Island, WA 98292. (360)320-1132

Camano Island State Park: 2269 S Lowell Point Road, Camano Island, WA 98292. (360)387-3031

Camp William T. Wooten State Park: 2711 Tucannon Road, Pomeroy, WA 99347. (509)843-1080

Central Ferry State Park: 10152 State Route 127, Pomeroy, WA 99347-9645. (509)549-3551

Chief Joseph State Park: contact Alta Lake State Park

Chief Timothy State Park: 13766 Highway 12, Clarkston, WA 99403. (509)758-9580

Clark Island Marine State Park: contact Sucia Island Marine State Park

Colbert House State Park: contact Fort Canby State Park

Columbia Plateau Trail State Park: contact Central Ferry State Park

Columbia River Property: contact Battle Ground Lake State Park

Conconully State Park: Box 95, Conconully, WA 98819. (509)826-7408

Cone Islands: contact Sucia Island Marine State Park

Crawford State Park: contact Mount Spokane State Park

Crow Butte State Park: Box 217, Paterson, WA 99345. (509)875-2644

Crown Point State Park: contact Steamboat Rock State Park

Crystal Falls State Park: contact Mount Spokane State Park

Curlew Lake State Park: 974 Curlew State Park Road, Republic, WA 99166. (509)775-3592

Cutts Island Marine State Park: contact Kopachuck State Park

D

Dalles Mountain Ranch: contact Horsethief Lake State Park

Daroga State Park: 1 S Daroga Park Road, Orondo, WA 98843. (509)664-6380

Dash Point State Park: 5700 SW Dash Point Road, Federal Way, WA 98023. (253)661-4955

Deception Pass State Park: 5175 N S.H. 20, Oak Harbor, WA 98277. (360)675-2417

Doe Island Marine State Park: contact Sucia Island Marine State Park

Dosewallips State Park: P.O. Box Drawer K, Brinnon, WA 98320. (360)796-4415

Doug's Beach State Park: contact Horsethief Lake State Park

E

Eagle Island Marine State Park: contact Jarrell Cove State Park

Ebey's Landing State Park: contact Fort Casey State Park

Elbow Lake State Park: contact Millersylvania State Park

F

Fay-Bainbridge State Park: 15446 Sunrise Drive NE, Bainbridge Island, WA 98110. (206)842-3931

Federation Forest State Park: Highway 410 E, Enumclaw, WA 98022. (360)663-2207

Fields Spring State Park: P.O. Box 37, 992 Park Road, Anatone, WA 99401. (509)256-3332

Flaming Geyser State Park: 23700 SE Flaming Geyser Road, Auburn, WA 98092. (253)931-3930

Fort Canby State Park: P.O. Box 488, Ilwaco, WA 98624. (360)642-3078

Fort Casey State Park: 1280 Engle Road, Coupeville, WA 98239. (360)678-4519

Fort Columbia State Park: contact Fort Canby State Park

Fort Ebey State Park: 395 North Fort Ebey Road, Coupeville, WA 98239. (360)678-4636

Fort Flagler State Park: 10541 Flagler Road, Nordland, WA 98358. (360)385-1259

Fort Okanogan State Park: contact Alta Lake State Park

Fort Simcoe State Park: 5150 Fort Simcoe Road, White Swan, WA 98952. (509)874-2372

Fort Ward State Park: 2241 Pleasant Beach Drive NE, Bainbridge Island, WA 98110. (206)842-4041

Fort Worden State Park: 200 Battery Way, Port Townsend, WA 98369. (360)385-4730

G

Ginkgo Petrified Forest State Park: contact Wanapum State Park

Goldendale Observatory State Park: 1602 Observatory Drive, Goldendale, WA 98620. (509)773-3141

Grayland Beach State Park: contact Twin Harbors Beach State Park

Green River Gorge State Park Conservation Area: contact Flaming Geyser State Park

Griffiths-Priday State Park: contact Ocean City State Park

H

Harstine Island State Park: contact Jarrell Cove State Park

Harvey Rendsland State Park: contact Belfair State Park

Helen McCabe State Park: contact Wanapum State Park

Hoodsport Trail State Park: contact Lake Cushman State Park

Hope Island Marine State Park: contact Jarrell Cove State Park

Horsethief Lake State Park: P.O. Box 246, Dallesport, WA 98617. (509)767-1159

Huckleberry Island: contact Sucia Island Marine State Park

Hyak Lodge State Park: (425)434-7120

I

Ice Caves State Park: contact Alta Lake State Park

Ike Kinswa State Park: 873 Harmony Road, Silver Creek, WA 98585. (360)983-3402

Illahee State Park: 3540 Bahia Vista, Bremerton, WA 98310. (360)478-6460

Indian Painted Rocks State Park: contact Yakima Sportsman State Park

Iron Horse State Park (Cedar Falls to Thorp): contact Lake Easton State Park

Iron Horse State Park (Thorp to Columbia River): contact Wanapum State Park

Isabella Lake State Park: contact Millersylvania State Park

J

James Island Marine State Park: contact Sucia Island Marine State Park

Jarrell Cove State Park: E 391 Wingert Road, Shelton, WA 98584. (360)426-9226

Joemma Beach State Park: P.O. Box 898, Lakebay, WA 98349. (253)884-1944

John R. Jackson House State Park: contact Lewis and Clark State Park

Jones Island Marine State Park: contact Sucia Island Marine State Park

Joseph Whidbey State Park: contact Fort Ebey State Park

K

Kanaskat Palmer State Park: 32101 Kanaskat–Cumberland Road, Ravensdale, WA 98051. (360)886-0148

Keystone Spit State Park: contact Fort Casey State Park

Kinney Point State Park: contact Fort Flagler State Park

Kitsap Memorial State Park: 202 NE Park Street, Poulsbo, WA 98370. (360)779-3205

Klickitat Rail-Trail Corridor: contact Maryhill State Park

Kopachuck State Park: 11101 56th Street NW, Gig Harbor, WA 98335. (253)265-3606

L

Lake Chelan State Park: 7544 S Lakeshore Drive, Chelan, WA 98816-9755. (509)687-3710

Lake Colville Shorelands: contact Riverside State Park

Lake Cushman State Park: P.O. Box 1399, Hoodsport, WA 98548-1399. (360)877-5491

Lake Easton State Park: P.O. Box 26, Easton, WA 98925. (509)656-2230

Lake Lenore Caves State Park: contact Sun Lakes/Dry Falls State Park

Lake Newport State Park: contact Mount Spokane State Park

Lake Sammamish State Park: 20606 SE 56th Street, Issaquah, WA 98027. (425)455-0710

Lake Sylvia State Park: P.O. Box 701, Montesano, WA 98563. (360)249-3621

Lake Wenatchee State Park: 21588A Highway 207, Leavenworth, WA 98826. (509)763-3101

Larrabee State Park: 245 Chuckanut Drive, Bellingham, WA 98226. (360)676-2093

Leadbetter Point State Park: contact Fort Canby State Park

Lewis and Clark Campsite State Park: contact Fort Canby State Park

Lewis and Clark State Park: 4583 Jackson Highway, Winlock, WA 98596. (360)864-2643

Lewis and Clark Trail State Park: Route 1, Box 90, Dayton, WA 99328. (509)337-6457

Lilliwaup Tidelands: contact Dosewallips State Park

Lime Kiln Point State Park: 6158 Lighthouse Road, Friday Harbor, WA 98250. (360)378-2044

Lincoln Rock State Park: 13253 SR 2, East Wenatchee, WA 98802-9566. (509)884-8702

Long Beach Seashore Conservation Area: contact Fort Canby State Park

Loomis Lake State Park: contact Fort Canby State Park

Lyons Ferry State Park: P.O. Box 157, Starbuck, WA 99359. (509)646-3252

M

Manchester State Park: P.O. Box 338, Manchester, WA 98353. (360)871-4065

Maryhill State Park: 50 Highway 97, Goldendale, WA 98620. (509)773-5007

Matia Island Marine State Park: contact Sucia Island Marine State Park

Matilda N. Jackson State Park: contact Lewis and Clark State Park

McMicken Island Marine State Park: contact Jarrell Cove State Park

Miller Peninsula Property: contact Sequim Bay State Park

Millersylvania Memorial State Park: 12245 Tilley Road South, Olympia, WA 98512. (360)753-1519

Moran State Park: 3572 Olga Road, Eastsound, WA 98245. (360)376-2326

Moses Lake State Park: 111 West Shore Drive, Moses Lake, WA 98837. (509)765-5852

Mount Pilchuck State Park: contact Wenberg State Park

Mount Spokane State Park: N 26107 Mount Spokane Park Drive, Mead, WA 99021. (509)238-6845

Mukilteo State Park: contact Wenberg State Park

Mystery Bay State Park: contact Fort Flagler State Park

N

Nolte State Park: 36921 Veazie–Cumberland Road, Enumclaw, WA 98022. (360)825-4646

North Beach Seashore Recreation Area: contact Ocean City State Park

O

Ocean City State Park: 148 State Route 115, Hoquiam, WA 98550. (360)389-3553

Ocean Shores Environmental Interpretive Center: contact Ocean City State Park

Olallie State Park: contact Lake Sammamish State Park

Old Fort Townsend State Park: contact Fort Worden State Park

Old Man House State Park: contact Fay-Bainbridge State Park

Olmstead Place State Park: 921 N Ferguson Road, Ellensburg, WA 98926. (509)925-1943

Osoyoos Lake State Veteran's Memorial Park: 2207 Juniper, Oroville, WA 98844. (509)476-3321

P

Pacific Beach State Park: contact Ocean City State Park

Pacific Pines State Park: contact Fort Canby State Park

Palouse Falls State Park: contact Central Ferry State Park

Paradise Point State Park: Route 1, Box 33914 NW Paradise Road, Ridgefield, WA 98642. (360)263-2350

Patos Island Marine State Park: contact Sucia Island Marine State Park

Peace Arch State Park: P.O. Box 87, Blaine, WA 98230. (360)332-8221

Pearrygin Lake State Park: 861 Bear Creek Road, Winthrop, WA 98862. (509)996-2370

Penrose Point State Park: 321 158th Avenue KPS, Lakebay, WA 98349. (253)884-2514

Peshastin Pinnacles State Park: contact Wenatchee Confluence State Park

Pleasant Harbor State Park: contact Dosewallips State Park

Posey Island Marine State Park: contact Sucia Island Marine State Park

Potholes State Park: 6762 Highway 262 East, Othello, WA 99344. (509)346-2759

Potlatch State Park: P.O. Box 1051, Hoodsport, WA 98548-1051. (360)877-5361

R

Rainbow Falls State Park: 4008 State Highway 6, Chehalis, WA 98532. (360)291-3767

Ranald MacDonald's Grave Site: contact Osoyoos Lake State Park

Rasar State Park: 38730 Cape Horn Road, Concrete, WA 98237. (360)826-3942

Reed Island State Park: contact Battle Ground Lake State Park

Right Smart Cove Property: contact Dosewallips State Park

Riverside State Park: 4427 N Aubrey L. White Parkway, Spokane, WA 99205. (509)456-3964

Rockport State Park: 51905 Star Route 20, Rockport, WA 98293. (360)853-8461

Rothschild House State Park: contact Fort Worden State Park

Ruby Townsite: contact Conconully State Park

S

Sacajawea State Park: 2503 Sacajawea Park Road, Pasco, WA 99301. (509)545-2361

Saddlebag Island Marine State Park: contact Sucia Island Marine State Park

St. Edward State Park: 14445 Juanita Drive NE, Kenmore, WA 98028. (425)823-2992

Saltwater State Park: 25205 8th Place S, Des Moines, WA 98198. (253)661-4956

Scenic Beach State Park: P.O. Box 7, Seabeck, WA 98380. (360)830-5079

Schafer State Park: W 1365 Schafer Park Road, Elma, WA 98541. (360)482-3852

Seaquest State Park: Box 3030 Spirit Lake Highway, Castle Rock, WA 98611. (360)274-8633

Sequim Bay State Park: 269035 Highway 101, Sequim, WA 98382. (360)683-4235

Shine Tidelands/Wolfe Property State Park: contact Kitsap Memorial State Park

Skagit River Property: contact Rasar State Park

Skating Lake State Park: contact Fort Canby State Park

Skykomish River Property: contact Wallace Falls State Park

South Beach Seashore Recreation Area: contact Twin Harbors State Park

South Whidbey State Park: 4128 S Smugglers Cove Road, Freeland, WA 98249. (360)331-4559

Spencer Spit State Park: 521A Bakerview Road, Lopez Island, WA 98261. (360)468-2251

Spokane Plains Battlefield State Park: contact Riverside State Park

Spokane River Centennial Trail: contact Riverside State Park

Spring Creek Hatchery State Park: contact Maryhill State Park

Squak Mountain State Park: contact Lake Sammamish State Park

Square Lake State Park: contact Manchester State Park

Squilchuck State Park: contact Wenatchee Confluence State Park

Steamboat Rock State Park: P.O. Box 370, Electric City, WA 99123-0352. (509)663-1304

Steptoe Battlefield State Park: contact Central Ferry State Park

Steptoe Butte State Park: contact Central Ferry State Park

Stretch Point Marine State Park: contact Jarrell Cove State Park

Stuart Island Marine State Park: contact Sucia Island Marine State Park

Sucia Island Marine State Park: Star Route, Box 177, Olga, WA 98279. (360)376-2073

Summer Falls State Park: contact Sun Lakes–Dry Falls State Park

Sun Lakes–Dry Falls State Park: 34875 Park Lake Road NE, Coulee City, WA 99115. (509)632-5583

T

Toandos Tidelands: contact Dosewallips State Park

Tolmie State Park: contact Millersylvania Memorial State Park

Triton Cove State Park: contact Dosewallips State Park

Turn Island Marine State Park: contact Sucia Island Marine State Park

Twanoh State Park: 12190 E Highway 106, Union, WA 98592. (360)275-2222

Twenty-Five Mile Creek State Park: 20530 S Lakeshore Road, Chelan, WA 98816. (509)687-3610/3710

Twin Harbors State Park: Westport, WA 98595. (360)268-9717

W

Wallace Falls State Park: P.O. Box 230, Gold Bar, WA 98251. (360)793-0420

Wanapum State Park: P.O. Box 1203, Vantage, WA 98950. (509)856-2700

Wenatchee Confluence State Park: 333 Olds Station Road, Wenatchee, WA 98801-5938. (509)664-6373

Wenberg State Park: 15430 East Lake Goodwin Road, Stanwood, WA 98292. (360)652-7417

West Hylebos State Park: contact Dash Point State Park

Westhaven State Park: contact Twin Harbors Beach State Park

Westport Light State Park: contact Twin Harbors Beach State Park

Willapa Hills Trail State Park: contact Rainbow Falls State Park

Y

Yakima Sportsman State Park: 904 Keys Road, Yakima, WA 98901. (509)575-2774

B. QUICK REFERENCE TO FACILITIES AND RECREATION

The following table provides a quick overall reference to park facilities and activities. For more specific information, refer to the individual park description.

Letter codes in the columns refer to particular features of the facility or activity in that column. For example, in the *Camping* column, the letter *S* refers to standard campsites (which have no power, water, or sewer hookups), *P* to primitive campsites, and *RV* to recreation vehicle sites (which have hookups), although some might not include all three types of hookups.

Swimming beaches are noted where specific swimming areas have been designated.

While *boating* or *paddling* are possible in virtually any park that fronts on a body of water, these activities are noted where they are particularly popular.

The *moorage* column includes only those parks where overnight tie-ups are permitted on floats, although a number of water-oriented parks with launch ramps have floats to aid in boarding boats.

Water sports includes water skiing, personal watercraft (PWC) riding, windsurfing, and surfboarding.

Field sports covers a broad range of activities such as volleyball, baseball, softball, soccer, tennis, horseshoes, and golf.

Nature study includes parks that have nature trails, or in which tidepools or bird- or animal-watching are a particular attraction.

Park and Page Number	Camping (Standard, RV, Primitive)	Picnicking	Group Camp (# Persons)	Group Day-Use (# Persons)	ELC	Dump Station (RV, Boat)	Disabled Access	Waterfront (Salt, Fresh)	Swimming Beach	Boating, Paddling	Moorage (Floats, Buoys)	Fishing (Shore, Boat, Pier)	Boat Launch (Ramp, Hand-Carry)	Scuba Diving	Artificial Reef	Shellfish	Beachcombing	Water Sports	Field Sports	Walking/Hiking	Rock Climbing	Equestrian Trails (Beach)	Bicycling	Off-Road Vehicles	Snow Sports	Nature Study	Interpretive Displays (Nature, Historical, Museum)
CHAPTER 1: THE OLYMPIC PENINSULA 19																											
Bogachiel State Park 19	S,P/RV	•	20			RV		F		•		S								•						•	
Dungeness State Park 20								S		•		B	R					•									
Sequim Bay State Park 21	S,P/RV	•	75	50/100	•	RV	•	S		•	F,B	P	R			•			•	•							N
Anderson Lake State Park 23		•						F		•		S,B	R							•							
Old Fort Townsend State Park 23	S,P	•	80	100		RV		S		•	B	B		•		•	•			•			•			•	N,H
Rothschild House Heritage Area 24		•																									H
Fort Worden State Park and Conference Center 25	P/RV					RV	•	S		•	F,B	S,B	R	•	•	•	•		•	•			•				H, M
Fort Flagler State Park 28	S,P/RV	•	40/80	100	•	RV	•	S		•	F,B	S,P	R	•	•	•	•			•		•	•				N, H
Mystery Bay Marine State Park 30		•				B		S		•	F,B	P	R			•	•		•								
Old Man House State Park 31		•						S		•						•	•										H
Shine Tidelands State Park and Wolfe Property 31	P							S		•		B	H			•	•										
Hood Canal State Park Tidelands 32								S								•	•										
Dosewallips State Park 32	S,P/RV	•		50/135		RV	•	S		•		S				•	•			•			•			•	
Pleasant Harbor State Park 34								S		•	F			•													
Triton Cove State Park 34								S		•		P,B	R														
Hoodsport Trail State Park 35		•																		•						•	
Lake Cushman State Park 36	S,P/RV	•	60			RV	•	F	•	•		B	R					•		•							
Potlatch State Park 37	S,P/RV	•				RV		S		•	B	S,B		•			•			•							

231

Park and Page Number	Camping (Standard, RV, Primitive)	Picnicking	Group Camp (# Persons)	Group Day-Use (# Persons)	ELC	Dump Station (RV, Boat)	Disabled Access	Waterfront (Salt, Fresh)	Swimming Beach	Boating, Paddling	Moorage (Floats, Buoys)	Boat Launch (Ramp, Hand-Carry)	Fishing (Shore, Boat, Pier)	Scuba Diving	Artificial Reef	Shellfish	Beachcombing	Water Sports	Field Sports	Walking/Hiking	Rock Climbing	Equestrian Trails (Beach)	Bicycling	Off-Road Vehicles	Snow Sports	Nature Study	Interpretive Displays (Nature, Historical, Museum)
CHAPTER 2: SOUTHWEST WASHINGTON 39																											
Schafer State Park 39	S,P/RV	•		50/200		RV		F		•			S														
Lake Sylvia State Park 40	S,P	•	120	200		RV	•	F	•	•		R								•						•	N
North Beach Seashore Conservation Area 42		•					•	S					S			•	•			•		•		•		•	
Pacific Beach State Park 44	S,P/RV	•				RV	•	S		•			S			•	•			•						•	
Griffiths-Priday State xk 44		•		75				S,F		•			S			•	•			•		•				•	
Ocean City State Park 45	S,P/RV	•	40			RV	•	S,F		•			S			•	•			•						•	
Ocean Shores Environmental Interpretive Center 45		•																									N,H
South Beach Seashore Conservation Area 46		•					•	S		•			S	•		•	•			•				•		•	
Westhaven State Park 47		•						S		•			S	•		•	•			•							N
Westport Light State Park 48		•						S					S	•		•	•			•							N
Twin Harbors State Park 48	S,P/RV	•	80	100		RV	•	S					S			•	•			•						•	
Grayland Beach State Park 50	P/RV	•						S		•			S			•	•			•						•	
Long Beach Seashore Conservation Area 50		•					•	S					S			•	•			•			•		•		
Leadbetter Point State Park 52		•						S					S			•	•			•			•		•		
Pacific Pines State Park 54		•					•	S					S			•	•			•						•	
Loomis Lake State Park 54		•					•	S					S			•	•			•						•	
Fort Canby State Park 55	S,P/RV	•				RV	•	S,F		•		R	S,B			•	•			•						•	H
Colbert House Heritage Area 58							•																				H
Fort Columbia State Park 58		•					•	S												•							H
Lewis and Clark Campsite Heritage Area 59		•																									H
Willie Keil's Grave Heritage Area 59																											H
Willapa Hills Trail 60		•					•						S							•		•	•				
Rainbow Falls State Park 61	S,P	•	56	150		RV		F		•			S							•	•					•	
CHAPTER 3: THE SAN JUAN ISLANDS 63																											
Patos Island Marine State Park 63	P	•						S		•	B		B	•		•	•			•							
Sucia Island Marine State Park 64	P	•	16/25					S		•	F,B		B	•	•	•	•			•							
Matia Island Marine State Park 66	P	•						S		•	F,B		B	•		•	•			•							
Clark Island Marine State Park 67	P	•						S		•	B		B	•		•	•			•							
Stuart Island Marine State Park 68	P	•				B		S		•	F,B		B	•		•				•							
Posey Island Marine State Park 69	P	•						S					B							•							
Jones Island Marine State Park 69	P	•	30					S		•	F,B		B	•		•				•							
Doe Island Marine State Park 70	P	•						S		•	F		B	•						•							
Moran State Park 71	S,P	•		100	•	RV	•	F	•	•		R	B							•		•	•	•		•	H,N
Blind Island Marine State Park 74	P	•						S		•	B		B													•	

Park and Page Number	Camping (Standard, RV, Primitive)	Picnicking	Group Camp (# Persons)	Group Day-Use (# Persons)	ELC	Dump Station (RV, Boat)	Disabled Access	Waterfront (Salt, Fresh)	Swimming Beach	Boating, Paddling	Moorage (Floats, Buoys)	Boat Launch (Ramp, Hand-Carry)	Fishing (Shore, Boat, Pier)	Scuba Diving	Artificial Reef	Shellfish	Beachcombing	Water Sports	Field Sports	Walking/Hiking	Rock Climbing	Equestrian Trails (Beach)	Bicycling	Off-Road Vehicles	Snow Sports	Nature Study	Interpretive Displays (Nature, Historical, Museum)
Lime Kiln Point State Park 74		•					•	S												•						•	H,N
Turn Island Marine State Park 75	P	•						S		•	B		B	•		•	•			•							
Spencer Spit State Park 76	S,P	•	9/30	50		RV	•	S		•	B		B			•	•			•						•	
James Island Marine State Park 77	P	•						S		•	F,B		B	•						•							
State Park Properties in the San Juan Islands 78								S		•			B	•													
Cone Islands 79								S		•				•													
Huckleberry Island 79								S		•				•													
Saddlebag Island Marine State Park 79	P	•						S		•			B	•		•				•							
CHAPTER 4: NORTH PUGET SOUND 81																											
Peace Arch State Park 81		•		300																						•	H,N
Birch Bay State Park 82	S,P/RV	•	40			RV	•	S		•		R	S	•		•	•	•	•	•						•	N
Larrabee State Park 83	S,P/RV	•	40	50/100		RV	•	S		•		R	B	•		•	•	•		•			•			•	
Bay View State Park 85	S,P/RV	•	64	175		RV	•	S	•	•			S							•						•	
Rasar State Park 86	S,P/RV	•	•			RV	•	F					S							•							H,N
Rockport State Park 87	S,P/RV	•	56			RV														•						•	
Deception Pass State Park 89	S,P/RV	•	32/64	•	•	RV	•	S,F	•	•		F,B	R,H	B,S	•		•	•			•						•	H,N
Joseph Whidbey State Park 93	P	•						S		•			S							•							
Fort Ebey State Park 94	S,P/RV	•	50				•	S,F		•			S					•		•			•				H
Ebey's Landing State Park 95		•						S					S							•						•	H
Fort Casey State Park 96	S,P	•					•	S		•		R	S,B	•	•	•	•			•							H
Keystone Spit State Park 97		•						S		•			S	•						•							H
South Whidbey State Park 98	S,P/RV	•	144			RV	•	S								•	•			•						•	
Useless Bay Tidelands 99																•	•			•						•	N
Camano Island State Park 99	S,P	•	160/180			RV	•	S		•		R	S			•				•						•	
Mukilteo State Park 101		•						S		•		R		•					•								H
Wenberg State Park 101	S/RV	•		150		RV	•	F	•	•		R	B					•									
Mount Pilchuck State Park 102																				•	•				•		H
Wallace Falls State Park 104	S	•																		•			•			•	H,N
Big Eddy Scenic River Access 105		•						F		•			S														
Skykomish Scenic River Recreation Corridor 105								F		•										•	•						
CHAPTER 5: SOUTH PUGET SOUND 107																											
Kitsap Memorial State Park 107	S/RV	•	32	75		RV	•	S		•	B		S	•		•			•								
Scenic Beach State Park 108	S	•	48	100		RV	•	S		•			S			•			•								
Twanoh State Park 109	S,P/RV	•	40	150		B	•	S	•	•	F,B	R	B					•		•							
Belfair State Park 110	S,P/RV	•				RV	•	S	•				S														

Park and Page Number	Camping (Standard, RV, Primitive)	Picnicking	Group Camp (# Persons)	Group Day-Use (# Persons)	ELC	Dump Station (RV, Boat)	Disabled Access	Waterfront (Salt, Fresh)	Swimming Beach	Boating, Paddling	Moorage (Floats, Buoys)	Boat Launch (Ramp, Hand-Carry)	Fishing (Shore, Boat, Pier)	Scuba Diving	Artificial Reef	Shellfish	Beachcombing	Water Sports	Field Sports	Walking/Hiking	Rock Climbing	Equestrian Trails (Beach)	Bicycling	Off-Road Vehicles	Snow Sports	Nature Study	Interpretive Displays (Nature, Historical, Museum)
Jarrell Cove State Park 111	S,P	•	64			B	•	S		•	F,B		S,P			•				•							
Hope Island Marine State Park 112	S,P	•						S		•	B		B							•							
Stretch Point Marine State Park 113		•						S		•	B					•											
Haley Property 113	P	•						S		•			B			•				•							
Harstine Island State Park 114		•						S						•	•	•	•			•							
McMicken Island Marine State Park 115		•						S		•	B		B			•	•			•							
Joemma Beach State Park 115	S,P	•					•	S		•	F,B	R	B,P			•				•							
Penrose Point State Park 116	S	•	50			RV/B	•	S		•	F,B		B			•				•						•	
Eagle Island Marine State Park 117								S		•	B		B			•				•							
Kopachuck State Park 117	S,P	•	•			RV	•	S		•	B			•	•	•		•		•						•	
Cutts Island Marine State Park 118								S		•	B			•	•	•											
Saltwater State Park 119	S,P	•	64	•		RV	•	S	•	•	B		B	•	•					•							
West Hylebos Wetlands State Park 120																				•						•	N
Dash Point State Park 121	S	•	96			RV	•	S	•	•				•						•						•	
Tolmie State Park 122		•						S			B			•	•	•				•							H
Illahee State Park 124	S	•	40	50/75		RV	•	S		•	F,B	R	B,P	•		•		•		•							H
Fay-Bainbridge State Park 125	S,P	•		50		RV	•	S		•	B		B			•			•								H
Fort Ward State Park 126	P	•						S		•	B	R		•		•				•						•	H
Manchester State Park 127	S,P/RV	•	•	150		RV	•	S		•				•						•						•	H
Square Lake 128		•						F	•	•		R								•							
Blake Island Marine State Park 128	S,P	•	80	50/50		B		S	•	•	F,B		S,B	•	•	•				•						•	H,N
St. Edward State Park 130		•		20/100				F	•	•										•		•	•				H
Bridle Trails State Park 131																				•		•					
Lake Sammamish State Park 133			200	100/300		RV	•	F	•	•		R	B					•	•	•							
Squak Mountain State Park 134																				•		•	•			•	
Olallie State Park 136		•						F					S							•							
Iron Horse State Park (West) 138	P																			•	•	•	•		•		
Green River Gorge Conservation Area 140								F		•			S							•							H
Kanaskat–Palmer State Park 143	S/RV	•	80	50		RV	•	F		•		H	S							•						•	
Flaming Geyser State Park 144		•		150/350	•			F		•								•	•	•		•				•	N
Nolte State Park 145		•					•	F				H	B,P							•			•			•	
Federation Forest State Park 145		•																		•					•	•	N
CHAPTER 6: SOUTHWEST CASCADES 147																											
Millersylvania State Park 147	S,P/RV	•	40	300	•	RV	•	F	•	•		H	B,P							•	•					•	
Matilda N. Jackson State Park 149		•																									H

Park and Page Number	Camping (Standard, RV, Primitive)	Picnicking	Group Camp (# Persons)	Group Day-Use (# Persons)	ELC	Dump Station (RV, Boat)	Disabled Access	Waterfront (Salt, Fresh)	Swimming Beach	Boating, Paddling	Moorage (Floats, Buoys)	Boat Launch (Ramp, Hand-Carry)	Fishing (Shore, Boat, Pier)	Scuba Diving	Artificial Reef	Shellfish	Beachcombing	Water Sports	Field Sports	Walking/Hiking	Rock Climbing	Equestrian Trails (Beach)	Bicycling	Off-Road Vehicles	Snow Sports	Nature Study	Interpretive Displays (Nature, Historical, Museum)
John R. Jackson House Heritage Area 149		•																									N,H
Lewis and Clark State Park 150	S	•	50	100	•		•													•		•				•	N,H
Ike Kinswa State Park 151	S,P/RV	•				RV	•	F	•	•		R	S,B					•		•			•				
Seaquest State Park 153	S,P/RV	•	50	150		RV	•	F											•	•			•			•	N,H
Paradise Point State Park 154	S,P	•				RV		F		•		R	S							•						•	
Battle Ground Lake State Park 155	S,P	•	32	150		RV	•	F	•	•		R	B	•						•		•	•			•	
Reed Island Marine State Park 156	P	•						F		•			S							•						•	
Beacon Rock State Park 157	S,P/RV	•	200	50		RV		F		•	F	R	B							•	•	•	•			•	N
Spring Creek Fish Hatchery 159		•						F		•								•									
Doug's Beach State Park 160		•						F		•								•									
Dalles Mountain Ranch 160		•																		•						•	
Horsethief Lake State Park 161	S,P	•				RV		F		•		R								•	•					•	H
Maryhill State Park 162	S,P/RV	•	192			RV	•	F	•	•	B	R	S,B					•		•						•	
Goldendale Observatory State Park 163																										•	N
CHAPTER 7: NORTHEAST WASHINGTON 165																											
Pearrygin Lake State Park 165	S,P/RV	•	48			RV	•	F	•	•		R	B,P					•		•					•		
Conconully State Park 167	S,P	•		350		RV	•	F		•		R	S,B					•							•		
Osoyoos Lake State Veteran's Memorial Park 168	S,P	•				RV	•	F	•	•		R	B,P					•							•		
Ranald MacDonald's Grave Heritage Area 169																											H
Curlew Lake State Park 169	S/RV	•				RV		F	•	•		R	B,P					•		•					•		
Crystal Falls State Park 170								F												•							
Crawford State Park (Gardner Cave) 170		•					•																			•	N
Lake Wenatchee State Park 172	S	•	80	100		RV	•	F	•	•		R	B,P					•		•		•			•		
Twenty-five Mile Creek State Park 173	S/RV	•	48			RV	•	F	•	•	F	R	B,P					•		•							
Lake Chelan State Park 174	S/RV	•				RV		F	•	•	F	R	B	•				•		•							
Alta Lake State Park 175	S/RV	•	88			RV	•	F	•	•		R	B	•				•		•		•			•		
Fort Okanogan Heritage Area 176		•																									H
Bridgeport State Park 177	S,P/RV	•	75			RV	•	F	•	•		R	B							•							
Crown Point State Heritage Area 178																											H
Banks Lake Recreation Area 179	P	•						F		•		R	B					•					•			•	
Steamboat Rock State Park 180	S,P/RV	•				RV	•	F	•	•	B	R	B	•				•		•			•				
Sun Lakes-Dry Falls State Park 182	S/RV	•	40		•	RV	•	F	•	•		R	S,B					•		•			•				N,H
Lake Lenore Caves State Park 183																				•							N,H
Summer Falls State Park 184		•							F				S														
Peshastin Pinnacles State Park 184		•																		•	•						

Park and Page Number	Camping (Standard, RV, Primitive)	Picnicking	Group Camp (# Persons)	Group Day-Use (# Persons)	ELC	Dump Station (RV, Boat)	Disabled Access	Waterfront (Salt, Fresh)	Swimming Beach	Boating, Paddling	Moorage (Floats, Buoys)	Boat Launch (Ramp, Hand-Carry)	Fishing (Shore, Boat, Pier)	Scuba Diving	Artificial Reef	Shellfish	Beachcombing	Water Sports	Field Sports	Walking/Hiking	Rock Climbing	Equestrian Trails (Beach)	Bicycling	Off-Road Vehicles	Snow Sports	Nature Study	Interpretive Displays (Nature, Historical, Museum)
Wenatchee Confluence State Park 185	S/RV	●	300	500		RV	●	F	●	●		●	●					●	●	●			●			●	N
Squilchuck State Park 187	S	●	160	100															●				●		●		
Daroga State Park 187	P/RV	●	100/100	75		RV/B		F	●	●	F	R	B					●	●	●			●				
Lincoln Rock State Park 188	S/RV	●		100		RV		F	●	●	F	R	B							●	●						
Riverside State Park 189	S	●	50/198	30/100				F		●		R,H	S,B							●		●	●	●	●		H
Spokane River Centennial Trail 193		●																		●		●					
Mount Spokane State Park 196	S	●	90				●													●		●			●		
CHAPTER 8: SOUTHEAST WASHINGTON 199																											
Hyak Lodge State Park 199																				●		●			●		
Lake Easton State Park 200	S,P/RV	●	50			RV	●	F	●	●		R	S,B							●			●		●	●	
Iron Horse State Park (East) 201	P																			●			●				H
Ginkgo Petrified Forest State Park 204		●																		●						●	N,H
Wanapum State Park 205	RV	●						F	●	●		R	B					●		●							
Olmstead Place Heritage Area 206		●		300																●							H
Helen McCabe State Park 207								F					S							●							
Indian Painted Rocks State Heritage Area 207																											H
Yakima Sportsman State Park 207	S,P/RV	●		200		RV	●	F					S							●		●				●	
Fort Simcoe State Park 208		●																									H
Brooks Memorial State Park 209	S,P/RV	●	50		●	RV		F					S						●	●					●	●	
Crow Butte State Park 210	RV	●	60			RV	●	F	●	●	F,B	R	B					●		●						●	
Moses Lake State Park 211		●		100/100				F	●	●		R	B					●	●						●		
Potholes State Park 212	S/RV	●	50			RV	●	F		●		R,H	B					●		●							
Sacajawea State Park 213		●		200			●	F	●	●	F,B	R	B,P					●									H
Columbia Plateau Trail 214																				●		●	●		●		
Lake Colville Shorelands 216												R	S												●		
Palouse Falls State Park 217	S	●			●															●						●	N
Lyons Ferry State Park 218	S,P	●				RV		F	●	●	B	R,H	B,P					●		●							H
Lewis and Clark Trail State Park 219	S,P	●	50/50	50/100		RV	●	F					S							●						●	H
Central Ferry State Park 220	P/RV	●	150			RV/B		F	●	●	F	R	B					●	●	●					●		
Steptoe Butte State Park 221		●																									H
Chief Timothy State Park 222	S,P/RV	●				RV/B		F	●	●	F,B	R	B					●		●							H
Camp William T. Wooten State Park 223					●			F	●	●			S									●	●		●		
Fields Spring State Park 224	S,P	●			●	RV	●	F					S							●					●	●	

INDEX

ABOUT THE AUTHORS

MARGE AND TED MUELLER are avid outdoor enthusiasts and environmentalists who have explored Washington's mountains, forests, deserts, and waterways for more than forty years. Ted taught classes on cruising in Northwest waters and both Marge and Ted instructed mountain climbing. They are members of several environmental advocacy groups, and are on the Board of Directors of Friends of Washington State Parks.

The Muellers are the authors of the popular *Afoot and Afloat* series also published by The Mountaineers, as well as a number of other books.

To do the research for the first edition of *Washington State Parks*, they logged several thousand miles by land and water, traveling to every corner of the state to visit each of the parks. For this second edition, they revisited each of the parks to update their information.

ABOUT THE MOUNTAINEERS

THE MOUNTAINEERS, founded in 1906, is a nonprofit outdoor activity and conservation club, whose mission is "to explore, study, preserve, and enjoy the natural beauty of the outdoors . . . ." Based in Seattle, Washington, the club is the third-largest such organization in the United States, with 15,000 members and five branches throughout Washington State.

The Mountaineers sponsors both classes and year-round outdoor activities in the Pacific Northwest, which include hiking, mountain climbing, ski-touring, snowshoeing, bicycling, camping, kayaking and canoeing, nature study, sailing, and adventure travel. The club's conservation division supports environmental causes through educational activities, sponsoring legislation, and presenting informational programs. All club activities are led by skilled, experienced volunteers, who are dedicated to promoting safe and responsible enjoyment and preservation of the outdoors.

If you would like to participate in these organized outdoor activities or the club's programs, consider a membership in The Mountaineers. For information and an application, write or call The Mountaineers, Club Headquarters, 300 Third Avenue West, Seattle, Washington, 98119; (206) 284-6310.

The Mountaineers Books, an active, nonprofit publishing program of the club, produces guidebooks, instructional texts, historical works, natural history guides, and works on environmental conservation. All books produced by The Mountaineers Books are aimed at fulfilling the club's mission.

Send or call for our catalog of more than 300 outdoor titles:

The Mountaineers Books
1001 SW Klickitat Way, Suite 201
Seattle, WA 98134
(800) 553-4453
email: mbooks@mountaineers.org
website: www.mountaineersbooks.org